Sweet Home Hinton Ampner

THE TENANT FARMER'S
DIARY FROM 2015

CHARLIE FLINDT

SWEET HOME HINTON AMPNER
The tenant farmer's diary from 2015

Text & images ©Charlie Flindt

ISBN 9781912821013

A CIP catalogue record for this book
is available from the British Library.
Published 2019 Tricorn Books
131 High Street, Portsmouth, PO1 2HW

Printed & bound in the UK

Sweet Home Hinton Ampner

Foreword

There are several types of farm diary.

Type A: the pocket diary, with a uselessly slim pencil that fits in a tube in its spine. The go-to version was produced by Farmer & Stockbreeder for decades, until that magazine folded. The countless pages of important farm facts (density of assorted cereals, gestation period of a goat) would be matched by the brevity of each day's entry by the diarist. Dad's diaries held no more information than "manured lower five-acre." September 3rd, 1939 merited little more than "Trouble in Europe." I have about seventy of these in the attic, destined for obscurity.

Type B: the diary kept by the niche farmers, those hardy souls who choose to farm a rare breed of unusual animal on wind-swept inhospitable hillsides using organic feed harvested by the light of the third blue moon of a leap year. I tip my hat to them, and love their diaries – but you wouldn't find me opting for that lifestyle.

Type C: a relatively new publishing phenomenon, the anti-farmer farm diary. An established author or celebrity buys or rents a bit of land, runs it in the style of a Type B diary, but then publishes a polemic against modern conventional farming from the moral high ground. They tend to be long on vitriol, short on fact. Reading one of these recently made it clear that what was needed was....

Type D: the day-to-day activities on a modern conventional mixed farm. Raising crops and animals using all the tools at our disposal, including modern machines and pesticides. So that's what I started writing about. Somehow, family life crept in, too. And the trials and tribulations of being in a third-rate covers band. And dealing with the tsunami of rural crime. And the medical stuff that starts to pop on the lifestyle radar once you reach your mid-fifties. And before I knew it, in a torrential hailstorm, 2015 was over. So here it is, my type D diary.

In the farmhouse
Charlie and Hazel Flindt, and their three children,
Anthony, Diana and Jonathan.

Pets
Fred and Monty - Flatcoat Retrievers
Joseph, Cain and Abel - cats

In the Churchyard
Charlie's father (aka Grandpa Flindt)
Charlie's mother (aka Granny Flindt) – although in 2015 she was
still on the shelf in the farm office in an urn, while it was debated
if she deserved an eternal break from Grandpa.

In the farmyard
2009 Skoda Octavia Estate
2007 Hyundai Terracan (aka Tigger)
2007 Mazda MX-5
(1999 VW Lupo 1.4E – arrived mid-2015)

In the barn
2012 John Deere 6630 Premium
2009 Massey Ferguson 5455 c/w front loader
2010 New Holland TC5070RS/SL
(Kubota 400ci RTV – aka Pig – arrived mid-2015)

Main farm kit
2006 Horsch CO3 seed drill
2014 Amazone UG3000, 24m boom
2006 Kverneland 5 furrow plough.

Secondary Farm Kit
8.3m Dalbo rollers
3m Terradisc
3m mounted discs
Assorted haymaking kit
Assorted harvest kit

Introduction

When we join Manor Farm, Hinton Ampner, the farming year is already three months and a day old - Michaelmas is the traditional starting point. Autumn 2014 was yet another wet one, and many of the arable jobs that should have been done and dusted were unfinished: the barns were still full of unsown seed, and the drill – and its operator – sat forlornly waiting for some good farming weather. But it rained, and rained, and rained…

Dedication

A mountain of thanks go to Hazel and the children, for their immeasurable tolerance and patience. I must also acknowledge John Lewis-Stempel, whose archetypal Type C diary, The Running Hare, did more than anything to make me keep a Type D diary.

And huge apologies go to Richard 'Dicky' Brooks, who, for five years, taught and instilled in me a love of physics. His pet hate was mixing imperial and metric units. This diary would enrage him even more than those two geeky pupils who wouldn't stop giggling over 'eddy currents' in 1977. Sorry, Sir.

Contents

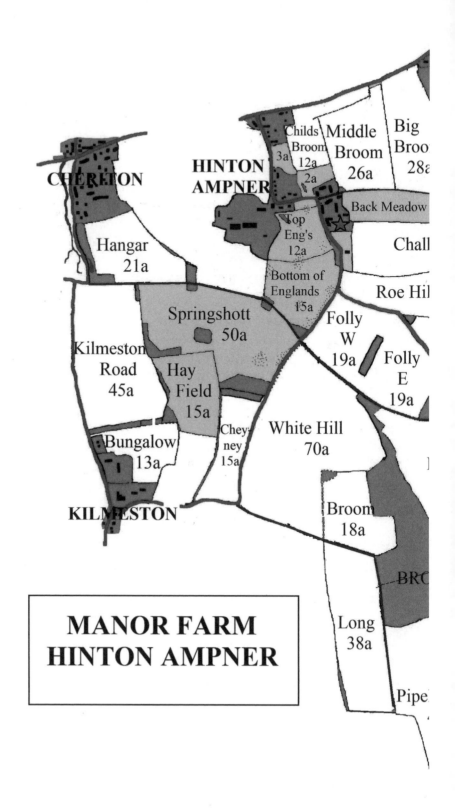

CHERITON

HINTON
AMPNER

Childs
Broom
12a

3a

Middle
Broom
26a

Big
Broo
28a

2a

Back Meadow

Hangar
21a

Top
Eng's
12a

Chall

Bottom of
Englands
15a

Roe Hil

Springshott
50a

Folly
W
19a

Folly
E
19a

Kilmeston
Road
45a

Hay
Field
15a

Chey-
ney
15a

White Hill
70a

Bungalow
13a

KILMESTON

Broom
18a

BRO

**MANOR FARM
HINTON AMPNER**

Long
38a

Pipe

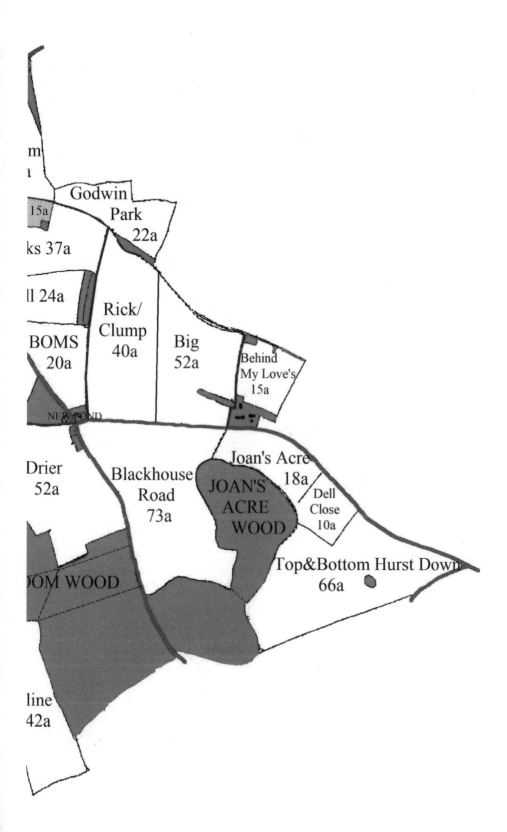

m
a

Godwin
Park
22a

15a

ks 37a

ll 24a

Rick/
Clump
40a

BOMS
20a

Big
52a

Behind
My Love's
15a

NEW POND

Drier
52a

Blackhouse
Road
73a

Joan's Acre
18a

JOAN'S
ACRE
WOOD

Dell
Close
10a

OM WOOD

Top&Bottom Hurst Down
66a

line
42a

A dozen farming thoughts.

Blessed are the pessimists; for they shall never be disappointed
Buy good grain trailers; use them for nothing else
Take those tractor weights off, and let down the tyres
Put something in the scrap skip every day
The fewer the grease nipples, the safer the second-hand buy
Rare breeds are rare for a reason
Avoid recreational tractor driving
You can never have too much hay/straw
Once a month, do something that baffles your neighbours
During harvest, bite your tongue and move on, no matter what
Ask yourself often whose life you envy
Excuses are the refuge of the incompetent

January 1st

2015 dawned dull and grey and damp – a shame after the glorious run of crisp cold weather we had last week. It had allowed me to sow a few more precious acres of winter wheat into the ground 'on the frost'. I nipped out and tried to get a bit more done yesterday, to end the year with a clear conscience, but the top was now an inch of greasy mud, and still frozen rock hard underneath. The Horsch CO seed drill pushed its sowing tips down a few inches into the ground where they met the frost, and twelve tungsten-tipped little anchors meant the tractor sat and spun, 4wd and diff lock proving utterly useless. So I had abandoned for the day - and the year - with a cloudy conscience. At least I had tried.

Thank God for Jools Holland, keeping us fifty-somethings entertained for New Year's Eve. Like many our age, we are quite content with the earliest of late nights, with the bare minimum of alcohol and a bag of expensive chocolates. *Hootenanny* has become an institution in many households, and it was nice to see no miming, only a few toe-curlingly embarrassing 'interviews', and not too many duff acts – not among the under-seventies performing, anyway.

So it was a reasonably late start, but no hangovers. Hazel was out doing her early constitutional flatcoat yomp when I got up. I was less full than usual of the 'new year/fresh start' feeling – probably a sign of getting older, or an unconscious acknowledgement of the reality of the challenges that 2015 will bring. The horizon is dark indeed. But I thought I'd try to keep my spirits up anyway, staggering down the stairs as brightly as I could.

It didn't take long for what little optimism there was in the soul to be firmly squished. At ten, the police sent one of their round-robin texts, warning of poachers in nearby Ovington – a gang of six this time. I didn't see the message until after lunch, and so I thought I'd have a drive round and see if the buggers were paying us a visit.

As is often the case, you go out looking for one thing, and find something else. Two horses had been up the footpath in Roe Hill, and then along the top, making a bit of a mess of my already sorry-looking winter barley. It's one of those situations where you are quietly relieved that a shouting match has been avoided, but seething that the age-old rights-of-way issue has once again reared its ugly head. It's almost daily nowadays. More fencing will be needed.

Further on I spotted that someone had tried to drive into White Hill. It's the poachers' favourite field, so I assume it could only be them. They had got their vehicle stuck on top of one of the old logs blocking the gateway in the Cheyney dip. You could see where a great deal of wheel spinning had taken place to reverse off it. Thank goodness they didn't get out into the oilseed rape. It's still mighty wet out there, and the mess would have been considerable.

A brief check of Drier Field showed it to be undrillable, and wind and rain was once again building. So I lit the sitting room fire, made a cup of tea and settled down in front of *Despicable Me*. I was sound asleep on the sofa within minutes, and slept for an hour. So much for the earliest of late nights.

January 2nd

A proper farmer wouldn't be woken up at 7.45am by the mobile phone ringing on the bedside table. He would have been up for hours, and probably just thinking about a mid-morning break at that time. This being the Flindt household, however, not a soul was awake. We were still in Christmas/New Year break mode, and, more importantly, we'd been up late again, this time trying to make sense of *The Dark Knight*, and the rest of the night had been noisily wet and windy. Leaping out of bed a couple of hours before dawn was most definitely not on the job sheet for today.

There are two options when the phone rings in this situation: answer it and try to sound wide awake (i.e. like a proper farmer), or let the damn thing go to the answerphone. I, of course, did the latter. I found my glasses, checked the number, and realised it was the local Massey dealers wanting to come out and fit a new throttle sensor to the loader tractor.

This important little gadget had been playing up for some time. Both the hand and foot throttle work for a bit, then give up, leaving the engine stuck at about 1400 rpm. Slightly unnerving, not least because the last time this happened on a tractor, it was the fuel pump on my Massey 6465, and that ended up being a four-figure repair job. I'm hoping that the new sensor will be slightly cheaper.

Hazel volunteered to get up and open up the yard for the mechanic, and I was left to doze and dream of days when replacing a throttle cable was about as complicated as engine speed control ever got.

As I set off to see if Drier Field had miraculously escaped last night's rain, the daily text arrived, this time from the NFU. It implored us to head for the web pages of the *Gloucester Echo*, and vote on their badger culling poll. I did – but, as ever, the Badger Lobby will have got there first and in higher numbers, so these polls reflect nothing except who can mobilise the most clickers nationwide.

Drier Field was, of course, sodden, so I checked out BOMS and Folly to see how the wheat that I had managed to sow in them was coming on. It has been in the ground for just under a month, and seems to be on the verge of winning the battle against the vast rook population. The wheat is almost visible in its Horsch-dropped rows, so I should be able to tell soon if the tramlining solenoids were affected when the pre-emergence marker solenoid burnt out in the middle of BOMS.

I always chuckle when I see a gathering of rooks – or is it a murmuration? Or a squadron? Goodness knows. They're a flipping nuisance – they cleared a good ten acres of the beans in Bottom Hurst Down last winter, systematically working their way up the rows. But I can still remember Dad reminiscing about rook control and how it was a job always done on or around his birthday – May 16th. A posse would walk round the farm, shotgunning the nests – and the young rooks inside them – to pieces. I chuckle because I wonder how far into that procedure we could get these days before the police arrive, summoned by outraged walkers.

Talking of which: as I drove home, four walkers and a dog were just climbing the stile into Bottom of Englands. They set off blindly across the middle of the field, down towards the old gate into Springshott. They realised there was no way out there, so headed up the western side of the field. Finding still no gate or stile, they lifted the dog over the fence, and then climbed over themselves. I made a mental note to check the fence for damage at a later date. I'll forget of course. At least they kept the dog on the lead.

Multiple attempts to book a table tonight at the local pub had failed. No one was answering the phone, but we needed to get out of the house for the evening while Anthony had a bit of a birthday gathering. So I jumped in Tigger and drove the pothole-strewn lanes through to West Meon. The pub was heaving, of course – that's why they'd turned the phone off. Luckily, they had a slot for four to dine tonight.

I spent an hour or so exchanging phone calls and emails with Tim at *Farmers Weekly*, getting the next article just right. It's a climate sceptic one again, so will open the usual can of worms and angry letters.

With an hour to spare before a stunning sunset, I thought I'd gave my new plough a bit of TLC. Armed with a paintbrush, some sturdy gloves and a tin of paint stripper, I set about getting the paint off the brand new No 28 bodies that had been fitted. As seems normal these days, the factory paint seemed astonishingly tough; either that, or modern off-the-shelf paint stripper has been neutered somewhat. It was strong enough to give me a fairly sharp headache after an hour – even though I was working outdoors.

And while the DIY bug was biting, I fitted the Cheek Eez pad to Jonathan's Browning. He'd got it for Christmas – I wasn't convinced that it was needed, so ordered the narrowest one available. Ten minutes with some surgical spirit, and some careful positioning, and he seemed happy with the result. We'll see if we can fit in a trip to the clay shoot on Sunday. If we get up early enough, of course. I might book an early morning alarm call.

We left Anthony and his mates getting the house party going, and headed for the pub, with only the slightest parental fear of what the place would be like when we got back.

January 3rd
One the best things about farming is that it gives the opportunity to own pets – lots of them. No farmhouse is complete without a selection of cats and dogs, and we're no exception. At the moment, we're on two dogs and three cats. They're all reasonably well trained – even the cats seem to know when to head for the back hall and settle down in assorted boxes and beds for the night.

It all went to pieces last night, during Anthony's party. The dozen or so 19- and 20-year-olds who were drinking and dining downstairs were being very civilised. If it hadn't been for the slamming of doors (something teenagers just can't help doing), we would hardly have known they were downstairs. Last night's pub meal was sitting a bit heavy on the tummy, along with a couple of pints of Tipster, but I was pleased to drop off at about midnight.

At about one thirty, Abel the kitten arrived in the bedroom. One of Anthony's mates had opened the door to the back hall, and the cat decided it was time to seek a warm duvet and some company. I was woken by the softest of claw-free paws pushing against my chin. As I stirred, the purring got louder and louder, as Abel realised he had found a chum for the night. I tried to ignore him to avoid getting up, but he shifted from my chest to my shoulder, to my armpit, and then over to Hazel. He was so thrilled to be with us. That was my cue to get up, pick him up (he still seemed thrilled) and carry him back downstairs. Luckily, a fresh bowl of biscuits averted any grudge-bearing.

The morning arrived very wet. Hazel and Jonathan had been booked to pick up and beat at Murph's shoot next door, so there was much gathering of decent coats and hats. I was very proud of Jonathan to be heading out, effectively on his own; he usually has a mate with him for company. Hazel is of course off with the pickers-up team, and the two teams rarely meet – especially on a proper shoot like Murph's.

The only farming job I had today was to get more calf nuts and milk powder. A quick phone call to Mole Valley Country Stores confirmed that they had a few, so I jumped in Tigger and drove into Winchester. The queue was horrendous, so I nipped down to Homebase to see if I could find some wood to make up the pheasant feeders that I'm hoping to build. The price of simple bits of three-by-one (or whatever the modern equivalent is) scared me out of that idea – I think I'll trim down some old fencing posts to make the legs for the barrels. Back at the Countrystore, the queue had all but vanished.

Back home, Anthony's sleepover gang had awoken, and were huddled slightly sorely around the kitchen table. I waited for them to leave before having lunch. Today's text arrived: Dave the Bass confirming that Sunday's Open Mic Night is on. Thanks goodness; I feel utterly under-organed at the moment.

Fred had spent most of the morning crying and howling after being left behind, so by 3.30 I thought it only fair that he had a decent walk. The rain had stopped, and a cold noisy northerly had started, so it was pretty chilly on my favourite Drier loop. The shooting gang got back before me – they'd all had a good day. Monty had been a star, and Jonathan had had plenty of ribbing. He complained proudly of being sent to the awkward corners in the beating strips – being 'the boy' on the line. He had a very handy wodge in his pocket to show for his troubles, though.

Poor old Fred spent the evening retrieving things for Hazel – bits of cardboard, beer cans, general party paraphernalia from last night. Anything to show that he can still do it, and it was quite unfair for him to be left behind. Somewhere in the house is a Monty Python 'I'm not dead yet!' t-shirt. We decided Fred could wear it. Ah, the joy of pets.

January 4th

Anthony's twentieth birthday – we are officially one teenager down. Was it really twenty years ago?

The world was still pretty soggy after yesterday's rain – no chance of any field work. Hazel and I walked out to the Folly to try and do something about the rooks. Monty had found an injured one in the hedge at Murph's shoot yesterday, so Hazel brought it back to do a bit of scaring with it. We cut a five-foot pole, attached the dead rook by one wing, and left it two-thirds up the hill in Folly East. Even as we walked away, there was a furious consternation coming from the Folly trees, with crowds of angry rooks making their displeasure loudly known. Or was it a couple of NT walkers?

The wheat is just about up in rows. Still not clearly enough to see any tramlines, but just enough to make you feel that there's a crop on the way, and to give the field a green sheen when viewed at the right angle.

We walked through Bob's Wood, to see if it ought to be a walked drive on the all-new Hinton Ampner shoot. Monty flushed half a dozen birds, so the answer is a definite 'yes'. We'll put a couple of guns in the Folly, and a couple in Drier Field. It should provide a good link between Caspar's and the Folly trees drives.

How long Bob's Wood will be there is, of course, a mystery. The National Trust had plans to clearfell the whole copse, with a view to it being their main base for the woodchip operation, supplying fuel cut in the main woods to the woodchip boiler up at the House. It has been on the cards for years, but nothing seems to have happened. The boiler itself is up and running, but fuel has to be brought in by lorry – not the greenest set-up. The felling of Bob's Wood seems to run into trouble with the local council, who seem to find a new bat or a significant tree with every inspection. It is now a slightly ghostly and melancholy place. There are signs of previous industry – well, gamekeeping – but now it lies like some sort of pheasant-rearing museum.

We walked back over BOMS, where the wheat seems a bit behind – odd, because it was the first of the late ones to go in. The stubble was a lot cleaner, and the field is lighter, so perhaps the seed went in that bit deeper. We crossed Roe Hill, where the winter barley looks a lot better on close inspection than it does from the farmhouse. Slugs have done quite a lot of damage, but it went in at a very high seed rate, and these new hybrid varieties are legendary tillers. This year will put that reputation to the test.

Anthony headed off to Petersfield for his birthday pub session, and I headed to West Meon for 'Open Mic Night'. Sometimes we get a dozen or more mixed musicians and a dozen or more eager listeners. Not tonight. Dave the Bass, Glynn and I spent four hours entertaining ourselves and four listeners – and half of them were the bar staff. Fi joined us towards the end and she and I mangled a vast selection of hits, from 'I know him so well' to 'Skyfall'. Always fun, even if no one turns out to listen.

Anthony needed picking up from Petersfield, so I went steady on the beer, knowing that Police are on the lookout for late-night dirty off-roaders. I finally got him out of the pub at eleven thirty, and got myself to bed an hour later.

January 5th

This time last year, the wave of rural crime that was washing over the countryside was enhanced by a spate of caravan dumpings. Ugly and moss-covered, they were appearing on the verges beside country lanes. The first I saw of it was in December 2013, when I saw a shiny new black pickup towing the mankiest of caravans along Joan's Acre Road while I was sowing beans in Dell Close. My first assumption was 'travellers', so didn't ring it in; I had no registration or anything useful to pass on. It was only a couple of days later that Keeper Mike said that an old caravan had been dumped on the Wheely Down Road, just the other side of Hurst Down.

A month or so later, I was heading home from the Drier, up past the entrance to Folly, when the distinctive black pickup/white caravan combination once again caught my eye, rounding the Cheyney bend. I pulled over on the Roe Hill Road, and pretended to answer my phone. Sure enough, the black pickup came past, towing the filthiest of caravans, and headed towards Brockwood. I jotted down the number, and then rang Mike to tell him that I thought another little roadside gift was heading his way. He happened to be at the bottom of Sheep Dip drive, and got a good look at it too. And, lo and behold, by the time I reached the Wheely Down Road, there was the freshly unhitched caravan.

It turned out that the pickup belonged to a London builder who was just finishing a huge contract renovating an enormous stately pile not far from here. It seemed that he was simply dumping the many caravans that littered the building site all around the local lanes. Quite how he though no one would notice, I don't know.

Anyway, the police visited the building site, and met the builder just as he was doing the very last jobs of the three-year project. Yes, it was his truck, he admitted. But, no, it wasn't him driving with the caravans; it was his mate Bob. 'Bob' had no other name, nor a contact number. He had just mysteriously appeared, taken away the caravans (all five for £300, apparently, and using the builder's pickup) and then vanished.

The local council weren't having this, and decided to throw the book at him – not just because of the dumping of caravans, but also because four of the five had been stacked to the gunnels with builders' waste. He decided to plead 'not guilty', and failed to show for a couple of court dates. He pleaded illness for another, until, finally, he was pinned down: the council have got him booked for a session at Fareham Magistrates' Court on Wednesday.

Mike the Keeper and I, as the accidental roadside observers, are also invited along. Which is why, late this morning, he and I, two officials from the council, and a lively prosecution solicitor could be found sitting round our kitchen table, discussing court tactics over coffee. Most of the discussion revolved around the apparent folly of his plea, and how it would in all probability be an open and shut case. We'll see. Dress code is jacket and tie.

After lunch I said "what the hell" and tried to finish the headland of Drier Field. Halfway round, all the rear wheels were completely bunged up, so I came back to the barn, angrily hitched off and drove the tractor home.

If I can't drill, I thought, then I'll give the new plough a run out. But, as ever, there were a few little jobs to do to the tractor first. Tyre pressures for a start. Front and back tyres had been 16 and 13 psi each, which were useless for the heavy weight block I was about to put on the front, and the five-furrow plough plus Packomat I was about to put on the back. I have a thing about overinflated tyres, so opted for 18psi all round.

I drove round to the diesel barn and filled up, wondering how I could put in some extra tanks to make the most of these crashing diesel prices. They can't go on falling forever, can they? I think Grandpa's old log store could come down, and a new, bigger, outdoor tank could go in on that corner. It would be nice to have it easily observable from the house – and even have a CCTV camera overlooking it.

I put the front weight block on – it's an old Ford wafer set, off the wonderful and much-missed 7810, twelve 40kg slabs and a base block, all mounted on an A-frame. Not huge by modern standards – I am staggered by the amount of cast iron some tractors are forced to haul around all day every day, even when not doing heavy draft work. Mine sits on the front linkage, so being stuck out well in front adds to its effectiveness.

Back round in the yard, it was Useless Farmer time, as it took me the best part of an hour to get the Kverneland on. You'd think with hook link ends, remote linkage controls, butterfly balls, and the small matter of thirty years' experience, it would be an absolute doddle to connect the two most iconic machines in the world of agriculture. But no; it was back, forward, out of the cab, back into the cab, a touch of WD-40, then too far to the left, to the right, back in the cab…

Just as it was getting dark, I had it all done: top link short enough to turn the five furrow without hitting the ground, but not too high so as to smash the window – it has no memory ram. The tyres still looked a bit squishy, but I'll see how they go.

Then just as a cup of tea had never looked more welcome, I realised Tigger was still down at Drier Field, so I begged a lift off Hazel to fetch it. And just as I could taste the honey sandwich that would go with the tea, I remembered that the truck was still full of music clutter from Open Mic Night, and there's an Old Gits rehearsal tonight. Shed 3b was a bit cold and manky, so I left the heater on once I'd unloaded all the kit, and headed in for a welcome cuppa. It's nice to be a bit busy again, even if I can't hitch a plough on.

January 6th

The morning started damp, and got a lot wetter. The National Trust's building supervisor, Paul, arrived in a downpour at eleven to take a look at Godwin's Yard. The Trust are in the process of overhauling all the ancient sewage systems in the village, and recently finished the redesign of the system leading out of Godwin's Farm Cottages. There's a family with two teenagers living in No 2, so it's well timed. The new system involved a powered tank, which sits and hums (as in noise, not smell) as it aerates and treats the sewage.

It seems wrong to have a powered sewage system. When the power cuts start, thanks to all the barking mad energy policies, it will be ghastly having sewage treatment plants not working. We'll all be yearning for the good old days of cess pits with their 'clean water' outlets (aka a brick taken out of the wall).

The contractors had done a pretty good job of tidying up and finishing off, but I wasn't happy with the last few buckets of waste soil, which had been crudely levelled out next to the feed troughs of the old cattle barn. This had turned into slurry when driven on, as well as pushing water into the cattle barn itself. Paul agreed that this needed finishing off properly, and suggested another scrape off, and some scalpings laid down. Sounded perfect.

Over a cup of tea, I signed the authorisations for the Trust to invoice me the two-thirds share of the costs of the external redecoration of the cottages and the bungalow – as laid down in the tenancy agreement. In the days of plentiful skilled labour, we would have had a man employed on the farm with handyman skills, and he would have done it, with the landlord paying the materials. The costs of such jobs usually came out at two-thirds labour/one-third materials, so that's what written into my tenancy agreement. I have the option, if I ever find myself re-employing anyone, to go back to doing it ourselves, but the system seems to work OK as it is.

It's just another aspect of the joys of being a tenant farmer. Millions paid in rent over a lifetime, and never an acre owned. Mind you, when the mathematical tiles on the front of the farmhouse needed replacing, it didn't come out of my pocket, thank God.

By now the sun had come out. I had planned to head out and try the new plough, but thought I'd procrastinate again, and took the dogs out for a Drier loop walk. The sun was actually warm on the face, and seeing the wheat in BOMS suddenly and dramatically greener was quite an uplift. And I could at last tell that all four seed cut-off solenoids had worked properly.

Back home, I noticed that our cess pit was overflowing, which was a coincidence after this morning's discussions. The smell on the southerly wind has been a bit ripe for a few days, which should have been a clue. I rang Botley Cleansing, who should be out on Thursday. Suddenly a new-fangled processing pit sounds a bit more attractive – humming or not.

January 7th

There's really no point in getting an early night; it never works. With a big day in court due today, I thought I'd get tucked up in good time last night, and get a nice solid night's sleep. Not a chance. It took longer than usual to doze off, and then all through the night I was checking the clock to make sure I hadn't overslept. By the time the alarm did go off, at an early-for-me 5.45, I felt anything other than refreshed.

It was rather odd to be doing an early start that didn't involve shooting. I had to stop myself from starting the shooting checklist (gun, squibs, belt, muffs, etc.), and had to keep reminding myself that all I needed for this most solemn of occasions was a tie – another chance to dig out the Agric Engineering tie from Newcastle.

I picked up Mike the Keeper (the other prosecution witness) on the dot of eight thirty, and we trundled down the A32 to Fareham. It's curious to think that in Dad's heyday Fareham was a charming little market town, and all his many farming prizes were won as a member of the Fareham and Hants Farmers' Club. The club recently dropped the 'Fareham and' from its name - acknowledgment, perhaps, that the town has become just another bit of Solent City.

And as for the courthouse – quite the most revolting block of concrete you ever saw. Some Seventies' architect probably got an award for it, but in the cold drizzle of a 2015 morning, it looked dated, dirty and dull. The interior wasn't much better. Too many misleading doors and confusing mezzanine levels.

We parked up and made our way through the metal detectors – Mike's rebuilt toes set everything off entertainingly. We sat nervously outside Court 4 with a handful of others, all eyeing each other nervously; were they the opposition? Should we acknowledge each other? Just what is the etiquette and protocol at these times? An oldish fellow with a walking stick sat down nearby. He was indeed the opposition. His legal team arrived and they went off to find some privacy in a separate room.

Our team then arrived, in good spirits. Our case was, after all, watertight. Our oppo, the builder, just had to be responsible for the fly-tipping this time last year. There was absolutely no evidence anywhere for the existence of the man he claims was responsible: 'Bob' (or 'Caravan Bob' as he swiftly became known). The only thing that could save The Builder was some paperwork to go with Bob's disposal/dumping of the caravans.

Which was exactly what we got – five minutes before the start of the trial. Their elegant, softly spoken lawyer presented our elegant, softly spoken lawyer with an invoice. If it hadn't been in the deadly serious surroundings of Fareham Magistrates' Court, we would have all gone Brian Blessed: "Caravan Bob's ALIVE!!!"

There then followed an hour's frantic meeting and debate – all done in the most elegant and soft-spoken style – about the invoice. I'm not saying it was dodgy – it's just that there was still no name for Bob on it, the phone number didn't work, and there was no record of his 'company'. Hmm.

It was agreed during the pre-trial discussions that Mike and I would not, after all, be questioned about our statements, and would not have to take the stand. The defence had accepted them completely. They agreed that The Builder's pickup had indeed been dumping waste-filled caravans around the English countryside. This rendered the existence or otherwise of Caravan Bob completely irrelevant: The Builder had been in charge of the caravans' disposal. The charges of not disposing of waste properly would be aimed four-square (or five-square) at him.

Mike and I were given the option of going home, but we quickly agreed to sneak in and listen to proceedings. It was my very first trip into a court, and it was all a bit quiet. I was expecting Kevin Costner/JFK levels of fiery oratory. Instead there was a lot of quietly spoken disagreement and pause-filled gentle argument. Even the occasional bureaucratic bungle was dealt with by the two sides in the smiliest and most civilised way. I suppose that's the result of hundreds of years of legal proceedings. Nothing works if tempers, voices and fists get raised.

We eventually left at about twelve thirty as the Bench retired to consider its verdict, only to find that I'd got a parking ticket. It had been a long morning.

Later in the afternoon, we got the verdict: guilty on all five charges. The fines were not as dramatic as they could have been – just over £3,200 including costs – but it was a conviction nonetheless. A victory for the council team – and, when they rang with the news, they certainly sounded pleased. I couldn't help feeling a bit sorry for The Builder. He was old, fairly unsteady on his feet, and his completely clean sheet was about to be tarnished with a criminal record and a fine – not to mention his extensive legal costs. But if you decide to be part of a scheme dumping waste-filled caravans out in the countryside, I suppose you have to live with the consequences of being spotted.

The evening bought battle of a similar but more light-hearted vein: the quarter finals of the Hampshire Growmore Club quiz: two teams of farming types, a quizmaster, two scorers, and a vast and enthusiastic crowd of two, all sitting in the West Meon sports pavilion. It's a quiz like no other, organised by a club that's the last of the network of Growmore Clubs that sprang up nationwide during World War Two.

We lost spectacularly. The force was not with us.

January 8th

It rained again. Yet another deluge. Several hours of really heavy stuff, that left the bottom of Roe Hill flooded again. Not really a lot to do on a day like this, so I did a few emails to press offices trying to organise another test car or two, and then Hazel and I set off down the Meon Valley to visit the Countrystore in Wickham. We picked up a dozen or so bags of calf feed.

I then spent the rest of the afternoon seething at the news from France.

January 9th

Right, I thought. That's quite enough not doing any farming. It's time to get that new plough up and running.

So off I went, on the long drive to Behind My Love's, the lightest field on the farm, and the only one that could possibly be workable after another sharp shower of rain early this morning.

I love a good challenge, and a second-hand plough that someone else has used in completely different circumstances, on different soil and connected to a different tractor, is as good a challenge as a Rubik's Cube. After marking out the headland on three sides, I started alongside our boundary hedge. I went up the hedge line with the Packomat still folded in, in what I assume is its transport position (I've got no book), right up against the plough bodies. I then set the Packomat out into its work position, and started on the complicated job that is getting a plough levelled up and working properly. It takes a few passes, and the secret is changing as few things as possible as little as possible.

First up was the front furrow width. The previous owner's tractor must have had his back wheels set a lot wider: the front furrow was only cutting about eight inches. Five minutes with the threaded bar soon sorted that out. But then the front furrow was still not cutting enough – it was too shallow. It seemed that the plough wasn't turning over far enough. I adjusted the stops to try to level up the bodies in that direction. Coming down the hill was ploughing a lot deeper than ploughing up the hill – the fresh chalk coming up was a giveaway. The two depth limiters for the rear wheel were different, so I got them evened up, too.

I then lost half an hour as Mike the Keeper couldn't contain his curiosity any longer, and appeared over the hedge to see how I was getting on. He was also dead keen to compare notes on our 'victory' in court earlier in the week. His opinion, like mine, was that the Bench had taken a dim view of The Builder early in the case. I agreed that all three seemed to listen to him with a slightly sarcastic look on their faces.

Back to the ploughing. The paint stripper applied earlier had done absolutely no stripping of paint, and the damp chalk was certainly not doing it. It was fairly unwilling to flow across the still bright red mouldboards, so it wasn't the best-looking job, even once it seemed that I'd got everything right in all the various planes and width settings. I stopped several times during the day to scrape the mud off, and for a turn or two there was a fantastic even finish, and as I wound the Packomat down another couple of turns, the field looked drillable.

The bulk of daylight hours had been dry with a fair gale, and the job was going better and better. As darkness approached, however, the rain came back, and everything got sticky on the top. Nothing would flow through the skims, and I was having to stop and lift mid-field to clear the blockages.

That was my cue to head for home. I'd forgotten how long it takes to de-mud a five furrow to ensure the roads are kept clean. It was a good half an hour in the heavy drizzle under the tractor floodlights. Just like the good old days.

It's funny to be out ploughing again.

January 10th

A foul, wet and windy morning. Hazel and Fred set off bravely to pick up at Tim Sykes' shoot. I assured her that the weather would get better, but I don't think she believed me.

The Editor called in, en route to doing a recce for pigeon. He always makes me chuckle: here is a man who, thanks to his job, gets to shoot every sort of quarry all over the world. He's been on every continent, mixed with everybody from royalty down to us tenant farmers – but nothing seems to light his hunter's fire like the prospect of a few windy hours in a Hampshire hedgerow, shooting pigeons as they blast in on the gale. Just as the squall line cleared us and blue sky approached, he set off on his bicycle for Drier Field and White Hill; I made a date with Mr Sofa.

Just as it was getting dark, the phone rang. It was the Editor. It had been a day of legend, apparently. He'd shot a dozen in White Hill. They had been drifting in from Kilmeston way, catching sight of his decoy pattern, and pausing in the trees in the Barracuda Dell – just above where he'd been standing. You never heard such excitement. I suggested a beer to celebrate – having not been to the Pots since before Christmas. Alas, he couldn't: he was off to see the new film about Stephen Hawking. I warned him not to expect too many rampant sex scenes or car chases.

Hazel arrived back; she and Fred had got wet, but had had another good day. Fred seems to be getting dafter as the years go by, and had lost the plot completely on one drive. He had behaved better after a good talking too, and regained some honour.

I, however, had caught up with some sleep, and enjoyed at least two beautifully remastered classic films through droopy eyelids. That's my idea of heaven.

January 11th

A dry and very cold Sunday morning, with a strong NE wind. The thought flashed across my mind that I ought to go out and check the Drier headland to see if it would drill. A millisecond later, the thought vanished. I had promised to take Jonathan clay shooting, and that takes precedence.

The fine weather had brought out the punters. Chalky Hill was as full as I've seen it. The queues weren't unbearable; clay shoots are places of enormous good nature, and the banter, advice and ribbing is continuous and heart-warming. I shot well, Jonathan shot even better, reaching 29/50. He seems to suit the second-hand Browning 325 20 bore that I bought before Christmas perfectly.

There was one long queue, to get into the dugout for the driven birds at the top of the field. I looked back down the site and saw an anti-gun campaigner's nightmare: a couple of hundred heavily armed people, unsupervised and in a public place. They were smiling, joking, civilised and safe. Even those of us beginning to feel the cold in the wait at the top of the field were uncomplaining as we chatted. A Guardianista's nightmare.

It was a long morning, and when we got home, Hazel's sister and her family had turned up for Sunday lunch. It was a real AGA-cooler of a lunch: massive joint of beef, all the trimmings, then lemon tart and apple and pear crumble. Let's not forget the cream, ice cream, and huge tray of chocolates. Someone quoted the advice in yesterday's paper about how to stay lean. 'Only eat when hungry, and stop eating when full.' It got the biggest laugh of the day.

The Editor turned up again. He claimed to be on pigeon patrol again, but I reckon he'd got wind of Heather's lemon tart. Unfortunately, he arrived too late to do any more than scrape the remains off the plate. I bet he doesn't do that with royalty.

January 12th

Another teaser of a morning – just about dry enough to think of popping out and seeing if there's some farming to be done, but with drizzle in the air and a horrendous forecast. I adopted my usual pessimistic attitude, and resigned myself to another day of office work.

Luckily, the session doing the accounts was interrupted by a 'damsel in distress' call. Our old friend the Lady Land Agent was stuck on the road through Cheriton Wood with a puncture. She, like most of us in our fifties, is suffering from an assortment of physical creaks and groans, and thanks to some quite serious neck problems would rather not get involved with changing a wheel. She had tried one of the emergency breakdown companies, and they wouldn't be there for ninety minutes – and she was on her way to an important appointment.

Well, who can say 'no' in these circumstances? I jumped in Tigger and raced up to Cheriton Wood. Thankfully, her old Polo had all the right kit: decent jack, wheel spanner, and – most crucially of all – a proper full-size spare wheel. There's nothing more absurd than a tube of glue and a feeble compressor sitting in the wheel well, and all for the sake of saving a bit of fuel.

I did my 'knight in shining armour' bit, and sent her on her way, telling her she owed me a beer. I couldn't help thinking, as I had a good snoop through Cheyney's farm on the way back, how in demand we farmers can be. During gales, we're the first people to get requests to clear fallen trees – we have the tractors and chainsaws. During the snow, we have four-wheel drives to help. In my youth, we had the village snowplough allocated to us. We're not needed much these days for food production, but at least a local lady land agent knows where she can find a certain farmer to help change a wheel: he'll be sitting indoors drinking tea.

The evening saw another rehearsal of The Thomas Lord Old Gits. A full strength one, too, although since Dan left, cutting our numbers by 16% and our talent by 40%, the shed where we rehearse isn't as crowded as it used to be. There were signs of optimism: rumours of gigs, and even one firm booking. After a drought of opportunities to get out and play, there's nothing like that sort of news to lift the spirits. As a result we played as well as we have for weeks. Mind you, we had to concentrate to hear ourselves over the thunderous rain that was by now coming down on the metal sheeting of the roof. Not a lot of farming tomorrow, methinks.

January 13th

Another ferocious rainstorm overnight. The whole house shook in the wind. We were all a bit disoriented by the lack of sleep – all except Jonathan, who was, as usual, up on time for school. I was baffled, being convinced it was a Saturday. Diana overslept, getting up with five minutes to spare for her babysitting duties over at the bungalow.

Hazel set off picking-up at Barrow Hill again, just as the clouds cleared and the loveliest of sunny mornings arrived. This time she took Monty, and Fred howled and groaned for some time. I managed to get some film of him up on Facebook. Poor old fellow.

I thought I'd make the most of the sun and put some rope bangers up in the OSR. The crop doesn't seem to be suffering too much from the pigeons, and it was the first time this year I'd thought measures to deter them were needed. Not like a couple of years ago, when the OSR was in Big Field. I had a gas banger out there at the end of October.

The debate about pigeon bangers and assorted scarers goes on year after year. What are the most effective? Rope bangers, gas bangers, or other non-explosive methods such as kites or rotating balloons or plates? Are they effective at all? Should we even bother before January?

I think we've tried just about everything over the years. I have fond memories of Dad trying the first of the rope bangers. I was very small, but can clearly remember him lighting one in the 'L' plantation in Springshott, next to Kilmeston Road. We all retreated a safe distance, as it says on the box, and he decided that halfway up the Hangar was safe enough. From that huge distance, the explosion seemed a bit weedy. Mind you, if you've ever had one go off close by, it's not very pleasant.

We went through a spell of putting the ropes inside half barrels; the theory seemed to be that this somehow amplified the explosion. Not sure about the physics behind that theory. I suspect all it did was leave another hazard for the combine driver to look out for come harvest.

Then we tried the delta-shaped kites. These were about four feet across, and hovered way up in the sky, bird-of-prey-like. They achieved great height thanks to the vast length of nylon string that came with them. There were instructions that came with the string: unwind the whole length, and check for weak points. I couldn't be arsed with all that, and went out to Rick/Clump with a brand new kite. I reeled out about fifty yards of twine, and got the kite airborne. As I allowed the kite to get higher and higher, I realised I should have worn gloves: the narrow white cord burned itself into my finger as the powerful uplift dragged the string out. To this day I can still remember the pain.

The pain was soon replaced by shock, as, with only a few yards of twine left to unravel, it broke. The kite, almost at maximum height, sailed away on the strong wind, over the trees, off towards Bramdean, and never seen again. I seem to remember getting an earful about that. Those kites weren't cheap.

We moved onto gas guns. The early ones were a triumph of Heath Robinson engineering. Incoming propane gas slowly inflated a chamber, and cocked a flintlock mechanism at the same time. Once the chamber was full, the gas supply from the cylinder was cut off, the chamber deflated, pumping gas into the barrel and the flintlock struck a spark, resulting in a fantastic explosion; what could go wrong? As it happens, everything. I spent many hours trying to clean out nozzles, or dry out or replace the tiny wet flints.

The flintlock mechanism was replaced with a spark generator system. A spring-loaded hammer, about three inches long, hit a piezo-electric block. This wasn't too reliable either. It did happen to work the day I had it on the back flap of the old Land

Rover, and Dad and I were twiddling with it. The barrel was full of gas. "What happens if I…" said Dad, flicking the hammer down. I blame the close range explosion for the ringing ears I still have to this day.

The gas guns then evolved into something more sophisticated. Complicated circuit boards controlled the gas supply, and converted the electricity supply from the now-compulsory 12 volt battery into a spark. Or two sparks, or three. They also controlled the time between bangs. All very sophisticated, but not foolproof. Early circuit boards were notoriously unreliable, and corroded easily. Mice chewed electric cables, and a £300 gas banger complete with car battery and propane cylinder proved awfully tempting for our friends in the white van fraternity, who frequently exercised their human right to help themselves. And who could blame them?

As Hampshire's biggest insomniac, I have another problem with gas guns. Even with the most sophisticated of light-sensitive on-off switches, they have a habit of keeping going all night. And I, as an insomniac living on top of a hill in a pretty-well silent part of Hampshire, can hear them from miles away. And then I get angry under the duvet. How can a farmer not hear his own banger? If he can't hear it, he's obviously an agribusinessman, not a farmer. If he can hear it, why doesn't he go and turn it off? I know some farmers who couldn't care even if they heard it (Dad would have been one of them) – but proper farmers wake for nothing. They work too hard to be woken.

I've lost count of the times I've realised that sleep is no longer possible. As soon as one set of bangs goes off, I'm counting the minutes till the next set. There's no point trying earplugs or diving deeper under the duvet. The thump reaches deep into the brain – especially if you're listening out for it. There's only one thing to do. Get up, grab wellies, a torch, possibly a map, truck keys and (crucially) a watch. I'm off to find it and turn it off.

The technique is simple. Stand in the yard until you hear it. Take a bearing. If it is going off, for instance, every twenty minutes, you've got eighteen minutes to head towards it. Then you stop somewhere quiet, turn the engine off, and wait. All being well, you'll find a new bearing, and be that much closer to it. Given four or five stops, you can track it down. Next step is to disconnect the battery, or turn the gas off. Then home to wind down over a bowl of Crunchy Nut Cornflakes.

I went through a stage of leaving little notes for the owner. They were rude and anonymous ones until a neighbour found out it was me. Very embarrassing. Then one day I got a furious phone call from a neighbour who had been kept awake by one of my gas bangers – and I hadn't heard it. I scrapped the agribusinessman theory – and the rude notes.

The electronics on gas guns have got more reliable, which is a huge relief – not least because a new feature of the guns is random timing of the bangs. There is no longer a fixed interval between volleys. This renders the drive 'n' wait tracking system all but impossible. I think it has been a couple of years since I did a night expedition.

Almost as soon as I got back from my rope banger hanging, the heavens opened again, and a series of heavy sleety showers blew through. Poor old Hazel, out picking-up, in all the wind and rain. I put the kettle on and had another honey sandwich.

January 14th

Things looked distinctly brighter this morning. It wasn't raining, which made a change, and it was the first day of the year that felt like it was getting longer. When I got out to White Hill to put out some rope bangers, not only were there no pigeons, but the late wheat in Folly and BOMS looked distinctly even and green. It was blowing a cold gale, and the odd flake of snow appeared from the blue sky. There were clouds to the south, so they must have come from them.

Neighbour Robert rang while I was out there, sounding better. His chest infection had died down a bit – it has been bad enough to send him home from our Christmas shoot without firing a shot. He said kind things about Friday's *Farmers Weekly* column – he was mentioned in the article, and he'd had some phone calls pulling his leg about it. Always nice when you get feedback.

Tod the agronomist rang to discuss plans for the spring. Let's keep on with the winter wheat acreage – there's a few weeks left of the sowing window. The February sown wheat for harvest 2013 surprised us all and rewrote a few rules on the latest drilling date. It was cheap to grow, too. So we'll persevere with the Scout in Top and Bottom of Hurst Down (TBHD), Joan's Acre and Dell Close.

The winter beans, pencilled in for Godwin's, are a different matter. Winter beans sown at this time of year are more unreliable than modern varieties of spring beans. He recommended dropping the winter beans – they may have just been cleaned and bagged up, but they can wait in the corner of a barn, and we'll use them next season. Only nine months till we think of putting them in. We decided to order some more spring beans, and get that drilling pressure off our backs.

There's only one thing nicer than starting to think about some farming, and that's getting back indoors and finding that the forecast has been rewritten for the next few days. We've still got all hell breaking loose tonight, but they are promising a more settled spell once that storm is through. Cold, too, which might give some firm, non-sticky ground which might mean I can get sowing again. Might I get all the planned winter wheat acreage done before the end of January?

First things first: we've got the third Hinton Walkabout Shoot tomorrow. The Editor and I (who are informal co-organisers) had a pessimistic chat about it via text earlier in the week, and were considering calling it off, thanks to the foul weather. When it looked like we'd have gales and scattered showers, we decided to go for it. I also thought it important that we showed a bit more commitment; I could just imagine the Trust on the phone, having heard that we had cried off. "After all that negotiation to get the shoot tenancy, and you can't even be bothered..." The most important chap to keep informed was Guy the Colonel, driving down from Glasgow for the shoot. Once he heard we were all systems go, he set off on the long trek south. I hope we find something for him to pull a trigger at.

I took a break mid-afternoon from doing the VAT (from our big double-entry day book – very old-fashioned and long winded) and made a bid for the Lupo that has been offered to us. It would be perfect for Diana's use, if she passes her test. It would

22

be lovely to have the dear old VW back here, because it was originally Granny Flindt's. She bought it in 1999, back when she was very much alive and with it. The story goes that Grandpa Flindt was huffing and puffing about her choice of colour – violent yellow. At which point, the salesman sidled up to Granny and said, "I think Madam should have her car in whatever colour she wants – don't you?" As the years went by she became afraid to drive at night, then afraid to drive at all – the hordes of bikers used to terrify her. I found it useful to use as a runabout, and sometimes would take it on long journeys for speaking engagements. It took me economically and swiftly to Liverpool, Somerset, and Hereford – and all at over 50 mpg. It spent more and more time in our yard rather than over at their house, and finally became ours. I'm not sure if any money changed hands, even if the documents did.

When a neighbour asked if it might be for sale a couple of years later, I had changed my farm vehicle to one more capable of doing long journeys (i.e. not a Land Rover), and the Lupo had become unused. So we sold it to him. He used it, his wife used it, his children used it, crashed it, repaired it and covered it with flowery stickers, but it now sits (de-flowered and freshly MOT'd) unused in his garage. He rang the other day to ask if we would like to buy it back. Of course we would; I can hear Granny murmuring her approval from the shelf behind me, where her urn still sits.

January 15th

January 15th

The storm arrived at about dusk yesterday and it was yet another big one. Funnily enough, I can sleep quite well through a constant roar of wind and rain, but when the guttering develops a leak just above our bedroom window, and there starts a 'tap tap tap' of waterdrops hitting the sill outside, then sleep becomes a problem. It's the mid-Hampshire version of Chinese water torture. The wind occasionally blew the drops off their cruel trajectory, and a few seconds of silence would raise hope that somehow the dripping had stopped; but no. Tap, tap tap…

If you had driven past the farmhouse at about 1am, you'd have seen me standing on the lawn, flat cap and wax jacket over pyjamas, shining a torch up into the deluge, in a vain attempt to come up with some way to stop the drips. If I'd seen me, I would have rung the police on the spot. Realising that there was nothing to be done, I headed back to bed. Somehow, I drifted off through the tap tap tapping.

I was up nice and early for the shoot preparations and was met by the Colonel, who is an even worse sleeper than me. I'm not sure whether that's in his nature, or part of the side effects of the Parkinson's or the associated pills. He seemed well, despite his horrific drive down to mid-Hampshire from Glasgow in some foul conditions. I thought I'd better lay on the apologies for what little shooting he might get. It's not like the grand shoots of yesteryear.

For decades, there has been a formal driven shoot here. In my childhood, we were nothing to do with it. As lowly tenant farmers, we had to endure the crop damage and wheel marks over the fields. We were rewarded (and I use the term loosely) with a brace of birds that were usually 'well shot'. Mum would dutifully serve them for Sunday lunch.

In the late Eighties, after the Trust had inherited Hinton Ampner, they let the big house, and the shoot, to a wealthy financier/businessman. Several years of hell ensued. He decided his shoot was to be the biggest and grandest in the country. There were keepers, under keepers, shoot managers, shoot consultants – and there were pheasants everywhere. Tens of thousands of them. Whole fields would vanish – not just the headlands next to the woods that we know so well ('partridge beetle' is the term used by agronomists). I can remember walking Drier Field one November and finding the complete crop had been skinned.

A whole book can be written about the battles that went on in those years. Chapters could be dedicated to how claiming for damage by game is all but impossible. Meanwhile the Hinton Ampner shoot developed a reputation for vulgarity that spread far and wide.

Suddenly, the Notorious Tenant upped and left. Rumours were rife about why he left. Some said the Trust, finally aware of the damage to their image, had been trying to evict him for years, and finally caught him out on unpaid rent on one of the little cottages he had also commandeered. Some said his financial acumen had deserted him, and he couldn't afford any rent at all.

I like to think that a grumpy tenant farmer had a small hand in it. One day, the shoot manager called over to the bungalow, where we lived at that time, and started the process of trying to lean on me to convert even more of my arable acres to shooting strips. "Look," he said. "I have a blank cheque."

"Sorry," I replied, "I'm not interested. I don't want any more game strips on my farm."

"You don't understand," he said, with a look of bewilderment. "I have a blank cheque for you. How much do you want for these extra strips?" I don't often use the word 'literally', but he literally had a blank chequebook, open on my kitchen table.

"No," I replied as calmly as I could. "No more shooting strips." He left empty-handed.

Not long after that, the Trust agent arrived. The Trust had decided to enforce the obscure clause in my tenancy agreement – the one about planting new blocks of woodland. And, to no one's surprise, these blocks just happened to be where the shoot wanted their new shooting strips. I made it clear that I thought this was outrageous. I would be monitoring these strips, and calling in legal help if a single maize plant appeared.

The first batch of tree planting took place. Not a single stem of maize appeared, and, best of all, we pointed out that a change in the area of a farm (due, for instance, to a block of woodland being planted by the landlord) re-set the three-year AHA rent cycle.

Soon after that the Trust agent left , the shoot manager was gone, and, most significantly, the Notorious Tenant left the village. Few mourned his leaving – not even the milkman, who was still chasing unpaid bills from Hinton Ampner House. The poor fellow had kept on supplying them, knowing that to stop doing so would have meant no chance whatsoever of recouping his money. And if you won't pay the milkman, what sort of a man are you?

So the shoot tenancy came up for grabs. The new man was from another local Big House (there's a lot of them round here) who wisely decided to work with the grumpy farmer. He too wanted shooting strips, but offered me half a day's shooting in exchange. By now I was getting invited onto neighbours' shoots, and quite getting into the whole thing, and so I jumped at the chance. Better still, when his son took over the tenancy, and started assembling a syndicate of youngsters, I was asked to join. It wasn't cheap, but you don't turn down the chance to shoot on your own farm. We kept costs down in all sorts of ways, one of the main ones being by hosting the lunches.

We tidied up the old estate yard workshop, where, in pre-Trust days, skilled carpenters and woodmen made doors, windows and gates for the village, using timber from the woods. There was a long shed containing a sawmill, powered by a vast diesel engine at the far end. Tree trunks were cut into planks and rails. A huge three-phase planer sat on a concrete plinth in the workshop, and an aged Rayburn sat on another plinth. Outside there was a huge pit full of creosote, perfect for treating fencing posts – when Dad arrived in Hinton in 1959, all the fences were re-done with treated oak posts. There are a still a few of them out there now.

It was a melancholy job clearing that place out, not least because of memories of being sent to play up there by our exhausted mother in those far-off pre-TV and pre-internet days. Ian and I would hang around the huge diesel engine as it roared deafeningly, hold sticks against the drive belt that went from engine to saw bench. We'd throw sticks into the vast creosote pit, and settle down to make toast back in the workshop, holding bread up to the open flames of the Rayburn with a fork fashioned from a spare piece of wire by the kind old carpenter. My brother and I must have been a flipping nuisance, but he always made us welcome. Back in the 1960s, Health and Safety was a far-off concept.

When the Trust took over the village, the estate yard was shut down, the site was returned to us (it was fully within our yard anyway), and when the youngsters' shoot started up, it became the perfect venue for the shoot lunches. A major clear-out and refurnish was needed. We lined the walls with cladding, put new windows in, and brought in another Rayburn to go on the site of the three-phase planer.

It was a major job, clearing out all the clutter. There were unused handbooks for assorted old trucks and tractors, curious tools (a 'chain' for field measurement – look that one up, kids) and, rather sadly, envelopes containing prize certificates from long-abandoned local shows. First Prize for a 'hunting gate', for instance. Oddly, and rather unjustly, owner of the village was named on the certificate as prizewinner – not the carpenter. No wonder the latter decided to leave them in the envelopes.

There were finds of a completely surreal nature: a canvas roll-up poster of a cross section of a woman, such as you'd find on the wall of a biology classroom. Were the young men of the village sent up to the estate yard workshop for a briefing before their wedding day? And as for the long and narrow strip of elephant hide that turned up in a drawer – I dread to think what sort of ceremony that was used for.

We finally got the workshop cleaned up and fit for hosting lunches. There were Saturdays when there would be thirty people, guns and guests, eating and laughing round the table, both Rayburns roaring away. I reckon the kind old carpenter would have approved – we were still using the very table he had built into the fabric of the building.

After eleven years of that shoot, the Trust started making noises about their plans for the estate – they'd like their woods back, please. You couldn't blame them for it: there was a fundamental problem with hundreds of acres of Trust-owned woods being shut to the public. The relationship between the shoot and the Trust wasn't improved when a Trust-led walk around the woods stumbled upon half-a-dozen members of the keepering fraternity, in full camo gear, waving automatic shotguns, doing a spring vermin shoot. A polite exchange may have smoothed the encounter, but aggressive demands of "What the bloody hell are you doing here?" – and not from the lips of the Trust or their guests – may have hardened the Trust management's attitude to the shoot, and hastened its demise. When the head of the syndicate couldn't agree to hosting the only sort of shoot the Trust would approve of, he walked away from Hinton Ampner.

And so, for a couple of years, there was no formal shooting at Hinton Ampner. This must have been for the first time in a very long time. The big pens in the woods were taken down, I brought all the shooting strips back into the rotation, and that, I thought, was the end of it. One day, however, as we were having a round-table discussion with the Trust, they said that they had never said 'no shooting'; there was a rough shoot to be had. And would we be interested?

I resisted the urge to suggest that their kind offer was a direct result of the bad press that had arisen following the demise of several pheasant shoots on Trust property, and said I would be very interested. My ambition for a farm shoot would be half a dozen guns, half a dozen beaters, a walk round the farm, a bag in the twenties, then late lunch in the farmhouse – or the pub. The Trust said that that was exactly the sort of thing they wanted. Perfect.

Ten months of negotiations followed. There were numerous attempts to get the geographical area of the shoot right; I was keen to get as much of the woods as possible, but the Trust have made walkways through them. These had to be kept separate. Paperwork went backwards and forwards, clauses went in and back out again – no one needs a Game Licence any more – until, finally, in mid-October, a five-year lease was signed. We only had time for four shoots this season, so very favourable terms were negotiated.

So we have had two shoots, today was our third, and we've one more at the end of the month. Each of them has been perfect to try this and that, to experiment with

26

where we go and how we drive bits of the farm.

Today looked a bit of a challenge. Keeper Lore tells you that the wind and the rain would have meant no flying at all today. Then one of the four beaters texted to say he couldn't make it. And when picker-up Julie turned up, she was down to one dog, and she had to be away by one o'clock. In the end, four guns, three beaters and two-and-a-half dogs (Fred was lame yesterday) set off with not the highest of expectations.

When we knocked off at one, however, there were eight pheasants and three pigeons in the bag, the sun had shone all day, the dogs had all survived and had the time of their lives, and spirits were high. Neighbour Rufus had driven past us earlier, and announced that he was idle for the day, so joined us in the farmhouse for lunch. A compact gathering (although Rufus boosted bodily weight by about 30%) enjoyed traditional farmhouse fayre.

Guy the Colonel set off back up the A34 in the evening, I headed for a date with my friend Mr Sofa, and everyone else collapsed in assorted corners of the house in contented weariness. And nothing does 'contented weariness' like a brace of flatcoats after five hours of beating. Bedtime for me was briefly delayed as Diana noisily whispered to me on the landing that a YouTube video of Hazel's snoring would most certainly not be a wise move. She's probably right.

January 16ᵗʰ

Not a great night. Nothing to do with gas bangers, mice, snoring or leaking gutters; I had just eaten too much of what I shouldn't have eaten. Long, weird dreams and a thoroughly restless night.

There was an early call from the head of the Trust's pet team of handymen who seem to have pretty well got all the construction jobs on the estate sown up. His team would like to come round and sort out the downpipes from the guttering on the south side of the kitchen block. Would that be OK, he asked. I said that would be fine.

This should bring to an end the longest building saga in the history of Hinton Ampner. The kitchen block is the one-storey bit of the house, but its gutters take a lot of the rainfall off the vast expanse of the rest of the house. Up until the Trust got hold of the place, there was no problem. Nice big gutters carried the water away relatively happily during nineteen out of twenty downpours. They were plastic, so I suppose they can't have been that old.

The Trust didn't like them at all – because they were plastic. So they were replaced with cast-iron ones. There were two problems with this idea. For a start, the first we knew of the Trust's plan was when a man in a dodgy van arrived in the yard and started taking down the guttering. Fellow inhabitants of Trust properties will recognise this scenario at once: the Trust seems to struggle to acknowledge that these houses are our homes. We certainly are rarely informed of any building work.

I think they would have changed their policy if they had seen the poor gutter-man cowering in the corner with two slavering Belgian Shepherd dogs waiting for the cue to rip him limb from limb – men in dodgy vans are their avowed enemies, after all.

The second problem was that the proper cast-iron guttering was too small. Even the tiniest shower meant an overflow, with water pouring through both back doors. Years of complaints (and threats to go down to Homebase and buy some of my own black plastic pipes to replace the approved but chocolate-fireguard metal ones) finally resulted in new downpipes to drain the flow more quickly.

The new downpipe was directed towards what looked like a soakaway – the square grid was still there, so there was much hammering and chiselling to expose what was thought would be a drain. In the end, it exposed nothing but a hole which seemed, inexplicably, to go back under the house, away from all the soakaways that we knew of. Undaunted, the builder's team dug new trenches out to the rainwater soakaways that cross the garden, taking water from the yard down through the garden to the bottom of the orchard.

The water supply/disposal system on the estate is chaos. It has been a source of wonder and confusion for as long as I've been here. In my office there used to be a big diesel engine, which was started up every morning to pump water, drawn from the farmhouse kitchen well, across the yard to an old thatched barn. On a platform in this barn was a huge tank. It was the high point of the water supply, and pipes led from it to every trough and many of the houses on the farm.

The pipes were laid down by Italian prisoners-of-war in the early 1940s, and started leaking and bursting in the 1980s. (I wish my Alfasud had lasted that long.) By then, memories had faded, but Dad and I spent many days with stopcocks and trial and error, working on a map of the water pipes, drawn up on the back of an old feed bag. Mapping the London Underground was child's play in comparison.

Give the Trust some credit – about ten years ago, they organised a new water main through the village, with nice new meters for each house. After years of trying to guess who had used how much water, and therefore who owed who how much, it was nice and rationalised and modern.

These pipes are still out there, though. When we were digging anti-poacher trenches, the 300+hp Fendt towing the massive single-furrow plough squatted and grunted as it came down the hill opposite Joan's Acre House. Up came a length of water pipe. Out came a fountain of water – brown at first, then crystal clear. After a couple of minutes, we realised that it was certainly a 'live' pipe. Luckily, the builder was in the parish, and managed to jam a length of wood up the end for temporary stop, but not before we'd had a good go at filling one of the trenches, turning it into a moat. Now, that really would stop the poachers. Why there should be a live pipe out there was solved by neighbour Robert, who pointed out that Joan's Acre Field would once have gone with Joan's Acre House, and would have been all paddocks and pastures. They would have been connected to the house, so mains feed would have reached all the pipes still underground, sitting there all these years later, waiting for a Fendt to rip 'em up.

The builder's mate turned up late this morning, finished off a bit of cosmetic work on the downpipes, and had a look at the infamous drip outside our bedroom window. Using nothing more than a very long ladder and a bucket of water (Health and Safety on line 2), he failed to recreate the problem, but having listened patiently to my description, agreed to come back and put some lead flashing to cover the gap between roof edge and gutter.

All the time he was listening, he and his sidekick were getting the flatcoat treatment. Lots of cuddling and fawning – not even the slightest growl. It could be because they've been round for so long they're not considered worth barking at. Or flatcoats make useless guard dogs.

The weather turned stunningly warm and sunny – but it was still too wet underfoot to try farming. I went over to Godwin's and chopped another barrowful of logs, and then took the dogs on a curtailed Drier loop. Curtailed because yesterday's bad eating caught up with me just as I got back. Having lit two candles in the downstairs loo for the sake of those who come after, I retired, once again, in some pain, to Mr Sofa. One day I'll learn.

January 17th

I didn't sleep well, and was up before dawn. My reward was the most stunning sunrise lighting up quite a hard frost. Frosts are always welcome when there's some late-sown wheat needing vernalisation. It seemed the sort of day that justified an early light of the log burner in the hall, but no sooner had I lit it than cloud moved in, all the frost vanished, and drizzle started. It was still nice to have a roaring heat source by nine in the morning.

It was a quiet Saturday. Still no chance of any farming, no shooting or picking-up to be done, and no children working. A good 'sit in front of the fire' day.

The dogs, of course, could only put up with it for so long, so I did the Drier loop just before dusk. At the far end of Roe Hill I found a CO_2 canister – the type used in air guns. I've certainly never used one out there – the only people I could think of who would have left it there are our poaching chums. Perhaps they may have dropped it during their deer chasing trips back in the autumn. I pocketed it carefully with gloves on. It might be useful to the Police.

I met Rufus and his two lovely collies at the New Pond junction and we walked together down Dark Lane. He was in a bit of stew. He'd had what he called a 'white out' – completely forgotten his lines – during his performance with the West Meon Players the night before. He got through it – the Players are one of the modern amdram groups who think the idea of a prompter is wrong; you're supposed to muddle your way out of a forgotten line. The ex-pro who taught us drama at school would be horrified at such an idea. If you forget your line, he maintained, a good prompter, who will have sat in on every rehearsal and performance, will notice, and will quietly prompt. Even a quietly spoken "prompt" by the actor will go all but unnoticed.

I remember just this situation from my days at the Cheriton Players. I knew I'd forgotten a line, and glanced down at the prompter. She sat there smiling back at me, with no book. Blind panic. I seem to remember picking up the nearest telephone and saying, "Yes Vicar?" It was nowhere near the correct line, but raised a huge laugh. The man playing the butler stepped in with the all-time classic amdram line: "What I think you meant to say, Sir, was…"

Rufus, in fact, had received a prompt from the director, which saved the moment, but it seemed to throw him for the evening. So much so, that on the way home he crashed his hire car into the muddy bank at New Pond. He was only using a hire car because the insurance company still hadn't finished deciding on the fate of his old but beloved Range Rover, which he'd crashed into a tree a couple of months ago. I wished him well for the last night, and, once we finally separated the jolly tumble of flatcoats and collies, we went our separate ways.

Back home, I put the CO_2 canister into a new food bag. I must make a note to tell the Police I've got it. They need an excuse to come round and coo over the kittens.

January 18th

A damp and cold Sunday morning. I went and put some rope bangers in White Hill, but saw few pigeons. Good. There was a yellow Labrador running loose across Cheyney, and a man walking along the edge of the field. On the way home, I had a quick word, and asked him to keep to the road. "I didn't realise there was a crop in that field," was the reply. Such are the country dwellers of central Hampshire.

I sat in the kitchen and made a determined effort to read the Sunday papers on the table, just like the old days. Most of the news is drivel, of course. Back on the internet, I shameless plugged my last *Farmers Weekly* opinion column on the Bishop Hill blog, where it got a good response. A curious mixture of old and new technologies.

After lunch, Hazel and I discussed some redecorating. The curse of living in the house in which you were born is that redecorating is hard – after all, I can remember the kitchen being done only recently. Well, when I say 'recently', I mean in the early 1980s. I suppose I'm a fan of the vernacular, too. If something works, there's no need to replace it. But having had more guests in our kitchen in the past couple of months than in the previous couple of years, thanks to the shoot, even I can tell that something needs to be done. The kitchen is old, shabby and tired.

Plans to replace the AGA have certainly been shelved, though. A couple of years ago, as oil prices soared, and we discovered the joy of burning wood, we had a plan to throw out the 1959 four-oven AGA – a solid-fuel-to-oil converted monster installed by my parents, and the object of immense affection from my mother – and put in an electric AGA. Next to it, we planned a wood-burning boiler, plumbed in where the old Agamatic is.

The Agamatic was an astonishing machine. It was plumbed into the water system by 2" pipes, and boiled up water as quickly as you could use it. Hot water was literally limitless. It wasn't until I went and stayed – and had a bath – at a friend's house that I came across the concept of 'using all the hot water' – and got roundly bollocked for it. Twice the Agamatic furred up and burst. The first time, Dad went to a scrapyard in the West Country to fetch another boiler. It, too, needed defurring, and he had many hours of fun pouring some lethal acid into it in the yard to remove the calcium. Just the sort of daily job he loved.

Some years later, this one burst, too. It was in the middle of the night, and, because the house is mostly downhill from the kitchen, the mess was biblical. It was never used again, and my parents switched to an immersion heater. They were alone in the farmhouse by then, so it was probably more economical.

There's much relief that we didn't crack on with this AGA masterplan. Oil prices have plummeted – electricity prices haven't. The old sky-blue AGA might have a few more years in the kitchen yet. One day we'll find the original receipt for it, which Mum tucked carefully into a book to flatten it out. She then forgot which book.

The weather had been too cold and damp to risk a trip out clay shooting, so I suggested to Jonathan that we get the chainsaw out and attack some of the bigger logs stored in the Godwin's barn.

Nothing sums up my farming career like a chainsaw. The old boys who worked here in the 1980s weren't terribly keen to pass on hard-earned skills to the boss' snotty cocky son, so I had to teach myself how to use one. My sharpening technique took some time to get right – there was no YouTube in those days. One thing I did learn pretty quickly was that poor performance was not down to a dirty spark plug. The old boys were always sending me down to George Cann Garden Machinery for new spark plugs. Cleaning out the air filter didn't cross the maintenance radar.

I shouldn't start pretending to be an expert, though. One day in the mid-80s, my brother (who was working on the farm for a brief spell) and I set off to clear some of the huge beech trees that had blown over at the very far end of Pipeline Field. It's a spot famous for its remoteness from the farmhouse, about as far away as you can get. We got there by tractor, which in the old days was half an hour's trip. Would the chainsaw work? Would it heck. The engine was going, but the blade wouldn't turn. Cursing and swearing, I climbed back into the tractor and set off home, then on past home and down to George Cann Garden Machinery. It had just been serviced by them, so I went in all guns blazing. "This effing chainsaw's just been serviced by you lot, and it doesn't work. What are you going to do about it?" Steve snapped the chain brake off and gave it straight back to me.

Thirty years on from that shame and I like to think I can prepare a reasonable chainsaw. Jonathan and I set about the log stack, and within an hour had a respectable heap of beech and pine ready to help us out through the cold snap that we are being promised. Jonathan loves a bit of splitting, and it's a joy to watch him wielding the axe with some strength.

We'd both worked up quite a sweat by the end of it. We would have to stagger the showers to make sure we all got a hot one. Where's that Agamatic when you need it?

January 19th

A cold but dry Monday morning. Right, let's do some farming. Before setting out to plough, I thought I'd have another go getting the paint off the mouldboards – the fluffy chalk in Behind My Love's wasn't having any effect at all. I'd tried Nitromors a couple of weeks ago, and that was useless, so I spent an hour this morning daubing on another brand. It looked like semolina, and bearing in mind that it had 'Enviro' in its name, I suspected that it would probably be about as useful.

Tod the Agronomist rang to say that he'd be in after lunch for a bit of a review of where we are farming-wise. There had been no spraying or sowing for weeks, and so it seemed a good to time to run through the recommendations he'd done. So, rather than set off ploughing for just an hour, I lit a couple of fires to keep the house warm for Diana, who seemed to be heading downhill with the inevitable cold.

Tod's message was 'Keep Calm and Carry on'– the winter wheat sowing window is still open for a few weeks, and now we've switched from winter to spring beans, that has also relieved the pressure. I told him I was getting cold feet about ploughing Blackhouse Road – was it really essential? He said it was; the brome out there would have been well knocked by the Roundup, but ploughing the field will finish the job nicely. As is usual, talk turned to the band and the gig he's organised in Greatham. It will be good to get playing again.

I finally got out to Behind My Love's, and finished the landwork. I ploughed the bottom headland 'in', and was just pushing to see how close I could get to the fence on the final turn or two when there was a spark and a flash – I had hit the recently installed telephone junction and manhole cover. I'd forgotten how far they'd put it out into the field, silly sods. A quick phone call to Murph established that he was still connected, which was a relief. I rang home and asked Hazel to get in touch with Openreach and report it. I never know who's to blame under these circumstances. I'm sure we'll find out soon enough.

I couldn't be bothered to go and do the top headland. I thought I'd drop into Blackhouse Road and make a start on it. Being 75 acres, it's going to be a long job. I started east/west, right alongside the road, and because it's had every man and his tractor and combine driving along it, the headland was pretty tough. Tough and soggy - the Packomat was on the limit, bunging up a few times. I did two-and-a-half turns, which made a nice start. It seemed to be going well, but it was getting pretty dark by the time I decided to go home.

It may have been tough going, but at last the paint started coming off the mouldboards. And the sight of shiny mouldboards is one of farming's little joys.

January 20th

A really hard frost and another stunning sunrise. I thought about getting some spraying done in the calm weather, but couldn't raise any of the usual contractors, and the water supply was frozen solid anyway. I assumed that drilling would be impossible on the hard headland of Drier Field, too, so decided to persevere with the ploughing.

That was blooming hard, too. I'd got as far as the old headland tramlines when I stopped yesterday, and the plough struggled a bit to get in the ground this morning. Once off them, and into the landwork, things went better. It was the usual game of tweaking this and turning that trying to get it all to match up.

The soil coming up was still very wet, so the Packomat was bunging up regularly. I jacked it up to its highest setting, which helped, but then it wouldn't flip over on its axle on the headlands. I had to lower it gradually, but then it started bunging up again. In the end, I let it cake up, and cleared it out very half an hour or so. Good exercise for the shoulders.

I still couldn't get the plough to match perfectly. The first right furrow always seemed too shallow, leaving a dip in the tractor tyre's furrow. Tomorrow I'll take a tape measure and go through all the link arm settings again.

Mid-morning, an Openreach van arrived at Joan's Acre, and the driver tromped off round the back to inspect my damage from yesterday. Nice to see they're on the case so quickly.

The frost went quite quickly as cloud and drizzle arrived – one of those situations when you hope for a bit more rain to justify not having organised the spraying.

Still, there's nothing like a trip to the Flowerpots to calm the nerves. Neighbour Robert was well enough for a beer or two, and, as is usual on a wet cold January Tuesday, we had the place to ourselves, until Hazel joined us after her keep-fit class in the village hall. Not sure a brace of ciders did much for her fitness levels.

January 21st
Mix beer and peanuts in the pub, ice cream and mince pies from last evening's tea, throw in some more heavy rain and wind, and you get a night somewhat short of refreshing sleep. Luckily, after all that rain, the world was saturated again. No field work today.

The postman brought a letter from Natural England, one of the many remote and mysterious unelected bodies that rule our lives. It was about our Entry Level Stewardship Scheme. We were late to the party on ELS. Bearing in mind that there was good money to be made from continuing to do what we do already, it was silly of us not to have joined up sooner. We tweaked our management options over the autumn – perfect for the newly resurrected shoot – and assumed the letter was just confirmation.

But no, it wasn't. It brought exciting news. There is to be a change in the way we submit the forms for ELS. Whereas one form on joining the scheme used to suffice, we will now have to submit a new form every year. As the letter explained: "New European regulations require a claim form to be submitted every year from 2015 onwards. This new requirement relates only to the payments for your land management options and land management activity to be carried out in the current calendar year." Not sure quite what the second sentence actually means.

The overall message is fairly clear. In order to get our money, we will have to do more bureaucracy. This will, of course, keep people in Natural England employed, and therefore the government will be happy. And the remote and unelected European Union is behind the whole thing.

My mind went back to an NFU meeting before Christmas, at the Winchester branch. A dismal five members turned up, and the NFU's glamorous Italian economist spent an hour trying to scare us out of thinking we should leave the EU. We should take the money and shut up. I tried pointing out the profoundly undemocratic nature of the EU (forgetting, foolishly, to mention how a technocrat was forcibly installed as Italy's PM some time ago), but it was blank faces all round. The 'take the money' line seems to be king. I also asked if the NFU's policy was still to join the Euro. Blank faces turned to denials that it had ever been. Hmm. Not what I remember.

It still rained after lunch, so Hazel and I did another run to the Countrystore. She needed to pick up the bag of calf feed that they failed to load the other day, and I needed some game cartridges for Jonathan's 20 bore; he's going on a boys' day down at Hambledon soon.

The dogs were jumping out of their skins late afternoon – the smell of new cartridges had obviously got to them. So we did the Clump loop backwards. Noel had been in for some hay from the cattle barn. Hazel had left the new gates open for him, and even in that short time, a horse had decided to take a shortcut across Chalks. It's probably best all round that I don't meet these people. Tempers might be lost.

Jonathan came home looking like death warned up – cramps and runny tummy. Based on the immediate inference that my troubles this morning were nothing to do with bad diet, I tucked into mince pies and ice cream again. I did stay out of the pub, however. That would certainly have been tempting fate.

January 22nd

Another lovely frosty start. Too hard to do any ploughing so I thought the time had come to address one of the biggest issues facing the farm at the moment: the landlord, and its policy of opening up the farm to unlimited public access.

A major argument has been raging for about eighteen months, and it boils down to two simple but utterly opposing positions. I believe I have the right to privacy on my farm. I have a tenancy agreement that says so. There are roads, footpaths, and bridleways that criss-cross the farm – these are as old as the hills, and form a network that mean access to this particular piece of mid-Hampshire countryside is fairly comprehensive. My view, not surprisingly, is that everyone should stick to the rights of way.

On the other side is my landlord, a fair proportion of its members and visitors, and the vast majority of the locals. Their view, and I've heard it ten thousand times in the past, is that the land belongs to the Trust, and therefore everyone can go anywhere on it.

It's one of the oldest debates in the countryside, and just at the moment, with food plentiful, it's hard to make the 'fields are for food, so please keep to the path' argument. However, I feel that I have the legal documents to prove that I have the right to privacy, and the Trust have been wrong to assume that they could hand out access rights over 'my' land.

I spent the morning writing and rewriting a long email to the Trust – in the form of its two agents based at Hinton Ampner House – putting forward this very argument. I phrased it as light-heartedly as I could, pointing out there seems to be a major misunderstanding when it comes to my tenancy agreement, and it would be wise, as the visitor season approaches, to establish exactly who can impose what on whom. I await a reply with interest.

I forwarded a copy of the email to George at the Tenant Farmers Association. There's a dilemma when it comes to calling for help as a tenant: the National Farmers' Union are constantly crowing about their services for their tenant members, but then there's the TFA, who never look after anyone else but tenants. The former might have more clout, but costs five times as much to join. I've had excellent dealings with George in the past, so I decided to stick with him on this one.

After lunch, I decided that more ploughing was in order, but that I would have to take the Packomat off – its constant bunging up was becoming a nuisance, and the soil isn't getting any drier. Ten minutes with a pallet or two, and a sledgehammer, and Hazel and I managed to get the pressure off the huge pin that connects it to the plough. We left the press balancing rather precariously on the pallets and a block of wood.

I then had a long afternoon back out in Blackhouse Road. The plough still isn't going perfectly: I was constantly changing settings to try and get a good match up. I forgot the tape measure, so was checking and measuring and evening up using the good old bit of baler twine that was among the clutter on the tractor floor. Was the front furrow really ploughing 14"? Let's tweak the adjuster. (Must order a hydraulic one.) Is the right link arm too short? Hard to tell with a slippery, muddy bit of plastic string. Occasionally, the job looked perfect, but then the soil or the slope would change again and there would be a dip in the furrows. It must be funny farming flat, consistent fields.

I headed home just as it was getting dark. As I looked back, I realised that I still hadn't made much of a hole in Blackhouse Road. Whose idea was it to have such big fields?

January 23rd

A really hard frost – minus seven, according to assorted car thermometers. Definitely too hard to plough or drill. And any spraying is well out of the question, with the water supply being one big lump of ice.

A good chance to hit the office, and finally get December's VAT return in. A nice easy online job these days. And we spent a lot of VAT in December, what with the rent, the first big tank of fertiliser and the new plough. Always nice to know that the best part of seven grand will be back in the bank account sometime in January, especially as the tax bill for January arrived in this morning's post. It's one of those farming paradoxes that I still can't get my head round – you have a really good year, take all the credit, feel all smug, and then get hit for £25K at the end of January. Luckily, the overdraft can handle it – for now. The pound has soared against the Euro, after the QE announced by the ECB. Not good for the short-term wheat prices.

Mid-morning, the Trust emailed a good natured reply to my message of yesterday, saying they'd love to come here on Tuesday. Let's hope we can keep the whole meeting as friendly as that.

Meanwhile, in my secondary email account was a message from the NFU, inviting us to get on and register for the new subsidy payment system that has just started. We have to ring a special number, and our identity will be checked using a selection of official databases. Horror stories already abound in the farming community of farmers who have never had credit cards or mortgages not existing as far as the verification agencies are concerned. I tried the first stages of the whole process, and then chickened out. That'll be for another day.

After lunch the frost had lifted, so I headed back into Blackhouse Road for what already seems the umpteenth time. In an attempt to get the tractor wheel furrow to fill in better, I lowered the rear depth wheel by a turn of the adjuster screw. It seemed to work – I was certainly pulling up less raw chalk, and for most of the length of the field, everything matched well. Only at the bottom did it still struggle, but it was on the gravelly loam, trying to flow over mouldboards that were still clay-covered from the top of the hill, and I think the plough was drifting away from the work, meaning the front board wasn't pushing far enough. That's my excuse, anyway. The John Deere seemed to be finding the 5 furrow not too much effort at all, and was using a lot less fuel than I thought. And after years of using a tractor with no suspension of any sort for ploughing, the smooth ride is a delight. But where the ploughing did match, it justified a pause and a photo. I might email it to the Lincolnshire Machinery Superstore who sold it to me. Not that they'd be remotely interested.

The evening brought an email from George of the TFA, thanking me for my message, and promising help if it's needed. Let's hope not. There was also a great deal of preparation for Jonathan's birthday tomorrow – most importantly, finding him the right clothes to shoot in. The drawers upstairs are full of extra-large moleskin breeks that have been, ahem, washed, and are only 'large' now, and therefore no good for me. We found a pair that fitted Jonathan perfectly. Next up, a check shirt, and a tie, and then a tear to be wiped from one's eye. My little Jonathan; over six foot and fifteen years old tomorrow. Where did it go?

January 24th

Another nice frosty morning. It was cold enough for us to dig out the old pocket warmers for the trip to Tim's shoot down at Hambledon. They're always a bit of a laugh – a carbon rod that you light and pop into a fireproof purse. Over the dozens of years I've owned them, I don't think I've ever got one to work properly.

I love Tim's shoot. It's not too far away, but the land is quite different to ours. It's sweeping chalkland – plenty of opportunities to tease him about farming boys' land. There are six or seven drives, all based on the one strip of woodland, with the odd monster arm of cover crop sticking out. It was the last day of the season, and there seemed to be a hundred guns and beaters milling around in the yard. Hazel and Alex were the only pickers-up, but I don't think they were expecting too much work.

I didn't take my gun – it being Jonathan's birthday, I said he should shoot the whole day. The Guns were split into two teams, but rather than beat and shoot, it was a case of back gunning then front gunning. Jonathan was suitably nervous – he had done a couple of beaters' days before, but this was much more formal than that. And rather than the trailer being full of rough/tough beaters, the Guns were very much the frightfully well-spoken south-mid-Hants types. He was quietly confident of hitting a target – several good clay days recently had sorted that out – but was very uncertain about etiquette and protocol on the peg. How would he know which was his? What would happen if he hit his neighbour's? When is a bird too high? All those questions that we remember from our first trips out. I'm glad that he got a chance to ask them at the age of fifteen.

He hit a good bird on the first drive and relaxed at once. He ended up with eleven against his name (at least one per drive) – including a pigeon and a jay, both of them firsts for him. The jay was a cracker, coming over from behind, and swooping. Most of his birds were good second barrels, and some were a fair distance away. I was bursting with pride at the end of it. A top 'proud parent' moment – up there with Anthony's two tries for Churcher's (one a pushover at number 8, and one a crash ball at a penalty) against Portsmouth Grammar School, and Diana's Cambridge interview.

As the day went on, it got warmer in both senses of the word. The late January sunshine kicked in beautifully (just as the hand warmer finally roared into life – a first – and had to be discarded) and the Guns all got chattier with each other. Word got around that it was Jonathan's birthday, and that he was shooting well. The backslaps and congratulations poured in for him. If he wasn't a complete convert to the bizarre and inexplicable joys of an English game shoot at the start, he was by the end of the day.

I thought I had done very well explaining to Jonathan some of the rules – especially on poaching. "On a shoot like this, never go for a neighbour's bird!" Just at that moment, the gun on our left, a gamekeeper from Bordon way, strolled over. "Feel free to go for mine!" he beamed. It was a lovely rewriting of the rules.

Thanks to the lengthening days, we didn't finish until four thirty, and got home well after five. There was just time for a sit-down and a slice of the birthday cake Diana had made and iced spectacularly. If university doesn't ever happen, there's an irony-laden career for a budding feminist.

Then it was off to Alresford for a pub meal. We'd booked Seni and her husband to join us, but hadn't told Jonathan. Seni was the third and last of Hazel's wonderful helpers when the children were tiny, and we've kept in close touch. Far too much food was eaten, but the steaks were magnificent, the sticky toffee pudding was an unusual ease to eat, the wine was excellent. Jonathan seemed to love the evening, and he and Seni get on famously. His girlfriends will all be like her; blonde, high-cheekboned East European types.

I couldn't help chuckling on the way home at the fact that my older sister, now a sixty-something granny, had met her husband in that very pub. You realise you've lived in one place a long time when that sort of fact emerges.

January 25th
A good Sunday sofa day.

If I had any worries about today's youth, they were completely dispelled this evening. We played Cards against Humanity with our two youngest. They are 18 and 15. They are terrifyingly well-informed, fantastically cynical and as capable of enjoying outrageously bad taste jokes as any world-weary fifty-something farmer. Utter joy.

January 26th
The whole farm is in shock: the Wool Board man came and took the wool. After months of telephones calls, email and texts, the two-and-a-half big rectangular bags finally got loaded onto a lorry and taken off the farm. We're not going to be holidaying in Oz on the proceeds, but it's all part of the new sheep enterprise – a first at Manor Farm.

Dealing with the Wool Board has been like dealing with one of the state monopolies of the 1970s – and it is a monopoly, because we can't sell our wool to anyone else. It has been like trying to get any action from the GPO or British Rail. Somewhere Hazel has a list of all the broken appointments and telephone calls. It seems to be run in a state of utter chaos. I'll have a small wager that the wool vanishes, or gets lost, and we never get paid.

Lynn and Mel, two policewomen from the Countrywatch Mob, arrived for a cuppa over lunch. They weren't there to help us cope with the trauma of loading the wool – it was just a social call, and a chance to catch up and have a well-deserved giggle about Caravan Bob from a couple of weeks ago.

We're in the middle of a golden age of policing at the moment. Very few people know my field names: there's immediate family, Tod the Agronomist, and the deer-control man. And then, amazingly, there's a good number of the Countrywatch Police Mob. If I ring in where the poachers have been overnight, then they'll know where I mean. That can't be bad. It has gone full circle from the days of my childhood, when there was a village bobby. The fantastically named Mr Lovelock patrolled the parish on a white scooter. He was straight out of the Level 42 song: 'a man so large, he barely fit his circumstances.' He certainly scared this six-year-old.

There was, of course, no crime. No, really. Doors and gates were unlocked, barns left open all day, cars with keys in all night. It sounds like a comedy sketch, but that's how it was. So, what was the point of maintaining a village bobby in a large (and valuable) police house? Police cover started to drop, and then became all but non-existent.

Not surprisingly, crime started to increase. Our friends in the poaching community discovered how easy it was to drive out to the countryside, and plunder our unprotected belongings while exercising their God-given right to drive over our field chasing hares and deer.

In autumn 2008, it came to a head. There were nightly visits, all over the farm. In at the Folly gateway, across dark lane into White Hill, out of White Hill into Long Field, on down to Pipeline and all the way back. One night, the poachers had to abandon a Toyota Corolla 4WD in the mud at the north end of Long Field. We stood round it in astonishment at their cheek. The police came out and had a look, and couldn't give a fig about it. They seemed horribly reluctant to agree even that a crime had taken place. We were told that no one would be back for the Toyota – we should tow it down to a barn somewhere and sell it.

I remember finding that the key was still in it, so of course I tried to start it. There wasn't enough power for that, but there was just enough to operate the central locking. So I locked it, and left it, planning what to do with a quite useful 4WD estate car.

It wasn't just me who thought it useful. Overnight, a large truck was reversed down narrow and rutted Stanmore Lane, getting as close as it could to the Toyota. This was then dragged onto the bed of the truck, and away they went. The job was obviously made that much harder by the fact that some farmer had removed the keys – and I doubt that a spare set existed. I knew that I'd upset them because, for the next three nights, a large dirty pickup continued to drive over the fields, throwing old tyres and wheels at random out into the crops. Quite bizarre.

There were plenty of farmers and gamekeepers being subjected to the same sort of thing, and things were escalating to the point where someone was going to get seriously hurt – or worse – taking these scum on; eventually the police got the message. A meeting was held in a function room at the old Alresford railway station. The police were stunned at the anger and fear that was filling the countryside. After three hours of quite violent and unruly debate, they knew exactly how we all felt. Shortly after that, the Countrywatch scheme was set up: a force of dedicated officers, with the brief to look after the countryside.

Seven years on, and the same team – more or less – prowl the lanes in an assortment of vehicles. We're on first-name terms with them, and I have their mobile telephone numbers on speed dial. So now we've effectively got several local bobbies – they just don't live in the village. We see less of them when things are quiet – I dare say the bean counters quietly shuffle them off somewhere – but just at the moment, while there has been yet another resurgence of poaching, we're seeing a lot of them. And a very good thing it is too.

The lunchtime forecast suggested that tomorrow would be a spraying day. In a fit of enthusiasm, I hitched off the plough, and then the weights (should I have left them on? Might be a bit soft out in Rough Field), did a major fuel-up and went and got the sprayer out of the Godwin's barn, where it has been sheltering from the frost. As usual, it took longer than it should have done: I didn't click the locking tab on one of the lower arm hooks, and the sprayer 'A' frame leapt out. It took another twenty minutes of manoeuvring to get it back into the hook. It would have been better if I had disconnected completely – pipes, PTO, the lot – and started again, but as usual, I am the living embodiment of Granny's favourite phrase: lazy people take the most pains.

January 27th

Finally, a spraying day. The concrete was dry, the light was brighter and the leaves were dry. The wind was calm, the sprayer filled up with fresh water, ready to go. Over an early breakfast, I made my usually hopelessly over-optimistic plans. I'd get the OSR done by lunchtime, then fly over the winter wheat up at Stanmore. Fantastic. Farming-a-go-go.

I made it out to White Hill at about nine thirty – as usual, it had taken longer than I hoped to get started. There then followed the traditional fight with the spool valve connectors. The hydraulic pipes from the sprayer just wouldn't seat in the tractor's connectors. I lost about twenty minutes jumping in and out of the cab, cleaning them, getting the mud out of the females, stopping and starting the tractor each time to make sure there was no back pressure. Finally, I had all the pipes cleaned and seated firmly in the right holes. I unfolded and set off.

Granny strikes again: lazy people take the most pains. I'm sure I had cleaned the sprayer to perfection when I put it away. Well, the state of the nozzle filters suggested otherwise. As I drove off up the hill, the majority of the nozzles were displaying a fantastic selection of pathetic dribbles. I persevered. Hoping they would clear. Of course, they didn't. There was only one choice: fold back up, and head back to the yard.

Removing nozzle filters and cleaning them out is pretty miserable on a warm day. On a cold January morning, it's particularly horrible. The water from the hosepipe is cold, the nitrile gloves are stiff and unyielding, and the clock is ticking against the short days. It's a dirty job, and there's only me to do it.

Finally – finally! – back in White Hill, and away we went, round the headland. The outside of Rough Field – remerged with White Hill after a break of a couple of decades – was pretty soggy, but I made it through. When the in-cab alarm beeped to tell me that the tank was empty, it was eleven thirty. So much for the day's master plan. Oh well. I got the second tank on after lunch, but it was a bit of a struggle. The middle of Rough Field was as soft as butter, and more than once I worried about getting out of the ruts I was making. Now I remember why we put Rough Field down to set-aside all those years ago. Mind you, the far end of Cheyney wasn't much better. And I really hate making ruts this early in the year – they are there for the whole season. But there's a time limit for the mix I was putting on, so there was little choice. If the weather forecast is right, there won't be another chance for some time.

The sprayer ran out almost perfectly – always satisfying – and I did a rinse out on the headland. I checked in the tank, and it was squeaky clean; Granny would have been proud of me. It was already hinting at dusk by then, and so I called it an early day and parked up. Half a day's spraying this time of year is better than none, I suppose.

I took Fred out on the Clump loop, and the day felt surprisingly mild. The winter barley in Clump itself is still yellow and waterlogged, and walking across it suggested that it would still be some time before a tractor could travel across it. Hazel and Monty got back from their walkabout day at Barrow Hill absolutely shattered: they'd done six hours of yomping on the Alpine slopes of East Hampshire for a bag of eleven. Now, that's dedication.

January 28th

I seem to spend a lot of time hitching onto implements and hitching them back off again, but that's the modern way on a farm with only two tractors – and one of them is on permanent livestock duties with its front loader. Effectively, one machine has to be able to switch from drill to sprayer to cultivator to hedge trimmer with the minimum of effort. Luckily, the 'hook' hitches that arrived many years ago made the job far easier (as long as one remembers to flick the locking tab, ahem ahem). I don't often do nostalgia for the old days of farming, but when I started in 1984, seven tractors were available for three men. It was easier to leave the implements on the tractor and swap tractors. The past is foreign country and all that.

Talking of 'foreign countries', in the evening Jonathan and I trundled up the A3 to Charterhouse for a public speaking competition. We think Jonathan's private day school in Petersfield is a bit swanky, but you can't help but be blown away by somewhere like Charterhouse. It's like the Surrey branch of Hogwarts, full of impossibly polite and impeccably polished students, all delighted to help a lost-looking farmer trying to find the debating chamber.

There was a curious system of mixing up the students into teams with complete strangers, and Jonathan seemed to do well. I missed most of it trying to work out what was better preserved: the historic buildings or the Charterhouse mums.

January 29th

A bright and frosty start for the last day of our first season in charge of the shoot at Hinton Ampner. There's always a tremendous sense of worry and anticipation when hosting a shoot, and even more so when you are the sole hosts. Where shall we go? Will anything fly? Have we cleaned out the stock that we inherited? I drove the tractor and trailer down to the Drier Yard just as it was getting light, loaded with bales for the ride home and sausage rolls and ginger beer for elevenses. As I went, I scanned the frosty fields for cock birds – our landlord decrees that this will be a 'no hen' day. I was damned if I could see any.

Julie turned up with her squad of dogs at ten past nine, and John and his dog followed her into the yard shortly after that. I was relieved to see John – he came along on one of the first days, and we failed to invite him to any more. It wasn't deliberate

41

– more an administrative oversight. Julie and Hazel both said, "I thought you were going to ask him!" Anyway, he seemed to be pleased to be back.

So our beater pack was complete: John, Julie and Hazel, and six dogs. The two guest Guns arrived at about nine thirty: my brother-in-law Keith and Graeme the vet. I went to school with Graeme forty years ago, and have been shooting with him for almost as many years. We had a relaxed cup of tea in the kitchen, and then set off across the farm.

The first drive was Keeper's Secret Drive, so called because, back in the days of the formal syndicate, several feeders were placed ever-so-quietly at the bottom of our garden, but the scrub and woodland there were mysteriously never touched on proper shoot days. Only at the end of the season, after all the days had finished, and after the beaters' day that normally marks the end of the shooting, there would be a 'bit of a walkabout' for the keeper and a very select group of locals. The first we knew of it would be when a couple of beaten-up Land Rovers would disgorge their contents into the farmyard, and half a dozen heavily armed types would sweep their way through our garden, and the guns started blazing as a good selection of birds, undisturbed for the whole season, were found. Our assorted cats, dogs, ducks and chickens didn't reckon much of this – neither did we, and eventually made it clear that we didn't. After that, we at least got a phone call's warning.

Keeper's Secret Drive had yielded nothing for us this year in our three previous visits, not a single bird, so I confess we strolled down to the old cattle barn somewhat nonchalantly. Inevitably, two fantastic cock pheasants got up and swept left, out in to Chalks. I was too far away on the old tennis court, but should have been twenty yards further on – and a bit more awake. Woulda coulda shoulda, as they say. I had an optimistic shot at both, but was pleased to miss completely at that range. 0 birds for 2 shots.

For Chalks Hedges, Hazel and I took the top hedge, the others took the bottom. We saw one cock deep in the hedge, probably one of the two that came out of the last drive, but he only just got up and flew lazily back down the hedge line – too low to shoot, and proving the 'they only fly well once' theory. At the bottom hedge there was nothing. Still 0/2.

For Caspar's (named after a member of the previous syndicate who had a red letter day there), I asked Keith to walk up ahead of us, and take position at the end of the copse. He had a shot at a partridge as he crossed from Roe Hill into BOMS, but missed it. The rest of us walked up through the trees and scrub. I was joined on the east side by a couple of elderly local walkers and their dogs, so unloaded and walked with them slowly, keen to do the PR bit for the shoot. Still nothing in the bag. 0/3.

We crossed BOMS and did Bob's Wood – named after Bob Coles, the keeper here in my youth. Keith and I stood in the Folly, and Graeme stood in Drier Field. At last, some action. Several birds flew out of the wood, and over to the Drier buildings – we should have got Graeme to hang back and walk with the beaters. (Woulda, coulda, etc.) I had an optimistic shot at a pigeon, and then had a nice cock bird right over the top of me. Graeme picked up a second barrel bird as it crossed over the track, and Keith felled a fantastic right-to-left way out in front of him – we very unscientifically measured it out at 45 paces. Huge relief for me, not just because we'd opened the scoring, but because everyone had a bird. 3/8.

For Folly itself, I took position at the bottom of the copse, and everyone else swept it from the top. I was so busy going 'Hello trees, hello sky' that I failed to notice the easy-peasy partridge coming out of the trees and back towards Bob's Wood until it was far too late. Must concentrate more. Graeme had a nice bird and missed a second one coming out of the east side of the trees. 4/11.

Much debate raged about what to do next. Elevenses (my choice) or Barracuda (which yielded bugger all despite hours of strategic planning last time we tried it). Enthusiasm to make the most of the long day and fine sunshine won over, so we Guns set off up the hill towards the Barracuda (named after the dive bomber that crashed there in World War Two). The beaters went left, up through the Trust woodland, and split into two teams, planning to do the two thick hedgerows that lead into the dell at the top of the hill. Julie and Hazel worked the southern one, and Keith had two clinical birds racing over him in the strong wind. Several other birds flew out, some back towards Broom Field, so I decided that that drive, like Folly, will be one to develop for the future. As we admired a dozen cormorants that inexplicably seemed keen to fly over for a couple of minutes, we realised that John had gone missing. We found him wandering around the woods, having misunderstood the girls' instructions as to where to go. There was much laughter and leg pulling ("If you don't want me to come, you only have to say so, rather than sending me off into no-man's land…"), but it was mingled with unspoken relief that someone on their own in sticky woodland hadn't tumbled over unnoticed. 6/13.

We did a sticky yomp across Drier Field to the trailer for elevenses – sausage rolls, ginger beer, Snickers – all good energy-giving stuff. I can never get the hang of vast quantities of alcohol when shooting – or even minor quantities. It just seems plain daft.

Fortified with E numbers and sugar, we set off for George's (no idea why it's called George's). Graeme and the dog team went along the road, and turned sharp right, sweeping the rough grass over the top. Keith and I took up position at the top of the hill. Graeme had a nice right-to-left as he reached the brow, but Keith missed a left-to-right well out in front – an overenthusiastic springer (is there any other type?) sent it the 'wrong' way, which was a shame. 7/16.

We thought we'd try a new drive next. After much discussion in a blisteringly cold sleet shower that sneaked up on us out of nowhere, it was decided to call it Pipeline South. (There's an aviation fuel pipeline that crosses the farm here, taking hot fuel from Fawley refinery to Gatwick.) Names that were briefly discussed included Headless Horseman's Gulch, Headless Horseman's Gusset, and so on. Hazel was keen to do this bit of woodland after numerous walks during which Monty would put up a couple of birds. We Guns took up position in the Pipeline Field itself, and in the end just the one came out, right over me. 8/17.

Julie keeps a couple of horses at Blackhouse Farm, and reported that there were birds in the woods there, so we thought we'd head there to finish the day. The dog team headed into the woods, and we guns stayed in Pipeline Field, to make sure we kept within the terms of our tenancy. Several birds got up early, just too far away for Keith, who was at the front. As we came over the brow, we could see birds flying out at the end of the woods, and heading over the south end of Pipeline Field, back towards Stanmore Farm – which used to have a big shoot. Hugely frustrating – if we'd known, we'd have sent Keith down there to start. Shoulda woulda coulda. Still 8/17.

We reached the V-shaped woodland block that we were allowed to shoot in, and did it in two sweeps, west to east down one arm on the V, then east to west to finish. On the first leg, Keith had another good bird going back, and I missed one far off to my left. On the return leg, Keith had two more – although one was a strong runner that headed south like a rocket past Blackhouse Farm itself. Despite the best effort of the dog team – which was beginning to flag a bit – it wasn't found. But we reached double figures. 10/23.

In fact, we were all flagging a bit. There may have been daylight for a yomp over to Cheyney or Kilmeston Road, but another grey cloud was rushing in from the west, everyone had shot something, the dogs were slowing to a crawl, so we decided to head home. Huge slobby sleet flakes were quite heavy by the time we reached the tractor and trailer at the Drier Yard, and hot food and a warm fire was definitely top of the request board once we finally reached home. Diana, relishing her role as shoot pixie, had the table laid and ready to go, and the chicken pie and sticky toffee pudding, fresh off the AGA, was just the job.

What a way to end our first season in charge of the Hinton Ampner shoot. In many ways, it couldn't be more different to the army of guns and beaters that assembled last Saturday at Hambledon, and that day's three-figure bag. But in one way, it was the same: it was huge fun.

Everyone was gone by five o'clock, and by six I was asleep on the sofa, missing two whole episodes of *The Big Bang Theory*. Perfect, although it did mean I was wide awake at eleven o'clock, listening to the mice scurrying about in the attic. I made the most of the thinking time to make plans for next season: which drives to work on, where to put the wild bird cover, and, of course, how to make sure everyone was in the right place at the right time. Woulda, coulda, shoulda.

January 30th

An interesting day of old and new.

First, the new: feeling slightly the worse for wear after yesterday, I thought it would be a good time to get on and register with Rural Payments Agency – the first step to take if we want to go on getting our subsidies. Do we call them subsidies these days? I lose track of the latest jargon. But whatever the fancy nomenclature, the EU intends, for now, to go on giving us farmers money which is entirely independent of our 'farming' in the old sense of the word, i.e. putting a crop in the ground and growing food with it. Every few years the whole system is overhauled and renamed, and the hoops through which we have to jump get moved, redesigned and resized.

The latest overhaul has just taken place. I suppose it was inevitable: the previous regime was getting dangerously simple. In its early days, the Single Payment Scheme (as it was then) involved the whole kitchen table covered in maps, page after page of handwritten forms and diagrams. We spent ages describing to the Ministry how old fields had been merged – the half dozen or so at the far end of Drier Field, for instance, that had been viciously bulldozed into one in the late 1980s. We had to do the acreages for them – or hectareage, I suppose the metric fetishists would call it. There was a panic about deducting ineligible areas. A dozen different land agents would give a dozen-and-a-half different verdicts on what to do about the bit where the bales were stacked that particular year, or if three trees quite close together constituted a wood.

Tracks and barn corners were easier to decide upon. These had to be removed. Hazel and I headed to National Trust regional HQ, where we pored over the large-scale maps to decide exactly where our boundaries lay. Round Blackhouse Road, for instance, some of the track that goes along the south and east boundaries were originally measured as part of the field, but the rest weren't.

The Godsend back then was my pride and joy: a Ford 7810, with radar area measurement. Once back from the map archive, I drove along the tracks, measuring and deducting as I went. It was a good few days' work. I can remember Dad coming into the kitchen to bring over our newspaper, as he did every morning, and taking a look at the kitchen table, completely covered in forms and maps. "I think I retired at the right time," he said – and his retirement was something he'd never mentioned before.

When that system seemed to be settled, we then had to become amateur cartographers and learn to renumber all our fields. Not that difficult, but another whole bunch of opportunities for mistakes. And it was still done on paper forms that had, I mean HAD, to be in on time. And that 'time' was around the middle of May. I used to take a day off, and drive up to Coley Park in Reading, where a drop-in and advice centre was held. Long-suffering civil servants would be slaving away in numerous Portakabins, trying to deal with farmers of assorted form-filling talent, not to mention assorted tempers.

And then, a few years ago, it all got very simple. Everything went online. And for a simple farm like us, it took not more than ten minutes of online form ticking to ensure that we got our monster but utterly vital subsidy cheque.

So it was never going to last. All that system has been scrubbed, and we start again. This time, there's a lot more emphasis on 'green' issues, and, to misquote Monty Python, every tree/hedge plant is sacred. But that's for next spring; first of all, we have to register the farm through the government's business gateway.

Earlyish this morning, I rang the helpline, got through the selection of security questions, and was given a ten-digit number (after all, we don't get given enough numbers these days) and a promise that another number – this one a code – would be emailed to me. This code would self-destruct ('expire' was what she actually said, but 'self-destruct' sounds better) in twelve hours. Eight hours later, nothing was in my email box. So I rang the helpline number again, went through all the security questions and said I hadn't received that all-important message. "Have you checked your junk?" she asked. I told her not to be so personal. It raised a laugh, which always helps with helpline staff. Then she spotted the problem. "Ah, you're with AOL. We can't get through to you via AOL. You need to get in touch with them and ask them to release the mail."

I have rung AOL in the past. It redefines the concept of a Kafkaesque nightmare. I never want to do it again as long as I live. "Well," said the nice lady, "What about an alternative email address?" I suggested my daughter. That would be no problem, apparently, and Diana could forward it to me, and then it would be all systems go. Hazel texted Diana to warn her, and, indeed, a few hours later the email, with its all-important code number, arrived. With baited breath, I clicked on the link. 'Service not available'.

It wasn't available for a couple more hours, but luckily, just after everyone had left the RPA office in Workington, the system started working. In went my ten-digit number, in went Diana's email (I had to use that for registration), in went the six-digit code, and up came our farm details. This is always a sticky moment: the RPA has been known to lose whole fields – Drier Field vanished from our official maps some years ago. But there appeared to be nothing wrong at all. Every field was there, our contact details were fine. All appeared hunky-dory. Quite a relief. It all seemed – AOL apart – easy. Too easy. And as they say in the war films, it's too easy, I don't like it… Perhaps when spring gets here, and the tree measuring gets going, we'll really know the battle has started.

The man from the South Downs Bloodhounds called in late morning to get a farm map which I'd marked up for their run round the farm on Sunday. With so much of the farm still unsown this year, I could offer him far more ground than usual, including what should be a lovely gallop right round the outside of Joan's Acre woods.

I emailed the Trust to say that the Bloodhounds were coming, and within minutes, my phone rang. It was Agent Mark. The Bloodhounds would need a licence. I pointed out that these were bloodhounds, so no animal quarry was involved – I was all fired up to wallow in the Trust's ignorance, but was pulled up quite sharply. "Yes, we know that," said Mark. "But because they look like an old-fashioned hunting hunt, we like them to have a bit of paper from us that they can produce if challenged by overzealous and ignorant witnesses!" That put me in my place. I apologised and promised that they'd get the paperwork in time for next year.

And now the 'old'. Hazel got back from another trip to the Countrystore with boxes of one of the oldest tools on the farm: mousetraps. One of the many reasons I'm not sleeping (apart from the wheezing and the painful hips) is the avalanche of mice running over the ceiling every night. I assume they're mice; as usual, at one thirty in the morning they sound like coypus. There were already some traps in all the usual places, but they're old, covered in an unsavoury mix of cake (Christmas cake, so quite alcoholic), Tracker bars and mouse blood/brain. Probably not that appealing any more. So, armed with a fresh set of traps, a fresh Tracker bar and my best torch, I ventured into the hidden recesses of the farmhouse where most of our furry friends seem to hang out.

It's always a thrill to go up into the attic, and imagine how it was when there used to be seven servants living up there. And then it was up above the kitchen where the false ceiling that Dad put in in 1960 hid the smoking chamber and the old ruined chimney stack above the office. One day, I'll take the ceiling down and reveal and restore all those features. One day.

Diana got back from a long day at the smart café where she's working, proudly boasting about her payslip. Well done her – café work isn't easy. I warned her about us having given her email to the Rural Payments Agency. If a load of inspectors suddenly arrive while she's trying to serve a double skinny latte thing, and demand to see her acres – or hectares – she can blame us.

January 31st

Twenty-three years ago, my rugby boots were sitting in a cupboard, dusty, crusty and unused. I'd had a thoroughly mediocre rugby 'career', playing for fun at school, university and at Winchester. Occasionally I would get promoted to play for the first or second team, and find the whole thing a bit too much hard work. The pre-match cigarette is too important. I gave up playing in the late 1980s when the sole ambition of my Winchester teammates seemed to be to have a fight – if they stopped swearing at the referee for long enough.

In 1991, Alresford started a rugby club. I heard about it, turned up to a training session, and found a group of players with just my sort of attitude. It was almost like student social rugby all over again, with just a hint more intensity. The first game I was chosen to play in, for instance, I turned up ten minutes before kick-off, cigarette in hand, wondering where everyone else was. Everyone was changed and gone. I had a slight panic. Had I got the kick-off time wrong?

I ambled out to the pitch at Perins School just as the pre-match running around finished. They appeared to have been at it for hours (definitely not my thing) and were on their way back in for a final chest-thumping group-hugging shouty psyche-up (still not my thing). I joined in as best I could – I thought that would be wiser than lighting another fag.

Finally, the game started. The oppo were a touring team up from the West Country, invited up by one of the founders of Alresford RFC. As usual for a prop, I have no idea what the result was. All I know was that I had the game of my life. Apparently, my opposite number was a county-level loose head, and he was somewhat shocked to be subjected to what rugby journalists call 'a torrid time' by a small-town tighthead. I was damned if I knew all that – I was just doing my thing. Funnily enough, my mate

Rupert – then a rugby journalist for *The Daily Telegraph* – came along with Hazel to watch. Sadly, we didn't get a mention in the broadsheet, though. In the Horse and Groom, then acting as a clubhouse, I was awarded, for the one and only time in my rugby life, Man of the Match.

I played for three or four years, until injuries and back pain meant I just couldn't do my day job any more. Through those years, the club struggled to find somewhere to train (any corner of grass in the town could be used), and somewhere to play. A kind local farmer in Bighton offered them a field for a couple of years, and they ended up playing there for two decades.

Today was a great day for Alresford RFC. After years of negotiations, rows, controversy, and furious letters in the *Hampshire Chronicle*, ground for new pitches had been obtained next to the existing Arlebury Park recreation ground. Today, they were to be used for the first time. You never saw such pitches: level, drained, smooth – they must be the best small-town pitches in the country. They had invited as many players, ex-players and officials as they could find to the opening. We had drinks in the clubhouse, speeches, lunch, an official tape-cutting ceremony, and then two games going on simultaneously.

I had to leave before the end to pick up Diana, although I was quite relieved; the north wind was scything straight through me, and I was freezing. And, for some reason, I could have murdered a quick cigarette.

Back home, I found that the Bloodhounds' preparation team had been in, preparing for tomorrow's yodel round the farm. Let's hope that it's dry enough for them not to chew the ground up too much. Hazel and Fred got back from their walkabout day at Barrow Hill, absolutely exhausted. Fred spent the whole evening upside-down on the sofa, grunting. I think that that's officially the end of the shooting season.

February 1st

Don't look now, but there's something funny going on with the weather. All three of my regular weather forecasts agree on something: we're in for a rain-free spell. The Met Office's forecast spell is five days, the BBC's is ten, and Weathercast's is fourteen. The wind is going to swing round further north, then east, and a run of dry and cold days is on its way; something we haven't seen since the start of October last year. Might I finally get the winter wheat sown? It's just about within the approved sowing window.

I do love online weather forecasts. They are as hopeless as the human ones on the TV, but have the added comedy factor of mistaking precision for accuracy. Weathercast, for instance, will confidently predict that in eleven days, we will have 5.2 mm of rain. Not 5.1 mm, not 5.3 mm, but 5.2 mm. You can bet that within a week, the forecast will have changed again, and there will be no rain at all – or a couple of inches.

I had a quiet Sunday morning. I was feeling a bit fragile after yesterday's rugby gathering. The thing I miss most about youth is being able to insert anything you like in the first bit of one's digestive season, and handling it effortlessly. By no stretch of the imagination did I overindulge yesterday, but I was horribly the worse for wear.

When the Editor bounced into the yard and almost through the kitchen window, demanding that we all go and watch the bloodhounds, I gave him a rude hand signal. Luckily, Hazel, Jonathan and the two dogs went with him down to the Drier Yard, where they had a grandstand view of the goings on. The best moment came when the hounds, having done the diagonal from The Neck to the oil compound in Blackhouse Road, found our dogs, and everything ground to a halt as canine greetings were exchanged. No wonder Monty and Fred looked a bit overwhelmed when they got back.

By mid-afternoon, the beer has passed, and Jonathan and I hit the wood stack to prepare for the week's cold snap. Two hours with a chainsaw and a splitting axe, and we had filled the tractor bucket. Another proud parental moment: watch one's son really showing some muscle and skill with an axe. And doing it without getting injured – unlike his father.

At tea time, I popped up to Kilmeston to finish the paperwork for the Lupo. The chap selling it was just starting his preparation for going back to work tomorrow. He's another of those poor souls who are on the sparrow's fart train from Winchester every morning. Not my thing at all. On a cold Sunday evening, tucked up in front of a fire raging with freshly split beech logs, the idea of getting up for a six o'clock train the next morning is the very definition of hell. Hurrah for farming.

February 2nd

I had such plans for Candlemas Day. Fine and clear it dawned indeed, so more winter is on the way; let's get this bloomin' wheat into the ground. First, I did an early run out to the oilseed rape to light a couple of rope bangers. There was a mob of fifty or so pigeons on the very south end of Cheyney – a site that is almost unprotectable thanks to the houses and horses nearby, but if that's the only corner getting eaten, I think we can live with it . I came back via Drier Field, and – at last – it was frozen but drillable. Perfect. Full speed home to get the tractor.

As I pulled into the yard, everything went a bit surreal. There, in the garden, just outside the office window, a large lurcher was wrestling a deer to the ground. The deer was shrieking horribly, the dog was growling and snarling – a ghastly sight. Somehow, the deer got free, and the two raced down through the garden. At that moment, Hazel and our dogs came up from the tennis court – Hazel looking as shocked and baffled as I felt.

What on earth was going on? If you see lurchers chasing deer, it can only mean one thing – the poachers won't be far behind. But I had just driven back through the farm and there wasn't another vehicle to be seen. Just then, the horrible noises of a mortal struggle started up again, just across the road. Hazel went through the hedge, dived in and found the lurcher. It wasn't quite poacher material – it was too dainty, too domesticated. "I know that dog," said Hazel, and named its owner. We grabbed the dog, put it in the back of the Skoda, and I set off in Tigger to find her. I did a full trip on road and on track, but there was no sign at all of the owner.

Then the phone rang. It was Hazel, having found, but not been able to catch, a second lurcher. Two lurchers is a sure sign of poachers – so I rang 999, gave the poaching codeword and my location, rang Mike the Keeper next door to see if he'd got any visitors (the second dog had set off hell-for-leather towards Brockwood), and then set off round the farm again. The increased certainty that it was poachers – even at this time of the morning – certainly made the heart beat a little faster in wary anticipation.

But once again, no one to be seen. No beaten up Transits, iffy Subarus, not even a rusty pickup. Then, just as I was heading home again, the phone rang, from a strange mobile number. It was a policewoman who had come out from Winchester (at some pace and very promptly, it must be said) who was now at Hinton Ampner House. I told her she'd got the wrong place. "No," she replied. "I'm here with a lady who has lost her dog." I told her I'd meet her in the farmyard.

It was indeed the lady that Hazel had named, and she was in a bit of a state. No one likes to lose a dog, and I probably didn't help by giving her an earful. But, I mean, really. She and a friend had taken their two lurchers for a walk, and let them run free. Really? I mean, *really* really? I tried to get across my astonishment, but I think it was wasted. The police, probably sensing that there was tension in the air, beat a hasty retreat. Hazel arrived in the yard, announcing that the deer hadn't made it and was dead, jammed up against the fence at the bottom of Englands. More words were exchanged, and off the dog owner went. There will be a good *Farmers Weekly* article to be had: 'Bring back pet rocks.'

I rang Mike with a 'stand down' message, and went back down to Drier Field: the frost had come out, and the ground was now as slippery as hell. So much for all that drilling I was going to do today.

I rang Tod the Agronomist to discuss options for sowing. He was uneasy about too much Scout going in the ground at this time of year. He suggested that I sow all the Scout I've got, originally meant for 94 acres (TBDH and JA/DC), on only TBHD (66 acres). That'll boost the seed rate to something suitable for February sowing and minimise the risk of it going wrong. We'll get some spring wheat in for JA and DC – some specialist milling variety. You never know, we might actually end up supplying some to the Trust for their mill in Winchester – an idea much discussed but one that never seems to get any further than discussion. We can give those two little fields another burst of Roundup, and get a really good spring seedbed later in the year. We also ordered the spring barley, which, rumour has it, is getting short. I think I'm not the only farmer with winter wheat sowings in disarray.

I spent the rest of the afternoon waiting for the spring beans to be delivered – our promised slot was mid- to late afternoon. At about four, he rang to say he wouldn't be here until six. I pointed out that it would be a bit late by then – mainly because daylight is needed to get a forty-foot articulated lorry turned in this old farmyard. Luckily, he was happy to park up overnight, and come down here first thing tomorrow. Seed delivery gets more and more complicated. I decided that if I was going to lose an hour unloading seed tomorrow, I'd hitch the Deere onto the drill this afternoon. It's more easily done in positive temperatures, too. Just for a change, it went on easily.

I then wasted another couple of hours trying to get the review of the Land Rover Discovery finished. For some reason, it has proved all but impossible. I nailed the majority – just the big finish to come up with. This evening's rehearsal with the Thomas Lord Old Gits should clear the creative tubes, and the words will fly. Tomorrow. Probably while I'm drilling.

Hold on, let's not make too many plans – there's a curious halo round the moon tonight.

February 3rd

So much for all those plans. Leaping out of bed relatively early, I was treated to the sight of Hampshire nestling under a shallow layer of snow. All a bit of a surprise, for two reasons: first, the forecast from only two days ago said that we were in for a prolonged spell of dry weather, and second, David Viner of the University of East Anglia Climate Change Research Unit said, quite specifically, in 2000, that we'd never see snow again.

It is now traditional whenever the snow (that we'd never see again) falls, to visit *The Independent*'s page which gives that story, and post it far and wide. It is, I believe, that paper's most visited webpage; it is up to us climate change sceptics to keep it that way.

Just when I was wondering if there was enough snow to finish off my drilling plans, the heavens opened and we had half an hour's heavy snow. Hazel made it back from the school run with reports of the roads being fairly dodgy. Just then my seed lorry rang and said that there was no way he was going to make it up the hill to the farm – did I have any ideas? Once upon a time, I would have organised unloading at another yard, like Murph's, but these days I work on the theory that if they send such stupid great lorries out to tiny farms, that's their lookout if they can't get here. My conscience is clear-ish. He agreed that it was hopeless, and said he'd be in touch to arrange another day.

Policewoman Lynn rang to discuss yesterday's lurcher incident. Did I want it taken any further? I thought it would be a good idea – if she called round with her specialist Countrywatch hat on, she could really lay it on thick about keeping hunting dogs under control. The best line she could use was that if two dogs had been found, and the owners happened to live in a certain type of camp, arrests would be in order. That might get the message home.

I had a fruitful office afternoon, finally finishing the Discovery article. I approved the proof of the Wrangler, and chased up a couple of press offices to get cars sorted for the rest of the year. The north wind was by now scything through the whole house, so I lit all the fires, locked up the yard and hit Mr Sofa just in time for the rerun of *Tipping Point*. How sad am I?

A long evening snoozing was interrupted by the phone, and if the phone rings between six and seven on a Tuesday night, it has to be neighbour Robert, keen for another trip to the Flowerpots. I never turn these trips down – I get out rarely enough as it is.

The children tease me mercilessly about my pub trips, claiming that we say the same things every week, but slightly louder as old age comes on a bit more. They've got a point, but this time we got onto talking about Doug Reid, who lived in my house and farmed this farm for the twenty-five years before Dad moved in – which would be about 1934–59. Dad had very few stories about him, apart from the farm being so poorly run it was nearly requisitioned by the War Ag during World War Two. It was said that he lived in just the one room downstairs, and the one room upstairs, was unmarried, and Mrs Debenham ('Mrs Deb' to me and my siblings when she became our nanny/housekeeper) looked after him. Most of the house had been untouched since Victorian times which is why, when we moved in, so much work was needed (hot water!), and so much damage was done in the name of improvement. Ice house? Bread oven? Who needs them – pass me the sledgehammer. Dad's only other story involved coming round the farm not long before the takeover, and Doug driving up White Hill with him. Over at the top of Rough Field, there was a man sheeting down his halftrack tractor – mid-afternoon. Dad asked who on earth was knocking off at this time of day. Doug said it was one of the 'senior' employees, who very much did his own thing. Dad said he made a mental note that he had a battle coming.

Robert managed to fill out the character somewhat. Doug was a tall man, 6' 2", and with a huge belly – Mrs Deb was some cook. He wore the most beautifully polished leather gaiters, but topped his work kit off with a scruffy brown overcoat, with the buttons always mismatched. He spoke with a tic of some sort, saying "putt putt" every few words – Robert did a superb impersonation.

Later on, in bed, as I waited for the beer and peanuts to settle, I couldn't help but feel slightly awed by the history of the farm – even though most of it seems unknown. Going back, there's me, Dad, Doug, someone called Cheyney (as in the field) – and then who? I know of John Spencer, but he was around 1870. Some historical research is needed. I wonder if they all came back from the pub and jumped on top of their 15-year-old sons, pretending to be drunk, saying "I really love you, you're my besht mate"?

February 4th

Just for a change, we did a bit of cattle work – the ground was still soggy from yesterday's snow, so there was certainly no arable work to be done. It was castration time for seven of Hazel's calves.

You never saw such an outbreak of professional calf handling. It helps that they have been reared by Hazel and two of the children, so they are calm and quiet, and it was only about half-an hour's job to slide them out of the pen, into a temporary crush (no more than a couple of sheep hurdles tied together) and let Graeme the vet get on with it. A quick injection to the scrotum, a quick injection into the flank, a flash of scalpel and a selection of bloody tasty morsels yanked and twanged, then thrown into the bucket. If only the dogs had known!

As usual, we three gossiped and chatted all the way through, covering everything from last week's shoot to Monday's lurcher incident, to what Graeme thought of Groenendaels – we're thinking ahead and looking for a third dog again, and this time trying to find one with a bit more bark that the flatcoats, but not as disastrously inbred as our last Malinois. Not surprisingly, Graeme knew little about them, but his only advice was to watch the inbreeding.

The slightly stunned and sore calves were quietly nudged back into their pen. Job done. What a bunch of professionals we are. Who needs tractor driving?

Back indoors, I found that *Farmers Weekly* had forwarded to me an email from a producer at Channel 5. He's putting together a documentary about grass-roots supporters of UKIP, and had come across my article last year proclaiming my feelings for them. Could he come down and have a chat about it?

My hackles go up at once in these situations. Some years ago, I had exactly the same proposition: could I help a company who were doing a children's TV show, where child presenters interviewed members of assorted professions. Would I be able to help? I jumped at it. A huge crew arrived at the farm, we gave them tea and biscuits, were polite and cooperative, and generally looked after them royally.

The first inkling I got that something was not all what it seemed to be was when, seconds before we started filming, I was asked to sign a confidentiality document, which meant I could not tell anyone about the event. I thought it was odd, but assumed it was standard practice. Then the filming started. We did stuff with cattle, we drove tractors, we sat on bits of farm machinery, and all the time a sweet bespectacled thirteen-year-old, William, fired questions at me off a clipboard. And every tenth question was really odd. The one that sticks in my mind, the one that suddenly made me realise that this was *definitely* not all it seemed, was "Do you think shooting at ramblers is a good idea?" I reined in my enthusiastic cooperation at this point, and I seem to remember that the day was brought to a slightly hasty end. I did cash their respectable cheque though.

Some months later, the show – *Little Friends* – hit the airwaves. The interviews were a minor part of proceedings. It was basically a foul-mouthed child-based version of *Candid Camera,* without any laughs. These child presenters would dupe unwitting members of the public into looking stupid while trying to be helpful. I sat up late to watch the show, being shown on a major commercial channel after a run on one of the minor channels, and my heart sank as I realised what was going on. The first of the interviewees was an estate agent, and the short interview was a compilation of all the bizarre questions. He looked very foolish indeed.

I never found out if my interview made it to the final programme. After only a few episodes, Ofcom ordered it off the airwaves after a storm of complaints. There's no sign of it on the internet – thankfully. All I know is that if I ever meet 'William' again, there will be tears.

I passed a concise version of this sorry tale to the man from Channel 5, and added that we all know what the establishment (including the media bubble) thinks of UKIP, and we know damned well that it will take any chance it can to portray it as clichéd nut jobs, fruitcakes and swivel-eyes loons – copyright David Cameron, I think. What assurances could he give me that we would be treated properly? I await his reply.

It was quiz time in the evening. We went up to the lovely old village hall in Privett for a light-hearted version of the Growmore Club Quiz, known as the Dalgety Shield – now in its 28th year. There were four teams, lots of insults, endless barracking, a couple of beers and finger food afterwards. We (Petersfield Wey) won the evening – despite my best efforts. Very jolly it was too – perfect to help forget that we *still* can't get any arable farming done.

The full moon looked a bit iffy – more weather tomorrow?

February 5th
It would be easy to get a bit fed up with the weather. Once again, just as the day looked right and the ground was dry, the heavens opened and more totally unforecast snow arrived. Another short but irritating blizzard – enough to make the ground slippery as hell and totally undrillable. Still, it's all good character-forming stuff. No tractor driving today.

The man from Channel 5 replied, promising that his documentary about UKIP supporters will be fair and balanced, although they'll have to make sure it's "entertaining for the viewers". Gosh, I wonder how they'll do that. Some selective editing to make us look like complete fools. I haven't replied yet.

There was then an email from the landlord, which was a delight. He agreed to all the points I made to him in my email a few days ago. Yes, it is true that our farm is not theirs to hand over to their visitors. Yes, they will have to change their publicity to reflect this fact. Yes, they will be doing some more fencing to keep people where they should be. I replied gracefully, saying how grateful I was, and how Shrek-like the past eighteen months had been. I genuinely felt a wave of relief wash over me – and only then did I realise how much the issue had been getting to me.

The next message of the day was from policewoman Lynn. She'd had a chat with the lady with the lurcher, who was reluctant to agree that her dogs had killed anything, although she did acknowledge that the dogs had been out of control, and that was wrong.

Tod was in just after lunch, with a pre-holiday (for him) wash-up and briefing. Forget any more spraying – getting the oilseed rape done was enough of a victory for now. Concentrate on the drilling – and stop panicking! Quite reassuring. There was much talk of the Old Gits, and potential gigs.

I then continued the good PR with the landlord by sending them the complete history of the Barracuda bomber that crashed in Rough Field, complete with a couple of old black-and-white pictures from my old photo album. I hope they use them in their 'about Hinton Ampner' material, which at the moment is a little short on accuracy.

A quick walk in the lengthening evening in the cold wind, and another non-farming day done. It seems absurd to watch the weather forecast after this week's efforts, but I suppose I'll give it a go. You never know, we might get busy soon.

February 6th

We were lucky enough to host the all-England mouse ten-pin bowling championships in the attic last night – or so it sounded. It started at bedtime – and I was having trouble getting to sleep anyway – and went on till about one thirty. I can't believe they're not interested in my brand new restocked traps. A couple of hours later, I was prodding Hazel in the back to try to persuade her to stop the snoring that her cold was causing. Then, at five thirty, the idiot flatcoats decided to wake up, with their usual cacophony of flapping ears, crashing down the stairs and tail-flapping against furniture. I abandoned all attempts to sleep, and had an early breakfast.

It was worth it. The ground outside was, at last, perfect for some wheat sowing 'on the frost'. I was up and running at a ludicrously early hour for me, and the ground was frozen dry and crumbling perfectly. Utter joy. And then, four-and-a-half turns round an eight-turn headland (all that was left to do in Drier Field) the 'low seed' buzzer went off. This was a bit of a mystery. I had been sure that I had enough in the tank – OK, I had pushed the seed rate up on the computer when restarting, but I was still somewhat surprised. It wasn't a problem – I had one more bag left in the barn, and I'm always happy to get the barn as empty as possible. It just meant a trip back to the Drier Yard, a drive home in Tigger, unlocking the seed barn, moving all the Scout seed that I'd carefully blocked that last bag of Panorama with, driving back down to Drier Field with the one bag on the front of the loader, and refilling the drill. No trouble at all.

The slight problem was that the ground, in that hour, had thawed, and everything was back to a slippery sticky square one. I persevered, doing a ninth turn of headland and then running the seed out next to the Broom woods. It looked a bit messy right at the end, but hey, I finished a field!

I drove the drill home round the outside of Folly, making a bit of a mess there too, and parked up in the yard. I was going to calibrate for the last bit of winter wheat – Scout in TBHD – but I thought I'd wait until plans were a bit clearer.

I spent the rest of the afternoon doing some serious machinery porn. It dawned on me that in March the last payment on the John Deere will go out of the farm bank account, and my tractor will join the combine harvester, the drill, the Octavia and the Varidisc in having been fully paid for in the last six months. This is all very well for cash flow – especially with prices heading seriously south at the moment – but the old and wise tell us that it's a good thing to have a couple of machines ticking away on HP. There's something complicated about capital allowances, which, as usual, goes right over my head – all I know is that the figures involved are well out of our reach.

Nonetheless, I have a hankering for a second big tractor. It would be handy to have another 150-ish HP machine to pull the new plough or the new sprayer, so I could leave the Deere on the drill when situations like this year arise. The local Claas dealer has a couple of old-ish machines, with just over 4,000 hours on the clock, priced in the mid-20-grand zone. I wonder if they would suit.

I'm also contemplating upping the drill size to a four metre Horsch. I just can't go on being caught out with the sowing unfinished. I'm sowing at double the speed that we were five years ago, but in two of the last three autumns, I've been found wanting. Going up to four metres would force a new tractor into the yard – 150hp wouldn't handle it on our ground.

And I found myself scouring the Skoda website, too. There's a lovely dark blue Octavia 4WD up in Buckinghamshire. I did an email enquiry, and got a phone call back very quickly, valuing our present Octavia at half of bugger all. I think I might drop that idea.

In fact, I shouldn't really be lured into machinery buying at all. If there is cash there, it should continue with the quest to improve soil indices. It's nothing like as exciting, but it is better for the farm in the end. I could invest it in an infrared mouse detector c/w heat seeking mini-missiles and 30 mm cannon. Or get some sleep earmuffs that work.

There is another way to get to sleep: pop down the Flowerpots, pick up a huge takeout of Perridge's Ale (and half a dozen packets of peanuts), then head down to Blackhouse Farm and enjoy watching England unexpectedly beat Wales in a thrilling opening to this year's Six Nations. So that's what I did.

February 7th

The beer trick worked. I slept in late, but then woke up with a thumping headache. I'll never learn. Once I'd recovered enough, I remembered that today is National Pigeon Day – the day when as many guns as possible head out to the countryside and take up residence in as many copses and spinneys as possible and shoot pigeons. The idea is to keep the pigeons on the move, never letting them settle. I wasn't up to shooting, but did my bit by filling my 85 acres of oilseed rape with a veritable forest of rope bangers.

As I stood on the headland of White Hill, waiting for the childish thrill of watching the bangers go off, I could hear shooting coming from all directions. Let's hope we do make a hole in the pigeon population, which has recovered in the last couple of years, after the curious throat parasite that was killing so many of them. You'd see them sitting cold and motionless, unable to eat, all over the farm, and then see a pillow-burst of feathers where a hawk of some sort had swept in and finished them off.

National Pigeon Day might not be called National Pigeon Day any more. They have to keep renaming it in a hopeless attempt to avoid outraging the professional outragees of the animal rights movement. Pointing out that pigeons are an agricultural pest, and present a threat to crop production, and therefore the nation's food, is a waste of time – especially in these days of full barns. I think the whole concept is almost by word of mouth only these days.

With my conscience clear that my oilseed rape wouldn't be a safe haven for the county's pigeon, I settled down for a long afternoon of rugby. Ireland vs Italy was dull, France vs Scotland excellent.

February 8th

Another cold and clear Sunday morning, but with enough wind to put the idea of spraying a bit of Roundup right out of my mind. We thought we'd go and shoot some more clays. Unfortunately, the north wind cutting across the Chalky Hill shoot meant that the long queues were harder to endure than normal, despite the general bonhomie and chit chat. Jonathan had his first score with the new gun that was lower than the last, and his head dropped too much as a result. Hazel suggested that it might have been due to his coming down from the sugar high that he'd enjoyed with two mates on Saturday afternoon – lashings of coke, pizza and Haribo.

More scanning of the weather forecast left me pondering what to do next. They still reckon it'll be dry for the foreseeable. I went and had a walk across TBHD. It was, for the first time in months, firm. Still damp on top, but a tractor would definitely travel. Should I do a day's spraying, then leave the Roundup undisturbed for another day, and only then get on and drill? If the pass with the Roundup totally eliminated a pass later on in the year, perhaps it would be worth it. As it is, I don't have that much faith in the forecasters. I think I'll get the drill ready.

I spent an hour or so at dusk shuffling seed bags. I put eight on the big blue trailer, two on the old wooden trailer, and one in the drill, ready for calibration. It also cleared space in the barn for the delivery of spring beans and spring wheat seed that's due tomorrow. Then just as I was reversing up to the rear weights, the hand and foot throttles went dead again, leaving me with an engine that will only idle. Bother – luckily, we haven't paid the bill for the last repair yet. Let's hope it behaves itself for tomorrow's unloading.

February 9th

A day of immense and intense frustration. It was all planned so nicely: get up early, and get some writing knocked off while waiting for the two morning deliveries, which are the seed and the Nissan X-Trail (this month's press car). And then, after lunch, race out to make a start in the dust of TBHD.

Just for a change, that's not how it worked out. By ten, I'd done all the writing, and there was no sign of any delivery. So I did some long-overdue drill maintenance: I put the new marker arm holder on, and did lots of greasing. Still no deliveries, so I did the diesel order.

I have a list of local fuel suppliers, and I ring them and ask for their best price on red diesel. That may sound like the most obvious way to do it, but a generation ago, that wasn't how it was done – not on this farm, anyway. We would ring our supplier (singular) and ask for a load to be delivered. No one did anything as vulgar as talk about the cost. It was only a couple of years after I took over that I thought I'd ring someone else for a quote – and promptly saved over £200 on the load. I think our account at the original supper was marked 'Never asks price – charge what we like!'

The crash in the price of crude oil has been reflected in the final price I got – almost exactly 25% less than the price when I last ordered. I did mull the idea of bringing another old redundant tank back into operation, and doubling the size of the order – but there's no saying that fuel prices won't fall further.

There was still no sign of a lorry or a Nissan, so I calibrated the drill, and filled up with diesel. By lunchtime, I was ready to go.

I rang the seed company, who denied all knowledge of any 'late morning' promise. Tough titty, I said. I'm out after lunch, so you'll have to re-do all your plans. They took the news better than I thought. Then an email came through from Nissan saying that their morning delivery had gone awry too – it would now be after four o'clock. That suited me; I could get some drilling done, and Hazel could take the delivery driver to Petersfield station as part of the school run.

The afternoon was clear, all mine to finally start the very last lap in the long race to get the winter sowing done. I drove down the roads to the Drier, across the stubble of Blackhouse Road, through The Neck and into the Top of Hurst Down. I dropped the drill into the ground and started the long 'marking out' turn, twenty-ish metres in.

It was like porridge. The tractor could only just get enough grip, and by the time I got to the corner opposite Murph's house, all the press wheels were bunged up with mud. It hadn't dried a bit. Yesterday's firmness is hopeless if the ground is still saturated. I parked the drill up behind the trees, hitched off and brought the John Deere home. The only consolation was to see that Murph's maize, over the hedge on similar ground, is also unsown. I might try some ploughing tomorrow, if the drilling is so utterly hopeless.

The Nissan arrived at four, so I took it on an early mission to Rod Gaskin's, to get more shear bolts for the drill marker arm. M8 should be better than the weedy M6 ones I've been using – these have been breaking, but only falling out when the arm goes into the upright position, and then the arm falls forward, hits the ground and gets bent and buckled under the drill. I couldn't be bothered to get the proper M8 bolts last time I shopped, and what was the saying about lazy people?

At band rehearsal, it turned out that Ian had missed last week's because he was passed out on the hard shoulder of the A3(M). He woke up in Frimley hospital A&E, fully wired up for a heart attack. We truly are the Old Gits. He seemed well enough to have to put up with a storm of sympathy-free abuse from the rest of us.

February 10th

I'm not doing very well with tractor work at the moment. Any plans to get on early were once again scuppered by a late-ish phone call last night from Adrian, the seed delivery driver. Could he pop in tomorrow with two tonnes of spring wheat? I agreed, of course, and it made a refreshing change when he arrived within half an hour of ETA.

We squeezed his ludicrously long curtainsider into the lane outside the barn, got it unloaded, and then (most crucially) got him turned round. "Right then," he said. "I'll see you in an hour or so with the spring beans." This was news to me, and I told him so. He was quite happy to reschedule if I insisted, but I told him to go and get them. When you've got a competent lorry driver who knows exactly where to come, and how to turn his behemoth around, you agree that he can come back.

It's always a good chance to do a bit of maintenance. I refilled the grease gun (bloody hard work in these low temperatures) and gave the loader a good greasing. I was in the middle of doing good farming PR with a couple of passing German tourists when the lorry arrived back. Can't say it wasn't a relief.

Just for a change, there was yet another complication. Whoever bagged the beans had used the sort of square bags you buy sand from the DIY superstore in. Very handy if you're trying to save space – they can almost be stacked like bricks – but they are completely impractical when it comes to moving them. They have a lifting strap at each corner, so the tractor can only pick up one half-tonne at a time, doubling the unloading time, and a man is needed to guide the straps over the lifting arms. This slows the job down even more and raises a selection of safety issues. Adrian would never win a Kate Moss impersonation contest, and was tumbling around in the lorry in a way that YouTube was invented for.

By the time we'd got all ten tonnes off, and got the 45-footer turned and sent on his again, it was well after lunch, and, once again, plans for a long session of drilling, or ploughing – or anything – were scuppered. I dropped Hazel and the dogs in Hurst Down, persuaded myself that it was still far too sticky to work, washed Tigger, and then settled down to do some homework on the accounts for the long trip down to Havant tomorrow.

The forecast has suddenly changed to a wet spell on Friday and Saturday. Ho hum.

February 11th

I finally got the next *Farmers Weekly* article sorted before nine o'clock, and sent it off. It's always a relief when a piece clicks, and seems to read well – but the final say is always with the magazine, of course.

After a bit of accounts-related homework, reminding myself of the queries I had with the draft set, I set off to Havant to see Richard the accountant. It's always a strange drive down the A3 to the coast, for all sorts of reasons. It will always remind me of Dad, because whenever he and I would go together, he'd have a nostalgia overload about when he was a 'pupil' on the farm that is now buried under the A3/M27 intersection. Stories of being in the Home Guard would pour out, none of them succeeding in removing the image we all had of Dad as the Pike of Portsmouth.

It's also good for a farmer to get out of his bucolic comfort zone and see where others work. The accountant's office is the dullest of square blocks in a part of Havant that might not win 'seediest corner' award, but would be in the top three. The place is a quiet buzz of activity, and Richard's office is minimalist and functional. I don't know how long I would last in such an environment. He has been our accountant since we started, and was Dad's from 1981, when there was a branch in Petersfield, which was far closer to the farm. He announced earlier this year that he will be retiring, which seemed wrong at the time, because it seems only yesterday that I set off down there to do my first set of accounts. It think that was the first time I really felt I'd taken over the farm, even though it must have been in early 1993.

We never know if Richard is the best man for the job – how can you, without submitting two sets of figures and getting two different sets of figures? It's a bit like children and schools – you never will know if you did the best – you just try, and hope you're happy with what actually happens. I know that there are specialist agricultural accountants around, who really will understand some of the jargon, not to mention some handy tricks of the trade, but we're happy with Richard. Especially if he books the band for his retirement party.

We sat down and had our usual chat, covering a multitude of topics, which included the accounts themselves. But we also did politics, the EU, Cards against Humanity, and lots of catch up on the children. He has, after all, been following our career progression for 22 years, so he loves the updates.

There were a couple of issues that will need changing, but they will still be nice and healthy. The biggest change is in the last page, where our capital account, having been bumbling along in the negative for seemingly endless years, has bounced gloriously into the black, thanks to Mum's legacy which came through at Christmas. And that figure is always the one the bank zooms in on. Not sure why – one day I'll understand accounting.

On the point of leaving, I took a deep breath, and asked his opinion on a Little Problem: for a decade and a half, we've had our old tractor driver paying rent in cash every week for a cottage. This cash hasn't gone anywhere except our back pockets – rather quietly. Having heard the other day on a shoot about a farmer having the book thrown at him by HMRC for just such a situation, I thought it would be wise if we took steps to own up. Richard agreed, and said he'd do some sums.

I got home to a message from the fuel company driver – he'd be here in an hour, and was just ringing to warn us, as we requested. I popped out and unlocked the multiple barriers to the fuel tank, and he arrived, unloaded and did the paperwork exactly as requested. How refreshing.

February 12th
I spent a long time out on the heavy brow of TBHD, staring at the ground, then kicking it, then staring at it again. The forecast for tomorrow was quite grim – possibly half an inch of rain starting at lunchtime. If I wanted to get the late wheat into this field, it would take me two days. If I started this morning, had a long day today, and then got out here early tomorrow, it might all get done – I'd certainly knock off the landwork.

But… the ground just wasn't quite ready. It was firm underneath, but still slippery on top – the week's dry, calm weather had, bizarrely, done absolutely no drying. Maybe I should have run a cultivator through it, to get some air into it. "Won't dry till it's moved," as Dad used to say. Should I get going anyway? There's nothing worse than starting a couple of acres and then abandoning – especially on one of the few fields that's visible by others.

I gave the ground one more kick, and soil stuck to the toe of my boot. Right, I decided. That's too wet. Better to go in well in a week, than make a mess now.

I hitched the plough on again, and set off to Blackhouse Road. The work from a couple of weeks ago had weathered beautifully in all that frost, but it showed that the plough still wasn't set up right. This time, I got serious. Out came the tape measure. I took an inch off the front furrow width, shortened the right-hand link arm by a turn, and then raised the left-hand turnover stop by a couple of turns. The other key change was to desensitise the Deere's draft control a bit, setting it to near as dammit pure 'position' control. I'd noticed that at the first sign of tougher ground, the plough leapt up – you can monitor it on the 'depth percentage' readout on the tractor screen. I set it so the reading stayed around 14%, and gradually, during the day, everything clicked into place. By late evening, the job was looking, even if I say it myself, fairly respectable, and I'd turned a decent chunk of the 75 acres brown (with occasional white strips where the old chalk dells and hedges had been). Best job in the world, ploughing.

I celebrated the joy of farming with Rufus in the Thomas Lord, where we agreed furiously about lots of things over a couple of pints and some pretentious peanuts.

February 13th

The weather still was set to turn foul at lunchtime, so I made an early-ish start (once the beer and peanuts had been dealt with) ploughing in Blackhouse Road. The Golden Hour on the radio was 1979, and musical nostalgia doesn't get better than that. I rang in with the right year, which is a mistake if you fancy getting on air. Get it wrong and put on a bit of a show, and they'll broadcast it later. But there's only room for one 'right' competitor. I'm not saying I ring the station too much, but they pick up the phone with "Hello, Charlie."

The sky blackened just after noon, and the heavens opened, so I called off, cleaned off (in a bit of a hurry) and headed home for lunch.

As the rain continued, I thought I'd head into Petersfield for my twice-yearly haircut. It's always a lottery at the appointment-free barbers. Will there be ten men all queueing, or will it be a straight-in job? Today, there was just one in front of me, so waiting was short.

I got away without being asked what I was doing today (answer: "Having my hair cut."), or where I was going on holiday (answer: "Every day is a holiday at Manor Farm.") Somehow we got onto the band, and she promised to look us up on YouTube. Confessing to being a farmer got its usual set of good-natured insults, which I take as a compliment. Some years ago, there was a loud and lively discussion, involving the whole shop, about the outrage industry, and how certain sections of the community should toughen up a bit. "You don't mind being called a fat smelly farmer, do you?" I was asked, to great guffawing. "Not at all," I replied, almost completely truthfully.

Every time I go, I mean to get it really short, for convenience's sake, but never do. You can bet your life that the cold weather would come back in a week or so, and I'd be mighty glad I didn't do a No 3 all over. I'd be even gladder if it got cold enough to do some drilling.

February 14th

A drenched Saturday morning. Had a lie in, made a trip to the Countrystore to buy some cartridges, and then watched rugby. Perfect.

February 15th

A slightly better morning. I thought I would try some more ploughing, and did the long drive to Blackhouse Road. Always a risk working on a Sunday these days, because of the certainty of seeing Trust walkers all over my fields, but a couple of hours' ploughing would shine up the mouldboards and polish my conscience for another session on the sofa watching rugby.

The Deere struggled a bit going up the hill on the first turn – I assumed it was a simple case of the ground being sodden after 19 mm of rain on Friday and Saturday. Coming down the hill seemed to be a bit of an effort, too, though. Up and back once more, and there seemed to be a heck of a lot of subsoil coming up. Hmm, I thought, this isn't right. Sure enough, when I got out and checked everything (as a good farmer would have done before setting off), the relatively flimsy and completely tread-free depth wheel was as flat as a pancake. That brought a premature halt to my ploughing for the day.

The rugby was another thriller though. It's funny to think that when I really got into rugby, in the late 1970s and early 1980s, when Billy Beaumont lead the England revival (aided handsomely by my all-time hero, Fran Cotton), a typical game would end 9–3, all points coming from penalties. There would be lots of loving lingering shots of Rob Andrew and his hyper-developed cheek muscles, lining up for yet another go at the posts, but not often a lot else.

These days it's a disappointment if there aren't forty points in every game. It's ten times faster, ten times harder, but it's ten times more painful to see the modern injures. This weekend seems to have been particularly bad. The thuggery seems to have almost gone; multiple cameras, officials and replays have got on top of that. The price we pay for the 'modern era' is all the razzmatazz: fireworks, opera totty screeching their way through the anthems, hyperbolic war-allegory build-up, and page after page of American Football-style statistics – as if anyone watching the intense mayhem of a modern rugby international can really keep count of 'missed tackles'.

It's lovely to have daylight after the final whistle, so Jonathan (still in pyjamas) and I took the dogs out on the Clump loop, just to confirm that everything is once again, very wet. The crops seem to be thinking about moving on a bit, though, and I could have sworn there was a green sheen on Drier.

Hazel met us in the garden with a long face: something has killed three of the beautiful, peaceful ducks. Could it be the springer that was terrorising them some months ago? No, two of the bodies had gone. It has to be the fox. Diana was not happy at all.

Also not happy was the Editor, who had set up in White Hill for a bit of pigeon shooting, only to see absolutely none. It's quite hard to make the right sympathetic noises when that sort of news is actually fantastic from a farmer's point of view. Not sure why the pigeons are avoiding my oilseed rape, but long may it continue.

February 16th
It was dry for an hour or so, then it rained. A lot. A good chance to set about the most important job on the farm: sorting out our registration with the Rural Payments Agency.

The countryside is buzzing with the sound of farmers and agents trying to log on to the RPA's system – and failing. I, for instance, spent half an hour trying to find the crucial bit of paper with my ten-digit number (ten digit? Are there really one short of ten billion of us?) and my password on it. I then tried several times to log on, and got numerous 'server internal error' messages. So many, in fact, that I thought I had better ring the helpline.

The helpline didn't help, as most bureaucratic helplines don't, and I was put on hold, and then asked for a number so they could call me back. There were lots of automated apologies, explaining that the system was running slowly. I abandoned the helpline.

I then, finally, miraculously, managed to get through on the internet, and set about… set about what, exactly? I'm wasn't sure what I was supposed to do. So I went through a couple of fields, changing the area from 0.00 ha, and filling in the 'land use' box, but then got to a field where I'm planning to put EF2 Wild Bird Mix in a corner. What should I do now? There appeared to be nothing on the 'options' to cover this plan. So I signed out and left it for another day, probably just like ten thousand (or one short of a billion) other farmers. Such is modern farming.

All that time in the office meant that I was able to oversee the departure of the Nissan (and even make a start on writing it up while waiting for the RPA helpline to answer), sign for the plough parts that I ordered on Thursday, and redirect Mr Tesco to Manor Cottage, catching him just before he started to wheel sister-in-law Anna's groceries round to our back door. I'm sure his computer told him he was at the right place.

February 17th

A stunning, frosty morning. I stomped across Drier Field, which was as sticky as hell, but the wheat in the land work was actually starting to show quite healthily. No sign of slugs, which is always a relief. In the trees above the old Conder bins were two red kites. Close up, they are huge – almost like roosting pheasants.

It's curious to think about the fuss that was made when the first kestrel was seen, in the Park. In the attic is a scrapbook, with drawings of the hole in the tree where they were spotted. That must have been in the mid-1970s.

And then there was the day all the tractors stopped in Pipeline Field to watch the first of the buzzards. Ian was working here then, so that must have been in about 1988. At about the turn of the millennium, I called Dad from the tractor to tell him to come and see the first red kite. Now they're all mundane. Don't see many songbirds, though. Funny, that.

The ground was too wet to do anything, but tomorrow looks better. In fact, the weather forecast is back to its depressing inevitability: tomorrow looks to be the last fine day for ages. So, now that the date has passed for getting back onto our overwintered stubbles, I thought that the time was right to hitch off the plough and put the sprayer back on. Before doing so, I had a session putting the new rear discs on the Kverneland. As usual, the non-original ones didn't seem the perfect fit – the recesses weren't quite right for the fixing plate. But I did them up tight enough – I hope. Both bearings seem a bit loose, so that'll be another job on the horizon.

Over lunch, I had another go at the new Rural Payment Agency website. I logged on fine, but once again didn't know what to do next. So I rang the helpline again, and got a very helpful lady who explained that I had done all I needed to do. I was registered, and all my fields were there. At this stage, that's all. Come March, a whole bunch of new 'functionality' will arrive, and we'll be able to do all the hedges, ditches, sub-divisions and tweaks that we want. Oh. Thank you very much, I said, and rang off.

My mood was spoilt by an email and phone call from the accountant. He had looked into our little 'undeclared income' problem, and it was now indeed time to come clean to the Inland Revenue. They are doing discounted penalties for just such situations, and he had come up with a figure. It was big. Big enough to spoil any holiday plans, or the new car, or the new gun, or any number of things. The cash flow might just about be able to take it, since nearly every machine we've got has just been paid off, or is very nearly paid off. If the worst comes to the worst, a loan will be in order. Not the best of news, but still better than being found out during a tax inspection, if and when that arrives.

After lunch, a manky old Renault Clio was parked outside the tractor barn. Two charming ladies and three children were climbing out. I was starting on my "Really? Must you park there?" routine, when they pointed out that the Clio had just broken down. They were somewhat distraught, so I switched seamlessly into "Don't worry, stay there, we'll sort you out!" routine. The Clio was completely dead – something major had gone wrong in the electrical department. I must have looked very impressive as I tested the healthy battery with my multimeter, but then looked pretty useless when announcing that I hadn't got a clue what the problem was.

Sarah, the driver, told a familiar story. The car had been in for a service, as it had been stuttering a bit, and the nice local garage had, ahem, topped the oil up. Oh, that'll solve any electrical problem. Sarah rang the AA, working hard to get help, since she was totally without any documents. She passed all their tests, though, and was promised a van in an hour. They set off to Hinton Ampner gardens to pass the time, I set off to take the plough off and have a cup of tea.

As I went round to Godwin's, Sarah was back, sitting in the sunshine on the fallen tree outside the barn, enjoying the fantastic evening. We agreed it was one hell of a place to break down. I did a bit of farming PR with the history of the village, and was rewarded with a brownie when the rest of her passengers came back from the House.

The AA man was baffled. There had been something quite serious to blow the main fuse, but he was damned if he knew what it was. He'd replaced the fuse, and got the Clio going, but wasn't entirely happy. Just before sending them on their way, he had one last inspection of the bonnet. With a triumphant cry, he gingerly lifted out a small torch, not more than four inches long, that had dropped down between the starter motor and the engine block, and been left there. It was fresh, and quite scorched where it had been shorting out. They were lucky to have just broken down and not caught fire, and lucky it was on a country bend (complete with charming farmer) rather than rush-hour on the M25 home to Chesham. He suggested that a phone call was in order to the local garage. The whole gang set off cheerfully, with big waves all round.

I hitched onto the sprayer, parked up in the yard, and started filling it, ready for tomorrow. I might get some farming done.

February 18th

Frosty and dry again, but the forecast said that the wind would get up later, so I pushed on relatively early with the spraying. Three litres of glyphosate and a litre of water conditioner per hectare for as many stubbles as I can get to.

First up was Kilmeston Road, which should have been straightforward, if some silly sod hadn't allowed the Wessex Historic Tractor Club to come and hold their annual ploughing match in it. They had turned a field that was at last completely free from decades' worth of ridges, furrows, veerings and ditches into a quilt of ridges, furrows, ditches and veerings. And they did the whole thing at ninety degrees to last year's tramlines – which I'd decided to re-use.

It certainly put the Deere's multiple suspension systems to the test – I was also quite relieved that the sprayer sets its own rate, using a sensor on the land wheel. I was speeding up and slowing down rather a lot, which would have caused chaos with the old flat rate system sprayers. The bizarre moment was realising that I had made it through the bottom of the field without getting stuck – or even sinking into ruts. Normally, this ground, next to the source of the Itchen, is waterlogged this time of year. We must, despite all indication to the contrary, have had a dry February.

Back home for a quick lunch, then refill for the Hangar. Nice and smooth, this one, and dry as a bone. Mind you, it is the chalkiest field on the farm. I made a mental map as I went round it of all the gaps where Joe Public and his missis and his dogs are merrily walking across the field. It looks a relatively small job – just a flipping nuisance. At some stage, the post driver will arrive, and I won't have to do my shoulders in.

Next tank was for Chalks. I decided to start at the top, so I drove along the Godwin's track and unfolded in the corner. A dozen or so walkers stopped and watched with interest, about four yards from the boom. I signalled that they should move a bit further away – I didn't want them to get a facefull, especially as the wind was picking up a bit. They moved, but I think they didn't reckon much of being asked to move on. When they were thirty yards away or so, I managed to hoot to get their attention, and give them big thumbs up and waves. Chalks was pretty clean, so I'm not sure it needed spraying, especially as I'm planning to plough it for the peas. All good stubble hygiene. I disturbed two woodcock out in the field, and four partridge down the bottom hedge. Where were they when we were walking it with guns?

With a couple of hundred litres still in the tank, I made my way to Joan's Acre/Dell Close (via the Drier to fill the clean water tank and enjoy the even greener Drier Field), to do the strips that I had missed back in October. Back then, I'd just done my lower back in, and had driven a 500-mile round trip in a day to rescue Diana from her false start at York University. Despite the test Jaguar's luxury seats, I'd gone from dodgy back to biblical spasm. But it was in the middle of one of those brief weather windows, and the fields desperately needed a pre-wheat clean up once I'd got back. I was in so much pain, I couldn't actually see which booms I had turned on or off. Consequently, I did quite a lot of headland and the first two turns up Dell Close with the inner left boom turned off. Today was my chance to finally eliminate the thick green strips of beans and weeds that had survived as a relic of those dark weeks.

I did a rinse out in the field, having decided that, despite the suddenly longer days, the winds were too strong for another tank, and I was aching like hell after the bumps and crashes of Kilmeston Road.

I noticed the birds singing like mad at dusk. A lovely sign of winter leaving us – although the forecast for the next week suggests that my optimism might be somewhat premature. A shame, because one more day like this and I'd be trying to remember where I left the drill.

February 19th

I found the seed drill. It was just where I left it, tucked behind the trees in the Top of Hurst Down (THD). I found it because I needed the stillsons that were in its toolbox. The local tyre supermarket had finally got everything I needed to sort out the depth wheel on the plough, so I thought I'd get that job done this morning, and maybe knock off a few more acres this afternoon.

Goodness knows when the last time the wheel had come off the plough was. I tried taking it off the spindle, but it wouldn't budge. So, rather than uncover and dismantle all the bearings, I decided to take the spindle itself off. Easier said than done. As usual, I couldn't lay my hand on the right size socket – my tools spend all their time spread out at random in all corners of the farm. It's pure fluke if the right socket is in the right place at the right time. My excuse for my untidiness is that no bugger can possibly nick the lot at once.

The only solution was to get the mighty stillsons. I drove up to THD, and kicked myself – the ground was firm and dry. I should have started up here yesterday. It wasn't worth doing it now – big rain was imminent. The stillsons and a five-foot extension pipe finally persuaded the whole depth wheel assembly to come off, and I loaded it into the back of Tigger, and set off up to Micheldever.

The tyre depot is a place of legend. It stacks 'em high and sells 'em cheap. Car owners will come from miles around – many, many miles – to fit a set of tyres here. The savings on four high-performance bits of rubber easily outweigh the petrol needed to get here. Mind you, its popularity means you sometimes have to wait a very long time. And there's an attitude from the staff which, while I wouldn't call it rude, borders on curt rather than business-like.

As I drove up through the countryside towards Micheldever, I resigned myself to a long wait, a humourless welcome, but a cheap tyre on the plough. As it happens, I was completely wrong. There was no queue, the whole job was done in ten minutes, and everyone seemed rather cheerful up there. Best of all, I didn't do my back in wrestling with tyre levers on the dirty floor of the tractor barn. Second best of all was seeing that there's still an awful lot of Hampshire countryside waiting for something to be done with it.

I reached home at the same time as the rain, with a sudden thick head, and a violent outbreak of snot and sneezing. I fixed the plough depth wheel back on, resplendent with its new tyre, carefully packed the tools away safely (can't remember where) and headed indoors, beginning to feel very sorry for myself. I made friends with Mr Ibuprofen and headed for the sofa.

February 20th

A very strange noise came from the Chalks valley as I was making my breakfast porridge. It was a subdued crack, followed by a long hiss, and then a thud. It was Jim the Deerman getting on with the long-overdue job off culling some of the roe deer that live in vast numbers on the estate.

Jim is ex-navy, with a broad Scottish accent, and a rifle/scope combo that is worth ten times what my entire gun collection is worth. He told me that it was his retirement present to himself. He has the invaluable stalker's gift: stealth. Very early one harvest morning I was greasing up the combine near the woods, in glorious isolation, when suddenly he was at my elbow – out of nowhere. Gave me the fright of my life.

He has not been well recently, which may explain why the deer population has boomed, but he's back here making the most of the lighter early mornings. It was comforting to hear that he, too, finds his day-to-day work hampered by the National Trust's access policy. Several times, he told Hazel recently, he has been up one of his platforms in the woods, ready to pull the trigger, only to find a walker or a dog in the danger zone. No surprise that now he's concentrating on the open valleys.

By the time the second crack-hiss-thud echoed across the valley, the garden was full of cats and dogs in assorted stages of worry and intrigue. After a moment's consideration, the cats headed indoors, heads and tails as flat as they could be. All three were soon to be found on my bed. Obviously the safest place to be. Meanwhile, the flatcoats decided that the noises were definitely the start of a pheasant shoot, and were unbearable all day.

The seed barley was due to be delivered just after lunch, so we parked the Massey loader tractor outside the barn ready for the lorry. By the time he finally arrived I had had a very productive odd-job session in the barn, doing all those jobs you only do while waiting for a lorry to turn up. I finally overhauled one of the bearing assemblies on the Varidisc, and found the back axle of the Massey to be woefully short of oil – no wonder the spool valve connectors had stopped dripping. It needed about fifteen litres.

It was a proper-sized lorry, with a sensible driver, and the most fuss-free unload of the season. I dread to think how many tons of stuff I have taken off lorries and stacked in that barn. Back in the Eighties, it was thirty-hundredweight pallets unloaded with the truly terrible two-wheel-drive Ford 6610. It had the disastrous 'Rubik's Cube' gear box, and was weighted down with a boiler full of concrete on the rear linkage *and* had both back wheels ballasted. It went through clutches several times a year. Out in the silage clamp in Springshott, yanking direct cut grass out of the heap to feed out-wintered cattle, it struggled in the mud, as the tiny narrow front wheels just sank. More than once, the acidic silage juice meant that the rivets in the wheel rim just rusted away, and the wheels broke off. Very scary. The primitive loader struggled a bit with what was asked of it. Twice the main lift rams buckled while attempting to rip another grab of long-cut silage out of the clamp.

In the late 1980s I persuaded Dad to buy a rough terrain fork lift: a Sanderson 622. This was a revelation: 4WD, four-wheel steer, fantastic lift capacity. It was also a death trap when driven by untrained fools like us. It's a mystery how we managed to avoid turning it over. It was also a mobile greenhouse, without aircon (or a radio), and was a nightmare to grease and service.

Our tractor driver wasn't at all happy to drive this yellow monster, and we were quite happy with that, but when Hazel first became pregnant in 1994, it was obvious that he was going to have to do loader work again. So I traded the Sanderson for a wonderful Deutz-Fahr 4.57, with drop-nose bonnet, down-swept exhaust, and a Chillton loader. The loader was so good that I kept it when we moved to a Fendt 309. I had always wanted a Fendt, but it was somewhat less than successful, proving expensive and unreliable. From the Fendt, we went back to drop-nose with the Massey 5455 – which is a little gem of a tractor: powerful, a bit noisy, and relatively reliable. As long as you remember to keep the back axle topped up.

Come evening, I adjourned to the Flowerpots with the Editor and neighbour Robert, and once we'd cleared the bar (as is traditional), we enjoyed some of Robert's encyclopaedic knowledge of the countryside through the ages. Stories of the 1930s, when whole swathes of Hampshire (and, I assume, the whole of England) were unfarmed. No one could make a penny out of agriculture in those days. The fields were untouched. Ganderdown, for instance, was a mess of gorse, juniper and sheep grazing. For the Editor, of course, this was an image of grey partridge heaven.

For farmers, it must have been anything but heaven. It shows just what a strong vocation agriculture was for Dad, who decided during those very years that farming was where his career lay. Of course, he reaped the fruits of his decision for the next fifty golden years. I'm not bitter, you understand.

February 21st

There's more big weather coming tomorrow, so I thought it would be wise to nail the top, sticky headland of Blackhouse Road before the deluge. The sprayer was still on the Deere, and I mulled hitching off in the yard; but the forecast suggests some serious frost tonight. So, in the new spirit of non-laziness, I backed it into the Godwin's barn and hitched off. A big fuel-up, a quick slotting on of weights and plough, and I was ready to go. Almost sounding professional.

I then spent three hours enjoying the fantastic view from the top of Blackhouse Road, as monster hailstorms swept down just to the west of us. Mid-afternoon, I had a nasty case of every tractor driver's worst nightmare: an electrical gremlin. Every time I pressed the foot brakes on (which on the Deere is how you disconnect the differential lock), the tractor's sidelights came on, along with the orange work light in the cab, and the whole dashboard dimmed slightly.

Alright – it's not really a tractor driver's worst nightmare, but an hour's contemplation lies ahead. Do I ring the dealer on a Saturday afternoon? No – it's not that serious, and it's a Saturday, for goodness sake. Ah yes, but electrical problems usually mean something: rodents in the wiring loom. I've got to the stage where I never park tractors indoors, to avoid our furry friends settling down among the loose straw and mud that lies on top of the axles and gearboxes. Have they got into the Deere's innards? And if they've chewed a cable or two, might there be a short circuit? A fire? You can tell I'm a bit of a worrier. In the end, nothing happened. I just kept ploughing.

Back home, Hazel, Jonathan and Tony the Shepherd set about worming the flock. It all went well until a sheep bit down a bit hard on Jonathan's fingers as he was holding a mouth open. Lots of blood and a couple of quite nasty fingernail-area cuts ensued. After a clean-up and a couple of pictures on Facebook, he seemed OK.

February 22nd

It was one heck of a frost. It made me glad I'd put the sprayer away. I headed out to Blackhouse Road to continue with the seemingly endless task of ploughing it. The frost lifted quite quickly as a huge dark front came in from the west.

Rather oddly, yesterday's electrical gremlins sorted themselves out. I can never decide if I should be relieved in this situation, or if I should be worried that it's going to come back even worse. I'll drop an email to the dealers and ask their opinion.

When the land work got longer at the Neck, I did the top bit of headland. Proper farmers leave the whole headland till last. I like to get them out of the way as they become available. The top of Blackhouse Road is particularly sticky, not to mention 'steep' opposite Joan's Acre house, and it took a bit of slipping and sliding to get it all finished. It made it all the more satisfying when the rain arrived, big time, just as I was finishing the last bit.

By the time I'd done a couple of turns back on the land work, the rain was really heavy, and the Deere was beginning to scrabble. It was a shame, because the job was looking better and better. It's a shame that no one drives up that no-through-road to see such quality ploughing. Satisfied with a long Sunday morning's work, I headed home.

After lunch, Jonathan and I hit the Godwin's barn log store. We had run out of wood, the horizontal rain had a bit of sleet in it, and the forecast shows no sign of spring. Poor Jonathan is the typical farmer's son: no chance of getting away on holiday, skiing or whatever if your Dad is stuck at home watching the weather on a daily basis, seeking a day's sowing/spraying/ploughing to catch up a bit. Still, a long session of manly log sawing and splitting together will have to do as quality time. He can always have a moan about it on Facebook.

February 23rd

Breakfast was interrupted by a lorry driver hammering on the back door. He was delivering a ton of feed for the cattle, and seemed surprised that we didn't know he was coming. We pointed out that he was supposed to ring an hour before arrival. He explained that he wasn't allowed to ring from his cab phone, but then sort of messed up this story by saying he'd rung the office to tell them to remind us he was coming. Life's too short to make any more of a fuss about it, so I said Hazel would be out in twenty minutes.

The Editor reported that he hadn't had any luck with pigeons over the weekend, but I thought I should put some rope bangers in the oilseed rape anyway. The howling wind meant that the first ones went off before I'd got back to the truck, and sure enough, only a couple of pigeons got up from the woods. Good news – a blitz by pigeons at this stage of the year does the most damage of all.

I had a quick snoop at the emerging wheat in Drier Field, and then had a chat with the National Trust lad in charge of the Monday Gang – a team of retired volunteers who come in on Mondays and do lots of cutting and felling. You can tell which part of the estate they're on by the vast plume of smoke they set up wherever they go. Apparently the big plan to clear-fell Bob's Wood and build the wood chip processing plant there has been scuppered by a rare bat. So now they're going to thin out the redwoods, and coppice the more open bit next to the lane. Fantastic news for our new shoot – the two times we went through it in January proved remarkably fruitful, and I remember thinking what a shame it was that the wood was going to be cleared. Once they've coppiced, and if I put a strip next to it, it will suit our purposes very well. As if I know what I'm talking about.

Then it was once again back to Blackhouse Road with the plough for another long session. I marked out the narrow south headland – narrow so that the land work ploughing would cross the outside tramline – and then did the first turn down the hill, just in case things were still sodden from yesterday. Luckily, it was still dry enough to travel, and as the howling gale went on, the ground got better and better. The flat ground at the top of Blackhouse Road was ploughing really nicely, and by the end of the day, I was just a couple of yards away from starting the short work.

I was entertained for the whole session by a couple of buzzards. In the air, they are the masters of graceful languid flight. On the freshly ploughed furrows, they look like small drunk men in buzzard costumes, stumbling and flapping as they chase their prey.

Another cold drying day like this one and I'll be out looking for the drill again. Where did I leave it?

February 24th

No need to go looking for the drill. It was bright, breezy and cold at dawn, but a monster storm had come through at about 3am and drenched everything again. So I dedicated the morning to getting the write-up of the Nissan X-Trail done, and once

I'd stumbled upon a theme, it was easy. It's always nice to be a couple of weeks ahead of deadline.

It was back to Blackhouse Road for another afternoon ploughing. There was a curious moment where the plough depth seemed to be going haywire – too deep, then too shallow, until I remembered that I was passing over the old veering.

Back in the mists of time, when the farm swapped from conventional ploughs to reversible, the received wisdom was that you still started with a veering. I've never worked out why – with reversible ploughs came the chance to be rid, once and for all, of ridges and furrows. I'm a great fan of starting on one side and going the same way over the whole field, and then moving it another way next year. Topsoil, said someone once, is like a duvet. Move it left a bit, right a bit, up a bit, down a bit, but move it too far one way, and you'll mess up the seedbed. A veering seems to me to be like moving the duvet into a ridge in the middle of the bed.

It was made worse on this farm when the ploughmen chose the same spot to make the veering, year after year. The line followed a distinctive tree or a gap in the hedge at the end of the field. I was once sowing Kilmeston Road, north to south, with the old 4-metre trailed Bamlett drill. The tractor almost ground to a halt. As usual, there was the panic about mechanical problems (it was a Ford 7610, after all) but once I looked round, I spotted that the wheels of the drill were perfectly straddling the veering, which was by then a substantial bank. The mound of earth was acting as a brake. Some years after that, we deliberately ploughed the two halves of the field either side of the veering away from it, leaving a deep furrow. With a couple more seasons of working, the ground finally levelled itself out. Mind you, that's the field where I hosted the old ploughmen in September, so all that good work was thoroughly undone.

The remains of the Blackhouse Road veering are still there, still in line with a silver birch in the edge of the woods, and they were just enough to flummox the Deere's highly sensitive draft control system. A nostalgic reminder of previous ways.

I finished the land work, the short top headland at the Neck, and the narrow southern headland. I did a couple of turns to start the long bottom headland (slow turns, too, as I was ploughing 'in' and so driving over the 'ins and outs' to start with). There was a good couple of hours' worth of work to do as it got dark, so I called it a day. I might finish it tomorrow.

February 25ᵗʰ

Yup, I finished Blackhouse Road. Good grief. It has taken weeks – not continuously, of course, but in three- and four-hour sessions as often as the relentless rain has allowed. As is usual in farming, there was no one there to appreciate the event with me except a floppy red kite. So I took a photo of him and put it on Facebook when I got home.

The reason the headlands take so long is that I'm very fussy about marking out and ploughing them. There are ploughmen who shamelessly mark out using the tramline wheel mark. This is accurate, but leaves the poor sprayer operator shaking himself to bits as he drives on the corrugated ground later in the arable year. They say you can tell when the ploughman and the sprayer operator are the same man, when the marking out is done well away from the first tramline. That's what applies on this farm.

But what does 'well away' mean? Well. You can mark out nearer the edge of the field, leaving a slither of a headland. The advantage is that the final headland takes no time to do, but the tractor has to do multipoint turns – and therefore goes through clutches more quickly. I prefer to mark out some way inside the headland tramline, giving ample room to turn. I try to mark out in the same place every year, whether ploughing in or ploughing out, working on the 'duvet' theory.

I still chuckle at the way things were done here all those years ago. Ploughing the soil downhill is easier. So, that's the way it was mostly done. The whole topsoil moved one way, year after year. The side effect of this bad practice is most easily seen in Roe Hill, where the fence at the bottom is almost buried, and the top consists of claggy clay soil which would once have been buried. The same applied to headlands. Ploughing out is easier, so that's what mostly happened. Ditches appeared fifteen or twenty yards into the field. It was hard work suggesting a change when I took over.

After all that work trying to eliminate all these bad practices, and waving goodbye to ploughing when I bought the Horsch, I couldn't help chuckle at the time (and diesel) I've spent in just one field, ploughing again – even if it is the biggest on the farm.

It was all go back at home, where the small-scale shearing gang were in. Well, when I say 'gang', it was one man in a Jap-import Toyota camper van, who set up his kit in the back barn and steadily worked his way through our little flock, trimming them up for impending lambing. It was very quiet and low-key, but that's the way we like these things with our animals.

After lunch, it was time for our annual insurance session with the man from the NFU. There's always hot debate about farm insurance; should we stick with the NFU, or should we switch to someone else? We're fully aware that the NFU are pricier, but they pay out. When I reversed the Amazone drill into the cultivator, and bent the pegged metering wheel beyond repair, they knew exactly what I meant on the claim form. Well, if they didn't, they still paid out. When Anthony backed his trailer into the diesel barn and took the door right off, they paid up without a query. And, most significantly, when my parents were burgled, the NFU's swift actions made a nightmare slightly less awful.

So we sat down and went through all the different insurances – tractors, in-store produce, and public liabilities and so on, and agreed a few changes here and there. Just before they left to crunch the figures and come up with a new monthly premium, I showed them my new desert boots that Monty had chewed a couple of years ago, and demanded a new pair, courtesy of my household insurance. It was gently pointed out, in the broadest Taggart brogue, that by the time they've deducted the excess, and then I've lost my no-claims bonus, it would be cheaper for me to go and buy a new pair myself. Tight-fisted so-and-sos. What was all that about paying out? I promised them a grumpy article in *Farmers Weekly*, but they didn't seem worried.

Talking of things quiet and low-key, in the evening I picked up neighbour Joe, and headed down to Romsey for the annual three-way quiz between Winchester NFU (us), Wellow Growmore Club and Romsey Young Farmers. Nine rounds of questions, some of them blooming hard – I don't often struggle with music questions. It was all very gentle and civilised, with a couple of pints and sandwiches and chips to round off the evening.

My favourite moment was during the second 'General Knowledge' round. "What country," asked our lovely question mistress, "is made by being surrounded by Rutland?" A deathly hush fell on the quizzers. Bafflement was written on all the faces. It made no sense – or did it? We were all too polite to make a fuss, and convinced, in that peculiarly English way, that we must be the ones at fault, all talked our way into putting 'England'.

The answer was 'Denmark'. "Ah," cried one of the quizzers, "You meant Jutland!" The lady quiz mistress was mortified at her error. But no one worried. No one minded. It had been the same question for all three teams. We pulled her leg mercilessly over beer and chips, and then got back to comparing notes on how much dry weather we needed before any spring sowing could start.

We won, by the way.

February 26th

It rained a lot.

The Manor Farm Dog Magnet is a mysterious thing. When in operation, it will attract dogs from far and wide. Sometimes they arrive here and just look for company, sometimes they arrive and kill our ducks. This morning it was time for a sweet little collie from Hinton Hill to pop in and say hello. We've had words with the owner in the past, and he was suitably sorry as he ran across the yard in pursuit of his untrained pet. Luckily, it just wanted to be friends with everyone, although the cats didn't reckon much of its presence.

In the morning post came a long letter from our vet. It said that they were abandoning large animal work. The reasons were many and varied – an inability to attract and keep staff, the bewildering chaos of losing the contract for TB testing, and the decline of dairy herds in the area – but the result was still as stark. We would no longer be able to call on them for help with lambing or cattle emergencies.

We go back a long way with this these vets. Dad dealt with them in his early days here, and the senior vet's wife and my mother were friends and magistrates together. I went to pre-prep school with their son. Scroll forward two schools, and there I was, aged fourteen, sitting next to a scraggy youth in a physics lesson. That same scraggy youth's signature was at the bottom of the vet's letter; forty years on from giggling at the idea of eddy currents, he is now the senior partner.

But we have to leave the nostalgia and sentimentality aside, and consider where that leaves us, with small scale beef and sheep production – lambing starts in a few weeks. The end of the letter contained an invitation to a meeting in Alresford, where we'll be able to meet the company who are offering to take up the work. Unfortunately they are based in Salisbury, although there's talk of them opening a satellite branch near here. We'll go to the meeting and find out.

We had a phone call from school: Jonathan had gone to see the matron because his finger (complete with sheep bites) was swelling and giving him trouble. She suggested that we book a doctor's appointment as soon as possible. Mind you, she was thrilled to write 'sheep bite' in her record book – it has to be a first in the long history of Churcher's College. I asked her to tell Jonathan that the sheep appeared to be fine. Poor chap – he must think that no one takes him seriously.

My heart sinks at the idea of getting an appointment with the doctor – experience suggests that it can be a couple of weeks before they can slot you in. Luckily, as soon as I went through the symptoms, the receptionist insisted that we whisk him there straight off the school bus. He was given antibiotics, some dressings, lots of advice on washing it, and a bit of a lecture about cleaning off a fresh wound more efficiently. He'd already had that last bit from everyone else.

February 27th

It was a stunning cold frosty morning, but the ground was saturated after yesterday's rain. I spent the morning writing, and then decided to head out to the chalky soil of Behind My Love's, and finish that awkward and wiggly headland.

Unfortunately, some poor soul wrapped their car round a telegraph pole in Bramdean, resulting in the closure of the A272 for most of the day. Traffic was diverted through our lanes – Hazel spent half an hour trying to get through in her Skoda. The vast majority of the population cannot reverse a car any more. I was damned if I was going to get the Deere caught up in a traffic jam of one-way commuters

I headed out to Chalks (accessible by track only) instead. My plan was to plough it uphill (what a good boy), and work parallel to the hedge between Chalks and the Back Meadow. So I used the satnav to plot the line of the Chalks/Back Meadow hedge, and then headed up to the top corner of Chalks. I then spent ten minutes trying to get the tractor parallel to that line. It should have been simple, but it dawned on me that the satnav system won't register the direction of the tractor unless it is moving. I suppose it needs two geographical points to be registered before it know where 'forwards' is.

Any passer-by would have been baffled to see me in my tractor rolling backwards and forwards, trying to get the system to register which way I was pointing. In the end, I dropped the plough and just made a start. Inevitably, by the time the work got long, I was quite a few degrees out. I mulled a couple of restarts mid furrow to straighten up, but decided I could live with any curve; better than unevenness, especially as the field is destined for peas, and the number one priority for peas (until they breed a variety that really does stay standing until harvest) is a smooth, even seedbed. I kept going in the dusk until I had got off the heavy land at the top, and the furrows were just beginning to get chalkier.

There was an ominous email from Crop Advisors about availability of pea seed.

Apparently, there's almost none left. I don't think we've ordered ours. That might throw a spanner in the spring drilling plans. I left a message on their after-hours phone wondering where we stand.

The four of us then sat down to a disgracefully enjoyable evening of Cards Against Humanity. Shocking. Fantastic.

February 28th
We must have left the Dog Magnet on again, because there was a pathetic yellow lab hanging round the back door at breakfast. Hazel's keen eye for dog recognition told her that it belonged to someone down on the main road, but we decided that it, and (more importantly) the ducks and chickens wouldn't come to any harm if we left it to make its own way home, rather than driving round the farm trying to find the owner. It had been given a good working over by the flatcoats, so was gone within moments of us shutting the door on him.

It rained a bit, then it rained a lot, then in the evening it rained torrents. I settled down on the sofa and watched Italy win in Scotland (having discussed with Jonathan the idea of a tenner on Italy before the game). In the evening, I drove Jonathan up to Godalming to take part in a drama competition – he and his chum Harry did a duologue from *Blackadder*. They got plenty of laughs but no prizes.

March 1st

A beautiful morning lit up a freshly drenched farm. We've seen that a few times this year. On the way to get the Sunday papers, Hazel met the Editor, who was out on pigeon patrol. After hearing a few shots, I thought I ought to pop out and see where he was, and how he was getting on.

I got to the entrance of Springshott just too late to intercept a dozen scrambling bikes, who were thundering along Dark Lane. They flew across the road just in front of me, and headed off toward the New Cheriton 'S' bends. Off they went, with much unnecessary gunning of engines through ineffective exhaust silencers. I watched them deliberately churning up the mud as they raced past walkers. I breathed a sigh of relief that no horses were on the track.

Dark Lane is a restricted bridleway, and marked as such, with 'no motor vehicles' signs displayed at every junction. The scramblers know this full well, and make sure their number plates are invisible. I have tried to stop them in the past, and got an earful and a worryingly close drive-past for my troubles. There used to be bigger signs, but these were mysteriously smashed down. I can't imagine who would have done this.

Some years ago, an organisation called the Trail Riders Fellowship started a campaign to open Dark Lane, and many other routes across the countryside, to scrambling bikes. It started with a curious letter sent to parish councillors. It was phrased as if some official legal document, full of threats and instructions. Luckily the parishes got together, took advice and told the TRF where to get off. In the end, the little motorised access to Dark Lane that had been permitted was stopped, and it became a restricted bridleway. Not what the TRF had hoped for. That's why when the scramblers come through, they have to keep themselves anonymous, as they chew up the lane and terrify everyone else using it.

I didn't find the Editor – it transpired later that he'd gone home in a huff, having found no pigeons at all.

I watched the disappointing England game in Dublin, which was made worse by the biblical squall line of rain that came through the farm, undoing all the good work that the dry weather had done until then.

Still, thanks to it being the first Sunday of the month, it was off to West Meon for Open Mic Night. I picked up Rufus and his keyboards on the way, and we all had a very jolly evening slaughtering an eclectic mix of tunes. It was still somewhat under-attended, but better than the last couple of months. As it gets warmer, we should have a few more coming along. I had another session on the drumbox, and only clobbered myself in the scrotum a few times.

March 2nd

Fine overhead, water running on the ground. But promises abound of better things to come in the week ahead. Yeah, right, as young people say.

I had another office morning, trying to sort out the pea seed (there's none anywhere, apparently), agreeing to take delivery of a small mountain of compound fertiliser (trying to stress to the grumpy transport manager that we need plenty of notice) and booking a doctor's appointment for myself. The children had insisted that my wheezing isn't right, and could I please do something? Well, you can't argue with that, can you? Saying to the receptionist that it wasn't urgent (a 'green' appointment) meant a wait of a month – suggesting that it might be a little more serious than that ('amber') got me one in three days. Let's see how that goes.

A quick lunchtime shower (still sweaty from my Buddy Rich impersonation last night), and then it was off to Sparsholt College for a briefing on the new payment scheme. Forty farmers sitting listening, jaws agape, eyes bewildered, as a well-respected local agronomist talked us through the nitty gritty of getting online and submitting our whole farm details to the Rural Payments Agency.

Most of us had, like me, registered, but it turned out that little more could be done. Despite the ten-week deadline for the details to be submitted, the system is still in cyber chaos, and the advice was that it's best not to touch it until its 'functionality' is perfect. If we were being paid by the 'hopefully', we'd all be rich men. "Hopefully, it will be working by the end of the week", "Hopefully, they'll have debugged the software" and so on.

Next up in the brave new world of modern farming was a guide to 'greening' and Environmental Focus Areas. These were apparently dreamed up by Euro-technocrats on their way to their plush offices in Strasbourg or Brussels. Looking out of their first-class railway carriages, they saw nothing but maize. They resolved that such things are 'bad'. So we must now grow a mix of crops. Not a problem for us, but serious trouble for a friend who has only a couple of hundred acres, and a neighbour farms it as a one-crop block. They've got to work out how they get round that one. Then there's the complicated arrangement whereby a certain amount of the farm (calculated using a complicated formula) must have 'greening' value. Hedges are good, fallow is good, legumes are good. I think, with my love of pulses, we should be OK on that one, too.

During the coffee break a fellow farmer and I both failed to get water out of the hot water flask. And we are the generation of farmers destined to get the bulk of our income using internet applications.

We moved onto the new Cross Compliance regulations, and a run through of the GAEC rules and sections. A thousand tripwires to avoid if you want to make sure you get your full payment. Lots of 'watch outs' for animal tags, animal movements, and correct procedures for muck heaps. Then there's soil erosion, wind erosion of dry soil (how we laughed!) and soil management plans. On and on and on.

Oh, for a run of bad harvests.

March 3rd

You can go off pets. I was late up, and the first thing I saw out of the bathroom window was Hazel setting off across the garden, whistling furiously. Thanks to the National Trust-approved windows (i.e. completely non-airtight), I was able to ask her what was going on. Monty had vanished. She continued down across the orchard, I got dressed in a hurry, grabbed my keys and started unlocking the yard. I was all set for a high-speed drive round, while resigning myself to the fact that missing pets round here means our poacher chums have made a sneak visit.

Just as I was about to jump into Tigger, a very relieved Jonathan shouted out of the kitchen window: Monty had been found. He had been sitting in the office, having somehow shut the door behind him. Panic over. Daft dog never thought to bark, or anything like that.

Once in the office, I found out what he'd been up to: the room stank of tomcat urine. I'd left the door open because Cain looked so comfy down by the heater last night. The local Tom had been in and given everything (including the electric piano and the printer) a good hose down. I washed down as many surfaces as I could, and then left the office windows open for the blistering cold wind to clear the pong.

To complete the set, another cat had thrown up all over the back of the sofa. Ah, the joy of pets.

We had a long session with the financial advisor from the NFU Mutual. We've fallen out of their net somewhat in recent years. Some dodgy farm years have restricted the sums available for pensions and investments, but things have picked up recently, so we called out their expert. I'm less suspicious of their advice than I was, thanks to the recently imposed lack of commission on products that they sell. It turned out that we were reasonably healthy: thanks to the fact that we have no fixed retirement date, we should be able to keep on investing into the pension pot as long as we want. The 25-year endowment we took out 23 years ago will boost the pot very nicely if we decide not to blow the whole lot. Full marks to the first advisor we had back in 1992, who insisted we took it out.

It was agreed that we should boost the monthly pension contributions a bit, and he's going to look into some projections of future pension levels. We might need to put some more in the pot after that.

I've struggled with these advisors in the past – I always feel I've just bought a dodgy used car after they've left, but the new one seemed straightforward and honest. Time alone will tell.

After a quick sharpen up of the chainsaw, Hazel and I headed down across the tennis court, to sort out the split tree on the top headland of Chalks. It was in the way of the ploughing I'd hoped to restart in the afternoon. It was a curious split: the first bit fell nicely on top of the hedge eighteen months ago, doing no harm to the fence, and not getting in the way. One day during last harvest, Noel and I were out in the barley in Chalks, checking if it was fit to combine. We were startled by sounds like gunshots coming from the tree, but thought nothing of it.

On the day of combining, I went merrily round Chalks once, and then, on the second turn, found that the rest of the tree had fallen out into the field. Spooky that it should fall at that time, and lucky that it hadn't happened as the combine was passing underneath.

With it sawn up and out of the way, I was able to continue ploughing, and had a good session finally getting the long work going, from the tennis court to the boundary with Clump. Well, it went OK until more electrical gremlins appeared in the Deere: it started disconnecting and reconnecting drive randomly. This is more serious than the odd side-light problem the other day, but worryingly seems to stem from the same area of the tractor, the pedals. A phone call to the dealer tomorrow will be in order. With fine weather promised – at last – I need a tractor that works.

Tod rang late in the evening to say that some pea seed had been found. A huge relief, not least because the sole reason I was ploughing Chalks was as an entry for peas. I then texted the Editor promising some world-class pigeon shooting once the field is sown. That'll get him going.

March 4th

The weather experts are more certain than ever that the weather is settling down. So it's time for a review of where we are and what needs doing.

First, there's the last 66 acres of winter wheat. That has to be done first – if it goes in too late, it won't be vernalised and will come up as a stem of grass rather than an ear of wheat. We could sell it for silage, but might not make a lot of money. But the ground still needs to dry a bit more.

Everything could do with a first dose of fertiliser. It's funny to think that we used to rush round the oilseed rape with 1 cwt/acre by the end of January to get it going. Latest thinking (a phrase to be wary of) is now very much against that. But, again, much of the heavy ground will still not support a full sprayer, so that will have to wait, too.

The December and January-sown winter wheat on the light ground looks healthy, but could do with a roll to get it to tiller a bit. That might come sooner rather than later. There are heaps of cultivating jobs in preparation for the spring-sown crops. I think I'll go straight into the Hangar, and ask neighbour Robert if he can give Kilmeston Road a pass with his Solo. Our Carrier or the Terradisc should be able to do Behind My Love's and Blackhouse Road. The spring beans in Godwin's will, I hope, be a 'straight in' job – I might get Tosdevine in to do that job.

It's all very well making plans, but that ground is still sodden. So I thought I'd have a nice long day ploughing in Chalks. I spent twenty minutes lowering the skims while the engine warmed up, and then fell foul of the electrical gremlins again – I'd be merrily driving along, and the drive would suddenly disconnect. It got quite unnerving, so I rang the dealer. The service manager said he'd get someone out after lunch, but that it was OK to keep going if I had to. I did, so I did.

Diana set off at lunchtime on another uni fact-finding/interview trip up north and the Deere engineer arrived just after that. The fault was traced to a dodgy switch in the clutch button on the gearstick, and as luck would have it, he had one in the van. That makes a change; normally it has to come from Brazil or Taiwan. It was all done in an hour.

A long session in the afternoon seemed to suggest that he'd nailed it, but the plough started to struggle to penetrate. The time had come to change the 'Quick Fit' Kverneland points. I managed to prise an old one off, but couldn't get the new one (non-genuine) on. Tomorrow's job might be to see if I can get hold of some genuine ones. If I can't, that might be my cue to hitch the plough off.

Things that could only happen in farming, No 34: as I restarted after lunch, I noticed what I thought was a white balloon in the furrow up ahead. Then I realised it was white feathers, and then saw what it was: one of the thousands of seagulls, diving in for worms, had been trapped for the whole of lunchtime by a lump of soil that had rolled back into the furrow. I rolled the soil off it with my plough paddle, but it looked a lost cause, moving only its head and beak. I got the heavy leather gloves from the cab, folded its wings down where they should be, and carried it onto a bit of ploughed ground that I'd stamped smooth. It pecked angrily at the gloves as I did so, ungrateful so-and-so.

I didn't give it much hope, and decided that if it was still there on the way back, I'd bop it on the head. However, in the ten seconds it took for me to get back into the cab, it was gone. I was almost completely sure it flew away on its own – if a red kite or buzzard had swooped, it would have had to be unbelievably swift and silent. No – it had to be a quick recovery, and a warm soggy feeling of satisfaction all round. Bless.

A full house for an excellent Old Gits rehearsal made for a good end to a long day.

March 5th

It really does look like the weather's settling down. I walked down to the tractor, which I'd parked next to the tennis court, and brought it home, hitched off the weights and the plough, and refuelled. I then took Tigger up to Hurst Down to see if drilling was possible; the frost was coming out, so it was fairly sticky. No drilling quite yet.

I had a bit of an office session, chasing up new plough points and hunting for a reasonably priced but not completely knackered power harrow. There's one at Oakes Bros, and our rep promised to have a good look at it and report back. I did a run up to Gaskin's for new bolts for the Terradisc, and left the Carrier bearing up there for them to mend. I think the big discs will be busy this spring. I was going to pull Rod's leg about losing the Deutz franchise, but luckily he wasn't there.

After a quick shower it was off to the doctor's for a chat about the wheezing chest. He decided we'd re-do all the tests we did last year: a chest X-ray, some heart tests and something which sounded like a Spirograph but probably wasn't. The last two would have to wait three weeks, but for the first I was able to hurtle up the dual carriageway from Medstead to the new-ish mini-hospital, and its walk-in X-ray department. I have memories of multi-hour waits in Winchester hospital – this is an utter joy in comparison. It is also slightly odd to be back to the very place where I was born, although it was called Lord Mayor Treloar Hospital back then.

After a quick cuppa once I'd got back, I drove the Deere up to reacquaint itself with the drill in Hurst Down. It was still a bit sticky, but the time has come to go whatever. I hitched on and did a trial blast across the field, and decided that it would indeed do –

tomorrow. Hazel gave me a lift home in Tigger, so I can come out tomorrow with the Massey and some seed and then I'll – hold on, let's not make too many plans.

March 6th

A day that went almost entirely to plan. We were all up early to see Jonathan off on a school trip to London, so I was out in Top of Hurst Down ready to go by nine. It would have been earlier, but it takes forever to drive all that way in the loader tractor.

I started the land work at an angle so as to give a perpendicular turn on the longest boundary edge, and worked from the Neck back. It was still a bit sticky to start with, but as the day went on, the sun shone, and a warm wind blew, and the rear press wheels on the Horsch started running clean. Even the calibration seemed to be right.

There were one or two hiccups: I thought the following harrows seemed to be uneven, so jumped off and checked them just in time: they were about to part company with the rest of the machine. Numerous cable ties were called for to make a temporary repair. I'm not stopping now.

Just after lunch, Phil the salesman arrived in the field in his BMW for a chat. I don't normally like unannounced visits, but Phil's always worth a chat. I casually mentioned my plan to go from a 3-metre drill to a 4-metre one, and how I'd have to boost the tractor hp to match. That got him going, and he was all over the Deere taking pics. I expect an email will follow pretty quickly.

Just as it was getting dark, all hell broke loose in the control box: lots of sirens and 'Comms error' on the little screen, followed by a list of all the components of the drill. A moment of great panic – such things are usually beyond being repaired by the crap farm mechanic (i.e. me) and any repair/replacement will not be cheap. I thought for a moment, and the messages suggested that all contact had been lost with the drill; a two-second check down the cable showed that a plug connector was on the point of coming apart. Huge relief.

I stopped having done 36 acres of the 66, just as I was about to meet the dell. All being well, I should finish it with another long day, although the sticky heavy brow is proving a bit of a struggle.

When I got in, I found that the forecast now said rain and wind on Monday. Where did that come from? It wasn't in the forecast only two days ago. It looks like I had better finish it tomorrow.

March 7th

Well, who would have thought it? We finally finished winter sowing. It's true that what's in the ground doesn't quite match the map that was drawn at the beginning of September, but the last of the winter corn is in.

The big question now is 'Will it grow properly?'. Sixty-six acres of Scout wheat is all very well going in beautifully, but it's the first week in March – the latest we've ever sown wheat. Tod claims he has a client who has sown Scout later in the year, but we'll all be looking for a good frost or two to vernalise it.

It all went rather well, in the end. Despite a late start and the need to refuel (that ground was very hard after all the deluges), I did a ninth turn of headland to run out the last of the seed in the darkness at about 7pm. All very satisfying.

We run the Top and the Bottom of Hurst Down as one field these days. Dad split it into two based on the marked soil difference. The Top field is flat and the best soil on the farm, being the highest. The Bottom is smaller, all sideland, with fingers of the toughest clay near the top of the field. There's a chalky patch at the eastern end, and there are traces of a couple of old Bronze Age barrows. There's hardly any sign of them now – just two slight lumps that seem to have an abundance of small stones.

One of the many joys of farming is the knowledge that you're not the first to work this ground. The farm is littered with YL42 plough shares, which seemed to come off at the drop of a hat in the last century. Horse shoes still turn up, each one telling the story of some poor soul having to plod all the way to the nearest blacksmith to get his horse re-shod. And as the tractor gently rides up and over the Bronze Age mound, a sense of great history seeps into the soundproofed, air-conditioned cab.

When set-aside was first introduced, the Bottom of Hurst Down was an obvious candidate, with its awkward shape, difficult soils and general remoteness. So it sat, unused for a season. Other eyes noticed that the field wasn't being used. For this was the early-Nineties, and the 'rave' culture was at its peak. These eyes also noticed that the Bottom of Hurst Down had good road access into it, and wasn't a million miles away from the A32 in West Meon. Plans started to be hatched.

The first we knew of anything was during harvest, when a police car arrived in the Drier Yard. "Is this your field, sir?" asked the policeman, pointing at a badly photocopied map on a flier. It was indeed BHD, marked with a big X. Next to the map was a mini-poster entitled 'Torpedo Town Free Festival', and it showed a list of obscure bands that would be performing. The blurb underneath went on: 'Site to be taken on Friday. Word of mouth only!'

The policeman explained what the position was. They had found this flier during a drugs raid in Portsmouth, and had wasted a couple of days trying to track down the site (map reading not being one of a Policeman's skills). The man raided had been one of the organisers, hence the map, when the venue should have been 'word of mouth only'. The festival was due to take place at the end of the week. We could expect heavy sound equipment, stages, and several thousand people – if not more. Ninety per cent of these people would be fine. The remaining 10% would be nothing but trouble. He advised us to take steps to halt the event.

What steps would he recommend? Ditches, he said, would stop them for ten minutes. "Could you make the ground uneven?" he asked. We could plough it, we suggested. That should be enough, said Plod.

And so it was, on an August afternoon, harvest was temporarily abandoned, and four ploughs – two from our farm, two from Murph's farm – set about breaking the world ploughing record. Mick, one of Murph's men, asked how we wanted it done. "Quickly!" I replied. We set off in convoy, starting next to the bottom road. The air of panic was joined by the faint whiff of Gramoxone – the contractors had just finished killing off the green cover for the return to cultivation.

As we stopped for a cup of tea, feeling more confident now that we'd got two-thirds of the way across, a white van stopped on the Wheely Road at the far end of the field. Someone jumped out, stomped out into the field, and stomped back to his van. He did not look pleased. We convinced ourselves he was also one of the organisers, and jeered him on his way.

It worked. We prevented the festival from taking place. The police put a huge operation into action intercepting assorted buses and cars which had 'heading to the festival' written all over them – metaphorically and literally. We clocked lots of strange vehicles driving through the farm, but one glimpse of the freshly ploughed field, and the huge ditches that a local JCB-man had come out and dug, was enough to send them on their way. We were lucky.

There are nostalgic websites listing the golden years of the Torpedo Town Free Festival. The year they failed to come to Hinton Ampner was the year the festival stopped. We really are party poopers.

March 8th
Rain was due this afternoon, so we made a Sunday morning trip out to Hurst Down. Hazel finished the rolling, and I brought the Deere and drill all the way back home, via the Neck, Blackhouse Road, Drier Field and the Folly, and finally back into the yard.

After an hour's swapping machines, I managed to get two loads of N35(S) fertiliser on the very hungry-looking winter barley in Rick/Clump and Big Field. There was nothing more than spots of drizzle as I went up and down, and, unbelievably (after five months' deluge), I found myself hoping for more rain. Typical farmer.

March 9th
We were woken for the first time this year by the dawn chorus. It's an utter joy for about a week, then you wish you had a gun handy.

The power was due to go off just after breakfast, so I did a whole bunch of writing early, and then carefully shut down the computer. We had to do a major rebuild the last time it had its power shut off when it wasn't ready.

It was then back to liquid fertiliser. Much as I struggle with some aspects of the Amazone sprayer, there's no doubt that the high-speed filling system is a boon. I can get 3,000 litres into the tank in about eight minutes. It used to be twenty with old machines – it was my main texting time. Eight minutes means there is no time to text or even indulge in anti-nostalgia about the old ways of doing things: Ken in the Drier barn with the Taskers Paterson Fertispread, hand loading hundredweight bags into the rear bucket, ready to trundle out to the field and weave his way across tramline-free fields at seven-yard intervals. And then there were ten thousand old plastic bags to be tied into bundles, ready for sale to the dodgy builders who would queue up to buy them. As I say, no time for any of that.

I managed to get the oilseed rape in White Hill and Cheyney done. Even the far end of White Hill (Rough Field) was passable without too much slipping and sliding. The pigeons seem to have rediscovered the rape – I must get some bangers out, having got the crop this far looking this good.

Lunch without power is odd. No computer, so no endless weather forecasts or World Cup cricket updates (not that we wanted them this morning). I polished off the three sudokus on the back of *The Times*, and far too much coffee cake, and, having nothing left to do, went out in the tractor again. I did the very iffy winter barley in Roe Hill, and the late-drilled wheat in BOMS. The wind picked up, with a bit of drizzle, so I thought I'd tiptoe up to Pipeline, and see if it was dry enough to drive over.

Not only was it dry, it looked very healthy. True, the weed population is also very healthy, but the wheat looks good, and, boy, are those lines straight. Things were obviously going well six months ago, before the wotsit hit the fan in the middle of October. I did the whole of Pipeline, and then did the headland of Long Field.

There's always a melancholy moment when working the site of the old Stanmore Farm. It used to sit at the southern end of Long Field, accessed by the track that runs off the Cheyney bends. It was empty when Dad came here, unoccupied since being rebuilt during or just after the war. There was a small farmhouse, a cottage garden, barns, a dew pond and a yard. Families had lived here, farmed here, and died here. You can track its expansion using vintage maps on the internet. In 1960, however, it played host to a couple of bulldozers, and was gone. Much building material was reclaimed from the house and used in Ken's barn – hence the fancy set of stairs that go up to the storage area.

What's left now? You can find the old dew pond by the strange soil that consists of huge flints and slabs of clay. The old garden soil always grows a better crop than the rest of the field. And every so often, the infill in the well drops another six inches, leaving a slight indent in the ground. Happened last year, and I hit the dip in my combine when working round the headland of Long Field. It gave me a heck of a fright. There's not much that doesn't feature on the internet, but apart from on old maps, the old Stanmore Farm is nowhere to be found.

When I got to the southern end of Pipeline, I was greeted by sixty pheasants and partridges, all gathered round the puddle that was still lying on the particularly wet spot. They must be a throwback to the late Denis Appleton's shoot, which would have been the other side of the hedge. As the wind got up, and the drizzle blew harder, I spent a couple of hours wondering how on earth we can tempt them north onto our patch. Something for the internet when I get home – assuming the power is back on.

March 10th

Tod the Agronomist came round in the morning for what was basically a 'clean sheet' farm walk. The only spraying that has been done this farming year was a bit of herbicide and fungicide on the OSR towards the end of January. All the brave plans for autumn pesticides were lost in the five-month deluge. There will be a lot to do.

Then the landlord's agent popped round. I had emailed him, asking if the NT's archaeologist would like to come out and have a check on whatever the curious feature is at the top of Blackhouse Road Field. It has been baffling us for ever: whenever the ground is ploughed, up comes a mix of bricks and burnt earth. This year, ploughing a bit deeper, the debris of whatever was there is ever more pronounced. There's no record on any of the maps of a building, and no sign of anything on the old aerial photographs that are now available online.

Dad had a theory that it was a wartime bunker – one of the network of 'last resort' guerrilla bases that dotted the English countryside. We used to pull his leg, saying that he might be overstating the strategic significance of New Pond junction. We won't half look silly if he was right all along. The man from the Trust said he'd pass the details and a picture or two to the relevant authorities.

Then it was fertiliser all afternoon. I finished the Claire in Long Field and Broom Field, and did Drier Field, where the very late frost-drilled Panorama looks good in some light, and pathetic in other.

I adjourned to the Flowerpots with neighbour Robert to moan about the dry weather.

March 11th

More dry weather; when will this terrible drought cease?

I reckoned on having just enough time to get the first dose of fertiliser on the Folly before the huge delivery of 0:26:26 arrived. I reckoned wrong. He made good time from wherever he was coming from, and I only had time to get the headland and the west side of Folly done. I popped back when he rang to say he was imminent, and swapped over to the Massey, fully prepared with back weights and torpedo bag lifters. I was only a couple of slurps into a cup of tea when he rang again, to say he was here. I must get my ears syringed, if I can't tell when a lorry is pulling up outside the yard.

We trundled down to the Drier Yard, and unloaded 47 bags, two at a time, each of them 600 kg. I got the lorry to stay on the Blackhouse Road, so we had to move once or twice for the little passing traffic going down the lane to Blackhouse Farm itself.

We got the whole lot off in an hour. It helped that the bag loops were all just right for the bag lifter. I had one scary moment: two 600 kg bags make up quite a load for that little tractor, even with weights on the back. I always drop the bags as close to ground level as I can as soon they're clear of the bed of the lorry. I did this rather enthusiastically at one point, while the tractor was still facing down the yard drive, and with a slight right-to-left lean. As the bags stopped in their downward travel rather suddenly, the rear right of the tractor came up off the ground – you can't argue with physics. Instinctively, I pushed the bags down further, and calm was restored. Luckily, no one was there to see it. It's like falling over the big vacuum cleaner pipe in the grain barn. You know no one's there to see it, but you still look round to check.

I left him to turn round his monster lorry, and popped back to complete my tea drinking. Then it was back to the Folly to finish it. Every acre with green crop growing in it has had 140 litres /ha of N35(S) – equivalent to 49 kg/ha of N, or about 40 units in old money. That should get everything going, and means I can concentrate on the spring sowing, if the weather holds for a few more days.

It would be odd to be a proper farmer, whose nitrogen application plans are honed to perfection, with dates, growth stages, ley lines, and the latest astrological projections all taken into account. Here, I do WICWIC farming: what I can when I can.

Back home for lunch, and there was a lost-looking man wandering around. It was the driver delivering the new post banger we've decided to invest in. There's a lot of fencing needs to be done, and the days of merrily wielding a sledgehammer are gone. We knew the lorry was coming, but a phone call would have been nice. And there's a phrase we farmers seem to use a dozen times a year.

I got him unloaded, and then spent a very jolly afternoon playing with the new toy. I had to change the hydraulic connections, but in an astonishing and thoroughly unexpected turn of events, had the right parts on the workshop bench. And that's a phrase I only use once in two decades.

March 12th

A frustrating day. It was dry, again, but blowing a fairly stiff wind in the morning. I had a plan to nip out and put a healthy dose of Roundup on Bungalow as part of our master plan to reclaim it, but it was too windy for that. So it was office time.

I rang Hampshire Grain to discuss my long overdue commitment forms, on which we foretell what stuff we'll be sending up there during the long months of harvest. As usual, I haven't got any real clue what's going to come off what field, but I fill it in as best I can, putting the quality stuff in the 'long' pool, and the feed wheat and barley in the 'off the combine' pool. I only hope I get near enough to the final result to not incur fines or penalties. The big debate is how the late-sown wheats will perform. Two seasons ago, they did spectacularly, but there's no guarantee that they'll do it again. I filled the forms in deliberately pessimistically – better that than the other way round.

While chatting to Michael the store manager, I asked for a guide to what our next cheque would be – the second instalment of income from the long pool of last year's harvest. He ran through the figures, which had all improved a bit on December's first instalment. We should get around £40k in the next couple of days, which will help the overdraft no end.

During all this faffing about in the office, I was popping in and out to sort out spray deliveries. The only downside of the new-ish buying system, which puts out all the orders to tender to numerous companies, is that numerous companies pick up little individual contracts, and three or four vans end up driving into the yard in the days after a crop inspection and chemical order. One vehicle drove in which set the dogs off in 'welcome' mode – it turned out to be the NFU pensions man, back for an appointment that I'd completely forgotten about. With Hazel being away, it seemed daft to hold the meeting. He was quite relaxed about it, and said his secretary would reschedule.

There were more phone calls. The company that supplied the spring bean seed replied to my grumpy email about the ludicrous seed bags they had used, with an awkward tiny loop at each corner. You can only lift one at a time, and it takes two minutes, and several trips out of the cab, to even get one on the front of the loader. "Ah," said seed man. "We had to buy them in from France, you see. That's how they do them over there." I was unconvinced. In fact, my bullshit alert buzzer went into meltdown.

Having got the new post banger all plumbed in, and feeling that getting out of the office was in order, I tried putting some new posts in just across the road in the Top of Englands. It was an astonishing success. The stone-filled clay soil on the top of the ridge is a nightmare for fencing, but the new posts were fully in after only three or four mighty thwacks from the massive weight. I was interrupted by yet more phone calls. The second load of P/K fertiliser will be coming mid-morning tomorrow; I talked the driver through directions, but I'm not sure how many got through. Then his boss rang from the office to say that the last batch of solid fertiliser (a compound mix for the pastures) would be hot on the heels of the first lorry. We'll see. I have a tenner on a late-afternoon delivery, with me having waited four hours.

I then realised that the wind had dropped. But was it enough to go spraying? I'm a terrible one for not going if the wind is too strong. A rustling leaf is enough to put me off if I'm not in the mood. Tod had put me in a bit of a panic about getting the poppy-killing mix on the OSR at soon as possible, and all the chemical was in, and the sprayer was full – but I still didn't reckon conditions were right. I may live to regret it if we lose four days and the OSR gets damaged by the late spray.

For a relaxing end of the day, I headed out to BOMS to give the December-drilled Panorama a roll, to try and get it to tiller a bit. It wasn't a great success; the ground is almost too hard, and I think I might be a bit early, but I did half, and it looked better. It also brings on memories of my very first tractor job ever. Dad decided to show me the basics of tractor driving, and so we headed out to BOMS to roll the wheat. I was probably fourteen or fifteen, and the tractor was – I think – an old Ford 4600. The rollers were the ghastly gang-rollers, that took hours and a couple of back injuries to get into V-formation, and the same again to pack up and bring home. We spent a less-than-successful couple of hours, Dad wedged up uncomfortably on the tiny toolbox on the left of the driver's seat (he was 6' 5"), getting crosser and crosser as I merrily chatted away and lost my way time after time.

Even with today's 24 m tramlines, and eight-and-a-bit metre rollers, I still managed to lose the line once or twice. I blamed it all on the crop not being quite ready, and the ground not being soft enough. It was nothing at all to do with me being still, after forty years, a crap tractor driver.

In the evening, I picked up neighbour Robert and we headed off to the Swan Hotel in Alresford (famous, allegedly, for hosting Jimi Hendrix on his way to the Isle of Wight festival – at least, that's what my big brother used to claim), for the official briefing from our local vet about the end of their services for farm animals. A couple of hundred concerned farming types crammed into the vaults under the hotel, and heard a slightly melancholy sign off from our vet, ending decades of efficient cosy service from a vet not more than a couple of miles away. You couldn't blame them for coming to the decision to end farm animal work. They are trying to be a general practice, and getting the staff is almost impossible. There seems to be a lot of politics and shenanigans about TB testing, but my old mate Graeme put it nicely: "I want to walk without a stick when I'm old!"

It was then time for what turned out to be a two-hour advert from the vet hoping to take over. It was all a bit evangelical, almost like a timeshare sale of the 1980s. My hackles went up as soon as we were addressed as "you guys". Only two questions seemed to matter to us in the audience. How long will you take to get to our farm, and how much will it cost? The latter brought reassurance that, for a while at least, they would be the same as our old vet. The former proved more controversial. They're based in Salisbury, "only an hour" away. When the head man said that an hour doesn't normally make a difference in a veterinary emergency, there was a sharp intake of breath in the room, and one or two heads were seen to shake.

Hazel and I chatted it over later, and thought we'd give them a crack of the whip when lambing starts soon. But, as they say, other vets are available.

March 13th

Let's get one thing straight. Today was supposed to be wet – very wet. A front was supposed to stall over Hampshire for the whole day. There I was dreading the idea of unloading yet more fertiliser bags in a deluge, with slippery ground and sliding tractors.

In fact, it was a beautiful day. Not exactly sunny, but calm and dry. Perfect for all that spraying I was getting into a stew about yesterday. But first there was the second batch of 0:26:26 which arrived an hour early, at 9.30. I got him unloaded, and hearing nothing more about the part load of grassland 20:10:10 that was due sometime today, set off to put the poppy killer on the OSR. Ten minutes into the tank, the phone rang. The second lorry had arrived – he was outside the barn. We had a sharpish exchange of views about him giving me notice of his arrival – he denied all knowledge of it, of course, so I said he'd just have to wait.

I emptied enough of the tank on White Hill to mean only one more fill up was needed, and popped home. It took only half an hour to get him done, and the right-hand lean-to down at the Drier Yard certainly looked full by the end of it.

After lunch, it was back out to finish the OSR in White Hill and Cheyney. The crop is looking better by the day – I must remember to keep on at the pigeons at this crucial stage. After a quick rinse out in the field it was time for Stage 1 of 'Reclaim Bungalow'.

The good people of Kilmeston who live around Bungalow have decided that it's their field. It's true that we have not done anything with it in decades, but we can't quite see the logic that says it's no longer ours. Hazel had a very unpleasant exchange with one of these residents at the newsagents a few days ago; his message was, "It belongs to the National Trust, you're not doing anything with it, so we're going to do what we want, and you can't do anything about it!"

Well, we decided that we could in fact do something with it. So it's going into spring beans. Stage one is a damn good dose of Roundup – it had 4 litres/ha, and I even used my satnav to get (I hope) nice parallel lines across the field. If there are any green strips unsprayed in a couple of weeks, I think Hazel and I will be drawing short straws to see who goes up there with the knapsack sprayer. Stage two will need lots of fencing posts and some barbed wire. Let battle commence.

The postie brought news of the second Hampshire Grain long pool payment. I was pessimistic by ten grand, which made for very positive news on what was a good day all round. Not bad for Friday the 13th.

March 14th

There's nothing like the anticipation of the first night of a new tour with the band. We've been reduced to a five-piece, so the winter has been spent testing out what we can and can't do. At one stage, we thought we'd have no gigs at all, but a few have come in.

There were also two big rugby matches to enjoy, so I spent the morning doing a bit of tractor/implement shuffling, just to clear my conscience for an afternoon and evening off. I took the sprayer off, and put the plough and weights on. I was more careful than usual with lynch pins and crush points; no point turning up at the gig with damaged fingers. Mind you, with my standard of playing, I doubt anyone would notice the difference.

The rugby was magnificent – I rang Tod to say he'd have to set up in the pub without me. I wasn't going to miss a moment of the Calcutta Cup match. Luckily, he didn't seem concerned.

I bolted my tea, had a quick shower, put on my band shirt (i.e. moody black), and was just about to get into the car for the long-ish haul up the A3 when my phone rang. It was Ian the drummer. "Don't bother coming," he said. "The pub's all shut up, in total darkness." It was a complete mystery. Tod had rung them to confirm earlier in the week. Through the windows could be seen a chalkboard with 'Live Music Tonight' on it. What had happened? We'll find out one day.

The only blessing was that I hadn't set off, and was able to turn on my heel, grab a bottle of beer and head for the sofa. It didn't make me any less cross, though. Ah well, there'll be another gig.

March 15th

A quiet-ish Sunday. It seemed wrong to waste yet another dry morning when the plough is all set up to go, so I went out to Behind My Love's, and finally polished off the north and west headlands. Both of them are a flipping pain – the north one is a series of square saw teeth, and the west one still has a massive oak tree down on it, left over from the St Jude's Day storm last year. It took ages of course, but there was the tiny ploughman's consolation of the chalk polishing up the mouldboards to a mirror finish.

It was then a long haul back to Chalks, via Big, Rick, BOMS and Roe Hill. I spent another couple of hours out there, and then settled down for the third rugby match of the weekend. Inevitably it was dismal – rain pouring down in Rome, and the ball as slippery as hell. Not much of a spectacle. We're getting spoilt if we expect all three games on a weekend to be as good as the two yesterday.

Robert Raimes called in to see if we wanted any help with spring work. He and his huge machines have caught up, of course, so are looking for things to do. I suggested going over my ploughing in Blackhouse Road with the Kockerling spring tine, so he popped out for an evening inspection, a cup of tea and a mighty fine whinge about farming in general. I bet that our ancient farmhouse kitchen has had a few moaning farmers in it over the centuries. He said that Blackhouse Road should go well if the forecast is right (just the odd shower), and Paul would be in tomorrow. He should knock off all 75 acres in one day. I could see the ghosts of those old farmers shaking their heads in astonishment.

March 16th

Well, the forecast was right for a bit. It was cold and dull, with light drizzle in the air. I polished off the land work of Chalks, and Paul turned up with the monster cultivator and started biffing Blackhouse Road into submission. The drizzle got heavier and heavier, and turned to moderate rain. I drove down to check with Paul, but luckily the soil was dry enough to start with so he could keep going.

Hazel and I went puppy hunting in Hurstbourne Tarrant. Since we had our Malinois put down in the autumn – too much inbreeding meant she was basically going mad, chewing the house and furniture, and completely unable to be without human company – we've only had the two ever-so-friendly flatcoats for company, and, more importantly, for security. Nothing persuades the members of the caravan-dwelling fraternity to get the hell back into their Transits and get off my farm quicker than an angry Malinois. Flatcoats don't really achieve the same effect.

We found a dog trainer, not a million miles from where we used to buy our Malinois, who has crossed one with a German Shepherd dog. Bearing in mind how keen we are to find a broader genetic base, a cross-breed sounded perfect. So we drove up to Andover, through thousands of acres of identikit matchbox houses (a lot of them on the site of the old Malinois breeder's farm – no wonder she gave up dog breeding) and found the kennels tucked away in a valley just off the main road.

We didn't see the pup for twenty minutes; we were given a right grilling first. What sort of dogs we had now, what did we do with them, how much training did they have, what sort of training – the breeders were very serious about what sort of home their pup went to. Then we went out into a pen to meet the little blighter.

My Golden Rule of puppy choosing is simple. Meet the whole litter, and take the one that rushed up to greet you. The problem here was that the pup was the last to go – it was only a litter of two anyway. And it was very distracted at first. It was upset because its sister had just gone, and the pen was surrounded with a comedy menagerie of chickens, pigs, doves and allsorts. And down the hill was the boarding kennel, compete with howling homesick hounds.

But after five minutes, it noticed me and Hazel, and would indeed run over when summoned. It took a distinct shine to me, trying to snuggle up into my coat. Aaah. We were introduced to the mother (Malinois) and father (GSD), who were like beasts from Greek mythology – huge, powerful and full of presence. That pup will be a big dog. The questioning and probing went on from the breeders, but they relaxed as the intro session went on.

No one made any decisions or promises, though. We talked it through on the way home. I was uneasy breaking my Golden Rule, but impressed at how it had eventually behaved. We ought to wait until the breeders decide if we're suitable first. We might not be the right stuff.

March 17ᵗʰ
A quick run round on pigeon patrol revealed no pigeons, Paul just finishing the last turns of headland of Blackhouse Road, and a tank full of liquid fertiliser. This must have been delivered by a driver who knew where to go, had the keys to the tank, and had a very quiet lorry. Good news – although it adds to the list of things that must be done ASAP.

Monday's rain is still in evidence, so there was no point going sowing yet. So I nipped out to Chalks and finished ploughing the two short headlands, and started the long southern one. I couldn't do it all – a session with the lopper is badly needed. That field is due to have peas, and there's a week or two until it warms up enough for them (assuming I've got all those other jobs done), so I'll pop back and finish that later.

I went out and looked at Behind My Love's. That one could have been sown, but, thanks to my dreadful efforts trying to get the new plough up and running, needs to be levelled somehow. Choice A is the Varidisc, but that still needs some maintenance. So I went and fetched choice B, the good old Terradisc, from the bushes. Low maintenance, high speed, huge ground disturbance if set deep enough – just right for leaving a somewhat leveller seedbed. In the hour before dusk I managed to get half of it done.

I had several false starts doing the next *Farmers Weekly* column in the evening. Four or five times I got halfway into a piece about fencing off the fields, but each time it came out a bit too rude about the landlord. That may not be wise at the moment; they've backed down on the public access issue big time, and even as I typed away, they were at a Parish Council meeting in Kilmeston, having promised to back me up if and when the hoary topic of rights of way was raised.

So I changed subject completely, and had a light-hearted moan about the ludicrous square bags that the beans were delivered in. Curiously, all 580 words came flowing straight out. Usually a good sign, but we'll see what Tim has to say when he has read it.

We agreed to buy the puppy.

March 18th

Today saw that most rare and wonderful of things – a repair job that goes to plan. Proper farms have meticulous workshops with shadow boards for tools, and probably a full-time mechanic to look after things. When I embark on a bit of farm DIY, it usually ends in tears, and more damage than there was in the first place.

Last summer, I overhauled the following harrow on the Horsch. Each tine is attached to a square bar with u-bolts, so no problem there. The bar itself is mounted to the drill by way of a thick vertical metal plate, up into which the bar fits, in a square slot. It is held there by another smaller plate going under the bar, which is bolted into place. Simple. In the overhaul, I failed to lock the bolts in properly, and realised, during a pee break last weekend, that the whole lot was about to drop off. Thanks to lots of cable ties and baler twine, I managed to finish last week's drilling in one piece.

I thought that before I set off on the spring drilling marathon, it would be wise to sort out the fixings. I had lost two bolts off one fitting, and the bottom metal plate. I would have to take one of the old ones out of the other side (actually an Allen bolt), get two new bolts of the same size, make another bottom plate, and refit the lot. First I found the right Allen key. Then I found a piece of bar to cut to size. The bandsaw worked properly. Then, astonishingly, I found a sharp drill bit. The pillar drill worked, too, and made two perfect holes. Then it was up to Gaskins for the M12 x 50 bolts; they had them in stock. Everything was ready. The only thing I couldn't find was the thread-locking compound, but I was damned if I was going to go all the way back to Rod's for that.

Everything fitted back on. I couldn't believe it. Fired up with enthusiasm, I decided to have a go at putting the spring wheat into Joan's Acre/Dell Close. Hazel helped to load up the drill with a tonne, then went off to finish the cultivation Behind My Love's. I calibrated the drill, then set off on the long haul to Dell Close.

It went beautifully. It was smooth and clean, and I bashed off Dell Close and half of the headland of Joan's Acre before the seed ran out just a fraction before the calibration suggested it should have done.

I can't remember exactly when we grew spring wheat. I think it may have been way back in the 1980s, when we patched up a square in White Hill that had been eaten by slugs. It may have been one of the first years after the ban on stubble burning, when the slugs were taking off. Not literally. The re-sowing wasn't a great success. Neighbour Robert always says spring wheat is a 'should have' crop: you end up saying either 'should have grown more', or 'should have grown something else'. The little 28-acre block I started today will be an interesting experiment. It might be the premium milling crop that the National Trust want us to grow so that they can use it at the Trust mill in Winchester.

As much as I struggle with the idea of working with them, this might suit quite well. We'll have to go back to drying it and cleaning it, and storing it, and haggling a price – come to think of it, let's put the whole lot on a lorry for Hampshire Grain.

I took the chance to check on last weekend's Scout up in Top of Hurst Down; it has an inch of root, and a quarter inch of shoot on it already. If we get the frosts that they promise in the next few days, we'll be able to relax a bit.

The sunset was staggeringly lovely, the following harrow stayed on, and the forecast still looks good. Hell of a day.

March 19th

Over early coffee, I mulled the sowing progress. I was halfway through the little patch of spring wheat, half the vast area of spring barley had been worked, but no barley had been sown. Tosdevine was booked to do the spring beans, but he wouldn't be here for a couple of days yet. The weather looked good, but we should know better than to trust the forecast. Neighbour Robert (Jnr) did mention that he was available to do some sowing if needed, so I texted him to see if he'd do the 75 acres in Blackhouse Road his team had worked down over the last couple of days. "We'll be there later this morning!" was the reply.

He would need seed, and lots of it. That huge Vaderstadt drill goes through seed like fresh air. So my first job was to get a trailer full of Propino down to the Drier Yard, ready for him to get going. The old bale trailer we use for seed cart is a single axle, six-tonne Warwick, and because it's now a bit old and rusty, I draw the line at five tons. I dropped that off down in the yard, thinking that that would see him through today.

I then got back to sowing JA/DC. The problem with doing small areas of a crop is calibration. The first tonne had run out almost right, but there was only one tonne of seed left. If the area came out as I'd planned, all would be well. If I'd been overly cautious with the seed rate, there would be a lot of unused seed in the bottom of the drill, which would have to be emptied out somewhere. But if I ran out early, I'd have to go and get a bag off neighbour Joe – and it would have to be the whole 500 kg bag (it's not the done thing to lift 100 kg out and return the bag), which I wouldn't use up, so it would sit in the corner of the barn gathering rats. The secret, of course, is to run out just at the end of the field. There's the skill.

I managed about half of the remaining field before lunch, and stopped on the way home to check how Paul and neighbour Robert Jnr were getting on with setting up. It seemed a bit fraught, so I headed on home. Robert had been hammering on the door at home, demanding more seed – the five tonnes wouldn't be enough, apparently, so Hazel let him into the barn, and he trundled down to the Drier Yard with another two tonnes on the front of the Merlo.

I carried on in JA/DC close after lunch. I dropped the seed rate as the afternoon went on; I really didn't fancy going on a hunt for more seed. I then realised that the top headland was almost upon me (I'd done the headland first in this field), and there was plenty of seed in the drill. So I pushed the seed rate right back up again. The field measured 12.5 ha when I'd finished – I'd calibrated for 13, so there was indeed a bit of seed in the drill. It was a satisfyingly small amount, though, so I nipped into Dell Close and double drilled the heavy clay headland at the top. Not sure if it's a good thing to do, but it emptied the drill and should give plenty of pigeon shooting for a very down-in-the-dumps Editor when he comes out.

It was late afternoon by now, so I brought the drill home, and had an early finish. Paul seemed to be going great guns in Blackhouse Road, so I didn't interrupt him.

It was quiz time – again – in the evening. This time it was a trip down to the Bat and Ball near Hambledon, for the Tony Hill Memorial Quiz. It was my first visit to the Bat and Ball since my cricketing days with the White Hunters. I remember keeping wicket on the famous pitch opposite the pub, and thinking, as another ball flew past my ear, rearing up from a length, that it was one of the worst squares I kept wicket on. You'd have thought that as it was the oldest in the world, that they would have had time to get it sorted.

Tony Hill was an immensely popular local farmer who died of a heart attack when in his thirties. The locals have been holding a quiz in his memory for the best part of forty years, and it was a great honour to be asked to be question master. I was even asked to set a round of questions myself.

It was the usual gentle and good-natured event. Four teams, a dozen or so spectators, five rounds of questions, a couple of beers, and sandwiches and chips afterwards. My round was supposed to be on agriculture, but, as I explained to the teams, my knowledge of agriculture is minimal, so I did a lyric round: I read out six lyrics, and the artist or song had a link to arable farming. It went down better than I had hoped. There were groans when I pointed out that Lionel Ritchie's hit 'Hello' had been released in the Far East as 'Harrow'.

At the end, there were kind thank yous, more beers, some leftover chips, and lots of generous compliments interspersed with piss-taking about the *Farmers Weekly* column. And just to finish off a lovely evening, the road home over Old Winchester Hill was dry and empty, and felt a little wider and smoother than normal.

And then, to round off the day, a text arrived from the NFU. The Rural Payment Agency has abandoned the online application system for the farm payments. It's hard to know what to think. It's a huge relief that the idea has been dropped – for now anyway. I had tried a few times to get my head round it, and been defeated by the sheer complexity of it. There's even more relief that I'm not one of the many farmers who have put many, many hours of work into doing it, and then found all their data wiped when they logged back on. And many farmers have paid someone else to do many, many hours of work – and all for nothing.

Then there's the anger of the cost of the whole thing, the fact that we all knew in our hearts that it would be a disaster. And then there's the 'civil servant apology game', where the first to spot the senior civil servant saying 'moving forward, lessons will be learnt, and we will do everything in our power to make sure it never happens again' wins a prize.

There will now be a paper-based system. There seems to be confusion over whether the paper will be prepopulated or blank. I suspect the latter, to ensure we can make more mistakes, and therefore lose our money.

March 20th

I'll never learn. All that beer (in truth, only a couple of pints), and all those chips – the inevitable consequence was a morning spent mostly indoors. It didn't help that Diana and Jonathan are both unwell at the moment, and Jonathan had been coughing heartily from 5am. We rang him off school and settled down to enjoy the world's least impressive eclipse.

If you start with a clear blue sky and a blazing sun, an eclipse is probably very spectacular. Today, however, the day went from cold, grey and dull to a bit colder, a bit greyer and a bit duller. It was so unimpressive I decided to go and put some rope bangers in the OSR. No pigeons to be seen, and the poppies seem to be keeling over nicely.

By lunchtime, I was feeling more human, so took the drill off the Deere, and hitched onto the Terradisc. I then spent an entertaining couple of hours in Kilmeston Road, trying to level out the ridges and furrows from the vintage ploughing match. The 'boiling' action did a remarkably good job. Just as I was finishing, neighbour Robert Jnr rang to say that Paul was available to come in tomorrow and do the whole lot again with the Carrier. I jumped at the chance, and asked him to do the Hangar at the same time. Let's get on.

Then the whole farm stops. The new puppy arrived. There's always something fascinating about a new puppy – taking it away from everything it ever knows, and dumping it in a completely strange environment. Manor Farm is the most animal-friendly place on the planet – we know that by how many stray and loose animals end up here – so it never takes long for a new pet to settle. It doesn't stop you from being worried about it for a few hours. It met the two flatcoats, got told off by one of them, met the cats, got told off by all of them, crashed round the house, chewed a couple of carpets, and by the time the breeders emailed to ask for a progress report, was sound asleep at Hazel's feet in the hall. Aaah.

March 21st

A big rugby Saturday. But it showed just how much the past five months of rain has got to me that I watched the first half of Wales and Italy, and decided I would be better off in the tractor, rolling the spring barley in Blackhouse Road. I tuned into Radio 5 Live, or whatever it's called this week, where they are usually covering some dull football match. They were indeed doing a very dull football match. The referee, being a f***ing w***er, had sent some diving, cheating spitting yob off in the second minute, No surprise there. The only problem was that the referee, being a f***ing w***er, had sent off the wrong diving, cheating spitting yob. And apparently that had killed the game, and it was never offside, whine whine, moan, moan.

Thankfully, they took a break from football every time something happened at one of the rugby matches. And because the rugby matches all featured an unparalleled torrent of tries, we hardly had time to hear what a f***ing w***er the referee was, because Joe McMoan would get as far as the 'f' of 'f***ing' and they'd cut back to

Rome or Murrayfield.

I finished the rolling just in time to grab a cuppa and a sandwich, and then head down to Rufus' to watch the England game. Which, as everyone knows, was one of the most extraordinary games anyone has ever seen. England won, but didn't get the points needed to win the championship. But it was just uncanny to see so much running and scoring, and the whole Six Nations Championship coming down to the last few minutes of the last game. Spooky.

There was time for a quick shower, then it was off to the pub for Diana's 19th birthday meal. Anthony was just back from Leeds, and we had a pleasant bar supper, with a couple of beers. I did, anyway – the children all had water. What is wrong with young people these days?

March 22nd

Despite the pub meal last night, I was ready to go reasonably early – for a Sunday morning. So I loaded up the bale trailer with 5T of Propino, ready to rush out to Kilmeston Road and the Hangar, which Paul had done with the Carrier yesterday. What should have been a reasonably straightforward job moving bags was made much worse by the fact that the rat population have decided that Propino is flavour of the month. Many bags had holes in them, so quite a lot of black tape was needed. I lifted one bag too close to the rough concrete pillar, and split it open – Lord knows how I'll patch that one up. I dropped it swiftly near the wall, to be sorted out later. I obviously wasn't quite as ready to go as I thought. I can still blame the rats, though.

I took the Deere off the rollers, filled up with fuel, and hitched onto the drill. The plan to give it a thorough greasing was foiled by the fancy grease gun refiller giving up. It's one of the expensive gadgets that fits on the top of a keg of grease, and cleanly refills the grease gun via a few strokes of the pump handle. In theory, no grease is ever spilt or wasted. There's a rubber seal on a plate that goes inside the tub – this had disintegrated. A shame – it's not very old, and it wasn't cheap. Attempts to repair it left me covered in grease, and fairly cross. I was damned if I was going shopping for grease cartridges on a Sunday morning, so I abandoned the idea.

Attempts to calibrate the drill for spring barley were also foiled, this time by Policeman Paul, who called in for a catch up and a bit of gossip. Sasha the pup was a huge hit, and by the time he puts the word out about her, we'll have to stock up with doughnuts for the Policewomen.

Finally, by about three o'clock, I was out in Kilmeston Road. Paul's work with the Carrier was excellent – it had done just the job, and I had a long and very satisfying afternoon and evening doing long turns in the fabulous cold light.

March 23rd

Hazel was up and away early – the lambing season is imminent, so it's that time of year when she's up at sparrow's fart to check the very pregnant girls in the back meadow. The dogs didn't reckon much of being left alone, especially the puppy, who left a huge dump in the kitchen doorway as a protest.

I had plans to crack on early in Kilmeston Road, but, as usual, they were undone by office-related stuff. I had to get hold of Mitsubishi; they were delivering a test car today, and I needed to know what time it would be coming, and if the delivery driver needed a lift to public transport. Out here in Hinton Ampner, buses and trains are a bit of a remote joke, and taxis never can find us. So I'm always on standby to give the driver a lift to Petersfield or Winchester.

By nine thirty, I finally had my answer: he'd be here just after lunch, and he would indeed need a lift.

Just after ten, I was back in Kilmeston Road, trundling up and down, trying to keep the line straight in our most visible field. Not that the good people of Kilmeston would know a straight tramline if it sneaked up and bit them.

The Shogun arrived right on time, just after lunch, and Anthony volunteered to take him into Winchester. I was able to head back out, and have a very satisfactory afternoon in the increasing dust, finishing the headland just as it was getting dark. A bit of rain, and a roll, and that'll be perfect – especially if the lines come up straight.

There was a band rehearsal, and Ian brought along a new guitarist who was inexplicably keen to join a fifth-rate covers band. Since Tod's two boys left us, we've been short of depth, and crying out for another rhythm/lead. Will joined us for the evening, and it went every well. He seemed to enjoy it and fit in, and let's hope he decides to stay.

What should have been a very good day was spoilt by the shadow cast by my landlord, in the form of Dame Helen Ghosh. She was on Radio 4 this morning, telling all and sundry of the Trust's plans for the next ten years. It was, as befits an organisation that has become a cheerleader for the Green Blob and is led by the ultimate Labour apparatchik, a tidal wave of envirobollocks. So much so, that even the BBC gave her a reasonably hard time. The future for us doesn't look good: the phrase 'traditional commercial mixed farming' didn't feature a lot in her list of ambitions and goals. We're going to be fighting harder than ever to keep on doing what we want to do. Thank goodness for our AHA tenancy agreement – wherever it is.

March 24th

A good-ish forecast: sunshine and heavy showers later in the day. Last night's useful rain wasn't enough to stop any plans, so things were perfect for getting the Hangar – 21 acres and light chalky soil – done. The trouble is that the Hangar is the most awkward shape possible. No matter which way you sow it, there's a vast amount of short work to do.

By lunchtime, I was only halfway through. And I didn't finish until five, in a heavy storm. I'd been interrupted by the bank manager, then having to stop to avoid running over someone's terrier which decided to come and attack the Horsch, and then having to top up fuel with the Jerry can. We got all the assorted tractors and trailers back to base by six, in a very useful downpour. There's always great satisfaction in getting those two fields done. If I can get back there in the next couple of days and roll them both, I'll be even happier.

In his phone call, the bank manager had seemed happy; he suggested continuing with our generous overdraft for another three months. We've got some fabulous accounts to send to him, now that the only two figures that seem to matter to him – the profit and the current account – are both so healthy. He seemed utterly unworried about our little problem with the taxman, seeming quite relaxed at the idea of renegotiating our huge 'consolidation loan' that we took out five years ago to include the surprise tax bill.

Curious days; not many years ago we were 'on remand', with a clueless 'emergency manager' wanting to know how much I budgeted every week for beer. Mind your own effing business, is what I nearly said. But didn't.

March 25th

Just what we needed: a reasonable rain last night, followed by a surprisingly hard frost. Good for all the crops, but especially for the late sown winter wheat. I was texting one word to Tod at 6.15: 'Vernalised!'

It was too frozen to head out to Behind My Love's to finish this year's mega acreage of spring barley, so I had another go at mending the grease gun filler. Clad in a pair of bright pink shoulder-length plastic gloves (mmmm, nice), and clutching a can of de-greaser, I prised the follower plate out of the bucket, and started cleaning it off. Just for a change, I managed to remove 95% of the grease without it getting everywhere. For the last 5%, I headed indoors, commandeered the kitchen sink and set about my task with hot water and Fairy Liquid. There's an advert lurking there somewhere – 'Removes kitchen grease – and farm grease!' says Farmer Flindt. Finally, I had the two components (zinc disc and large washer) squeaky clean. I left them on the drainer to dry while I had a think about how to reconnect the two.

The next job, if I was to finish the spring barley, was to rescue the split seed bag. I tipped it over so that the split was uppermost, lined the inside with a 50 kg seed bag and did some sewing with a long length of baler twine. Granny Flindt would have been proud of me. And it worked: the last of 28 bags went smoothly into the Horsch. Mind you, it was probably slightly less than fourteen tonnes in total, judging by the heap that was left on the barn floor after all the rats and splits.

After an early lunch, it was off to Behind My Love's – 15 acres of multi-cornered awkwardness. Half of me had wanted desperately to go up to Twickenham to support the Churcher's 1st XV in the Natwest Schools Plate, but the weather forecast suggested that my time would be more profitably spent in the tractor.

It went perfectly. Not only did the seed run out in the very last ten yards, but I was also able to get out there with the rollers and get it all smoothed off. And Churcher's College won.

Our enormous acreage of spring barley is complete. Blackhouse Road was ploughed, heavy tined, Vaderstadt sown, then rolled. Kilmeston Road was part ploughed (using ancient ploughs), Carriered and then drilled with my Horsch. The Hangar was only

Carriered, then Horsch drilled. Behind My Love's was ploughed, then Terradisced, Horsch drilled and finally rolled. Now, that's a good mix of trial seedbeds.

In an ideal world, I'd have got the lot rolled. I'm never quite sure that it's essential, but you can't help thinking that the seed is better firmed in a bit. In a slug-filled autumn, seedbed rolling can save a crop. Unrolled triangles in Cheyney back in the Eighties vanished dramatically, converting even Dad to the idea. I also work on the theory that good barley will lodge nicely, so the combine needs to be low, so those pesky flints need bashing into the ground. Somehow they keep on coming up to the surface. The old boys were convinced that they grew, and you can see why: they would pick the biggest out of the fields and throw them in the hedge, and within a couple of years another set would appear. Stubble burning and power harrows kept them down a bit, but these days there's nothing to bring them down to size. And if one tumbles gently into the combine header, you'd better hope it stops there.

Hazel was hosting Book Club, where the ladies sit around and discuss God knows what – no one believes it's the book – so I picked up Rufus in the Shogun, and we adjourned to the Thomas Lord to agree furiously for a couple of hours.

March 26th

The atmosphere in the Westley Suite at Sparsholt College was not very nice. Several hundred farmers had gathered – again – to hear a senior member of the Rural Payment Agency explain to them what the bloody hell was going on with the new subsidy system. All we knew was that last week, the highly sophisticated and expensive online scheme had been abandoned by the RPA. It would be back to paper forms for this year, at least.

Full marks to the man from the RPA. He didn't actually apologise, but he talked us calmly through the new paper form that would be coming our way soon. They would be 'pre-populated' – in other words, all the fields' details would be on them – but there would be more detail needed from us. The big change from the last years of old system is the introduction of crop codes. The dear old OT1 code, which covered almost everything we grew, is gone, so patching up a corner of winter wheat with spring barley will need new measurement and maps.

His message was 'be patient, call for help, we're here to help, all will be fine' seemed to get through. I spent the last half hour regretting all the cashews and pints of Tipster in the Thomas Lord last night, and was mighty relieved – in more than one way – when it was over.

Last night's big rain had cleared, but the ground was still too wet to catch up on rolling, so I had a long agronomy session with Tod, and then nipped up to Rod's in the Shogun to get some pop rivets for the grease gun filler repair job. He had what I needed, my cunning plan worked, and I filled up as many grease guns as I could lay my lands on just in case it fell to bits again.

My drive back from Rod's happened to coincide with the school bus dropping off at the West Meon Hut – in theory. There had been a huge accident on the M27, and traffic had headed inland. The A272 was at a crawl, and queues stretched for miles east and west. I sat in the petrol station car park for forty minutes, and watched the world go by – slowly.

I watched the world's dodgiest chainsaw sale take place, right next to me. A large man stood outside his van, watching and waiting nervously. A second man arrived, the van slid open to reveal an Aladdin's Cave of farm tools, all not quite in the original boxes. There was a hurried exchange of words, a wad changed hands, and a chainsaw was handed over.

Then a huge lorry pulled in to the lay-by just next to the crossroads. The driver jumped out, and immediately started exchanging loud words with two lads in a beaten-up old BMW. The body language was aggressive, the language was fruity, but for the life of me I couldn't work out who had done what to whom. They all piled into the shop. Lorry driver came out again, clutching multiple packs of fags, and drove off. Two minutes later, a fraught member of staff came hurrying out, as if in pursuit. The BMW driver pointed him towards the lay-by, but the lorry was well gone. Another mystery; what had he done?

Next excitement was some yob in a BMW X5, who needed to get to the petrol station, but was stuck in the long queue approaching from the west. He decided to overtake the queue (normal rules tend not to apply to BMW owners), and blasted down the wrong side of the road. A head-on crash was just avoided; traffic going the other way had to slam brakes on to avoid the idiot. Horns were sounded, fists were waved, and the traffic stuck on the centre of the crossroads was still there when the light changed, adding to the general chaos.

It dawned on me, after half-an-hour's observation, that I am the last person in the country who slows down and stops at the sight of an amber light. Today's rule is to keep crossing a junction until traffic starts to emerge from another way. It's the airbag culture in action.

I also couldn't help remembering Ken the tractor diver's recollections about his days at Hinton Ampner primary school. Back then, in the 1940s, the A272 was effectively part of the playground. The children would play cricket on the road, and just occasionally have to pull up stumps when a car came. As I watched Jonathan patiently wait to cross the road from the bus disembarkation point, it struck me that the chances of bowling a couple of overs of off-spin on the modern A272 were fairly slim.

March 27th

After a day out of the tractor, today would be our last spraying day for a bit, if the forecast is to be believed. So I dropped off the rollers, and hitched onto the sprayer again. I got a tank and a half of Liberator on Blackhouse Road, which completes a fairly comprehensive and expensive assault on the grass weeds that have taken hold out there. We left the stubble for ages, gave it a big dose of Roundup, ploughed (reasonably well), and have now done a pre-emergence anti-grass-weed spray. I hope that's given it a good sorting out.

After lunch, it was the winter barley's turn. A mix to clobber the grass weeds and the broadleaf weeds – there's plenty of both out there. The Retriever in Rick and Clump is still a bit sorry for itself up on the top of the hill – I think it's just waterlogging. The spray mix will be a fairly hot one, so I hope it copes OK. I had a curious moment half way through Rick/Clump: I couldn't for the life of me remember if I'd put the right amount of Axial in the tank. It was supposed to be 11 litres per fill-up, and it comes in 5-litre cans, so I should have had a clear recollection of taking just one litre out of a can, and returning the opened can to the store. But I didn't.

A slight panic ensued. Did I only put two full cans in? Not a great problem – just a slightly underdosed field. Did I put three full cans in? Slightly more of an issue – a seriously overdosed field, and a good chance of a lot of dead barley. Just as I was making contingency plans involving forty more acres of spring barley, a flash of memory resurfaced of me returning a part-full can to the store. Of course I had put the right amount in. It's just that after thirty years of spraying, it's very easy to go into auto pilot, and go through the motions.

Big Field was a nightmare. Noel had worked the wheat stubble with last year's tramlines E–W, and I drilled it at 90 degrees, going N–S. Big mistake. It was seriously rough. Luckily, I was able to slow down, and the sprayer controller sorted out the rate. It didn't stop me feeling like I'd been in half a dozen scrums afterwards.

Nothing had happened in the lambing department yet. But after a day rolling Kilmeston Road and the Hangar (which I thought we wouldn't get done, so was a bonus), Hazel summoned Tony and his pack to bring the flock into the barn. She'd heard the forecast for the weekend, and didn't reckon it was worth leaving them out. If the weather turns out better than expected, we can always let them back out.

On Fridays, the Editor works from home, which normally means he can be seen prowling the farm in a hideous turquoise Toyota, pigeon spotting. Hazel rang me with reports of thousands out with her on Kilmeston Road, and I mischievously passed the message on to him. "You should get out there now," I said. "Hazel has just finished – the field is yours, the gates are open." Very cruel of me. He managed to resist the temptation. I promised him a gale tomorrow as consolation, and then had a stream of "I'm so excited!" texts through the rest of the afternoon. As I often say to his wife, it's good that a man has a hobby.

March 28th

A damp and windy Saturday, so definitely a day out of the tractor. Spare a thought for the Editor, who flew in, grabbed the carefully prepared map of Kilmeston Road (entrances and exits, padlock codes, best places for decoys and most likely feeding spots for countless hordes of pigeons) and got out there to find not a pigeon to be seen. He upped sticks after an hour or two and moved to Dell Close, from where I got occasional morose text updates.

I had a quiet day, feeling somewhat knackered. A bit of domestic DIY – trying to sort out the stiff tap in the bathroom – ended up with the inevitable trip to Homebase to buy new ones. I popped down the road from Homebase to pick up a couple of drums of sodium hypochlorite from the Countrystore. I used Ally on the winter barley the other day, and it's one of those herbicides which will wipe out oilseed rape unless even the slightest traces are bleached off the inside of the sprayer. Looking at the forecast, my next job might be more fertiliser on the OSR, so it would be wise to have the machine cleaned out properly. Having got the crop looking this good, it would be a shame to ruin it.

Diana had a friend over for the day, and the two of them sat in front of the fire and played Scrabble, and then spent the afternoon in the kitchen baking. Young people today – outrageous.

March 29th

It should have been a quiet sofa Sunday, what with the gales and driving rain, but the sheep took their cue from the weather to start lambing. One had twins, and one decided she was very close indeed, and rather fancied being in a pen.

I left Hazel to deal with all this, and did indeed spend the best part of the day on the sofa, nursing a very stiff back – it's funny how it gets worse when the work dies down. By afternoon, I was fed up – the winds were playing havoc with the loose aerial cable, and hence the TV signal, so the feed of drivel on all those channels was very limited. When BBC1 started rerunning the Grand Prix, that was my cue to fall asleep, but a brace of police turned up just as I dozed off properly, lulled by the inaction of modern Formula One, and the sound of the moped engines they seem to use these days.

PC Paul and Shivi were treated to tea and biscuits (thanks to yesterday's baking), and a long session cooing over the puppy. Latest Countrywatch updates revolve around the mysterious door-to-door Irish chainsaw sellers (that's the sellers that are Irish, not the chainsaws) that Policeman would really like to have a chat with.

I realised that the Shogun is due to go back tomorrow, so had a final drive round, including some serious off-roading up the tracks to Stanmore. It seemed to struggle occasionally – the Tesco tyres didn't do it any favours at all. But all in all it's a lovely old-school off-roader, and shouldn't be difficult to write about.

I was just settling in for tea and sandwiches when neighbour Robert was on the mobile. His straw barn on Ganderdown was in flames. Did I fancy coming up and gawping at it with him? He came over and picked me up, and we drove up to the remote and windswept chalkland. In the middle of a treeless arable plain is a simple barn that – until that moment – was stacked to the rafters with barley straw. It was now a twisted steel skeleton, with a heap of charred and smouldering bales, occasionally flaring up as they fell open to reveal fresh straw.

Brother-in-law Noel had been ferrying sheep past the barn, along the well-used South Downs Way, and noticed, on one run, a champagne bottle left on one bale. Twenty minutes later, he saw the smoke pouring out of the barn. By the time assorted tractors got there, very little was salvageable – straw fires are inevitably left to burn out.

Robert seemed relaxed about it. I would have been cursing and swearing – he shrugged his shoulders and put it down to the joys of having the modern public walking through your farm. He did seem keen to have a look at our huge stocks, which might suit us very well indeed. So much for a relaxing Sunday.

March 30th

A grey and breezy Monday morning, with worse promised, so time for a bit of a review of what needs doing.

There's 85 acres of spring beans to get in. They could sit for a bit longer, but the sooner the better. There's grass weed spray on the Stanmore wheat to do. There's a full tank of fertiliser down at the grain store, and the OSR could really do with another dose, but I can't touch it until I've bleached out the Ally that I used the other day. Right, it's going to be the spring beans first.

I had checked the central heating/AGA oil tank over the weekend, and we were almost running on air, so I did the usual ring round on prices. Like red diesel, the price of kerosene has come down 25% since I last ordered, which is good. It was also nice to note that we haven't had central heating oil since September. It's true that we've had a mild winter, but we've also had the log burner going flat out, which is a delight, and obviously saves us a bob or two.

Having placed the order, I decided to fill the sprayer with bleach, and leave it for a day or two to clean it up. Then I can go onto fertiliser if I need to with a clear tank. I hitched onto the drill, ready for the worst job on the farm: taking off the Horsch Duo coulters and putting the Solo bean legs on. Luckily more police arrived – Lynn and Mel – to spend an hour cooing over the puppy.

Once we'd finally got the farm free of cooing constabulary, I was able to get under the Horsch, armed with my Nike floor mat, a 24 mm spanner, a 7/8" socket on a ratchet (complete with water pipe extension bar), a wire brush (for cleaning up bolt threads) and some Loctite. Several hours later, it was all done – and, miracle of miracles, I seemed to be uninjured. A quick change of the feed roller, and the drill was ready to go. By then, it was getting dark, and there was the small matter of a Thomas Lord Old Gits rehearsal to be done. Will, the new guitarist, had come back for more, so we had another two-hour session trying to teach him how we murder a wide range of classic hits, from the Sixties, right up to the present day.

March 31st

One heck of a gale got up well before dawn, which meant everyone was severely underslept. Luckily, I was up in time for the oil delivery man, who did exactly what was asked, and gave us thirty minutes' notice of his arrival. It's important because we mix a magic green bottle with the '28 second' heating oil to help avoid the aged AGA coking up. Fifteen or so years ago, the oil seemed to change, and the AGA would die within a matter of weeks. A bit of research suggested that an additive would help – I also learnt how to service it myself, so it might be down to that. The previous service team seemed to find a 1960 solid fuel/oil conversion too much to handle.

Rod Gaskin turned up mid-morning with the Kubota UTV he's trying to sell us. I'm not convinced we need one, but it would certainly come in handy for assorted jobs round the farm. They get stolen on a daily basis around the country, so it would need to be locked away very securely – which inevitably means you end up jumping in the truck instead. Rod agreed to leave it with us for the day. He went away to do some sums on trading in our old but almost unused Massey Ferguson/ Arctic Car ATV.

I spent late morning converting the continental bean bags to single loops, by using some old blue rope and farm tape, and then decided to double check that the right amount of beans had indeed been sent; ten tonnes seemed a heck of a lot for 85 acres. I had a very jolly hour in the kitchen hand counting beans, and then weighing them. In the end, the results were spot on: exactly the right amount had been delivered for 50 plants per square metre.

So, after lunch, I set about putting spring beans in Middle Broom. I managed to get the beans well down in, even though I was drilling up and down the hill. There was a curious calibration conundrum: the first bag ran out right on time, but the next ton slowed right down. There was much head scratching in the cab. Had the seeds changed TGW? Has the drill been playing up? All I could do at this stage was keep on playing with the seed rate setting until everything catches up again.

The gale was quite scary. There were huge showers flying by to the NE, but here we had fantastic sunshine and a wind that was shaking the tractor. As I headed north, the increased pressure in the cab as the wind came in through the open side window made my ears pop. Hazel and Jonathan spent the afternoon in the Kubota, doing more soil samples, and they too found conditions somewhat breezy – although that might have been a combination of no windscreen and Jonathan's right foot.

Just as I was finishing Middle Broom, neighbour Robert called to suggest the inevitable Tuesday trip to the Flowerpots. It seemed foolish not to.

In the pub, he asked if I'd seen the death notice in last week's Hampshire Chronicle, of an Italian. This chap was an Italian prisoner of war, allocated to Grange Farm in 1942, who had happily 'gone native'. He had worked on the farm for three years, and after compulsory repatriation at war's end, had come back, spending another couple of decades there. He had been joined by his childhood sweetheart, and they had married, and had a son – who now practices law in Southampton under an anglicised name. After the Italian had left the farm, Robert had lost touch with him completely, and seemed very melancholy to have seen the announcement after all these years. I could have sworn I saw a watery eye as he told the story of the Italian making a set of toy buckets as a present for him in 1946.

April 1st

I'm oversensitive about April Fool's Day for two reasons. Many years ago, I fell completely for one of the excellent BMW adverts – it was the one about soap flakes in the paint which mean self-cleaning cars when it rains. I repeated this faithfully for many years, and it was only when I mentioned it on a press car launch, and someone said, "That was one of their best ever April Fool's ads!" that it dawned on me. I agreed hastily, and laughed a bit too heartily, but I'm not sure I got away with it.

And then there was the April Fool's morning phone call from a 'Graeme Hopkins', claiming to be from the Ministry, announcing a snap inspection of all our store cattle ear tags – and back then we had a lot of store cattle around the farm. I played along with it for a bit – Graeme is my vet and oldest chum, 'Hopkins' is his wife's maiden name. Eventually, I burst out laughing, said "Very funny" and hung up.

I left it for an hour, and then rang Graeme – the vet – back, and congratulated him on a good try. "I think you ought to know," he said solemnly, "there really is a Graeme Hopkins who works for the Ministry in Guildford." I had to find a phone number a bit quick (this was well before the days of 1471) and get hold of Mr Hopkins. He saw the funny side – eventually. It didn't stop him coming out and doing the inspection, though. We used to get far more than our fair share, but consoled ourselves with the theory that we were on their list as compliant, not on the fiddle, polite, and happy to do tea and biscuits after the inspection. No wonder they headed out to us so much.

The day was windy and cold again, and the rain looked like it would arrive late, so I headed out to Big Broom to do bean sowing. It went fantastically, and I had it finished by tea time. I had to summon Hazel several times. First to tell her that the pea seed was coming – completely unannounced of course. I'd given the lorry driver (who did at least ring to say he was thirty minutes away) a bit of an earful, so he was particularly helpful when she unloaded him. No sooner had that finished than poor old Hazel had to console a distraught walker, who, armed with her telephoto lens, had spotted a dead lamb in the field. It was a huge stillborn lamb, so there was nothing that could have been done, but the walker had been desperately ringing the National Trust offices to raise help. We must get some signs printed up to help inform and educate.

Having finished Big Broom, I dropped into Child's Broom, with a view to getting an extra eight acres in by dusk. Once again, it was time to summon Hazel, this time for a jerry can of red diesel. The Deere was getting worryingly low, and the last thing you need with modern diesel engines is a run out. Twenty litres in a tank of 240 doesn't make much difference on the gauge, but I felt a bit safer.

As the sun set, I got to the very last two turns of land work (having done the headland first), and promptly ran out of seed. All it needed was 10 kg – probably less than that, but I thought Hazel had had quite enough running round for today. I'm going to have to come back this way to do School Field at some stage, so I'll do those last two turns then.

April 2nd

April? I don't think so. It was cold and wet. It was like February again – cold enough to see your breath, and make every bash of a fingertip twice as painful. Not really the best morning to change the filter on the diesel station, but a new one had been delivered, and needed to be done. Diesel flow doubled.

Then it was back to changing implements again, from drill to sprayer. The plan was to get a slightly overdue second dose of nitrogen onto the oilseed rape, but I was still wary of the Ally. Unless cleaned out properly, it can wreck broadleaf crops. The other day I'd emptied the tank in Big Field, and done a 350-litre clear water rinse out on the headland. Back home I'd refilled the sprayer to the brim and added 20 litres of hypochlorite, and left for a couple of days while drilling. So, this morning I drained the bleach, and then refilled with another 350 litres of clean water, and rinsed that out. Clean enough? I thought I'd head out to the winter barley in Rick/Clump, and give that a dose of nitrogen, which should finally mean the tank is clean enough to venture into the oil seed rape.

A long afternoon saw fertiliser on the winter barley in Rick/Clump, the oilseed rape in White Hill, and the late drilled winter wheat in TBHD, which looks fantastic up on top. What you could do with a whole farm like the Top of Hurst Down – flat and level, with a bit of quality soil.

Late in the evening, two emails arrived from Tod with attachments. A couple of phone calls established that they were OK to open – they were the results of the first batch of soil samples. Quite reasonable reading they made too, with very little to worry about, and quite a lot to be pleased about. The phosphate indices have benefitted enormously from a couple of years of major TSP application, to the point where we could have got away with a potash-only application this year. However, since the barn is full of 0:26:26, that's what will be going on.

April 3rd

Good Friday. Cold – again – and very wet. Wetter, I'm sure, than they promised. I nipped out to Cheyney to finish the fertiliser on the oilseed rape, and realised that ground conditions weren't suitable for a long day. So I had a short day, and hit the sofa, played Scrabble and watched *The Alamo*. And no one mentioned Jesus. Funny how the world has changed.

April 4th

Easter Saturday, and a good day to stay out of the tractor and let a very painful right shoulder calm down. I can't decide if it's too much operating those very stiff controls on the Deere or just a flare up of the rugby injury from November 1981.

Lambing has kicked off properly, with twins and triplets arriving. It could still be a bit warmer for the poor little blighters – we had the first couple arriving on top of the AGA in a cardboard box.

April 5th

Easter Sunday, and a slightly melancholy morning as the lambs who were found just before dusk last night were both dead in the dawn. Somehow they just hadn't fed. That's lambing for you. Still, plenty more are on the way.

There's talk of spring arriving big time this week. A huge high pressure is imminent, and it dawned on me that it would be a good idea to get out and put all the fertiliser I still had on assorted fields, while the soil had a bit of dampness in it. So I had a long day putting nitrogen on Big Field (looking good except for the stripes from the Amazone's poor boom suspension), BML's (no spring barley through yet, but looking a treat), Blackhouse Road (barley coming through quite well, but a bit uneven thanks to my crap ploughing) and Drier Field (in places, almost bare, in places quite healthy). The best thing that could happen would be for the whole farm to enjoy a couple of weeks of fine warm weather – and that's what they're promising.

The Trust's visitors were out in force. I had a nice chat with one couple, and asked one lot who were taking pictures of me to send me a copy. I only had one mother/son couple running away with hands melodramatically over their mouths. I nearly chased after them to talk them out of it, but decided it wasn't worth it.

Should I have been working on Easter Day? Unthinkable in older times, but these days, when you've got to go, you go. The Good Lord had plenty of opportunities to send us fine weather from October till early March, and He chose not to. So my conscience is clear. At Open Mic Night, someone who had been out and about today said the whole countryside was buzzing with tractors and sprayers, so it's not just me out there.

The best moment at OMN was the return of Steve the uberguitarist. He, Dave the Bass and I resurrected our plans for a blues band, and I pointed out that Shed 3b was at everyone's disposal for rehearsals.

April 6th

The weather has gone into compensation mode. As if to apologise for all those months of rain and general foulness, Mother Nature is now sending us the most stunning early mornings. A touch of frost, gorgeous sunrises and mist-filled valleys. Perfect for lambing and general arable work. However, lots of worthy tractor-based plans for Easter Monday were abandoned when sister-in-law Heather arrived for lunch. The new plan was heavily food-based, and included lots of chocolate, and then a slightly tipsy gather round the telly to watch *Tipping Point*. What better way to spend an afternoon.

And there's no better sign than the flatcoats being too hot when sitting out in the sun, and having to come back in. Add the gentle cacophony of a dozen village lawnmowers, and it's safe to say that spring is here.

April 7th

Another fantastic morning: not quite a frost, but cool. A pin-sharp sunrise, a deafening dawn chorus, and wisps of mist down in the Springshott valley. It's enough to make even me get out of bed early. Hazel had already been up for some time, on lamb patrol. I've completely lost count of who's had what. All I know is that the field is gradually filling up, and becoming more photogenic by the day.

The spring beans in Middle Broom have got the tiniest of roots on them already, so I thought I would get on and get them rolled. A curious thing, rolling. It's hard to say exactly why we roll the seedbed: it covers the seed better, and leaves a flat layer for the pre-emergence spray to work on. I hope it will dissuade the rooks a bit – they have a habit of arriving from the rookery near Hinton Ampner Lodge and cleaning out beans by the row. If this weather goes on, we might be pleased that the rolling saves a bit of moisture. The most important thing about it, of course, is that it looks nicer.

I was back late morning, and ordered some more red diesel – down another two pence per litre. I also put in an order for more liquid fertiliser, which should arrive later in the week, just to keep things frantic. Then it was back to spraying, and two tanks on the only forward wheat we've got, the Claire, in Broom, Long and Pipeline – collectively known as Stanmore. It's a heck of a hike from home up to these fields – two tanks took the best part of the afternoon. It looks reasonable up there, and is still home to an astonishing array of pheasants; we must hatch a plan to get them back our way – or work out some drives down there, of course.

After finishing Pipeline, I did a clean water tank in the field, then back to the Drier and filled up with another 300 litres of clean water, which I rinsed out on Drier Field. Then it was home for a brim full and some more hypochlorite. I hitched off the full sprayer, and quickly switched back to the drill. The plan is to knock off the spring beans in Godwin's tomorrow. But we all know about farm plans.

April 8th

Indeed – so much for farm plans. The early start to finish the spring beans went horribly wrong when I tried to recalibrate the Horsch for the final push. The feed roller at the very bottom of the hopper kept on jamming. It would only do a couple of turns before locking up. Not very good for the very expensive motor that drives it. I did what I could as a calibration, and then rather optimistically headed out to Childs Broom, when it refused to work at all. So I came home.

I stood and stared at the drill for some time, but no matter how hard I looked, the truth was inescapable: I was going to have to empty the tonne of seed I'd just put in. Luckily, I had a keen teenager to help. So we went to work. First of all, I washed out the big general purpose loader bucket, and parked it carefully next to the hopper. Then Jonathan and I took it in turns to lift out as much as we could with little plastic buckets. Once we'd filled the loader bucket, we had to transfer it to an old seed bag, and start again.

Four-fifths of it was reasonably easy. The dregs, down in the bottom of the inverted pyramid of a hopper, down among the pipes and cables, was impossible. So we tried using the feed roller, but after ten little buckets' worth struggling their way through a constantly jamming roller, we decided to sacrifice what was left in the hopper. We took the plates off the sides of the roller unit, and let it spill everywhere.

Closer inspection of the feed roller showed that three consecutive flutes had broken off. This had to be why the roller kept jamming, and why I couldn't get the seed rate right a few days ago. I assume it was sheer old age, and the plastic getting brittle. Anyway, it was nice to find a reason. It was the hottest day of the year, and so I sent Jonathan to have a shower, while I less than optimistically started the hunt for a new fluted roller. My spare parts book didn't have it listed, but a brief search on the internet came up with a number, which I rang through to Oakes Bros, who just happened to have one in stock. Wonder of wonders. "Put my name on it!" I cried. "I'll be up this afternoon."

Also on the internet was a cross email from *The Field*, demanding my June car review today. The deadline has been moved forward to the beginning of each month, now that they're shorter staffed than they've ever been. I rang them and begged for another half day to finish it. Hazel then announced she was on her way to get Diana from work, and could do Oakes Bros on the way. Perfect – I sat down and bashed out the Shogun review in a matter of twenty minutes. It helped that the car itself was interesting, with plenty of points to write about, and that I've been sitting in the tractor writing the piece in my head for about a week. It was on the screen and down the email tubes in no time.

More plans fell into minor disarray when Robert Raimes rang to put off doing the application of 0:26:26 that I'd hoped to start today. No huge problem – it would be nice to get the rest of the soil samples done before we dose the fields, and the forecast suggests that anything we do spin on will be sitting on the surface for a bit, so a week's delay is no trouble.

Then tomorrow's plan to MOT the sprayer was scrapped when Hunt's rang to say that the tester man had been involved in an accident on the way back from holiday. Terrible bad luck for them, but it means that if I do get the drilling done, I'll have a longer opportunity to get the pre-emergence on them.

Rod Gaskin then turned up to look at the stripes in the barley caused by the Amazone sprayer still flapping its boom backwards and forwards, resulting in uneven liquid fertiliser application. This is an issue that has been rumbling for some time, and Amazone had been out and done a major overhaul of the booms, but with little effect. I showed Rod the stripes, and suggested he ask Amazone what they suggested was the next step. He had another go at selling us the Kubota, and I nearly agreed when he upped the trade-in value of the old ATV, but it's still not quite enough.

Meanwhile, Hazel was back with the drill part from Oakes. Two minutes of reassembly, five minutes of recalibration, and I was ready to go. I finished the two short turns in Child Broom, flew through a nicely moist School Field, got Hazel to drop another bag in as I passed the muck heap, and then headed off to Godwin's Broom. I got most of the headland done, and headed back to fill up the tractor with diesel, emptying the barn tank for tomorrow's delivery.

A hot and sweaty day. And just in case I'd been thinking of finally getting everything drilled and sprayed in the next couple of days and having a quiet spell, the lorry load of liquid fertiliser arrived mid-afternoon. Never complain about being too busy. Not ever.

April 9th

Another stunning morning, but another mysterious dead lamb. Once again it was the huge one of a pair of twins. Hazel developed a selection of theories, as she wrapped the smaller one in hay and put it in a box on top of the AGA. Were conditions so good this spring that the lambs are just too big? Was Elvis the ram not such a good 'un? Who knows? It's a shame, in these perfect conditions, to be losing any at all.

I started another attempt to get the spring beans in Godwin's finished. I had a good run until about eleven, when I ran out of seed with only a couple of triangles left to do. I opened the last 500 kg bag carefully, to let the seed trickle out. I let it trickle, and trickle, and trickle, until I guessed, using my multi-decades of experience and wisdom, that I had put the right amount in the hopper, and off I went, back to finish the corners.

Inevitably, I got it wrong. I needed just a few kilogrammes more. Back to the field entrance, where Hazel had left the loader tractor with the bag on the front. All went well until I tried to trickle just a bit more in. Plastic seed bags are notoriously difficult to control unless you get a bit of string high up on the outlet chute, which most bags come supplied with. These annoying single-skinned bags had no such control, and with a whoosh, the whole lot fell in. At least I definitely had enough to finish the field now.

Which I did, and as I drove back to the farm, I decided that I was not going to go through the bucketing routine to empty it again; that seed would have to stay in, and so the next bit of sowing I did would simply have to be Bungalow.

Hazel dropped in behind me after lunch and got the whole lot rolled, and the 85 acres of Godwin's could not have looked better. With the hot dry conditions, I'm pleased I cracked on with the 'go straight in' sowing policy; the idea of ploughing and working down would have left a seedbed crying out for moisture.

The next job is to get the pre-emergence herbicide on. I couldn't do it while Hazel was out there, so I took the opportunity to get the PTO shaft on the sprayer mended; it had gone a bit banana shaped when the tractor 3-point linkage had lifted a bit too far. I took the 'tractor' end up to Gaskin's, where they somewhat reluctantly said they could do it on the spot. I enjoyed ten minutes of small talk with Dave in stores (during which he managed to sell me two new mirrors for the Massey), ten minutes of small talk with Mike the workshop manager (during which we covered most of his family history), and then ten minutes of the usual insults and banter with Rod (during which he once again nearly sold me the Kubota UTV, and filled me in on his work getting Amazone to see sense on the floppy boomed sprayer.) By then, the PTO shaft was finished.

Back home, I put it all back together, and swapped the tractor back to the sprayer. Another bleach rinse out and clean water flush ensued, by which time I was knackered. I did a bit of late evening pressure washing of sprayer and tractor – nothing major, just a mud blast-off, but great therapy anyway. The pre-emergence spraying can wait until tomorrow.

April 10th

Many farming jobs are stressful, but today's was high on the list of nerve-wrackers. My mission: to get the pre-emergence herbicide on the spring beans in the Godwin's block of fields. Slight issue number one: the herbicide being used is bright yellow and very smelly. Issue two: the Godwin's block has the highest concentration of footpaths on the whole farm.

Still, when you've got to go, you've got to go. It was another perfect morning, crisp and clear, with a slight east wind. I was out there early, so based on the theory that the Ladies who Walk would still be indoors, I thought I'd start in Park (the one with the most public access), and work back towards the farm buildings.

It all went perfectly. I didn't see a soul, and I quietly went about turning the satin silver finish of smooth straw-mixed soil a nice shade of gaudy yellow. In and out of Park, no trouble, no walkers, no fists shaken at me, then in and out of Big Broom, easily picking up the new tramlines with the help of the satnav. It was back to the yard for a refill, and then in and out of Middle Broom, complete with its vibrant hare population. For Child's Broom, I stepped up the flow rate a bit – I was running a bit full.

Two great moments of satisfaction ensued: I needed about twenty yards to run out the excess, and a huge batch of walkers could then be seen heading up the far side of Middle Broom. I felt very smug as I did an in-field clean water washout.

I then had yet another cancellation phone call. The fuel company couldn't deliver the diesel that they'd promised today – could I wait till Monday? It was no problem, of course – but very odd to get so many rescheduling calls in one week.

I had a strange feeling of being slightly up together. 336 acres of assorted crops done in a month and a couple of days, as well as a lot of assorted spraying and fertiliser application. On a proper farm, that's a couple of day's work, but here that's an achievement. I should have got on with some more fertiliser, what with the forecast being damp for tomorrow, and several bits of the farm needing another dose, but Tod turned up for a crop walk. Inevitably we ended up feeding lambs (with his nipper) and then heading into Shed 3b for a session trying to get the new mixing desk ('New'? £9.99 off eBay!) up and running, with some success.

Hazel and Jonathan rang from the M3 to say they'd be late back (they'd gone shopping in preparation for his trip to Spain next week), and they asked if I could pick up Diana from work. I jumped into the MX5 (all these weeks of work have left me a bit more flexible than I was the last time I tried to get in it) and whizzed off to Alresford. Then it was on to the doctor's to pick up (and pay for) her pills. Now, there's a remarkable stage in life: standing in a dispensary paying for your daughter's contraceptives. From there, I completed a triangle down the A32 to Rod's, to buy a new battery for the electric fencer, and to finally agree to buy the Kubota UTV. We've spent a long time discussing all the things it would be handy for, and that's before we got onto the traditional jobs like slug pelleting and spot spraying that were horrible on the old ATV. And it will be a fun toy as well.

I treated myself to the rest of the afternoon off, and drank too much tea and ate far too many custard creams. I'll never learn.

April 11th

A dull and windy start, and then a reasonable band of rain blew through. For a couple of minutes I contemplated yet another Saturday at the wheel of the tractor, but decided to stay in. Then the rain cleared, and bright sunshine joined the strong wind. Terrible weather for liquid fertiliser. Well, that's what I persuaded myself as I dozed on the sofa, watching the Boat Races, whose political correctness was only matched by their dullness. Then yesterday's custard cream frenzy caught up with me, and I was very glad not to be out in the middle of Kilmeston Road.

Hazel took Monty down to the New Forest for a day's training with the Flatcoat Retriever Club. All the great and the good of that world were there; famous names from the trials world and England team members. Luckily, Hazel and her big black sidekick are good enough to hold their own in such company.

A significant moment came when the assembled dog owners were discussing how to introduce one's flatcoat to gunfire. "We have a rough shoot at home, and I pick up on three or four formal shoots," explained Hazel. Suddenly, she was the envy of the class. It came as a bit of a surprise to her that her easy access to real live shooting and picking-up was a rarity. Most of the others, despite their world of gundogs, never got the chance. A very pleasant surprise.

Not half as much a surprise as the blind ewe who had produced twins this morning decided to produce a third lamb at tea time. Sheep everywhere.

April 12th

A cold and breezy Sunday, and they reckon it was going to get breezier as the day went on. So I headed out to the two bits of spring barley that haven't had any nitrogen. Despite this, they – Kilmeston Road and the Hangar – are romping away, so I'm late with the first dose.

Spring barley fertiliser dates are always a good topic for debate. 'Get it on by the end of March' used to be the rule, but a bit difficult in these days of freezes and floods that mean no barley is in the ground by then. 'A third when you can first see the tramlines, the rest at three leaf stage' is as good as anything these days. Especially as the maltsters seem more content to take higher nitrogen malting barley than they used top, so early fertiliser to get the ultra-low grain nitrogen isn't so vital. My overall policy is, as usual, to do what I can when I can.

Kilmeston Road looked stunning in the sunshine, and the Hangar a bit scruffy. I managed to get them both done in time to rush home and say goodbye to Jonathan, who was off on his school trip to Spain for a week. Towards the end of the Hangar, the wind was getting silly, with the fertiliser flying out of the nozzles horizontally, so I abandoned for the afternoon and slept in front of the snooze fest Formula One.

Today's lambing success was Hazel doing a random check and finding a lamb suffocating in its birth sack. She was just in time to save it, although the ewe had already given up on it. The lamb was very quickly another member of the orphan pack.

By five thirty, the wind had dropped, so I did another tank of fertiliser, getting a first dose on the spring wheat in Joan's Acre and Dell Close, and a second dose on the Panorama wheat in BOMS. A very satisfactory few hours trundling around the farm, a far cry from the angst of five weeks ago. Mind you, we could do with some rain.

April 13ᵗʰ

Time for a Monday morning review of what's going on. All the spring barley up and away, and all has had its first dose of fertiliser. There's only Bungalow left for spring beans, but that needs ploughing and working down. Then there's the pea ground in Chalks, but we've got to do some lopping on the bottom headland before I can finish ploughing that. What is ploughed is getting harder by the day – not ideal for working down for a fine pea tilth. There's no spraying, but there's still plenty of fertiliser to do, and plenty in the tank, so that's what I decided to do.

I did spend an early hour tidying up the spraystore, just in case Tod's recommendations from Friday start to arrive; there was hardly room with all the empty boxes and randomly scattered cans. By the time I'd finished, there was plenty of room. The next lorry of red diesel was safely delivered –let's hope this lasts a little longer that the last load.

I headed off to give the oilseed rape another batch of fertiliser. It wasn't the best weather for application of liquid nitrogen on a broadleaf crop – a bit warm and scorching, but it's a job that's a bit behind, so I thought I'd get on anyway. I managed two tanks on the whole 85 acres in the morning, and planned to get up to Stanmore and do the Claire in the afternoon.

Unfortunately, just as I was filling up the first tank after lunch, the Subaru test car delivery driver rang and said he'd be here in half an hour, and no, he didn't have a wingman to take him to the station. I'd have to do it. I drove back to the yard with the full tank, and waited for him.

By the time he'd arrived and I'd run him into Petersfield, it was too late to do any more fertiliser. I had managed to get an appointment with Jane the Physio to try to sort out this painful shoulder at five o'clock, and a good shower was much needed to make her job less unpleasant.

Most of the farming community of central Hampshire rely on Jane to keep them going. In another time and culture, she would have been worshipped for her magic hands. The best cheque you can write – or Mr BUPA can write on your behalf, if you're willing to jump through all the hoops – is for 45 minutes having bits gently put back where they should be.

Within moments of me describing the symptoms, she had a diagnosis, and a solution. Did I say 'gentle'? In the name of increasing blood flow to the affected area of the shoulder, enormous pain was inflicted. "Ooh, I'm bruising you!" she announced proudly halfway through. There's usually a lot of chat and gossip during the course of a treatment, and if you feel there's not enough effort being put in on her part, you raise some important local issue – like poachers. Jane is a long-standing parish councillor. The therapy gets a bit more thorough when controversial matters come up. But this time, I couldn't talk. I was blacking out with the pain. Jane assured me it was vital.

She was right. By the time the Monday night rehearsal of the Old Gits was in full swing, the shoulder was already feeling much better. She's a miracle worker.

The rehearsal was good. Will the new guitarist couldn't make it, but we five had a very tight evening – the Mudansha Tour dates made it onto a sheet of paper on the wall, and that always seems to concentrate the mind a bit.

April 14th

Sometimes you wish you had smooth farm tracks and a high-speed tractor. The idea of swiftly getting two tanks of fertiliser on the Stanmore block in the morning were undone by a delayed start (too much beer at rehearsal and a surfeit of ginger cake at tea) and the long haul up to Long Field. I got the one tank done, and then had a think. I could rush down to the main tank, try and hurry another load on Pipeline, and then dismantle all the pipes and fitting off the fertiliser tank, so that when I got back to the yard, I could fill up with water for the spray MOT test that was due this morning. Or I could go home now, have a clean out and a filter blast off (and a cup of tea), and let the water fill up from the hose for an hour. I chose the latter.

Phil the salesman turned up almost as soon as I'd put the kettle on, and we had a very jolly half-hour chat – without a lot of selling going on. Tod called in to pick up yet another tray of soil samples – the last of the whole farm test that we've done this year. The yard was a flurry of white vans as all of Tod's recommendations were delivered.

The man from Hunt's arrived to do the sprayer MOT, and as expected, the nearly new sprayer passed. There's a lot of groping of pipes and timed flow through assorted nozzles, but at this age there shouldn't be any frayed pipes or worn hoses. I was rewarded with a sheath of paper and stickers for the office. Such is modern farming.

I finally got back to the fertiliser, finishing the second tank on the Stanmore block, and then emptying the last of the main tank onto Roe Hill. Somehow I ran short on the southern headland, but no doubt I'll be back that way again soon. I came back via the spring beans in the Godwin's block and found the early drilled field about half an inch away from emergence. Sowing them with the minimum of soil disturbance has certainly paid off when it comes to saving moisture. Deep down is still very soggy. If we'd ploughed and worked down, the ground would have been dry as dust, and there's no rain promised for a fortnight.

April 15th

The ghosts in this farmhouse have a mischievous streak. They know very well that I have a thing about 'nelsons' – multiples of 111. I had to get rid of my bedside digital clock when I kept waking at 1.11, 2.22 and so on – I assumed I was reading the time through half open sleepy eyes. But even without the clock, it still happens. This morning, I was woken (not the same as 'I woke up') while it was still dark. There was no noise, no roaring cars, no shouting sheep. Something had metaphysically tapped me on the shoulder. I decided to get up and have a pee. Hazel's digital clock – invisible until then, said 4.44.

That's just the sort of time to make getting back to sleep impossible. The dawn chorus kicks off soon after that, then dawn itself arrives, then alarm clocks start going off. So get up and make some very early porridge.

Any chance of a stunningly early start to more spraying was dashed by the heavy fog. It brought a tiny bit of much-needed moisture to everything, but sopping wet leaves tend to shrug off expensive spray applications. By nine, the day was drying rapidly.

And then the phone calls started. First up was the Police Chief Inspector, wanting to discuss the new meetings he's planning with the public. They sound perfect: very informal, a committee of just half a dozen concerned citizens (yuk) getting together with him to make complaints and suggestions. I warned him that I haven't done much committee work since Castle Leazes Rugby Club at Newcastle University. I was treasurer. We did five minutes of business, then got drunk. I'm not sure that these meetings will be the same. While I was on the phone to the Chief Inspector, PC Jon went flying past in his Land Rover. Typical – you wait ages for a policeman, and two arrive at once.

Once off the phone to the Chief Inspector, I rang Jon, just in case there was stuff going on down the valley at Brockwood, and an extra pair of hands was needed, but got no reply. So I finally got spraying.

Well, not for long. I got most of the way round the headland when the Editor rang, wanting a chat about nothing in particular. I managed another few hundred yards when SEAT rang, offering me a press car at the end of June. And then Jon rang back wondering why I had rung. All of the chats go on for about ten minutes, and I have to turn the tractor off to hear what's being said, and the cab turns into a greenhouse – and it was the hottest day of the year.

I finally got the fungicide on the OSR, and then set about the biggest job of the year: passing the ACCS inspection. A nice inspector comes and sits down in our kitchen, and gently goes through all the stuff we should have done to earn our Assurance stickers that go on the grain 'passports' that go with each lorry when we load them up at harvest. These stickers tell the world that we are safe farmers. As usual, we failed on a couple of minor bureaucratic points, but did quite well in others. A few hours of form filling and we'll be able to get our sheet of stickers.

I should have gone out and done yet another tank of spray, but there wasn't quite enough time – we'd promised Diana we'd be out of the house by the time her friends came round for a late birthday party. So we booked a table at the Thomas Lord, and headed down there with Rufus and Ali for a lively and loud evening.

April 16th

A curious day. First of all, we had a dead single lamb. It was another brute of a beast, and had been dead for some time by the time Hazel found it. Once again, it was frustrating to have such perfect lambing weather going to waste. Then, my test car

– from a Japanese manufacturer legendary for its reliability – started flashing orange warning lights at Hazel as she did the paper run. I got hold of the PR team, who promised a replacement tomorrow.

I did a bit more spraying, getting Folly and BOMS done – although the last corner of BOMS proved too far for what I thought was a perfectly calibrated tank. I did Roe Hill after that, which looks better and better by the day, and then hitched the sprayer off.

Time for Operation Reclaim Bungalow Part Two: the ploughing. The Roundup from a few weeks ago had been moderately successful, so it was time to get the whole field ploughed. It's a heck of a long way up there, but I thought I'd do it in a couple of sessions, especially as all the annoying short work is very trying. I started on the west headland, and managed to get the block nearest the houses done, and was just starting the first long turns when the Deer's gearbox started playing up again, doing horrid drive disconnection at random. Hugely frustrating, because it was only mended a few weeks ago, after doing the same thing.

It was well past six o'clock by now, so not worth trying to raise Hunt's to send out a mechanic. I'd have to do that in the morning. Annoying. I limped all the way home in 'Get You Home' mode. It's a long way at half speed.

April 17th

Yet another frustrating day got off to a bad start at midnight, when I was woken by a convoy of lorries hurtling through the village – well, three lorries, but that counts as a convoy in Hinton Ampner. I got out of bed to watch where they were going. They went over Roe Hill, and down towards the Drier. What on earth was going on? As usual, I ended up putting two and two together and getting several hundred: it had to be serious industrial fly-tipping in the yard down there, or someone was helping themselves to our fertiliser, or it was equipment being delivered for an illegal rave in the barn. The options were numerous and terrifying.

When one came back, I could see it was an empty tipper; this narrowed down the explanations, and I persuaded myself that they were finally doing the roadworks up Brockwood Bottom Lane. I wasn't quite sure why they should be doing it at midnight, but it was enough for me to get back to sleep.

I had a drive round in the early morning, and found that it was in fact Murphy next door having his long drive re-laid with motorway planings, and these are only produced by night-time motorway roadworks. Hence the odd delivery hour. I'll be interested to see how it goes for him – we've got plenty of tracks and corners needing some sort of filling in.

At 8am on the dot, I got hold of Hunt's service department, and explained my tractor's problems. Someone would be out soon, they promised. So I faffed around for the morning, doing some fertiliser sums, and checking on the spring beans, which were just starting to emerge nicely. There's a stiff cold north-easterly keeping things nice and fresh out in the Godwin's block. Let's hope it keeps the insect activity down until the beans get away properly. Still no sign of any rooks – long may that last, too.

Subaru sent out a replacement car mid-morning, but there was still no sign of any tractor mechanic by lunchtime. So I made another call, and it seemed that the eight o'clock message had got lost. But a mechanic really would be out today at some time. I confess I harrumphed a bit on the phone.

I gave up on any farm work, and showered ready for the big heart and lung tests at the doctor's – I'm still trying to shift this wheezy chest. I did the lung capacity and strength test, and came out with the lungs of a 42-year-old, which is pretty impressive (just so long as he doesn't want them back). I smoked thirty a day from aged seventeen until the day we got Hazel's first pregnancy scan, and have spent my whole working life in dust and chemicals.

The nurse couldn't give me any results from the ECG – that would be up to the doctor. But we talked about the inhalers, and she seemed sure that I should have a steroid version rather than the traditional one I'm using a lot at the moment. Her diagnosis was asthma caused by an allergy, so steroids would be better. I'll wait to see what the doctor says.

The Deere mechanics turned up late afternoon, and found exactly the same problem: the manual clutch button in the gear stick is playing up again. I pointed out that it was a brand new one, so it can't be that. We agreed to isolate the switch (I never use it anyway), and see how it goes. I couldn't help thinking that there's a wiring glitch somewhere – I've never forgotten the strange afternoon when applying the brakes switched on the sidelights. Mice in the loom? I do hope not.

April 18th
Another broken night, as Jonathan was coming back from the school trip to Spain at the ludicrous time of 4am – too late to stay up for, horribly early to get up for. Luckily, Anthony was easily persuaded to do the run for us, and did it perfectly. It didn't stop Hazel doing the old parental trick of waking up to check that he'd woken up. I remember August 1980, when a friend and I had booked a three week post-A-level trip to France. He and I spent the evening in the Red Lion in West Meon (gone, I'm afraid), and came back a bit tiddly. I had a big row with Dad, and we all went to bed a bit late. The holiday was saved when Dad, like all the best forgiving fathers, got up to check we'd got up, and found we hadn't. Thank goodness for his good-natured hammering on bedroom doors, and we managed to get the cross-Channel hovercraft (gone, I'm afraid. As has Dad. And my school friend Max).

All the comings and goings didn't make for the smoothest of nights so we were all up a bit late. Luckily there was no sheep crisis. Drummer Ian and his family turned up for a look round the farmyard – his six-year-old wanted to see lambs and puppies and tractors and sprayers (not sure about the last one), and it's always a joy to take enthusiastic children (of any age) round a tractor cab. I wished I'd been ploughing a bit nearer than Bungalow, so a proper ride would have been possible, but we made do with some noisy start-ups and plough turning in the yard. And there's nothing like a relaxed lunch with some completely non-farming types, comparing notes on lifestyles and situations, to have you counting your blessings.

I managed another few hours in the tough ground up in Bungalow, just about getting to the short work. As I got to the field, a lady and her dog could be seen sprinting for all she was worth out through the broken fence in the corner, so the message that we'd rather it was private has obviously got through. Some fence mending (and not the metaphorical version) would certainly reinforce the message. The tractor gearbox behaved flawlessly though. The Deere might have had a reprieve.

Then it was back for a big tea, to mark Anthony's last day before he heads back up north to Leeds University tomorrow. It's only a short term, and then he'll have finished two years. Already. Where does the time go?

April 19th

The perfect Sunday would involve some very old friends coming over for lunch, which would be home-produced lamb and Diana-produced cheesecake. There would be a surfeit of nostalgia, gossip, yearning for the ability to play cricket again, and general wine-induced nonsense. And that's what we got.

April 20th

Time for a Monday review. We've got one more fine week before it all breaks down, with, perhaps, some welcome rain. Priority number one is to get Bungalow ploughed, worked down a bit and then drilled. There's also some spraying which ought to be done this week if unsettled weather is coming. Then there's the 0:26:26 to go on. And the peas to go in, once we've lopped the bottom headland and finished the last bit of ploughing down there. And the game cover needs to be bought and sown, once I've sprayed off where it's going. And then there's the subsidy forms…

I rang Graham Tosdevine to book the spraying, just as Robert rang to say he'd be in tomorrow to do the 0:26:26. That was those two organised. There was the complication of a car going and a car arriving, so I couldn't set off for Bungalow in the morning. Instead, I sat indoors and wrote the next opinion piece for *Farmers Weekly*. The gang delivering the Isuzu arrived (with a puncture and a dent from a minor prang on the way down), and then the Subaru went away. The day was at last clear.

I set off for Bungalow after lunch and had a long afternoon finishing it. I had to stop several times to clean off radiator screens – it was a hot day again, and all the Roundup-ed grass and dust was clogging things up every hour or so. But at about six o'clock, with the fuel gauge shouting warnings at me, I finally finished it. Very smart it looked too.

Band rehearsal was somewhat muted – Will, the new guitarist, had decided that he would not be joining us after all, so we're back to a fivesome. Not to worry – we'll get by. Although we may have to play a bit better than we did tonight. I think the mood was somewhat down (deeper and down).

April 21st

Having failed to get hold of a power harrow to knock down the ploughing in Bungalow, I thought I'd go out there and use the Varidisc instead. It took a couple of hours to get it all greased up, and then to find that the new bolts I'd bought in bulk don't fit the holes on the legs which hold (or should hold) the replacement bearings. I decided to get on without one disc.

Robert and Paul arrived to start the phosphate/potash spreading, so we had a good old gossip in the kitchen – mainly about the vet situation, which seems to still be troubling the livestock men of central Hampshire. Once we'd all had a good moan, I packed them off with a farm map.

Hazel and I spent an hour planning a bit of a plumbing job on the fence line across the middle of Englands. The old cattle troughs are useless for sheep, so we're planning a couple of low level ones instead. Hazel has a plan to put one in the bottom of Englands fifty yards away from the old cattle one, to take it away from any public access. It's a brave plan, but I'm not sure it will work. I sat down with a list of bits (pipe, elbows, tees) and ordered them up from APM. I also ordered new base plates for the Horsch – I'm not sure that the old ones qualify as totally worn out, but I work on the theory that the Duo coulters come off once a year (for beans), so let's get new plates on then and there.

One again I had the phone struggle to avoid being called 'Charlie'. It's 'Mr Flindt' to you, you young whippersnapper. Young people today.

Then, at last, it was off to Bungalow. The Varidisc, with one missing disc, some iffy bearings and a few twisted legs, was never going to make an onion bed, but did a reasonable job. The early ploughing had baked to bricks, and yesterday's was still pretty soggy. But I got it all finished, and hoped that the deep tines of the Horsch, followed by a good roll, and the promised rain, will end up with a reasonable-looking job.

Operation Reclaim Bungalow seemed more apt than ever when I arrived – the Slovakian au pair was escorting her employer's springer out into the field for a huge dump. Another exchange of views ensued. Grrrr.

April 22nd

A frantic day. Graham Tosdevine sent his sprayerman over to do the Stanmore wheat and all the winter barley. He arrived in his new toy, a self-propelled sprayer that has absolutely no chance of getting down the vast majority of our roads. It had to be as tall as the combine. We stood round and admired it for a moment or two, and then I gave him the map, complete with how to get where he was supposed to go without using roads. I'll have to bear that in mind as the year goes on, and road travel is the only way. Robert Raines turned up to finish off the application of 0:26:26. He said I'd miscounted the tonnage of fertiliser, so would be upping the rate on Stanmore.

I loaded up the drill with another tonne of spring beans – some of our home-saved seed, probably from a couple of years ago or more, so I pushed the seed rate up a bit

– and off I went to Bungalow. It was rough going, but the tines were set deep, and the final seedbed looked fairly respectable. I was expecting it to be more unpleasant, but I reckon my memories of sowing anything in Bungalow are tarnished by the awful years of the mid-1980s. I can remember a terrible wet day, with two ploughs fighting their way through the mud, a power harrow desperately trying to beat the sodden slabs into submission, and a Bamlett drill uselessly trying to finish off the job. Today's job was considerably more successful than that.

On the way home, I noticed wheel marks in the Folly – not all over it, just a bit round the outside. Was it night-time poachers again? I had a late run round everywhere on the way back from picking up Jonathan from school, but there were no tracks anywhere else. It did make me think that we're getting complacent again – we must put those telegraph poles back in the field entrances. They're not going to stop any Subarus if they're pushed off to the side.

April 23rd

Today's plan was very simple. I would rush up to Bungalow in the morning and get it rolled, then switch over to liquid fertiliser in the afternoon and get a whole bunch of spring barley done.

What actually happened was somewhat less productive. Mac turned up to put some 20:10:10 on Springshott. While that should seem simple enough, it inevitably means the kettle gets put on, and an hour is wasted nattering. All the usual topics were covered: the new single farm payment, the ongoing local vet situation, Trust visitors dumping in the woods (the latest manifestation of the joys of public access). Less productive, but great fun nevertheless.

By the time we finished coffee, Hazel had to go, and so I volunteered to get Mac loaded up and then take the old bale trailer down to the field with the remaining eight bags on it, and leave the tractor so he could load himself and avoid lots of trips back to the farmyard. By the time I had walked back, it was lunchtime.

After lunch I headed up to Bungalow, where I seem to have spent every waking moment of the last couple of weeks, and rolled it. Tod arrived just as I was finishing off, and we both commented on how well it looked where the overlaps meant it had been rolled twice – so I rolled the whole field again, at 90 degrees-ish to the first pass. It certainly looked a better seedbed. I stopped for a natter with neighbour Mike, who was trundling round on his lawn on an aged ride-on mower.

We had lengthy chat – he's always interested in what was going in, and what the machinery was that we had been using over the last couple for weeks. I took a chance to pick his brains on some of the history of Bungalow. Was it true, I asked, that the little grass patch in the middle of our farmyard was built using soil from Bungalow – the really fine bit of it that used to be a fruit garden? Could be, said Mike – but more likely from his father's walled garden, where the soil was six-foot deep silt brought up from Portsmouth harbour.

"And is there a Hurricane somewhere under here?"

"No!" he scoffed. "But there are the remains of a Doodlebug just over the hedge in Corbett's field. It blew up, damaging my house and the two next to it." That made sense to me. In the Sixties I was told that the plaster damage in the southern attic room of the farmhouse was cause by a bomb blast in Kilmeston. So Granny Flindt might have been right after all.

I finally got going, only for Tod to ring again, in a bit of a panic. The Volume winter barley in Big Field was going into 'survival' mode, putting out awns far too early. It was the first sign of the crops beginning to suffer after the long dry spell. There's nothing to be done for now, though, and let's not complain about the long dry spell. So I finished Bungalow, and it looked a real treat. And there's a phrase I haven't said in my thirty years here.

An evening's sheep moving beckoned, with the lambs and their mothers heading down to the bottom of Englands, leaving the non-pregnant ones and the late lambers behind in the back meadow. They moved very easily, helped by Tony's dogs. I abandoned the plans to do any fertiliser, and headed down to the Flowerpots with Robert for an evening of beer and peanuts. Again, not as productive as the original plan, but far more fun.

April 24th

The phone rang quite early. It was David, neighbouring farmer to the south of us, and the only other farming tenant on the Trust's estate. One of his barns is occupied by a local mechanic, who has built up a fine reputation as an independent garage with the ability to handle today's high-tech cars. Unfortunately, the barn he uses was broken into last night and comprehensively cleared out. The thieves smashed their way through a selection of very sturdy locks and gates, stole a Land Rover that was in for service, and filled it to the brim with everything they could find. Rather curiously they then made their way away from the remote yard using fields and gates that only someone who spends the autumn poaching across this land would know. Sheer coincidence, I'm sure.

I had a drive round to see if we'd been hit too, but there was no sign. The buggers had had to manhandle the ten-foot cultivator that had been parked in the Stanmore Lane out of the way, so it must have been a gang. Poor old David sounded quite shaken.

Then it was back to fertiliser. The drill came off, and it was back onto the sprayer, and two tanks in the afternoon, finishing the second small dose on Blackhouse Road, and doing a slow final dose on Behind My Love's.

By tea time, I'd come over all queasy (last night's beer and peanuts, probably), and decided on an early finish. We even cried off another pub trip, to the Thomas Lord for Rufus' birthday. I was asleep by nine thirty.

April 25th

Much excitement for a Saturday morning: Rod, fresh back from his long holiday in Cuba, was on his way to deliver the Kubota RTV. It was enough to get Jonathan out of bed before ten. I thought I ought to get our old ATV ready to be swapped, so I put the battery on charge, pumped up a couple of tyres, and started taking off all the paraphernalia it had collected over the years: the connections for the slug pellet spreader, the sprayer tank I had optimistically started bolting on, and the handlebar hand warmers.

I felt rather sorry for it. It has sat, not terribly loved, in the barn, coming out on rare occasions – it has only notched up 450 miles in a dozen years. Mind you, it was uncomfortable to ride, hell to start, and, like all ATVs, a constant risk to life and limb. The UTV, with its bigger dimensions, roll-bar, bench seat and steering wheel, should be more comfortable and convenient – assuming yesterday's thieves don't come back and relieve us of it first. Despite all that battery charging, the ATV failed to start, and was unceremoniously pushed round from the barn to Rod's trailer. Very rarely for me, I felt no pang of sadness as it left. I usually get irrationally fond of old machinery – but this ATV never found its way into my affections.

As usual, Rod sat down for a long cuppa and a natter – ideas of how to get out of the mess with the present Amazone sprayer flew backwards and forwards. He said he'd go away and think about them.

Back to fertiliser, ready for tonight's rain. I got the spring barley in Kilmeston Road and Hangar done. While in the Hangar, I noticed the new owner of the kennels that adjoin the field hanging over the fence eager for a chat. I stopped and we introduced each other. Within moments we got onto the subject of Trust walkers. They are heading up across the Hangar, going over her fence, and crossing her paddock on the way to the pub. When challenged, they tell her that it's a new public footpath installed by the National Trust. Some more emails will be in order, methinks – as well as the new fence we're planning round the whole of the Hangar.

The fertiliser ran out just right, and I rinsed out in the field, ready for the bleach tonight, which would mean I can safely go into the OSR with its dose, and the beans when necessary, without causing damage.

Back in the yard, just as the sprayer filled to the brim with an ominously steaming solution of hypochlorite, Bev, our nanny/mother's help from fifteen years ago, arrived with her boisterous pair of boys. That was my cue to knock off for the day, and a very noisy and unhealthy tea ensued. Far too many chocolate chip muffins.

April 26th

A nice soggy cool Sunday morning – just perfect for yet more fertiliser on the oilseed rape without scorching it. I did White Hill and Cheyney, and then did a final dose on the spring barley in Blackhouse Road. There was just enough in the main tank to do a second dose on the spring wheat in Joan's Acre and Dell Close – or there would have been if I hadn't convinced myself that there was more than enough, and upped the rate. I ran out with a tiny bit of JA left to do. Oh well – I'll be passing that way again soon.

April 27ᵗʰ

The Monday morning 'state of play' review went something like this: the fertiliser tank is empty, the spray that Tod prescribed on Thursday isn't here yet, and the pea ground is still too hard to work down. Mind you, it was lucky that there wasn't any tractor work to do; I was incapacitated after a weekend of eating the wrong thing. It wasn't just a sofa morning, it was a sofa with duvet morning.

Luckily, I was up and about again, feeling a bit better, after lunch, but had already decided that a whole day out of the tractor would be in order. So Hazel and I sat down with the maps of the farm to plan the wild bird strips that we're going to put in. They're all part of the ELS re-jig that we did, swapping overwintered stubbles, which were becoming a pain, with 25 acres of field corners and edges sown with a mix of bird-friendly crops and flowers. Rumour has it that these strips are famously pheasant-friendly, too. Luckily, my head was even clearer by the time Rod came round with another sprayer quotation. We might be getting somewhere.

By evening, I was fit enough to head down to the Fox in Bramdean, for their Open Mic Night. As usual, it's impossible to predict how these things will go, and there seemed to be a surfeit of guitarists of a good vintage jostling for position in the tiny bar corner. Dave and Richard started the evening off quietly, then there was a run of assorted fifties rockers, and then the main band came on – three guitars and a drummer. They saw Dave playing bass, and asked him to join in with them. Dave then insisted, bless him, that I was asked to join in too. I squeezed in behind my keyboard, and promptly played my socks off. It was a very raucous and late finish.

April 28ᵗʰ

A bit of a dilemma this morning. I had promised to pop next door, where my neighbour had summoned the sitting Tory MP for a grilling. However, the winter barley was romping through the growth stages, and the growth regulator had to go on – soon. I chose the latter. I texted Joe to apologise, and then rang his wife to confirm. Luckily, being farmers, they knew that spraying sometimes has to be done – especially as it looks like being the last settled day of the week.

They were probably quite grateful. My loathing of all of the mainstream parties is hardly a secret, and I would probably have wrecked the meeting by getting into my anti-EU routine. "How did Neil Kinnock, after being comprehensively rejected by the British people as their leader, end up as one of the most powerful men in Europe?" "What happened to Cast Iron Dave's referendum?" All that sort of thing.

I got the winter barley sprayed, but it has to be said that the conditions weren't perfect. A proper farmer wouldn't have worried about the wind, which was fairly strong at times, but I always have kittens about drift and the industry's image. I shook myself to pieces again in Big Field, as the tramlines go across last autumn's cultivation lines. It was made worse by the fact that I'd decided to do the whole lot with two tanks, so was running at a fairly low water rate – I plugged 125l/ha into the computer. With the nozzles I've got, that meant a low pressure at my standard spraying speed; too low

January 24th

February 2nd – the dead deer

February 3rd – snow from the back door

March 3rd – tidying up the fallen tree

March 7th – rolling the wheat

March 16th – choosing the puppy

March 19th – loading up with seed

March 20th – historic ploughing match aftermath

March 29th – barn fire on Ganderdown

March 31st – bean sowing

April 7th – rolling the bean seedbed

April 8th – hand-emptying the seed drill

April 15th – fungicide on oilseed rape

April 22nd – fertiliser on the pastures

April 22nd – evening view towards Tichborne

April 28th – mysterious black soil

April 29th – April showers

May 24th – rope bangers on the peas

June 7th – open farm Sunday

July 11th – raking up hay

July 11th – three wise heads make a decision

20th July – Was it the googly?

August 4th – spring barley in Blackhouse Road (Ali Warner Photography)

August 7th – opening up BML's

August 26th – that should keep the dust down

September 10th – late wheat combining

September 21st – equinox sunset

October 12th – perfect callibration

October 24th – poachers in White Hill

November 28th – plumbing with Monty

December 5th – poachers' handiwork

December 17th – the first partridge

for the computer, setting off its alarms. The only solution was to go faster, which was fine in Roe Hill and Clump/Rick, but a real challenge in Big Field.

Just before I started the second tank I got a call from Hinton Ampner House. This is not always good news, and spraying on a windy day in full view of Trust visitors always makes me expect an angry phone call. However, it was good news: the Trust archaeologist was in Hinton, and could he come and look at the curious feature in Blackhouse Road that I'd shown Mark the agent a couple of months ago? The only problem was that they didn't know where it was, and only had a little hatchback to travel in. It took very little persuasion to get me to turn off the tractor and volunteer to give them a lift up to Blackhouse in the Isuzu test car which I still had here.

He was intrigued. Although the lush spring barley had hidden the dramatic patch of darkened earth, we easily found brick and burnt earth. We chuckled at Dad's 'wartime secret bunker' theory, and all did lots of *Time Team* impersonations. But his verdict was fascinating. He reckoned that there was something quite significant there. He found bits of slag and clinker – evidence of something quite industrial. I pointed out that there was no evidence of anything on the maps I've looked at. "Ah," he said mysteriously. "It could be older than any of those! Ever wondered why this field is called 'Blackhouse'?" Fascinating. He said he'll be back with a geophysics team, and go from there. It is just like *Time Team*. Well, Tony, we only have three days…

On the way back to the farmyard, we met several sets of Trust walkers, shuffling with assorted haste along the lanes. We slowed down and gave them a wide berth, and were rewarded for our troubles with nothing but cold, bitter glares. I think Lou from the Trust was somewhat surprised.

The 'two-tank' theory on the winter barley worked out perfectly, so I rinsed out in the field, ready for switching back to yet more fertiliser if it turns unsettled. The winter barley in particular looks like it is outgrowing its supply, and has gone a sickly pale green. I might be straight in again tomorrow, going over those lumps and bumps again. Oh well.

April 29th

Another two-places-at-once dilemma. There was another meeting at Sparsholt College to discuss crime issues, which would be followed by an update on our Rural Payment Scheme forms. Both of these are issues close to my heart, but there was another whole bunch of fertiliser to go on, and the conditions – sunshine and showers – were perfect. So I chose the tractor-based option, having rung the NFU to apologise for missing the meeting.

Just before I set off, Rod rang back with yet another offer on changing the sprayer. It was so good, it took me by complete surprise, and I must have sounded very rude, insisting that I had to go and think about it for a bit. By the time I was halfway through the final dose on all the winter barley, I realised that I ought to get on and ring him back to apologise for looking a gift horse in the mouth, and agree to the deal. So I did.

By late in the evening, the winter barleys were all done (joining the oilseed rape and the spring barley), leaving the wheats as the only crops without complete fertiliser. I made a mental note to check what the recommended rates were for the assorted wheats before ordering what might be the last lorry load.

April 30th

It dawned on me that those beans in Bungalow might have come through – they'd been in ten days, and the soil was mighty warm when they went in. So I jumped into the Isuzu (which had had its loan period extended until after the bank holiday) and drove up there. There wasn't a bean to be seen, even after extensive digging. My pre-emergence prescription was still valid.

There was also a fairly lively WSW wind, which would be perfect for the application of a whiffy cocktail of Stomp and Defy, keeping the smell away from the houses. It was a fairly awkward job in the end – Hazel and I had chosen the Eastern bank as the site for a wild bird strip, so I had to avoid spraying that bit. I used the satnav to create a new headland 24 metres in and then set about the rest of the field. Just for once, it didn't go entirely to plan, and I had misjudged the amount of water in the tank and ran out in the short work nearest the road. It was only a couple of very short turns, and would make an interesting little trial. I was certainly not planning to pop home and fill up with about ten litres of mix.

We spent lunchtime preparing for the visit of some Rural Payments Agency trainees. We'd agreed to help our ACCS inspector, who organises training sessions at Sparsholt College for anyone who might end up involved in dealing with farmers. His latest batch was from the RPA, so we jumped at the chance to take them round a hopeless farm.

Hazel nipped down to Bramdean House to shamelessly raid their supply of chairs and their tea urn, and I photocopied the farm map and made some guidance notes. By the time they arrived and we piled them into the old shoot shed, laid out with tea, coffee and custard creams, it looked quite welcoming.

I had absolutely no idea what was required of me for the talk, so I just stood up and described our farm, our lives, our hopes and problems, and what we thought the future held. They seemed to enjoy it, they laughed at the funny bits, and seemed to take on board some of our problems. I apologised on behalf of farmers everywhere if the RPA staff had been shouted at – which I bet they had.

After an hour in the shed, we wandered round the yard, talked through some of the machinery, and cuddled Sasha who had come out to greet everyone. Graeme the ACCS man seemed pleased enough with the visit, and after handshakes and a kind round of applause, they set off back to Sparsholt. I'll probably never know how useful I was to them.

I headed off to the doctor's at Medstead for the follow-up appointment to discuss all the tests I'd had the other day. Great lungs, but we're worried about the heart, was the verdict. Was there any history of heart trouble in the family, I was asked. It killed my father and grandfather, so I had to say 'yes'. One mention of the jaw ache I get after moderate walking was enough to provoke a flurry of appointments and recommendations for more tests and investigations. Hmmm.

On a more positive note, lambing finished.

May 1st

May's here but it was still bloomin' cold. On the list of things that should really be done before the bank holiday were the peas (although they really don't want to be sown into wet and cold ground), a bit of spraying (not urgent yet), and three loads of fertiliser still in the main tank.

There was also the July motoring copy to send in to *The Field* a bit sharp-ish, because the new-look skeleton staff up there get in a bit of a panic about late submission. So I polished that off early in the morning, and had it down the wires at four minutes to eight.

The fertiliser should have been a quick job, but I was finishing off Top and Bottom of Hurst Down, doing an unfinished length of Joan's Acre, and then trying to do the whole of Folly – all on one tank. Not surprisingly, it was lunchtime before I got all that geographically diverse set done. Over lunch, I checked with Tod what the nitrogen rates were for spring sown winter wheat and proper spring wheat, and did some sums on the kitchen table. He recommended 200 kg/ha for the winter wheat, and slightly less – 180 kg/ha – for the spring wheat, so I totted up what would be needed once the main tank is empty again. It came to another lorry and a bit, so I ordered another lorry-load. They offered to deliver over the weekend, but I said I needed a weekend without anything to do.

I headed up to Stanmore to do the block of Claire, and was greatly cheered up by the state of the crop. Good old Claire; we've been growing it for decades, and it loves early drilling, tillers like crazy, and this year is the only cereal that looks like it should look on the first day of May. I ran out of fertiliser on the very last bit of Stanmore Broom and did a quick in-tank water rinse, and drove home as quickly as I could: Jonathan's cricket season started tonight.

After a quick sandwich and a cup of tea, we set off for West End, another part of Solent City that was once a village outside Southampton. It is now an almost uninterrupted sea of modern estates – not ugly, but somehow ruthlessly conformist, right down to the road names: 'Lark Close', 'Sparrow Avenue', 'Dingly Dell Lane'. I suppose it's good to acknowledge that it was once countryside.

Poor old Jonathan. He went in to face the third ball of a potential hat-trick, being bowled by a wily Asian off-break bowler who was having the game of his life. Being left handed, Jonathan was facing a leg-break bowler, and, even though he stopped the hat-trick, lost his off bail to his second ball, and trudged back off. When the time came to field, he was despatched to the boundary, and I really thought that was that. I was sitting on the boundary in the semi-darkness, freezing my nuts off in a biting northerly wind, reflecting on the lot of the keen cricket parent whose boy seems to be mediocre, if enthusiastic. I was destined to travel round the county to watch second ball ducks and two throws to the keeper in the course of a long evening.

Luckily, he was given a couple of overs to bowl, and it was a delight. None of the traditional teenage overlong run-up and scatter gun 'fast' bowling. It was three paces, and fantastic upright slow action, bowling well-placed leg-breaks. The only runs he did give away were off outside edges down to third man. A thrill to watch. I still needed some hot food and a very hot shower when we got home. Is it really May?

May 2nd

The farming-free bank holiday weekend started with a trip to the hospital for an X-ray on Jonathan's lower back – even though it hadn't troubled him on the pitch yesterday. There's much debate about his stance and posture – the osteopath he saw recently insisted that there is a problem in his hips, while I think he's growing like a weed, and at the same time refusing to stand up straight. I sound like my father.

Private medical insurance is a huge monthly bill. Is it worth it? We took it out when the family started, and pay it religiously, but is it still needed? Back when my own back started to creak and fall apart, an X-ray session in Winchester hospital was like a visit to Soviet Russia in the 1960s – chaotic organisation, vast queues that made a mockery of appointment times, and X-rays getting lost. A trip to a private hospital made the extra money worth every penny.

Today's trip was the same – the hospital is quiet, free parking, and we were in and out within minutes. The dilemma is that the NHS has caught up so much. My trip to the walk-in hospital near Alton a few weeks ago was just as easy and organised. Is 'private' still worth the money? I once discussed this with a surgeon who came on the old shoot. His theory was that successive governments had hosed down the NHS with money, determined to cut the dreaded 'waiting times' (often using, ironically, the private hospitals to cut backlogs), and had done a great job. His warning was that it might not be ever thus, and holding onto private medical was still a good move, perhaps with some adjustments of excess payment and so on. Luckily, a couple of good years on the farm have meant that we're not looking to cut back on such things just yet.

May 3rd

Finally, the Thomas Lord Old Gits' 'Mudansha' Tour started at The Bull in Bentley. Those who know their martial arts will spot that 'Mudansha' is the term for those who are without a 'dan' in judo. We are without Dan (an incredibly talented guitarist and vocalist, who decided he'd had enough of old men playing songs from the Seventies, and left us) so it seemed the perfect name for the tour.

Without Dan, we're down to five in the band. We still outnumbered the audience. According to the landlord, everyone was in the other bar, and thought we were very good. Hmm.

May 4th

The frenzy of gigs continued with the Star Wars Gig (hey, if it's funny once, it's funny a hundred times), at The Fox in Bramdean. Somehow, we'd been allocated the afternoon slot, and the outside tent. So, in the freezing cold wind of a May bank holiday, we played our hearts out to a couple of dozen punters who had dropped into a country pub for a peaceful pie and a pint. Highlight of the gig was looking up to see a row of four nippers, watching slack jawed and utterly unmoved by our artistic endeavours.

Oh well. We enjoyed ourselves. And that's what counts.

May 5th
I definitely overdid it at the weekend. All attempts to start the big overhaul of the feet of the Horsch CO3 floundered in a sort of hungover mist. It didn't help that I didn't have exactly the right bits of kit that I needed. The internet beckoned, and I managed to track down what I needed and order it. By lunchtime, however, I gave up altogether, and headed for the sofa. It worked its miracles again, and by the evening I was fit enough to head down the pub with Robert. Good thing I'm self-employed.

May 6th
These are the days of instant shopping, of instant ordering, of 'it'll be there tomorrow!'. Only sometimes it isn't there tomorrow. I stayed in and around the house all day today, waiting for the oversized pop rivet gun that I'd ordered yesterday to arrive. I stripped down the last of the Horsch Duett coulters, and then put the new base plates on. And all the time I was on tiptoes, looking over the gate for the DPD van that was due to swing into the yard and deliver the crucial new toy that was needed to pop the new plastic side plates on.

By late afternoon, I resorted to getting out all the paperwork for our BPS scheme, and getting my head round how to fill in the new forms. The big question is about mapping: how many maps are we going to have to laboriously draw and submit? The tracks around the outside of, say, Blackhouse Road are now 'eligible', but because the boundary between them and the field itself is permanent, a map seems to be in order. Or does it? Further advice is needed.

By early evening, there was still no sign of any pop riveter, so I hit the phones. DPD knew just from my phone number that a parcel was due here, but the nice lady said that there was no sign of it in their system. I logged onto the Amazon website, put in a phone number, and pressed 'ring me now'; within five seconds my phone rang. Astonishing.

The nice lady at the other end was oh so sorry, but mostly incomprehensible; I think I got her message (apart from being oh so sorry) that I'd get more free 'Prime' membership and blah blah blah. Fantastic PR and crisis management, but all I wanted was my pop riveter.

The next call was to neighbour Robert, who of course had an oversize pop riveter, and I was free to borrow it. I should call in tomorrow, but make sure it's late morning – they're electro-ejaculating the bull in the early morning. At least, I think that was what he said.

May 7th

I like my breakfast. I have a big breakfast: a big bowl of porridge, lots of (soya) milk, and disgraceful lashings of brown sugar. And, to follow, three poached eggs and three slices of bacon. And three cups of tea. Rather sadly, it's the same every morning, but it's probably a Flindt thing.

So if I have to skip my morning feast, there has to be a good reason. This morning's trip to the doctor's was a good enough reason; more blood tests were needed in the hunt for whatever is making me feel knackered, and these blood tests had to be 'fasting' tests. Thanks to the huge tea I had yesterday, I made it to the surgery without fainting – and even got through the needle-in-vein bit (which has sent me crashing to the floor before) without incident. So the feast of porridge and bacon and eggs had to wait until eleven-ish, and somehow they didn't taste quite right. I had them all anyway.

I rang Robert to see if he'd finished fluffing the bulls – he had, and so I nipped down to Tichborne to pick up the riveter, and had a very jolly afternoon giving my shoulders a good work out, riveting the new plastic side plates onto the Horsch drill coulters. Unfortunately, the wrong number of rivets had been sent out, and I ran out.

So Hazel and I went lopping along the bottom headland of Chalks. We put a big bale on the blue trailer, tuned up the chainsaw-on-a-stick, and worked our way along under the four or five trees that now present a danger to tractor lights and exhaust pipes, not to mention leaving green patches of unripe corn underneath them. It's a bit of ground destined for a wild bird strip, but it's a job that needs doing. Once we'd done that, I dropped the sprayer off, put the plough on, and finally finished that headland. It was a good chance to shine up the plough before a long period without work.

Then the main business of the day began. Rufus had cried off the all-night General Election party, but the Editor was keen to stay up for a bit, so we headed down the pub to get warmed up. We were on the sofas, fire lit, popcorn and takeout beer ready by eleven – he had a brace of adoring dogs on his lap for good measure.

We abandoned at about two in the morning, safe in the knowledge that the appalling left-wing know-it-all intelligentsia had been utterly ridiculed by the results as they came in. All the pundits, pollsters and predictors had turned out to be completely wrong. It was turning out to be a great evening – and I don't normally like the Tories.

May 8th

I spent the whole morning watching the live coverage of the election results, relishing the bloodbath. By lunchtime, Cameron had a majority ("no way!" the experts had said – including Ladbrokes, who last week were offering 13/2 on it). Three leader of political parties has resigned, and the BBC spent the whole day in funereal mode. Joy of joys.

Hazel, on yet another hike round the county getting children to where they should be, called in at Oakes Bros and picked up more rivets – but not the complete set. I thought I'd get most of the worst part of the job done, and refitted the eight overhauled coulters to the Horsch. It's always a challenge, rolling round on an exercise mat, trying not to bang your head or injure your back while wielding sockets spanners and extension bars. I got the vast majority of it done, ready for bashing in the peas.

In the meantime, Robert Raimes had flown in with his Carrier, and given the ploughed land in Chalks a good working down. The rest of the rivets were then delivered by an Oakes Bros man on his way home, and my internet purchase riveter arrived too – two days late. But now there's no excuse for not getting going tomorrow.

May 9th

A windy night led to a blustery and quite wet morning, perfect for a Saturday lie-in to catch up after the election shenanigans. The sun burst through at lunchtime, and it dawned on me that conditions would be perfect for getting the peas in. I had to do another hour's maintenance – getting the last of the overhauled coulters on, and then repairing yet another bent marker arm. I seem to have gone through a heck of a lot of these recently. This latest replacement is made of much thicker tube that the last ones – I wonder if Horsch knocked it up especially for me?

After a calibration and a grease up, I headed out to Chalks. The first thing I had to do was mark out the two wild bird strips at the top and bottom, which I did by 'sowing' 12 m of headland with the seed turned off. Once I'd done that, I was able to crack on with sowing proper, and the conditions were just about perfect. The rain on the ground that Robert had worked down with the Carrier yesterday could not have been nicer. I got the headland done, started the land work at the bottom, and ran out of seed just as the low sun was making drilling east-west slightly difficult. Home for tea.

May 10th

Fellow bad-back sufferers will know exactly what I mean when I talk about 'the moment'. It's the instant when you realise that three or four days of suffering lie ahead – the moment your back 'goes'. Mine has a horrible habit of 'going' under the meekest and mildest of circumstances: a slight change in position when driving, for instance, or reaching the wrong way in the combine cab. It never happens when wielding a sledgehammer or lifting a 2cwt sack.

This morning, Hazel was about to set off with Monty to another Sunday morning flatcoat masterclass in the New Forest. Her Skoda has a slow puncture on the rear left tyre, so I decided to pump it up for her. You may think that that was when today's injury occurred – but no. We were checking the pressure tables on the inside of the fuel filler cap. I leant forward just slightly – and there it was. A slight popping sensation about three vertebrae up from the bottom, and that's it. I knew I was now due for a few hours of mild pain, and then it would all seize up in a spasm, and a good couple of days could almost certainly be written off.

Unfortunately, there were peas still needing to be sown – so it was off to meet my great friend Mr Paracetamol and his cousin Mr Voltarol, who comes in a tube. I used to use Mr Ibuprofen – my whole rugby career was done hand-in-hand with him – but

I think fifteen years of several a day finally trashed my gut. With them swallowed and applied, I managed to finish sowing the peas in Chalks. It even worked out pretty well, with probably 100 kg left in the bottom, which I used to double drill the northern headland – the clay had baked out horribly despite yesterday's morning rain.

While the painkillers were still working, I brought the drill home, walked down to pick up the seed trailer and the Massey, and headed back out with the rollers. I did all the tramlines and all the heavy land at the top – Hazel wanted to finish it tomorrow, so I thought I'd leave her the filling-in bits. Then it was off to the sofa to feel very sorry for myself.

Mind you, not as sorry as Ali down at Blackhouse Farm. A nasty accident with a hand-held blender and her left index finger has us all doing the sharp-intake-of-breath routine.

May 11th

Not a good night's sleep. Back pain, something slamming doors at 3am (no one owned up to it) and the bloomin' dawn chorus not long after that. It was definitely an office morning.

I ordered 6 hectares' worth of Wild Bird Mix for the shooting strips, managed to get an appointment with Jane the physio for Wednesday, did lots of email replies, and then had Rod and the man from Amazone come round to try and finally sort out the exact spec on the new sprayer. It's never simple – the tyres will be different, more spool valves will be needed, and inevitably, more money will be required over and above what Rod and I had agreed. I asked for a week or so to consider my options. Not that I have any real choice in the matter

Another batch of pills'n'cream gave me a few more hours, so I hitched the drill off, and put the sprayer back on ready for another influx of work. I booked Tosdevine to do the oilseed rape, not just because his high-clearance machine is probably the best thing for the rapidly growing canopy, but also to give me a couple more days to recover. He promised he'd be in tomorrow, if the morning stays dry.

Hazel finished rolling in the peas, and the field looked an absolute treat. As is traditional, I just had to text the Editor to tell him of the impending pigeon frenzy. Rather cruel of me to do so on a Monday. Will he be able to wait until the weekend?

May 12th

As ever, a bad back isn't a one-day ailment, and I was feeling very sorry for myself this morning. Graham Tosdevine had texted late last night to say his sprayerman would be in first thing, but a breakfast-time glance at the wonderful rainfall radar suggested that it would be worth waiting until late morning. There were showers lurking in Hampshire which looked meaty enough to wash an expensive cocktail of chemical straight off the leaves of the OSR. Luckily, Graham is incredibly flexible, and agreed to wait a few hours.

You have to marvel at how we get our weather info these days. A hundred years ago, the farmer looked out of his window at dawn, and made an informed guess based on what he saw, using his years of experience – and gut instinct. TV and radio brought weather forecasts – I remember the solemn silence that was vital as the weatherman spoke his predictions. These days, the weather forecast has descended into light entertainment, with the 'forecasters' frantically overegging their performances, desperate to get that daytime TV quiz show job. So, what do we farmers do first thing in the morning? We look through a frame of glass for inspiration, just like our ancestors did – OK, it's a computer monitor rather than the bedroom window, but in a way, we've come full circle.

By late morning, the weather looked more settled, and the job got done after lunch. It was a small victory, but little consolation as I lay on the sofa waiting for the painkillers to work.

May 13ᵗʰ

A perfect spraying day (quite a frost early on), but I was off to Jane the Physio mid-morning, to try and get this back sorted out again. Jane spent most of the session ranting and raving about the evils of big private medicine companies – she has just fallen out with the biggest, and will be turning down their business from now on. Mind you, she always puts an extra 50% into her kneading and probing when she's ranting, so I think every bit of spine and rib was back where it should have been within ten minutes. I was certainly feeling well enough to get back in the tractor as soon as I got home, and headed out to do the vital pre-emergence spray on the peas in Chalks.

This job presented a challenge. It's just the one field of peas, so there's no extra chemical in the store if I run out too soon. I know what the drill reckoned the size of the field was, but would the sprayer agree? I'd drilled the field across the slope, so the drill will have drifted down the hill a bit, but how much? Enough to mean considerable overlap, but was it enough to justify shutting off the end nozzles? I looked at how much water was in the sprayer, divided it by the drill acreage, wound it back by a couple of litres per hectare, and set off.

Just as I got onto the short work on the top of the hill, something told me I wouldn't have enough, so I hit the 'cut by ten per cent' button on the controller, and had the huge satisfaction of the sprayer running out right in the very last corner. It's a delight when farming instincts work. A quick flush of clean water round the headland, and Chalks was all set for the deluge that is promised tomorrow.

I had planned to try and get all the late wheats sprayed as well, but news that Dave the Bass wanted to launch the new blues band tonight meant a short evening. In the end, I only got one tank on, on Top and Bottom of Hurst Down. There's half an hour's travelling to be done to get there and back, and I lost another ten minutes helping some residents of Brockwood Park get a grip of the concept of private land. It was five o'clock when I got back – no time to get another tank on.

The new blues band session went well – even if there was far too much Bob Dylan going on. Steve the Uberguitarist brought along his mate Doug to join in with me and Dave, and we had a very jolly couple of hours in Shed 3b running through an amazing selection of songs, including, joy of joys, Green Onions. The Hammond clone organ coming into its own at last.

May 14th

A proper wet day. Real good, heavy rain – and there's a phrase I never thought I'd use again. It started slightly later than forecast, at about 9am, but then went on for most of the day, with a pause in mid-afternoon. Perfect for those peas: sown on Saturday/Sunday, rolled on Sunday and Monday, sprayed on Wednesday and a deluge on Thursday.

Perfect, too, for sitting down and taking a good look at the new SPS forms. There were a couple of questions that had been bothering me. We have lots of tracks and grass strips round the outside of our fields. These were ineligible under the old scheme, but are now eligible. However, any boundary between something temporary (i.e. a crop) and something permanent (which I assumed would include a grass strip) has to be measured and mapped. I thought I'd ring the NFU helpline to check what the exact procedure is – the last thing I need is to have to do a new map for just about very field.

The NFU had good news. Strips of grass round the outside, including tracks and footpaths, could be assumed to be part of the main field. That would make life much easier. What about our EF2 wild bird strips? What should the code be for them? The NFU's answer was even better: these, too, can be assumed to be part of the whole of the field – as long as they don't make up too large a proportion of the field. So, once again, no mapping, no measuring – a whole lot less hassle.

Relieved that the whole job might be turning out to be a lot less trouble than we all thought it would be, I shoved all the forms back in their envelopes in a joyful act of procrastination, and headed down the pub with neighbour Robert.

May 15th

Everything was still nicely drenched after yesterday's rain, but by late morning the leaves had dried out enough to get the herbicide on the late drilled wheats. I finished the Top of Hurst Down, did Joan's Acre and Dell Close, and then, after lunch, did Drier Field, and then called an early finish.

It was off to St Cross Cricket Club to watch them take on Jonathan and the rest of his Ropley teammates. It was cold and drizzly – very satisfying for those of us who had stopped spraying mid-afternoon – and quite dark by the time Ropley wrapped up a good victory over the prestigious Winchester side.

May 16th

A bright but very breezy Saturday – breezy enough to rule out spraying. So it was a big hello to Mr Sofa for the BTCC highlights, interrupted only by yet another visit from the Editor, on fruitless pigeon patrol. I also tried to fit the new battery on the recently-bought Kubota UTV (it keeps mysteriously going flat), but Gaskin's had sent the wrong one.

An evening walk showed that the peas in Chalks have inch-long shoots, despite only being in for six days. As soon as they peek through, that's when the pigeons will really move in. The spring beans in the Godwin's block have leapt another couple of inches and look magnificent. An evening browsing *Farmers Weekly* and its dour outlook for prices soon brought me down to earth.

May 17th

One heck of a dilemma: the wind had dropped, the weather was perfect for starting on the five pages of spray recommendations that Tod had sent through the other day, and the forecast for the best part of next week is not good. I should have jumped into the tractor and set off, without a backwards glance.

However, I had signed Jonathan up to play in his first ever game of cricket for the White Hunters, and I had agreed to keep him company and do some umpiring, and probably have a few beers. It was a case of 'cricketing vs farming'.

Cricket, of course, won. We set off through the stunning valleys of the Hampshire Hangars to Hawkley, and found a selection of motley cricketers of varying size, age, and quality. It had to be the White Hunters. After a lunchtime pint, we adjourned to the lovely pitch, and enjoyed English cricket at its very best: admirable levels of incompetence mixed with a good-natured attitude, but with just enough competitiveness to make sure it was a game. Jonathan bowled a bit, fielded well, and batted for just the one run. He didn't make a fool of himself in any department, which in White Hunter cricket, makes you a bit of a star.

Even my umpiring seemed to go well. No controversy, no temper tantrums (not from me, anyway), and much friendly handshaking in the evening as the last White Hunter wicket fell pathetically with a small matter of a hundred runs needed.

It was enough to make me determined to get back into full whites, but I'll be needing that new hip (or two) that I've been promising myself, and a six-month 'get fit' campaign. Trouble is, sitting in the club bar downing a couple of pints of Moondance complete with peanuts isn't the best way of starting a 'get fit' campaign.

May 18th

A windy and wet Monday morning, as forecast. No farming possible, except for more office stuff, but with tonight's heart examination, I couldn't concentrate too much. And I was feeling a bit sorry for myself after yesterday's efforts – seventy overs of concentration and standing.

Much of the day seemed to be spent on the phone sorting out medical stuff. I finally got some feedback from the doctor on the hip and lower back X-rays that Jonathan had had a couple of weeks ago. Everything looks normal, apparently, which backs up my verdict based on watching him run round a pitch a couple times. He's just growing like a weed, and taking time to catch up with himself.

The next job was to get authorisation numbers for tonight's heart examination. The whole family is subscribed to one of the country's leading private medical insurance companies, at full whack (although they claim we're on a discount, organising it through the NFU). We don't do any excess agreements, or any other tweaks that might drop our bill; we pay a good few hundred quid every month, without fail.

But the curious thing is that the insurance company seems to be reluctant to pay out these days. I had a mini-op on my spine a couple of years ago, and ended up paying for the anaesthetist. Jane the Physio announced she's leaving them after another wave of bureaucratic nonsense. Diana's therapist, who is helping out with post-A level issues, announced the same.

So I wasn't terribly surprised when I rang them this morning, fought my way through the labyrinth of phone options, finally got to the treacly-voiced operative, and was told that the man I was off to see was on their 'sharp intake of breath' list. On this list are medical professionals that the insurance company will not pay in full.

Now, I'm just a farmer, so I don't get the whys and wherefores, the politics and economics behind this decision; all I know is that my GP keeps suggesting we go to higher medical authorities, and despite being insured up to what I would consider the eyeballs, I seem to end up paying.

I finally got my 'authorisation number', but it came with caveats of more phone calls being needed if more work or tests were needed.

In the end, no further tests were needed. The charming heart specialist took a look at the ECG that had been sent through, listened to my chest for a bit and did some ultrasound scanning. He then pronounced my heart to be strong and healthy. We had a very jolly session, having turned on the 'sound' that goes with the ultrasound, debating if the noise was the intro to 'Voodoo Child' by Hendrix or 'Is This a Love Thing?' by Raydio. His final verdict (medical, not musical) was for me to get a steroid inhaler to beat the wheezing. He did suggest some exercise, but we glossed over that silly idea nice and quickly. Then it was back home for chips, ginger cake and alcoholic ginger beer.

May 19th

Another medical-ish morning, this time to the dentist in Winchester, for a six-month check-up. No hygienist this time (how did the world go round without them?), and no trouble to report, apart from being scolded for over-butch brushing pushing the gums down. All very dull.

Trundling back along the lovely Parchment Street, I spotted the world's emptiest barbers, complete with a rather optimistic sign outside saying 'Book your appointment now!' I popped my head round the door, and asked if I actually needed an appointment, or could I have get a cut now. "Of course you can have a cut now," said the nice lady, turning off her laptop, on which she'd been catching up with the latest from *Emmerdale*. I had the world's fastest haircut, shortish round the sides, and almost untouched on top. It should do for another few months.

Hazel needed some fencing done in the back meadow – the cattle have to go out soon, even though the cold days aren't providing much in the way of lush pasture. We hitched on the new post banger and headed for the far corner, where we pummelled in, with varying degrees of accuracy, a corner post and few normal posts. We then repaired a top strand next to the dell, and the field was once again cattle proof.

It was then back to the office for a lengthy session making up cash flows. We're not far away from Peak Overdraft, and some convincing (if not entirely accurate) spending projections will be needed for the bank manager.

May 20th

The day was well planned: it was to be fine and dry, so a long session spraying was in order. The puppy decided to change things, however, by chewing a lump of lead (as in the toxic metal, not the bit of string you attach to the collar). She'd been enjoying the sun, lying on top of the drain cover, and decided to chomp a bit off the corner while she was there. I realised what she was doing as I passed the open back door – I immediately tried to get the bit out of her mouth, but Sasha, being a puppy, scooted off with her tail tucked between her legs, and swallowed the offending lump.

I pondered this for a moment; inert lead should be no problem, but what about stomach acids and lead? A quick call to Graeme the vet was needed. "Bring her in," he said. "We'll get it out of her!"

Hazel was taking Diana up to work at the playgroup, so her car and the cage were unavailable. I carried the other huge sleeping cage into the back of Tigger, persuaded Sasha into it, and we shot off to Alresford. There was a sense of urgency from Graeme and his team, as we weighed her, and he gave her what seemed like a tiny injection. We then adjourned to the back yard, and a hastily spread out square of old newspaper. After a moment's waiting, the whole of Sasha's breakfast emerged on to yesterday's racing results. Graeme donned some blue gloves, and had a rummage; sure enough, out had come a slither of silvery grey metal. Mission accomplished. Off he went to sort out the next emergency. The nice Welsh nurse and I chatted while Sasha made an astonishing recovery, cuddling up to the nurse to show there were no hard feelings. We were home before Hazel.

The wind was still too strong for spraying, and Hazel had put many hours work into making a run so the big cattle could get from Godwin's barn to the Back Meadow via the muck heap corner, so we thought we'd get on with that. It went almost perfectly, with only one old girl looking like she fancied a run across the beans in Godwin's. Always a nice feeling when all that preparation works.

I'd emailed the bank manager, suggesting that we needed to talk about the cash-flow limit. We were on the point of tripping over our existing one, and thought we'd do better to discuss our needs before we set off all the alarms. He was on the phone within minutes, saying he had a cancellation tomorrow – could he come round then? I was happy, but realised I had better get on and finally come up with a cash-flow forecast – always a fun job. I got half of it done before getting utterly fed up, and realised that the wind had dropped enough to go spraying.

I managed to get Big Field and Rick/Clump done, and was just finishing the latter when Hazel rang to say that the blues band were in the yard, waiting to get going, I'd forgotten all about it – I was sure Dave was still giving it large in Cannes with his other band, Different Place. I told them to get set up, and wolfed some tea, and joined them twenty minutes later. We ran through a list of blues classics, talked through a couple of gig opportunities, but still are short of some basics, like a drummer and a name. No doubt both will appear eventually.

May 21st

In Friday's *Farmers Weekly* there was a long letter from someone whose life was being made unbearable by gas bangers, pleading for their more responsible use. I remarked to Hazel that this was the first winter and spring I could remember when I haven't been disturbed by one.

At 5.05am, I was woken by the distinctive triple thump of a gas banger – a long way away, but enough to disturb me. Inevitable really. The dawn chorus was also in full flow, so I abandoned sleeping well before six and headed down for an early breakfast. The mist was still in the valley, so I took a picture for the now very busy Facebook page.

The consequence of all this early activity was that I was ready to spray as soon as the dew was off – I should get up early every day, like a proper farmer. I nipped out and did Roe Hill, which, for a field that was at one stage on the point of being Rounded-up and ploughed in, looked a treat.

It was warm and sunny, we had an hour to spare, so it was perfect for the livestock event of the year: calf turnout. Not quite the drama of thirty years ago, when eighty or more were released from the claustrophobic and overcrowded calf pens into the back meadow, but still fun, as Hazel's dozen gingerly tripped out from the new barn to meet the old girls who had got out there yesterday, ran around for a bit, ran back into the barn, back out again, and then decided it was too hot, so stopped running around and grazed. That's why it's best done on a hot day.

I headed indoors too, for more creative maths with the cash-flow forecast for the bank manager, who was on his way to discuss the overdraft renewal. He arrived a bit late – the major roadworks on the road past Springshott held him up. I should have rung them in to the local radio station for a laugh – the most significant thing to happen in Hinton Ampner since the Roundheads marched through on their way to the Battle of Cheriton in March 1644.

We chatted for a bit, did lots of small talk, and then I pitched for our substantial increase in borrowings. It's still tiny compared to most farmers, but we tenants have to work harder – there's no vast tract of Hampshire land to borrow against. But I made a great song and dance about how many acres we've got sown (true – the most ever), how good everything looks (true), how hard we'd worked this spring (true), and how confident I was of a barn-bursting harvest (nearly true). We wouldn't know until later in the day what the bank computer said, and it seems to run the show.

Off to Blackhouse Farm to pick up poor old Ali, who had got a swollen knee to go with her partially severed finger. She also has a husband who can't drive at the moment, so I volunteered to take her up to Basingstoke for a private appointment. What should have been a short trip ended up taking the whole afternoon, and scans and further tests were needed. I sat in Tigger and listened to the cricket and dozed, so had a nice peaceful afternoon. They were suitably grateful when we got back, so there's a favour in the bank for later.

Late in the evening, munching fish and chips and browsing *British Farmer and Grower*, I read of the farmer charging the public a tenner a head to watch cattle turnout. We missed a trick there.

May 22nd

The day was perfectly planned: two tanks of spray before lunch on the people-heavy spring barley in Kilmeston Road and Hangar (important to get them done before the bank holiday), and then two tanks on the rest – Blackhouse Road and Behind My Love's. There would then have been enough time to nip out and get a bonus tank on the wheat somewhere. I hadn't counted on the weather, which, despite the earnest promises of dry skies by the Met Office ladies (still available to view in all their cocktail-dresses glory, thanks to the internet), turned thoroughly damp. It was more than just damp, it was a heavy drizzle from about nine until well after lunch. Hugely frustrating, having lost a good day yesterday doing my Kindly Neighbour routine.

As it happened, I was struck by a vicious headache and gut rot that ruled me out of any tractor work. Not sure if the frustration caused it, or if it was something I ate. Luckily, by mid-afternoon, everything had cleared, and I nipped out to Kilmeston Road and got that done. The leaves were still a bit damp from the earlier rain, and the clouds threatened more at any time, but I think I got it on with enough of a dry window.

Back to proud cricket Dad in the evening, to watch Jonathan at Ropley, batting beautifully but still somewhat missing the concept to being hungry for runs. Attempts to coach him in that department just after he'd come off the pitch did not go down well.

May 23rd

A windy and dull Saturday – not weather for farming. So I didn't. I did help the Editor get set up for some shooting over the newly emerging peas, but he abandoned after an hour or so – they obviously aren't that hungry. I had a good sofa day, enjoying the cricket.

May 24th

There was talk of rain or drizzle this afternoon, so I thought I ought to get on and polish off the late fertiliser on some of the wheats. So, after putting a few rope bangers out in Chalks, I set off up to Stanmore, on the early drilled Claire. Most of it was already well in ear, so I'm not sure what use the late dose of nitrogen will be – it might boost protein, I suppose, but I suspect it's too late to have any yield effect. Should have got up here earlier. I did it all anyway, aided by some riveting cricket on the radio. It was exciting enough for me to keep going later than I had originally planned, and did BOMS as well. The next job might be the herbicide on the beans, so I did a bleach fill up and left it to clean overnight.

May 25th

Bank holiday – again. I did a rinse out of the bleach, and then finished off the fertiliser, running round all the late wheats. It left most of them on a total of around 170–180 kg/ha, which might not seem enough, but it should be safe to add the 20 kg/ha or so of residual nitrogen from the previous bean and pea crops, bringing the total up to something more respectable. Most of them aren't going to be barn-fillers, and there aren't many tillers per square metre, so that should be a suitable dose. We'll see. I had an enthusiasm by-pass after tea, and headed home with the last dregs of the big tank on board. I'll spread what's left on Folly tomorrow.

Hazel and Jonathan set about Tigger with brush, vacuum and pressure washer, getting it ready for MOT tomorrow. I hardly recognised it. Late evening, we nipped up to North's Garage, and dropped it off. It's always a tense time; I don't look after Tigger very well, and it's not the sturdiest off-roader ever built, so there's usually an advisory or ten with suspension ball joints and rubbers.

May 26th

I so nearly got the Folly absolutely right – there was an undosed bit of headland next to the road down to Springshott, but I was buggered if I'm ordering another cubic metre or two just for that. If I were doing another 30 kg all round I could sort it, but cash flow suggests that quite enough fertiliser has been bought this year. I did get a lovely burst of drizzle in the middle of it, which is a handy anti-scorch measure.

Then it was back to spraying, and a long day doing long-distance stuff. There was fungicide on Stanmore (we abandoned the straw stiffener as the ears are so far out), and then the broadleaf weed killer on the Godwin's beans. They look as good as any beans I've ever grown, and I don't think I've even seen Godwin's Park look so good. Let's hope they continue like that for another few months.

I took a break to go and fetch Tigger, which had amazingly passed its MOT. As suspected, there were plenty of advisories, but no mention of the expensive propshaft replacement that was mooted by the garage at the last service. It certainly rumbles a lot on the road now, so it should be done at some stage.

I managed to negotiate Godwin's, the most footpath-laden corner of the farm, without upsetting anyone, which, on a fine if breezy May afternoon and evening, is a bonus. A good end to a good day. I'm knackered.

May 27th

It was supposed to be the last decent day for spraying for a bit, so I cracked on reasonably early, heading up to Bungalow to finish the spring beans. It looked fantastic – even and healthy, with only some small patches of rook grazing. It's even better when you remember it was sown with manky old re-cleaned seed that had been sitting round the Drier barns for two – or it is three? – years, being moved from floor to pit to trailer, getting mankier and mankier.

Then it was over the Hangar for a good dose of all sorts, and the wind had just begun to swing round to the WSW, perfect for not upsetting the locals down there. After lunch it was two more tanks on the spring barley, finishing Blackhouse Road and Behind My Love's. The wind was getting up a bit, almost over my limit for spraying, but really wanted to get it all done. After a cuppa and sandwich, I loaded up for the last trip out, doing Folly and BOMS in one trip. I did a rinse out in the field and drove home.

Back in the yard, it hit me: I had nothing to do. All the arable work was up together, for the first time since... since when? We started drilling in early September, but you could go back even earlier than that, and say that there was tractor work to be done the day after we combined a field that didn't need baling, and that was probably late July.

But all the spraying is done (but there will be more to come, of course), all the fertiliser is done – there's the shooting strips to be sown, and a whole bunch of paperwork (the BPS forms, the Subaru review, the next *Farmers Weekly* opinion piece), but tomorrow, for the first time in nine or ten months, it'll matter not what the weather is. I will not be wondering if it's suitable to do some tractor work. Fantastic.

Hazel and Jonathan had a very productive session with the sheep, rounding them up using the Kubota, and giving them a good dose of something in the pen they had built in the Bottom of Englands. The joy of watching a 15-year-old becoming something really quite useful on the farm almost beats the joy of an even crop of beans in Bungalow. No, not 'almost' – 'definitely'.

May 28th

A lazy day, waiting for the wind and rain to materialise. It didn't. I did some paperwork, monitored the pigeons in Chalks, had yet another trip to the doctor's to talk about wheezy chests and – a new one – a blooming painful shoulder. I then hit the Flowerpots with Rufus and Robert. Rufus was especially loud and jolly. It is also dawning on him, and all of us, what a narrow escape Ali had with the infection in her knee. After I took her up to Basingstoke last week, there had been a bit of a panic, and she was summoned for surgery to drain the knee and get the vicious infection under control. Rufus was feeling quite pleased that he'd stamped his feet to get the private tests done, after the hospital and the doctor had shuttled her pointlessly from one to the other. And there we were thinking about cancelling our private health insurance.

May 29th

Another quiet day – the good Lord chipped in with some serious rain to help things on a bit. A squall came through mid-morning that shook the house, and it was followed by a couple of hours of good downpour. And then the evening was fine and bright – but still cold, so cold. It doesn't bear thinking about that the days get shorter in three weeks' time.

Rod came out and we finally agreed to go for the 'replacement' sprayer – I agreed to pay the extra for a steering valve for the oversized wheels, he agreed to pay for a spare 3" pipe so I wouldn't have to keep packing one up every time I moved from water in the farmyard to liquid fertiliser down at the Drier Yard. Poor old Rod just looked fed up with the whole thing. Apparently, the phone has gone awful quiet in the office – we farmers are having a bit of a panic about the next couple of years. Interesting times.

May 30th

Like most farmers, I have a terribly boring wardrobe. I wear the same type of black jeans, from dear old Marks and Spencer. I have four or five pairs, which I wear until they need changing or I might be in exceptionally smart company – in which case there's a suit at the back of the wardrobe. There's wedding kit somewhere, which did a lot of miles during those 'Four Weddings and a Funeral' summers of the 1980s. I was the farmer in the Land Rover – but without the wealth.

Tonight's do was a chum's leaving party – she has found God, done all the exams and is heading north to take up being a proper vicar. Rare and unusual these days. The occasion did justify some smart-ish clothes, but the only pair of decent, clean trousers were the ones I'd been wearing during a huge sprayer bleach out, and I had got a bit splash-happy with the hypochlorite. The result was a series of random white spots on my otherwise pristine black jeans.

How odd it must be to be in a job for which you have to dress smartly. It must be strange having a wardrobe with different sections for workwear and leisurewear. Mind you, I suppose city gents must think it odd that we seem to spend all day every day in the same classic county wear – check shirts and jeans (even if they are covered in bleach spots).

May 31st

Jonathan and I were enjoying a typical end-of-May Sunday in front of the TV. The fire was roaring – again – and I was snoozing on the sofa. Joseph the old ginger-and-white cat was on Jonathan's lap, and all seemed well. There was then a quite bizarre moment: Jonathan looked at the cat. The cat looked at him. And then, totally without warning, leapt at his face, locking on – *Alien*-style – with all four claws-out paws. There was a heck of a rumpus as Jonathan fought him off, and the cat fled from the room hissing. Jonathan's cheeks were quite badly scratched, and he was furious; my suggestions that Joseph was an old cat who was starting to go slightly dotty fell, not surprisingly, on deaf and angry ears.

Late in the afternoon I popped up to Kilmeston to see how a non-farming mate is getting on with the restoration of an old Ford 3000 he inherited from his mother's smallholding. He's making fantastic progress with it, with panels and parts being repainted to a lovely original finish. He said it was amazing how easy it was to still get parts form assorted sources around the country - including dealers who sold Fords back in the 70s and 80s still carrying a few parts. He's taking the whole job slow and steady, and getting it just right. I'd have got bored months ago.

June 1st

Monday morning, a new month and still so, so cold. Time for a review. All the fertiliser is done, there's no spraying outstanding, although no doubt Tod will be round with a new bunch later in the week. There's lots of EF2 wild bird strips to be put in, but the corners where I had planned to put them have mostly recovered too well to be ploughed up. A bit of a dilemma. We haven't done our Basic Payment Scheme forms yet – there have been so many changes so late in the day, we almost feel afraid to commit to them.

Today was my deadline for writing up the August motoring review for *The Field*, and having had the spark of inspiration overnight on how to start it (always the most difficult bit), it was polished off and down the wires by 8am.

There's big rain and wind on the way, so we did a Countrystore run late morning to get some fencing posts and some more sodium hypochlorite. I spent most of the afternoon trying to assemble some pheasant feeders, because we'll be getting our ex-layer pheasants in soon. Suddenly the shoot gets more serious. I made one feeder, and then decided it would be far better to get Robin the Beeman to do the shaping of the legs using his carpentry skills – usually reserved for bee-related constructions. I was making a right cock-up with my jigsaw. The badgers will die laughing if they try to nick wheat out of the one I made.

Late afternoon, I put more bangers out in the peas, and then did the Drier loop walk, as part of the campaign to get fit and shift this bloody wheezy chest. I paused for a rest in the cattle barn on the way back, and was stunned at how little hay and straw there is left. Another eighty big bales are being taken away this week by an enthusiastic customer, who is much relieved to find we've still got some. The barn will be almost empty after that. Dad always used to say you can never make too much.

Shed 3b was still chilly for the band rehearsal, but we soon warmed it up. Mainly by standing around saying how old and ill we all are.

June 2nd

An early morning call came in from Jan, next door's keeper's wife. Did we know that there was a camper van parked up the track at the far end of Blackhouse Road? I thanked her for the info – it's always a relief that it's not anything to do with travellers – and set off to have a word. I think I was unnecessarily shouty and unpleasant, but I wasn't feeling well, and needed someone to shout at. The daft thing is that if a camper van comes and knocks on the door of the farmhouse, we'd be happy to find them a level corner, some water and let them use the loo.

Diana failed her driving test. No real surprise – they just don't want teenagers on the road these days. If the examiners let them through, the insurers do their best to keep them from getting behind the wheel. It's the norm for youngsters to go through three or four tests before passing. It's a pain to have to keep on giving them lifts to go anywhere, but it's also nice not to have the worry of them alone out on the road. The roads aren't what they were thirty-five years ago. Come to think of it, I failed three times.

If there was a surprise in her failing, it was caused by one of her 'black marks' – she had failed to overtake slow lorries on the dual carriageway. "But we were nearly at the slip road!" was her fail excuse. I think a word with the driving instructor might be in order.

I went up to the Alton walk-in X-ray centre for a couple of pictures of my shoulder, which is still proving troublesome, especially at three in the morning when I roll onto it. I called in at Rod's at the way back to discuss a bit of a consolidation of cultivators. We've got a motley selection of kit – the Varidiscs, the Vibraflex, the oversized Carrier – that really ought to be culled in favour of one simple machine. Rod's eyes lit up and he promised to be in touch.

The disgracefully short Test series against New Zealand ended one-all. No sledging, smiles all day every day, great cricket – it's what the White Hunters would play if they could.

June 3rd

Hazel hitched the Massey onto the enormous heavy-duty flail mower (bought in the days of reclaiming scrub-filled set-aside) to give the pastures a bit of a haircut, although sometimes the flails hit a bump, and it moves from haircut to scalping. I had a long productive session making more pheasant feeders, while waiting for the man from the specialist soil testing company to arrive.

His sales pitch was simple: blanket application of fertiliser (of all sorts) is wasteful. His company will take hundreds of samples, all over the farm. The results are fed into a computer, and then fed to the machine spreading the product. It raises or lowers the application rate using the info and GPS. It sounded fantastic; the savings would be enormous, he claimed.

Naturally, I enquired about the initial investment: the sampling, the computers, the specialist spreading equipment, the GPS system. The answer very quickly persuaded me that blanket applications would have to do for a few years yet.

Another rehearsal with the blues band yielded some good tunes and a name: the Hog Lane Band. Catchy.

June 4th

Today was *Farmers Weekly* opinion piece deadline day, and I managed to get it done and sent off before 9am. It wasn't brilliant – more of a rant and rave about how much I dislike the antidemocratic nature of the EU. Usual stuff, but getting more and more topical now that the whole idea of a referendum is becoming more acceptable.

Once that was done, I decided that the time had come: I just had to go and get the wild bird strips sprayed off in preparation for some 'pheasant and finch' mix to go in. I'd been putting it off for too long, mulling over the wisdom of it – all that nice healthy crop that was going to be destroyed. But in the end I convinced myself that a good day's shooting next winter would make it all worthwhile.

So I put enough water in for about ten acres, and a respectable dose of Roundup, and headed off. I shut off half the sprayer (to do 12 m strips), and did the south and east headlands of Roe Hill, all round the Folly tree strip, except the southern end, the White Hill headland that adjoins Broom Field, the eastern slope of Bungalow (daft, after all that work getting it back into cropping), and the old game strip in the SE corner of Kilmeston Road.

It wasn't the quickest of jobs, what with all that folding and unfolding, not to mention locking and unlocking gates. It did work out perfectly, though, and I did a rinse-out on the last bit in Kilmeston Road.

After a late lunch, the wind had got up too much for the only remaining spraying job – tidying up Springshott pastures. It wouldn't have been right to put a smelly mix of CMPP and 2,4-D with the wind howling up towards the grounds of Hinton Ampner House.

An early shower beckoned before tonight's cricket, and then Jonathan, Rufus (coming along to see what the White Hunters are all about) and I set off for the lovely drive over Harting Hill to the equally lovely Goodwood Estate pitch. Well, it's normally lovely, but the Festival of Speed was imminent, and the pitch was surrounded by a thousand smart tents and enclosures all in the process of being built. It should also have been an idyllically quiet spot, but even the noise of the construction traffic was drowned mid-game by a World War Two American fighter doing acrobatics over the pitch, all laid on for some event at the House itself. It was deafening. What a couple of dozen in a dogfight seventy years ago would have sounded like, I don't know.

The White Hunters won in a very close and exciting finish. Jonathan didn't bowl, but he fielded well, and struck two lusty blows with the bat – and was caught on the boundary off the second. He got back to the pavilion to a hero's welcome, which was lovely. He'd been told by the captain to hit up or get out, and got a cheer for doing both. Rufus enjoyed himself, fitting in perfectly with a bunch of middle-aged ex-public schoolboys whose love for cricket was matched only by their incompetence.

My umpiring didn't cause too many rows, although I spent an awful lot of time drifting away from the game, and forgetting little things like head-high no balls from square leg. But, hey, it's White Hunter cricket. Who minds?

The drive home was stunning, with a spectacular sunset – just what Granny Flindt would have called 'a weather maker', and the forecast for tomorrow suggests that she might have been right.

June 5th

The promised deluge of fierce thunderstorms headed east of us, and hit Kent and East Anglia. We had a shower or two, and it was unpleasantly humid, but the sun broke through late morning. It was too windy for spraying, so I did office work in the morning and knocked up a few more pheasant feeders in the afternoon, and then ran out of M6x38 coach bolts.

By evening the sun was fully out, but a blisteringly cold north-easterly wind had set in. I went up to Ropley to watch Jonathan play cricket, and froze my nuts off watching him get one run and bowl one over. I confess I came home in a bit of a huff, but such is the lot of the father of a journeyman teenage cricketer.

June 6th

I spent a busy Saturday morning assembling the last of the pheasant feeders, while Hazel and Jonathan were equally busy, setting off in the Kubota (now known as 'Pig' after its sheep herding skills) to assorted corners of the farm, to leave the newly assembled feeders and some freshly made water bowls where we reckon some wheat and some water might attract some birds, and hold the new birds we're planning to bring in in the next week or so. All very productive and exciting. It's like we're all proper keepers.

After lunch, Hazel set off for yet another dog training session, and I sat down to get the BPS forms done once and for all. The hours of researching and questioning some of the finer points seemed to have paid off – the fact that grass strips round the outside and shooting/ELS strips can both be incorporated into the main field made life infinitely easier.

I would have finished sooner had the Editor not turned up to shoot a few pigeons over the peas. We hadn't seen any out there, so didn't hold out much hope for him, but there were a few shots during the afternoon, and Hazel got home just in time to be summoned with some flatcoats to help retrieve seven or so pigeons from the hedge and the tall winter barley in Roe Hill. You never saw anyone so happy.

I had a lovely evening yomp with Fred, because he was looking miserable.

June 7th

The first Sunday in June can only mean one thing: it's Open Farm Sunday. It's the tenth year of this brilliant idea – a selection of farmers up and down the country open their doors to the public, and welcome them in. It's a chance to show them what we do, and explain a bit about why we do it.

I'm not brave enough to do it on my farm, but Joanna and Mark in Cheriton are, and a whole bunch of the local farming community turn up to help. I've missed it for a few years, but this year I was back on trailer duty, riding round the farm in a trailer full of general public, stopping occasionally and having a chat about what we could see.

First stop was at the corner of a field of wheat, with a wild bird strip alongside it. So I introduced myself and whoever was driving the tractor. I thanked our guests for coming along, and paying half of my wages through subsidies. I then talked them through the idea of subsidies, the years of 'grow more at all costs', followed by 'grow less'. I then did my well-worn 'wheat fields are killing fields' to try and cure any vegetarians on board. Without giving anyone the chance to ask too many difficult questions we'd move on to the next stop.

Up at the top of the hill, we had a lovely view, up to Cheesefoot Head, across to Hinton, and down into the site of the Battle of Cheriton. I gave a quick resume of the battle, including the claim that the whole thing took place in our valley, not this one. There was a nice sprayer miss in the wheat alongside, so I could point out the merits of crop spraying to keep yields up, as well as avoiding ergot getting into the bread.

Behind us was a grass crop that had had a cut of silage taken off it, so I was able to do a bit about the chemistry of silage.

On to the calf yard, where I confessed to knowing nothing about dairying, but asked the assembled trailerfull my favourite question: "If badgers were rats, would Brian May care?" It always raised a murmur – not sure if it was approval or disapproval, but when everyone disembarked back at base, the thanks seemed genuine.

At the end of a long but not too tiring day – there were more talking farmers than trailers, so we could do shifts, and the weather was just perfect – the numbers were produced. It was estimated that 4,000 had come to the farm, and nearly 1,500 had been on the trailer rides. And this last number was no estimation – Sarah and Hazel had been using a clicker to count them on. All round the rest of Middle Farm, the burgers had sold out, the ice creams had been cleared out, and everyone was exhausted, but justifiably chuffed at the day's proceedings.

There was bad news, however, when we realised it was Sunday, so the legendary Alresford chippie would be shut. The plan to get a huge packet of fish and chips to slump over would have to be abandoned. Instead, we had a fried egg and ginger beer frenzy, followed by the earliest bedtime I can remember. The whole house was tucked up by nine thirty. It was still daylight – a fact not lost on the dogs, who mistook the evening pre-lock-up turnout for the beginnings of another long walk, and were not pleased when they were herded back in and sent to bed.

June 8th

I had a plan for this morning: I would give the Kia delivery driver a lift into Winchester station, and then find the Natural England offices, just along from the station, to hand in my BPS forms. And just for a change, it all went to plan. The charming driver was half an hour early, so I gave him a lift into town, chatting away. He was a proper musician, who travelled Europe playing church and cathedral organs in the big cities. He had been a music teacher, but had been defeated by the endless paperwork and targets. Curious that my BPS forms were on the back seat of the Kia at the time.

After dropping him off, I drove down to the old market car park, and then walked down the Andover Road to Cromwell House, where Natural England were receiving the precious forms. Up a flight or two of stairs, pausing only to try to help a poor old couple searching, somewhat frantically, for somewhere that "deals with tax", and, after following all the 'BPS forms this way' signs, ended up in a slightly dreary office, with two perfectly pleasant chaps processing my application. All seemed in order – I seemed to have filled in all the right bits, hopefully with the right stuff, and I got my receipt. They reckoned about 60% had come in, and were dreading the rush that would no doubt take place in a few days.

It was all relatively painless – much more complicated than the online system that did us so well for the last few years, but far more simple that the nightmare first few years of IACS. And the Kia was a delight to drive in and out of town.

Early afternoon was pheasant pen time. The ex-layers that we've ordered will be arriving soon, and the wisdom seems to be that to avoid them vanishing off the face of the earth – which ex-layers are prone to do – we need to pen them for a couple of days. Luckily, physical remnants of the old shoot could still be found round the farm. Several partridge pens had been taken down, but not moved, and Hazel and I spent a couple of hours reassembling two in the Folly trees. They should just be enough, with a feeder and some water, to feel like home for a few days. That's the plan anyway. Hazel had been up to Kilmeston Road this morning, and found one still intact and untouched, so she's treated that one to a bit of a clean-up. We'll see if they work at holding some of the birds.

The Trust weren't keen on us buying in any birds when they drew up our lease, but it was pointed out that it is very bad form indeed to run a rough shoot without putting down birds when surrounded by big commercial shoots. Word gets about very quickly that you are simply drawing off your neighbours' birds. We pointed out to our landlord that, after all the controversy involving the Trust and shooting in recent years, it would be a good move for us to be allowed to buy a few birds to make sure that our Trust-approved shoot wasn't seen to be just poaching from next door. The Trust saw the light and agreed that we should be putting our share down. We're in close contact with assorted members of the keeping fraternity locally, and they all now know our plans. We've done the sensible thing and asked for lots of advice, making it clear that we're going into the whole thing as complete pheasant beginners. So far, we've had nothing but a good reaction. I hope we keep it that way.

At three, Hazel went off to get Diana from Alresford, and I sat in and waited for the delivery of the new microwave. The AGA went out last week, and we needed something to help out the simple electric ring plates that have taken over – especially as Anthony is due back this week, and the extra cooking facilities will be much needed.

I was mid phone call to Tod, checking what might be desperately urgent from Friday's spraying recommendations, when the dogs barked, and crashed their way out of the gate. Their barking was friendly, so I didn't hurry to see who it was, but when I got to the kitchen window I was just in time to see a white van leaving the yard. It was a small van, something like a Fiat, and it got my hackles up. It left via the corner gates, and wasn't delivering any of the huge heap of spray that was arriving in lumps today. The landline had rung while I was on the mobile to Tod, so I put two and two together, and got four, or maybe five: the white van had been trying to deliver the microwave, but had been scared to get out when he saw the dogs in the yard, so had driven off, having failed to raise the house by phone. I even rang back the number that had been trying to ring earlier, to confirm my theory. The worry was that missing the delivery slot meant extra delivery charges, and we didn't want that just because he'd not got out of his van. After the fourth ring back, Anthony answered. He'd been ringing to check what our plans were for the trip north, and a bit of moral support and advice for an interview tomorrow – he has been offered an undefined job by an old friend of ours in Bradford. Anthony wasn't sure exactly what the job might be, or what to wear, or how to buy a tie, or... I told him to relax, be himself, be polite, be interested and interesting and do a whole bunch of research on the company before tomorrow. But the white van remained a mystery.

There was no sign of the microwave by the time Hazel got back, so she took over waiting, and I went and put weedkiller round the grubbiest bits of the pasture in Springshott. Twenty-five acres' worth covered a full turn of the headland, round all the copses and most of the ground between the footpath and the gate. I rinsed out thoroughly in the field, and came back to fill up with a bleach mix; the next trip out will be into the beans, and everything needs to be squeaky clean before I hit them with assorted fungicides.

Halfway through the Springshott job, Hazel rang to say a proper liveried van had delivered the microwave, which was a relief in a way, but still left the nagging feeling that the other white van had been up to no good. Well, they should have had a close-ish encounter with all three dogs, even if the latter were grinning and wagging their tails.

A mostly good day, although I spent the evening nursing a sore knee, which got jarred while we were carrying bits of pheasant pen this morning. That'll teach me to tell the White Hunters the other day that my knees are the only things still working properly.

June 9th

I love a long drive. I do it most days of the year in the tractor, but every so often it's nice to do it without turning 180 degrees at regular intervals. In other words, it's nice to go somewhere.

Today's 'somewhere' was Leeds, where Anthony had finished his second year of university. He was also changing house up there, so couldn't leave any stuff behind for the summer holidays. He asked if we could drive up, pick him up, have a look around Leeds, and bring him and all his clutter home. Well, I'd got the Kia specially, and cleared with Tod that nothing couldn't wait for a few days, and off we went.

It used to be a nostalgia fest, driving due north; I'd revisit all the towns and villages that used to be on the route to Newcastle in the early 1980s. It was a bit of a shock when I tried it six or seven years ago, and found most of it gone, or, in the case of the A1 when we went up to York with Diana last year, rerouted. You suddenly realise that Hinton stays the same, everywhere else moves on.

We had a lovely drive up, the Kia was splendid and comfortable, and it took exactly four hours to reach the little hotel just south of Leeds. It would have been quicker if most of the nation's motorway network wasn't being ripped up and rebuilt as 'smart motorway'. There we all were, driving at the steadiest 50 mph you ever saw, all aware of the threat of 'average speed cameras'. It made for good fuel economy and relaxing cruising – you're no longer on the lookout for psycho BMW drivers hurtling up behind you.

The other joy of a long drive is to snoop on the farmers who have the misfortune to farm next to the motorway. They can get away with nothing. Then there are the farms, and indeed villages and hamlets that have ended up yards away from the vast ribbon of tarmac. There's one farmyard that is so close that you can see a fine clock built into a stable block, now rusted and broken. Then there's the scattering of stately homes on hillsides, whose views of lovely valleys now have 10,000 cars an hour speeding (or dawdling at 50 mph) through them. Still, I was one of those cars today, enjoying the convenience of a modern motorway.

After a snooze in the relaxed little hotel, I had a bath. The first bath I've had for years. There is a huge bath in the farmhouse, which thrived on limitless hot water from the Agamatic, and, when that blew up, from an old-fashioned immersion heater. When that gave up, however, we moved to a modern immersion, with its health-and-safety heat settings, i.e. cold. It became impossible to have a hot bath. We'd had a nice new shower unit installed in Jonathan's room by then, so the bath became little more than a store for clothes and nail clippings. And spiders.

Anyway, the hotel had limitless hot water, even after Hazel had had her go, and the bath did air bubbles, so I was in there for a long time. Rather longer than I had planned, after finding I was now so unfit and inflexible that it took me about ten minutes to work out how to get out. Very embarrassing.

Finally, in the early evening, we set off for Headingley. It was a slight culture shock, having set off from Hampshire, the land of gentrified and Bodenated housing, to find row after row of slightly chaotic houses, in states of repair ranging from shabby to squalid. It seemed to be a thousand acres of student hovels, once proud and with a hint of ornate decorations – black railings here, a stone face over the doorway there – and now looking thoroughly unloved. Anthony said all who lived there were happy. It made our little flat in Ellesmere Road, Newcastle seem eminently civilised. Mind you, the first thing we did when we moved in in 1982 was repaint the place. The landlord seemed delighted, and even supplied the paint.

Having seen round the house, we then walked up to the legendary Otley Road, and had a very nice beer and a gammon and chips supper. Opposite the pub was a spectacular Victorian church, looking slightly in need of a scrub, and a war memorial, which sat unnoticed in the middle of a busy junction. One beer in one pub on the Otley Road was enough for me to claim to have done the Otley Run – the old man's version, anyway.

Anthony had had his job interview that afternoon. He'd gone and bought a proper shirt, some trousers that weren't jeans, and some leather shoes for the occasion. If the interview leads to nothing more than him wearing smart clothes for once, it will be a triumph. But Anthony reckoned the chat had gone very well. I had told him to be interested and interesting. We'll see what comes of it.

It was astonishing, walking back along Headingley Lane, to see huge, solid, grey stoned houses, empty and open. Number 57 stuck in my mind: magnificent gates, huge chimneys, but utterly unwanted. Not even the vandals could be bothered to do anything with it. Winchester, it ain't.

We left Anthony for his last night in his house, and headed back to the hotel, dozing off to the unfaltering roar of the M621.

June 10th

It should have been a lovely sleep. The bed was perfect, the duvets and sheets were top class, but something in the gammon and chips wasn't sitting very well, and by the time the hotel took its first delivery of essential stores, which was about 5am, I was thoroughly restless and sleep-free. Still, a change is as good as a rest.

It didn't stop me indulging at breakfast. Two packs of Crunchy Nut Cornflakes, with milk, then toast and jam, and a full Yorkshire breakfast. A perfect set-up for another long drive south.

We drove back into Leeds, having said a fond farewell to the hotel, and loaded up Anthony's stuff. He tried to Hoover the room with the world's most knackered student Hoover, which involved him pushing debris from one end of the room to the other. There was a sense of melancholy as he left. He'd been there a year with a whole bunch of company, most of whom were vanishing on assorted work experiences all round the world, and he was moving out to a small house with just one friend. There seemed to be a sense of a big change taking place, and he seemed more nervous about it than he had when he set off to Leeds two years ago. We left the big old four-storey house in a terrible state. The kitchen in particular needed a skip rather than just a couple of bin liners. The shelves and cupboards were still full of student-style essentials. It looked thoroughly disgusting, and most unlikely to satisfy the landlord when the post-move out inspection took place – I dread to think if the girl who was last one out would have to finish the job off.

I couldn't help comparing the whole experience to what we did in the break between our second and third years at Newcastle. As far as I remember, we locked up 194 Ellesmere Road, leaving most of our stuff there, and went home. And then came back a few months later, unlocked, and continued with student life. Simpler days.

After a quick stop in the centre of Leeds to let Anthony drop off some essential paperwork at the uni, we headed south. It was another uneventful drive, four hours door-to-door, with a couple of pee breaks, and a disgraceful Big Mac Meal for me. As if the gargantuan breakfast hadn't been enough.

Late afternoon and evening was spent safely back home on the sofa, but feeling somewhat the worse for wear, as Big Mac met Full Yorkshire Breakfast, which was itself still engaged in a battle with gammon steaks and chips. I'll never learn.

June 11th

There was no time to enjoy a lie-in to get over Kia-lag, because the pheasants were arriving this morning – an exciting new venture. Even more exciting was the pile of disassembled pens that Hazel had spotted in the old keeper's yard, perfect for putting together a couple more temporary pens for the ex-layers to find their feet in.

So it was an early start to unhitch the topper from the Massey, pick up the old wooden trailer and head off to pick them up. I thought it would be wise and diplomatic to email the Trust's man in charge of clearing out the old yard to double check that it would be OK, and then we set off.

We put one pen up behind the cattle barn, and one in the estate yard, and very smart they looked too. Even better, the Trust's man had replied by email, telling us to take whatever we fancied. Not sure what we would have done if he'd said 'no', but there we go.

And then, just after eleven, the birds arrived – ten crates, about twenty per crate, delivered in the typical mucky doublecab, just the sort of vehicle that in other circumstances would have you dialling 999 at double quick speed. After a chat and a cheque handover, we were official gamekeepers. I could hear Grandpa chuckling away in the graveyard. After all those years of fighting the shoot at Hinton Ampner, here we were looking at a big heap of our very own pheasants.

There wasn't a moment to lose. First couple of crates went round the back to the estate yard. The golden rule was one cock bird per pen, and each crate seemed to have a couple of cocks in. So Hazel's job was to carry the crates in and play 'rummage for the cock'. Once found, they would be let free via the pen's door, manned by the one with the bad back – me.

It all went smoothly, with only a slight pause while we reinforced the netting on the roof. One or two of the hen birds had gone off like Exocets, clean through a tiny gap we'd left. We also found that if we let them walk slowly out of the end of each crate, they stayed a lot calmer, and did a lot less frantic flinging themselves against the wire.

It was then simply a matter of loading up Tigger with a couple of crates, a bag of wheat, some water to top up the drinkers, and heading off to the pens: one in the top on Kilmeston Road, two in the Folly trees, and then the one behind the cattle barn. By lunchtime, we were done, and feeling quite proud of ourselves. The next debate is how long we leave them in the pens. The shorter the better, to avoid Mr Fox finding a very convenient packed lunch, but long enough for them to develop some sense of territory. That's the theory, anyway.

The rest of the afternoon was horribly hot and humid, so no spraying was possible. I took the opportunity to rinse the bleach out of the sprayer, ready for bean spraying when the wind dies down. The day was complete with a trip to the Pots with neighbour Joe.

June 12th

The dawn chorus was brought to us this morning by a ewe, who stood outside our window and bleated monotonously for about half an hour, starting at 4am. The birds joined in just after that. Suddenly, the unceasing but somehow soothing roar of the M621 seemed like a distant memory.

It was another hot and windy Friday, constantly threatening rain and thunder. There was a lot of pheasant work, popping out to the pens and seeing if our latest babies were OK. They all seemed to have settled down OK, and the debate raged about how long we should keep them in.

Hazel set off with the flail mower to trim the areas we've got pencilled in as game strips/wild bird covers. Some were thicker and easier than others to do, and some were so full of blackgrass and brome that a crop of hay could have been taken off them. I took advantage of the hot weather to have a comprehensive filter clean on the sprayer.

It was off to Ropley in the evening for what should have been another cricket match. Unfortunately, it had been cancelled, but the message about the cancellation hadn't reached the nine Ropley players who turned up or the three Trojans players (and their parents) who had made the long Friday rush-hour trip up from Eastleigh way. There might be a grumble or two over the weekend.

I'd cried off a pub trip with Rufus to watch the cricket, and by the time I got hold of him to say I was actually available, he was collapsed with a thumping headache, and didn't want to go anywhere. Probably best not to add to the headache with three or four pints.

June 13th

The farm missed a deluge last night by the narrowest of margins. Petersfield was drenched, and the nice lady who rang early on the Saturday morning to apologise for the cricket mix up (an email had got lost in cyberspace, apparently) said that Ropley had a deluge at about 11am. It's a shame – we could have done with a really good soaking.

Hazel and I set off round all the pheasant pens, topping up feed and water, and releasing half of the birds. The vast majority just hopped out through the open door, without a hint of panic. Time will tell if they stay close.

It was still too windy for spraying, so I hitched the Terradisc onto the Massey and did the strips that Hazel had mowed. Some went better than others – how that rain would have helped.

The Editor rang over tea time to ask if I would be a referee for his shotgun and firearm renewals – I said we should discuss it in the pub. He said he would if we brought our other halves. So we had a very jolly foursome in the Flowerpots.

June 14th

A big shoot-related Sunday. Hazel and Jonathan set off in the Kubota to top up water, and let all the birds out. All went well – the birds seemed calm, and there were plenty hanging round from the mob that had been let out yesterday.

My half of Big Pheasant Sunday went slightly less well. I hitched off the sprayer, hitched onto the drill and did a calibration for 50 kg/ha of bird mix. I had left the bean metering wheel in, but it was dispensing a bit too fast – my minimum speed, according to the onboard computer, would have to be 12 kph. So I emptied out the seed, and changed the wheel to a smaller capacity one, and recalibrated. All seemed well.

The Editor dropped in to do the licence paperwork and have yet another Saturday gossip, and once I'd sent him on his way, I drove the tractor and drill out to Chalks with a view to nailing the shooting/wild bird strips. It all went horribly wrong. For some reason, the Horsch decided to quadruple the seed rate I thought I'd set, and all six bags of expensive wild bird mixture flew down the pipes and out of the drill in the first acre of ground. It's a bit of mystery what went wrong – perhaps the rubber flap that's supposed to hold the seed back as the metering wheel turns is old and inflexible, and the seed managed to work its way past it, helped by the rough shaking of the machine (which doesn't happen in the yard during calibration). I came home in a bit of a huff to have a think about it. Half of my expensive seed had gone.

Luckily, with no rain forecast for the foreseeable, there's no hurry to solve the problem. But it would be nice to solve it anyway.

June 15th

Right – time to sort the drill out. I removed the red metering wheel that was proving useless, and put the two small oilseed rape sowing wheels in, hoping that the two combined would have enough volume to dispense 50 kg/ha at a reasonable forward speed. It calibrated OK – and with much trepidation, and all six of my remaining bags of seed, I tiptoed out to the Folly. Things started well when the drill seemed to make next to no impression on the wheat we were driving through (the full width tyres on the back of the Horsch should have rolled the crop down completely), and then got better when the metering system behaved itself impeccably.

I did the horseshoe shape around the Folly trees, then went and did Bob's Wood. Then it was off to the long strip up at White Hill, next to the old Barracuda drive, and then across Springshott to do Kilmeston Road and Bungalow. There was quite a bit of bunging up in the bits where a thick crop had been chopped down, and the sowing could be described as adequate. Only Bungalow went in well, having been ploughed not that many months ago. I didn't bother with Roe Hill, because the seed had run out just right in Bungalow, but also because it was a forest of trash, and the drill would be very unlikely to get through it.

Back indoors, I ordered two more bags of seed, just in case I get a rush of enthusiasm and end up doing Roe Hill, and maybe redoing Chalks where I think the incontinent drill may have emptied out early.

Band rehearsal was a quiet affair – Ian was away on a course, and we had a very subdued but excellent run through. Tod told his sperm bank joke again.

I did some sums to try and work out what the last Hampshire Grain chunk of money will be at the beginning of next month. I rang them up to get some sort of indication of the final prices that they've achieved selling our stuff throughout the year. It wasn't brilliant news, but not terrible either. And once again, I have full faith that they and their fulltime professional agents are doing a better job than I would do trying to sell it.

The farming papers are full of gloom again. Tractors sales are down by a scary percentage – Rod Gaskin had said the same the other day; we farmers are battening down the hatches big time. There are lots of articles about resizing and changing the nature of one's enterprise – pursuing more acres at all costs is now not wise, apparently. Well, some of us have been shaking our heads at the mad scramble for more land for years. Getting one's farm down to a size that one person can handle most efficiently is the way forward. Funny to think that we've been there for years. All I know is that Churcher's College have seen our last accounts, and ramped up Jonathan's fees by 33% by abolishing the generous bursary we've enjoyed for some years. And if the next set of accounts are terrible it will be too late – he'll be leaving them next summer.

Hazel, Diana and Jonathan spent a very fruitful hour rounding up the sheep in the bottom of Englands, and penning them up ready for the shearer tomorrow. Who needs an expensive private education?

We dropped the Skoda down at the local garage for a much needed brake overhaul and a puncture repair. I dread to think how much that will all be. Mind you, it has done 80,000 miles, so deserves some TLC.

June 16th

Not terribly well this morning. I had awful ringing in my ears – and it wasn't band rehearsal that had done it. And then my right ear went almost completely deaf. Horrible. So I sat indoors and felt sorry for myself, fielding the latest wave of Alresford Show phone calls ("I sell organic llama droppings – is it too late to have a stand?") – Hazel is in charge of the trade stands. It was worth being in to take delivery of a bizarre range of goods. There was an unknown box for a neighbour who wasn't in, Jonathan's new hoodie and the two extra bags of seed for the game strips, which had been rushed out here from Salisbury at express rate. I really didn't feel up to jumping in the tractor and doing any sowing, but I was quite content to use the 'I might go sowing' excuse to stop me from hitching off the drill and doing some of Tod's huge list of spraying.

The battle with the pigeons in the peas in Chalks had recommenced. I've been trying to find a way of stopping the firecrackers in the rope bangers from dropping to the ground. The problem is that the fuse holds the banger itself in the rope, and once the fuse lights, the banger drops down into the peas, where it is muffled and takes out half a dozen plants at the same time. I tried Sellotaping them together so that they stay in the air. All that did was blow all the nearby bangers off the rope completely, or blow out the smouldering rope altogether. I might have to put up with a few square feet of bare soil and some slightly quieter bangs. It would be nice to think that the pigeons will be giving up on the crop soon, although I seem to remember that they like peas right up till harvest.

The shearer arrived on time, but then sat quietly at the back gates waiting for someone to find him. And then, by the time he'd slowly worked his way through our little flock, and a few of Tony's from the next field, most of the day was gone, and Hazel seemed a little less keen on the whole small-scale shepherdess concept than she had been this morning. I had to give Tony a lift home (he's off driving after having had what they call 'a funny turn') and then drove to Petersfield and get Jonathan from school, and Anthony from the station after his night away. Anthony was thrilled that he'd been offered the internship up in Bradford – eight months, starting after harvest, with real money while doing it. It will mean I can indulge in my all-time favourite habit: used car buying.

We went and picked up the Skoda – four new discs with pads, and two new tyres, all for £550. I reckon that's good value – and a bit of a relief.

June 17th

There's a day in June when the farm reaches puberty, and as I did my three tanks of late fungicide on some wheats, I realised that that day had passed: the crops no longer look sweet and innocent; they have gone all adolescent. Weeds that have somehow survived the herbicide are now showing above the wheat in the Bottom of Hurst Down. The winter barley in Rick/Clump looks hideous, especially on the overlaps. Drier Field has gone a shocking shade of yellow, especially on the gravelly ground. It's no wonder that farm competitions take place early in the month.

June 18th

After another couple of tanks of wheat fungicide. It was off to Basingstoke hospital for another consultation to try to sort out the chestiness and breathlessness. The heart had passed with flying colours, so it was time for a more detailed look at the chest – the early bog-standard X-rays had shown nothing.

Round the back of the grey monstrosity known as Basingstoke hospital is a brand new private clinic, complete with fancy name, hideous colour scheme and the feel of an airport terminal. Every table had leaflets strewn on them with proud claims about the new clinic, how it was an NHS initiative, and how it would be a valuable asset to the community. There was a particularly odd claim about the services being provided in 'safety' – which makes the rest of the hospital grounds sound particularly unsavoury. It was almost empty, and the whole atmosphere was laid back and relaxed. The doctor chatted about my health, the children, rugby, and then decided more blood tests and a chest CT scan would be in order. The blood tests were done on the spot, and the CT scan was booked for next Monday. They're obviously not very busy.

The blues band rehearsal, due tonight, was cancelled. Dave the Bass had been on the phone earlier, suggesting that the whole project might be on hold while Doug's health issues are sorted out. I tried Rufus to see if he was up for a pub trip instead, but wasn't feeling well, either. We are all getting old.

June 19th

Time to spray the beans. Not a great job, thanks to all the footpaths in Godwin's, but it's got to be done. They look magnificent – I've never seen a spring crop of beans like it. They look even better with the footpaths carefully mown. Hazel went out there with the ride-on mower and trundled slowly back and forth to make everything legal.

In the end, I met no walkers at all, and managed to get a fairly potent and smelly mix on to knock out the wild oats and aphids. Then it was off to Bungalow to do the beans up there. They're slightly behind, but still looked good.

The last tank of spray of the week was on the peas in Chalks, to knock out the broadleaf weeds. It's always a scary job – if the peas aren't waxed, they can be taken out too. There were dozens of pigeons out there too, so I must get serious with the rope bangers again.

A complete change of scene beckoned in the evening, as Jonathan was playing for Ropley against Trojans down at Southampton Sports Centre. This venue is a curious one – numerous cricket and football pitches cut into the hillside of a valley taken over before World War Two as a leisure facility. I found somewhere to sit, high on a bank overlooking the pitch, where I read my *Spectator* in between deliveries. I had plenty of company – every couple of minutes, another pitbull/staffie and its owner would snuffle their way past. Then there were the teenage courting couples, the reluctant children being hurried back to catch the bus by a fraught mother, and the girl telling her father that she was a farmer because she had a bit of grass in her mouth. I couldn't resist joining in and telling her that I was a real farmer, and she looked just right.

It was a lovely way to spend a warm Friday evening. Ropley won easily, Jonathan didn't bat, didn't bowl, retrieved two boundaries and did two bits of fielding, but he seemed to enjoy it nevertheless. I did a bit of grumpy Dad routine as we headed back up the M3, suggesting that we should find a club where he might get an active role on the pitch. I probably spoiled his day a bit.

June 20th

A nice quiet Saturday. Too windy to contemplate putting the two last tanks of fungicide on the beans, so no tractor work. The pigeons were still giving the peas a hard time, and the Editor was stuck clearing up after his daughter's 21st birthday party, so I put another set of rope bangers out in Chalks. The peas were showing the classic symptoms of having just been sprayed with a herbicide that was a bit 'hot' – all the tendrils were curled, and the leaves had turned down. Basically, the whole field was shouting 'Ouch, that hurt!' I walked through the plants, trying to reassure them that it was for their own good. I came back via one of the game strips where I had applied the dregs of the herbicide, confident that there was no way that any of the seed would have grown in these dry conditions, only to find that some had just started to grow, and was looking very unhealthy. Maybe it was a good thing that I had quadrupled the seed rate.

We decided to bring the pet lambs down from the pony paddock just outside the farmhouse and put them into the bottom of Englands with all the other sheep. Being so tame, they were easy to move, following a bucket down the hill on the road. The only danger was traffic on a fine weekend day, but we only met one car, who followed behind and helped move them along.

It was another good little job to take Diana's mind off her big trip to Europe tomorrow. She's still not a good traveller, so the less time she had to sit around and get in a stew, the better. Hazel set off in the afternoon for another training session with Sasha, so I took Diana into Curry's in Winchester to buy her a portable DVD player for her trip, to help while away the long train journeys. It was cheap as chips, and will no doubt conk out in twelve-and-a-half months' time.

Back home, it was hello to Mr Sofa while listening to a thrilling finish to the England vs New Zealand ODI. It will be astonishing if the rest of the summer can keep this level of entertainment going.

The promised rain never materialised. There were a couple of brief showers, but nothing to help the crops. Monday is now our best bet for some significant moisture.

The curse of the late night music struck again, just as I was drifting off to sleep. Just loud enough to be recognisable as music, but not clear enough to work out what is being played. The trouble with this farmhouse is that it picks up sounds from miles around. On a quiet calm June night, it could been five miles away. Luckily, I dozed off in the end.

June 21st

After weeks of preparation, Diana set off for her short trip round Europe. She'd organised it with a friend, and the two of them were dropped off at St Pancras station by her friend's parents. It was a bit of a nervous moment for Diana, but we hoped that a mini-break round some of the capitals of Europe would do her good.

I had a lazy Fathers' Day after that. Granny Flindt used to get very cross about 'Mothering Sunday' becoming 'Mothers' Day'. But she never demanded that 'Fathers' Day' should be 'Fathering Sunday'. Probably because it sounds a bit rude.

Anthony suggested a trip out in the evening for a meal, and I managed to get an early table at the Thomas Lord. The two boys ditched garish T-shirts for the evening, changing into smart shirts and shoes, and looked infinitely better for it. I was very proud.

June 22nd

The latest test car arrived mid-morning: a SEAT Leon X-perience – yet another variation of the 'family estate car with four-wheel-drive' concept. The delivery driver was very grateful for a lift back to Winchester station, and I soon spotted he was from the north east. It turned out he was from Wallsend, so we had a fantastic nostalgia-fest about Newcastle. I established that stotties are indeed still available (Anthony, on one of his trips to visit a friend up there, claimed not to have seen one anywhere). Newcastle Amber, alas, is no longer available.

The afternoon was taken up with another long session with the NFU Pensions guru. He'd been away with the facts and figures that he collected last time, and come up with some projections for the future. Even with the proposed additional lump sum being paid into our pension fund every month, we're not going to be skipping off into a lucrative sunset come our 65th birthdays. Looks like we'll still be driving tractors.

In another year, the Churcher's fees will have stopped, and then the 25-year endowment (started at the insistence of the first NFU pensions man we dealt with all those years ago) will mature – so there should be some cash to boost the pensions pot. And there's always the Golden Age of Farming which is imminent. Like it has been for thirty years.

June 23rd

A big medical day – again. Off to the Candover Clinic in Basingstoke, this time for a CT scan. And once again, it was prompt, professional and fuss-free. The only slight issue was me trying to get comfortable face down on the sliding bed, with my arms 'up', as if diving into a pool. I hope I didn't wobble too much as the bed stopped and started. It might have made a mess of the pictures. Anyway, I was in and out within half an hour.

After lunch it was back to the doctor's in Medstead, for an update on the shoulder. The X-ray showed nothing but wear and tear, so the doctor was happy to do a chunky injection of anaesthetic and steroid to try and get things healing up. I was less than happy – me and needles don't mix. Luckily, he did the huge jab from behind, into the depths of the shoulder, so apart from lots of pain, most of it imagined, it wasn't too bad. I have been known to keel over at the sight of an injection. I was once trimming the loose sole of a shoe, with it on my left thigh, using a Stanley knife. Just as the blade reached the edge of the tough sole, it dawned on me what was about to happen – but I was too late: a two-inch long gash appeared in the muscle. Lucky, back then, I was still propping, so had plenty to spare. I drove bravely to the Ropley doctors (in the days when you could drop into your doctor's surgery), didn't blink at the clean-up and the butterfly stiches. When the tetanus jab was produced, everything went dark and I ended up on the floor.

The advice after the shoulder jab was awkward – avoid lifting if possible. Not much good with all the outstanding spraying, and haymaking imminent. I'll just have to work my way round it.

Then it was down to Blackhouse Farm to watch some live cricket, as the England vs New Zealand 20/20 finished off a fantastic early summer tour. What an utter joy to watch live cricket, too. Getting Sky would be fatal for me, though. I'd get out of the house even less.

June 24th

Right, that's quite enough medical stuff; time to get back to some farming. I put fungicide on all the spring beans and a tank on the spring barley in Kilmeston Road. Hot and sweaty work.

June 25th

More spraying. The Hangar and then a tank on Blackhouse Road before lunch. That's seventy acres, which is what I could get sprayed in a day with my first sprayer, an Allman, with a 12-metre manual folding boom, a 150-gallon tank, and mounted on a Ford 6600. Now THAT was hot and sweaty. No air con, no radio, and ten acres at a time. I remember stamping my feet until Dad upgraded the controls to in-cab electrical – I wasn't going to be leaning out of the back of the cab to turn it on and off. Old Ernie, who did the spraying before me (what little there was of it), was less than healthy at this time, so that may have had something to do with my decision. Let's hope all these lung tests don't reach the same conclusion.

Tod turned up over lunch to walk the last few fields before we shut all the gates, and to have an early think about next year's cropping. The first wheats are easy, but everything else is a bit of a head scratcher. Are we going for oilseed rape? We managed to grow it this year without the neonicotinoid seed dressing – will we be so lucky again, especially as the beetles are savaging the kale in the game strips with a vengeance? It got too complicated, and I needed to keep spraying, so we agreed we'd come back to it.

I finished the fungicide on Blackhouse Road, did BML's, then the two earlier bits of Panorama in Folly and BOMS. And I was once again up together with spraying jobs. With the forecast suggesting rain tomorrow, I headed to the Pots with neighbour Robert to celebrate.

June 26th

A very lazy and sultry Friday. I lost a couple of hours recovering from last night's pub trip – my excuse, m'lud, was that it was supposed to be raining today, and it didn't. By late morning, I was feeling myself again, so decided to get my head around haymaking, which is the next big job. The first thing to be done was to get the Massey cleaned up and given a bit of a going over ready for a week's intensive mowing and tedding. Hazel hitched off the topper and then brought the tractor round to the yard, where I set about it with the pressure washer. The back axle is constantly covered in oil and dirt – the spool valve connections are a weak spot on that Massey, and drip constantly. Luckily, it was so warm today that it blasted off easily. I always struggle with the dirt that collects on top of the axle, under the cab. It's a forest of wires and pipes and it's next to impossible to clean off. The mud clears, leaving the straw and grass, which always looks a bit of a fire hazard – or good nesting material for the pied wagtails who find their way in there.

Hazel went off and did the last of the footpath mowing jobs – the short one across Roe Hill. Because she didn't think she'd worked hard enough this week, she did it with the strimmer. Silly girl.

That particular footpath always makes me chuckle. Back in the mists of time, probably twenty-five years ago, it was our only path across arable land. Nobody walked it in those days, and Dad wasn't even aware of it. I pointed out our responsibility to keep it mown, and he wasn't impressed. "If a path is used enough, it keeps itself short. If it gets overgrown, it obviously isn't needed!" There a nice logic to that argument, but, these days, massive deductions in subsidy make mowing it the best option. We are now fully 'mown up'. Next month, I gather, is Rambler 'Shop a Farmer' month (aka 'The Big Pathwatch'), so the timing is perfect.

Jonathan was on a short day at Churcher's, so I volunteered to pick him up, and go via the Massey dealer and order two new spool valves for the tractor. I had a quick snoop at the new tractors, exchanged insults with some of the staff, and then headed into Petersfield to meet Jonathan. Most of the town centre was crawling with schoolchildren, but being nice polite yoof, the atmosphere was carnival rather than riot. We had a strawberry milkshake each on the way out from the MacDonald's drive-through. I only just stopped myself ordering the full Big Mac meal.

I got back in time to commiserate with the Editor, who had taken today off to hit the pigeons in the peas, but they had not been playing at all. He'd had a handful of shots all afternoon. He seemed relaxed, though – an afternoon in a hedge is good therapy for a stressed fifty-something with a lot on his mind. Once he'd gone, Sasha and I went out and lit three more rope bangers to keep the field free of pigeons. Sasha was much taken with the concept – so much so that she vanished later in the evening, and had us all calling and shouting for twenty minutes in a slight panic. She was found down near the peas. Mind you, she did smell strongly of fox poo, so perhaps it wasn't pigeon patrol that she was on.

June 27th
A quiet Saturday, but in anticipation of more rain overnight and tomorrow, I popped out to Roe Hill with the Horsch and drilled the last of the spring-sown game strips. It's a bit of a lottery this late, but everything was set up and ready to go, so I thought I'd get it out of the way.

June 28th
In a perfect world, all Sundays will be like this one. A cool and damp morning, nothing to spray, and the world's best game of cricket in the afternoon. The White Hunters were hosting the Old Grumblers up at Brockwood.

The pitch, as ever, looked like a green velvet dream. The opposition were a touring side down from London, who were a lot better than the White Hunters, but quickly adapted their game to suit us – even giving us their captain for the day because we were a man short. And it was one of those increasingly rare things – a declaration game. This meant that when the Grumblers had notched up a healthy few hundred for not many wickets, the White Hunters could dig in after tea and get a draw.

The Grumblers got to 205–8, and declared at tea, as is the convention. The highlight for me as umpire was watching Jonathan being given a healthy six over spell, and getting two wickets. True, they were 'bought' but he was thrilled. The Hunters, in reply, got to 182–8, looking, occasionally, like they might reach the total. But then the Grumblers would bring on the stronger bowlers to limit things.

We adjourned to The Fox in Bramdean for a beer and peanut frenzy to round off the perfect day. When the world is sorted out, all games will be like this.

June 29th
Much of the day went missing after last night's dietary indulges. Luckily, all was clear for yet another hospital trip, this time for another set of lung function tests. Once again, I passed with flying colours, having enormous lung power and capacity. It would be easy to start to wonder what all the fuss is about. A much more productive band rehearsal rounded off a good-ish day.

June 30th
Fiendishly hot. The hay gang cut Springshott, which worried me – the forecast suggested downpours. The storms did arrive very late on the evening, but missed us by a whisker.

July 1st

So there I was in the office, a bit dozy after last night's wind and thunder (but, alas, still no rain), when I noticed a bee had come through the office window that I had opened to try and cool the room down a bit. Then I noticed another one. Then another ten, then they came pouring in, just like the cockroaches in *The Mummy*. Now, I don't get on very well with things that sting, so there was a bit of a panic. As I leapt up to shut the window, I noticed a whirlwind of bees just outside. It was an enormous swarm. I got stung on the wrist, so I beat a hasty retreat, slamming the office door, and then ran round the house shutting all the windows I could find.

After ten minutes of being under siege, we noticed that the swarm was settling in a tree over the chicken run. There's only one thing to do under these circumstances: ring Robin the Beeman. He was in his shed, not a hundred yards away, and was over like a shot. While he sized up his unexpected prize, I opened the office window, and let all the 'scouts' back out. They headed straight off to join the swarm.

Robin filled me in on what was going on. The swarm will have left a hive nearby, either a natural one or a man-made one, probably due to the heat and the hive getting too small. They'll have mulled around in a big airborne bunch, with the scouts checking out suitable new sites – hence all the blighters in my office. Once somewhere suitable is found, they'll up sticks and head for it. Robin's job was to get them into a suitable container before they find something better.

He got all white-suited up, climbed a wobbly ladder that he propped up against a none-too-safe base of shrubs and young trees, and lifted down the huge brown scrotum of bees that was dangling from the branch. Once safely back on the ground, he realised the swarm was bigger than he thought – a bigger box would be needed, so off he went to make one. By the time he'd persuaded them into the larger home, they were all still in a bit of a tizzy, so he left them on the lawn to get used to the new box and calm down a bit.

I asked about the etiquette of finding a swarm. Might they belong to someone, and is there a system of notifying local owners? Apparently not – it's 'finders keepers'. If your swarm has decided it's time to leave home, it's a fault in your husbandry. So there. Beeman finished the day quite pleased. I watched the whole thing from a respectful distance, nursing my sting like a giant five-year-old.

It was fiendishly hot and windy, no good for those dregs of spraying I've got to do. The Springshott haylage gang were in, obviously deciding that the grass had dried enough in these conditions, and probably having looked at the forecast for tomorrow. They had the whole lot baled by evening.

July 2nd

Yet another trip up to the Candover Clinic in Basingstoke brought some significant news. The scan had found something quite dramatic: bronchiectasis. Quite a large section of the left lung was knackered and infected. All the wheezing made sense.

There was much talk of aspergillosis, too, and asking if I struggled in the autumn with dusts. Struggle with wheat dust? It's the story of my life. He said that it would be controllable with steroid inhalers, or surgery if it got out of hand. I was from now on to have a flu jab every year, and buy proper dust masks – if I insisted on continuing to farm!

It was a curious drive back. A heck of a lot had been explained by that short meeting. In a way, it was quite a relief. When I got home and read the literature that he'd given me, I found myself shouting 'yes' at mentions of inability to exercise, and endless joint pain. Mind you, it could also be because I'm idle.

It was good to get out of the parish again, and this time it was a drive up to Heathrow Airport, Terminal 3, to pick up Diana and her mate after their ten-day cross-Europe trip. I always dread the M25, but this time it was the M3 that was a nightmare. It, too, is undergoing the massive change to 'smart' motorway, and so we crawled up most of it at a scared 50 mph. The M25 was clear as a bell, and getting into Heathrow and parking was a doddle.

The other great modern joy is the level of information available. I'd monitored Diana's flight taking off on a website before I left, and the screen inside the terminal itself was constantly updated. As soon as Diana had landed, she texted to tell me so, and I was treated to updates until the two of them walked out of the arrival doors. While waiting, I sat and surveyed the scene in the arrivals lounge. All the nations of the world, all on mobile telephones in a multitude of different languages. I confess that I caught the eye of another white Englishman, and we nodded to each other, as complete strangers.

The drive back was lovely in the sunset, even when we found that the M3 had been shut completely. We were forced off at Basingstoke. And so I chose to wind our way back through the lanes – a route I'm well used to after the endless trips to the hospital.

July 3rd
Very hot, very sweaty. Not a lot going on – I got a late tank of spray on once it got cool enough. And that was all.

July 4th
A proper farm-free day. It was Hazel's godson's 18th birthday, so we headed to his house up at Beauworth for a noisy garden lunch, which somehow dragged on until 6pm.

Then we headed to the Flowerpots. The godson's father (now separated from his mother) had come up for the weekend for the occasion, and we offered to host him and another godparent. The godson's father is also a very old drinking and rugby companion, having lived in one of our cottages for a few years after the separation, so it threatened to be a major reunion in the pub, but I didn't want to get my hopes up too high – think 'Fun Bobby' in *Friends*. I dug out the Editor and neighbour

Robert to join us, and we set to.

Luckily, it was as daft and childish as ever, and far more fun than I dared to hope for. It has been a very long time since I couldn't talk for crying with laughter. Anthony kindly offered to pick us up, and I can just remember him sitting in the bar, looking at us with a mixture of horror and embarrassment as we said 'bum' a lot and wet ourselves laughing. Much of the late evening vanished from the memory, except for neighbour Robert looking hard at his Land Rover, while slightly unsteady on his feet, and then announcing solemnly that he would walk the hundred yards to his house. Apparently we all said "Shhh, it's a library" a lot on the drive home, but I don't believe that for one moment. It would have been too silly. We are, after all, in our fifties.

July 5th

Not altogether surprisingly, it was a slow morning. There was an egg and bacon frenzy for everyone, and then our guests left by nine. One assumes it was safe for them to drive. I retreated to the sofa in time for the British Grand Prix, which denied me any sleep by being interesting. There was overtaking and even some occasional moments of excitement. And the heavy rain shower towards the end confirmed my suspicion that Formula One would be infinitely better with the introduction of randomly-operated garden sprinklers on every corner.

Despite the lack of sleep, I popped down to West Meon sports pavilion for Open Mic Night. It was well attended, and I played OK. There were multiple offers for new projects – a jazz/funk outfit with Dave, a Sinatra bar band with Richard, and some acoustic folk with Glyn. They're great ideas at the end of a boozy weekend, but the cold light of day will probably extinguish them.

July 6th

A very quiet day indeed. The wind refused to die down enough to do the only two tanks of spraying needed, so I tidied up the spray store, dealt with a couple of deliveries, changed the mirrors on the Massey tractor while generally feeling a bit over-boozed from the weekend. I thought a good walk round the shooting strips to clear my head would be a good thing, but all it did was make me cross that we hadn't had any of the promised rain.

I spent some time in Blackhouse Road, studying the curious lines that the very dry weather is throwing up in the spring barley. I looked and looked, but they just seemed to be random wobbly strips, a couple of yards wide and perhaps forty yards long. I must book a flight over it with Murph to get a better view. It'll probably leave me none the wiser, though.

July 7th

A flow of showers and high winds meant that I still couldn't get the two last tanks of spray on the wheat. So I sat indoors and knocked up the latest opinion column for *Farmers Weekly*. It was witty, incisive and honed to perfection. *Farmers Weekly* decided it was rubbish, and sent it back. I went for a long walk round the wild bird shooting strips in a huff.

In the evening, Jonathan played for the Ropley U15s again, and this time got to take part, rather than just sit on the boundary for half the game, and in the pavilion for the other half. He batted at six, got a few runs with his trademark agricultural swipes, and was out to a slog with his head way in the air. He then bowled two very tidy overs of left arm spin and took a fantastic catch at long on. And to think I nearly didn't bother going to watch him.

It's great fun watching that age group. There are the still-little squeaky things that roll around on the boundary fighting, and there are the almost-grown-ups, who have deep voices and full frames, but can still burst into tears if they're out. There's a lot of trying hard to look cool, and doing what they've seen the professionals cricketers do on the telly. The ball gets thrown round as many team members as possible on its way back to the bowler, for instance. Each one gives the ball a polish and throws it to the next man, who drops it, undoing all the hard work. It also means that the game drags on twice as long as it should do.

Still, I was happy, wrapped up in cap and coat, sitting under the trees to get some shelter from the wind and driving cold drizzle, with a copy of the *Spectator* to fill in the long gaps between deliveries. And a big smile at Jonathan's performance.

July 8th

I spent the whole morning wrestling with the rejected *Farmers Weekly* article, trying to get the same message across. I think I managed to do it – Tim wasn't in the office, so I'll know tomorrow. Meanwhile, Hazel dug out the haymaking kit and dusted it off, so having given up any chance of spraying in the continuous high winds, I set off to the Hay Field and mowed the headland.

It was a bit of a gamble – as haymaking always is – but they reckon the weekend might be unsettled. I'm keen to get the job out of the way, though; the barley is turning rapidly, and it won't be long before we're dusting down the combine.

July 9th

Haymaking is usually an utter joy – a throwback to the good old chemical-free days. A chance to do some slow-speed farming without examinations or certificates, spray suits or risk assessment. It should have been perfect – the day was dry and windy. The slight problem is that the Met Office have slightly revised the forecast to the haymaker's nightmare: three wet days, starting on Sunday. And having cut the headland last night, there's not much point in stopping now. I kept going, with steam coming out of my ears. Thanks goodness for the start of the first Ashes test to keep my spirits up.

I took a break from the mowing for a heavy chat with the two lads from the National

Trust. I'm not sure which of them is actually my direct contact, but they seem to work as a team. We went through the usual gripes about public access and paths, but, as usual, parted on good terms.

In fact, the whole discussion cheered me up a bit, and I headed back out to mow the rest of the Hay Field. The weather forecast didn't get any better, though.

July 10th

A busy farming day. I nipped out and finally put the last two tanks of fungicide on the wheats in JA/DC and Hurst Down. Hurst Down also had a late herbicide to clobber the assorted weeds that had remained untouched in the cold spring.

There was a general panic on the hay – the forecast is getting worse and worse, so we rang Mac to see if he could round bale tomorrow. He said he should be OK for it, and Hazel turned the hay twice, once early, once late.

Thunderstorms rolled in late in the evening, giving a short burst of rain as they skidded past to the north west of us. There was major thunder and lightning, which stopped mysteriously just as it seemed to be heading over the top of us. It was as if they'd been served a Noise Abatement Order.

July 11th

A perfect haymaking day, but the last one for some time, and the hay wasn't 100% ready – nearer 90% dry, I reckoned. There were frantic phone calls between Hazel and Mac, as a plan was hatched. He was happy to bale it for us into big round bales – these are less sensitive to not-quite-dry grass than the small square ones we'd hoped to do. But his baler needed big thick swaths to work well, not the piddly little ones our tedder would make. We would have to borrow his huge spider-wheel tedder.

That was all very well, but he would be using it to row up the grass in Kilmeston that he's also in charge of. That left us with a nervous three or four hours, watching the weather forecast, wondering if we'd get it done today.

Luckily, he was finished with it by lunchtime, and dropped it off in the Hay Field. I hitched off our little tedder, and headed up there to play with this strange machine. After a couple of turns, I'd cracked it, sweeping seven metres of spread grass into one thick swath. Hazel then came up and took over, determined that the hay would be her project.

I went home and supervised Anthony's build up for his little party tonight, took Diana down to her party in Durley, and dropped Jonathan off at the Hinton Arms for his long shift being kitchen monkey.

The air got heavy, the rain got closer, and then Mac's baler blew up. Luckily, thanks to the network of farming neighbourliness, a couple of urgent phone calls were made, and another baler arrived. Mac switched to wrapping his crop in Kilmeston, and also the dampest of ours. Late in the evening, all was done. Eighty-three unwrapped big round hay bales, and 25 wrapped. Not the easy-to-handle lucrative small square ones we'd wanted, but baled hay nonetheless.

And all through this, the Spitfire Sisters were performing just across the field in the grounds of Hinton Ampner House – a great soundtrack for a summer afternoon.

July 12th

The rain arrived – not a lot, but quite steady for most of the day. A good chance to snooze and have a break after all that haymaking franticness. Diana arrived back from her sleepover in Durley in one piece, and we didn't see much of Anthony after his gathering.

I walked out to check on the winter barley late in the evening, to see if it was ready for its pre-harvest Roundup. The retriever in Rick/Clump was a bit of a patchy mess, with some ears necked, and many ears quite soft. Luckily, the forecast means there will be no spraying done for a couple of days, by which time it might have evened up a bit, and be fully ready.

July 13th

Overslept.

Not much happened. Hazel did more bale cart, after we'd had a long session tightening up the top tines on the loader grab. A lot of WD-40 and extra-long bits of hollow tube on the end of ¾" T-bars were needed. I then headed indoors with a headache – there's something doing the rounds again.

Band rehearsal was good though – we were all in, and sounding right on the button. There was much discussion of an email Tod had got, thanking us all for agreeing to play a festival which we've never heard off. Even worse, idd's a charrideee one, so no money will be involved. Whoever our mystery agent is, he needs a good kicking.

July 14th

Whatever the latest bug going round is, it certainly knows how to hand out a headache.

I spent most of the day in a fuzzy mess, wondering how long it would be before I could take more painkillers.

Everyone else was busy, though. Graham Tosdevine's man came in and sprayed the oilseed rape with Roundup, Diana failed another diving test, and Hazel went and fetched the last of the round hay bales. By evening, late drizzle scuppered my plans for a bit of spraying myself, so I took Diana and Jonathan into the Peter Symonds's Sixth Form College open evening. Diana was bursting at the seams to show her little brother round, so she must have enjoyed herself there.

July 15th

A damp and quite drizzly morning, but luckily I got the writing bug – the headache must have cleared – and did the two press releases for the Alresford Show. It's in September, and the secretary likes to get some publicity out well before then, and every year I volunteer to write a few hundred words of nonsense that she can send out to the local papers. It's always fun trying to come up with a fresh write-up for what is fundamentally the same show. The *Hampshire Chronicle* went through a brief stage of using my copy as an article, and one of their journalists would put his name at the top. I soon stopped that – I made my piece ruder and ruder until he couldn't bear to put his name to it. Job done.

The drizzle stopped after lunch, and Hazel, Jonathan and Diana set off in the Kubota to have a massive sheep session in the bottom of Englands – lots of tagging and drenching. I set off in the sprayer, and put a very complicated mix of fungicides, graminicides and insecticides on the peas in Chalks, and then put Roundup on the Retriever in Rick and Clump, and the Volume in Roe Hill. The harvest clock has really started.

So it was good to see Luke from Garwood's giving the combine its service. I called in to see how he was getting on. He said that there wasn't much to do – a belt here, a bearing there, but nothing major. One of the header lift ram seals was leaking, and he reckoned he'd get that done and fitted tomorrow – then it will be ready to go.

July 16th

The pre-harvest lull has officially started. Nothing to spray, nothing to combine. And even if it rains, the wild bird shooting strips could benefit. We took children here, there and everywhere, and then there was a very lively thunderstorm at bedtime. Perfect for those strips.

July 17th

The editor of *South East Farmer* came out to interview me for a feature they're doing. This is a great honour, and I can't really believe I justify their attention, but if they think otherwise, who am I to argue? I thought it might have been a bit of a heated interview, because SEF are about as green a magazine as you can get in the much-diminished world of the farming press, and my views on the Green Blob are quite well-known.

But we had a lovely morning, chatting away, sometimes with the tape recorder on, sometimes off (so I dread to think how much will be noted accurately). We covered a thousand topics: fracking, Skodas, the band, the National Trust, peak oil, ramblers – all the usual farming stuff. I showed him the copy of *Southern Farmer* from 1976, in which Dad was profiled, and challenged him to come up with as good an opening paragraph. "The tall debonair Peter Flindt could easily have been a film star if he hadn't taken to farming at such an early age..." We went round the farm, and took plenty of pictures. It must have looked a bit of a mess compared with the modern flash agribusinesses that he usually goes to, but that's the way we are. We gave him a good lunch and sent him on his way.

The Cheyneys were kindly hosting a party for everyone who had helped with Open Farm Sunday back in June, so we headed down there for a very jolly evening. It seemed odd that they should be hosting – they put all the hard work in in the first place.

July 18th

A very lazy Saturday recovering from last night, and being relieved that the England cricket team were back to where we expect them to be. Not to forget cursing that I didn't take Ladbroke's 7/4 on Australia winning the series, which they were offering after England won the first test. The Aussies are now 2/1 on.

July 19th

Another pre-harvest lullday. I went and played with the combine for a bit, digging out assorted covers and dividers that inevitably seem to spread their way round the farm. I checked the barley in the drizzle, and realised that harvest is still a long way off.

July 20th

Another damp morning, so I set about assorted press offices to get the next batch of cars sorted out. I tried Porsche for a Macan, Fiat Group for a 500x and a Jeep Cherokee, and Mazda for a CX-3. I came up against a lot of 'out of the office' and 'in a meeting', but finally managed to get the Mazda sorted.

We hadn't done the traditional pre-harvest stock-up, so I had a leisurely drive to APM at King's Somborne, and bought a new broom, some super-strong dust masks, a selection of black and silver tape, and the inevitable cans of WD-40. I love the drive through to King's Somborne. It's one that I've done hundreds of times in the last quarter of a century, and is a great opportunity for a bit of a think. I remember doing it when Hazel was pregnant, doing it with excited toddlers, and now doing it with teenagers stuck at home, faces glued to screens, not remotely interested in a drive out to an agricultural Aladdin's cave. Such is the way of the world.

I came back via the Claas dealer in Micheldever to have a look at the new Arion 430 that they've got on the forecourt. At some stage, we're going to replace the Massey loader tractor, and I quite like the look of the green machine. Good cab, nice steps, and sensible controls. Shame about the Adblue – but I suspect we're going to have to bite that bullet one day.

The evening came on damp, just as Diana set off to see some ballet at the Theatre Royal in Winchester, and Jonathan set off to cricket, for the last game of the season. They won, and he got a couple of overs of bowling in, which made all the difference. He finished the U15 season having enjoyed it.

July 21st

A nervous morning – the new vets were coming to do the first half of the TB tests on the big cattle. We've had the same vets for as long as I remember, but back in the late winter they announced that they were abandoning big animal work (except the lucrative horse market), so we had to call out the new lot for today's test.

It went well, even though the big blighters are still reluctant to go anywhere, being tame as heck. But the diminutive vet was quick, efficient and friendly, and the whole lot was done in half an hour. We'll see if the horror stories about being charged by the minute apply.

Meanwhile, over in one of our cottages, the electricians were checking the electrical system. The new tenant seemed convinced that the whole lot was dangerous and asked that an electrician get out there as soon as possible. It struck us as odd, because we'd had the whole place checked out only recently as part of our duty to make sure the letting of our cottages is all by the book – not least, to keep the Trust happy.

The day turned hot and humid, so I thought it time to set about the last bits and pieces on the combine. In went the de-awning plates – a nightmare on those TC combines, unless you're a small-handed gynaecologist. Off came the assorted bean elevator covers, and on went the lifters. I dug out the dividers and put them on, and set the drum and fan speeds for winter barley. She was ready to go. So I went home for lunch.

After lunch, I helped Hazel put hydraulic pipes on the 'wrapped round bale' grab. This attachment for the loader has been sitting unused in the yard since we last made round bale wrapped silage – which must be well over ten years ago. It was an object lesson in not selling stuff, even though you think you'll never use it again. Hazel then set off to gather the bales from the Hay Field.

I drive up to Clump to check the Retriever winter barley. It still wasn't hard as nails, and the Roundup had only been on six days, so combining it wasn't legally an option. The Volume in Big Field is the other option, but we're selling the straw, and I'm scared of swathing in unsettled weather. It can be there for months afterwards if it's not cleared quickly enough. I chatted through my harvest plans with a dozen ramblers who had stopped to see what I was doing. They seemed delighted to hear all about it.

There was nothing left to do except sweep the barn floors, so, clutching my new broom and my super-strength dust mask, I sweated my way down the left-hand lean-to and the main Drier barn. A fine workout it was, too. And then, still seized by an odd bout of enthusiasm, I hitched the sprayer off and fetched one of the big green trailers, brought it up to the yard and started greasing it up. Luckily, tea beckoned, and put a stop to that.

The electrician reported back: nothing whatsoever wrong with the electrics in the cottage. I win that one.

Hazel and the rest of the gang from her weekly 'keep fit' club had a long evening of beer and chips in The Fox at Bramdean, which sort of defines irony.

July 22nd

Would we start harvest today? Mac called in to see if we were going to, because he'd got the job of baling the winter barley straw for the buyer. As usual, any sense of harvest urgency vanished, and a lot of tea was drunk. I said I thought it unlikely, because it still didn't feel settled enough. Mac agreed, and headed off to try and get some hay done somewhere else. It then rained for quite a lot of the day, which made me feel quite relieved that I'd called it right.

The forecast also deteriorated, so I'm not sure how long any feeling of relief will go on. When it does dry up, we'll have lots to do.

It seemed a good time to sit down and address the tiny issue of the bursting overdraft, and how we're going to pay some substantial tax bills and some even more substantial chemical bills on a fairly limited cash supply. The tax has been sorted with a six-month loan from the bank – good thing money's cheap at the moment – and so it meant we're going to have to ring up and grovel to the chemical companies. I rang the buying group and got some names and contact numbers in assorted accounts departments, but chickened out of starting the cap-in-hand routine until another day.

July 23rd

We started harvest. I tried to find excuses not to – I drove out to Rick and Clump and rubbed some barley out, and it had dried perfectly after yesterday's rain. I'd swept all the floors, hitched onto a trailer, got the combine ready and the Retriever was now through its post-Roundup harvest interval period.

Luckily, Phil Tickner came to look at the big cattle, with a view to buying them. By the time he and Hazel had finished that, and we'd sat and drunk tea and moaned and gossiped, it was well past three o'clock. By the time we finally got out to Rick and Clump, it was four o'clock.

I did a turn on the bottom headland without the chopper to test for thrashing, and then set off round the headland with the chopper on. Where it was thick, it was very thick. Where it was a bit thin, it was very thin, but we managed six trailers off six-and-a-bit hectares. There was no real way of judging bushel weight, so no idea how much is in a trailer. But it would be nice to think it was about eight tons. If that barley – the lower yielding one of the two – manages three ton/acre, I'll be pleased.

We kept going until after eight. I had to turn down a pub trip with neighbour Robert, which took some determination. I was in half a mind to push on into the night, with the forecast of biblical rain, but there was damp in the air, and the combine was beginning to complain a bit, so we abandoned with a clear conscience. Well, almost clear.

July 24th

The rain arrived at about 9am, just late enough for us to think they'd got it all wrong again. But arrive it did, and it was long and steady. I was mighty pleased not to have swaths of straw on the ground.

The cattle passed their TB test, and there was a harsh (but quite accurate) letter in *Farmers Weekly* having a go at me. I snoozed a lot, although I sneaked out in a short break in the rain to take the dogs for a walk.

The forms arrived from the bank to set up a loan to pay the tax bill, and three chemical companies agreed to us holding back some payments on their bills. I think the overdraft limit should be safe.

And then, most bizarrely, in the last week of July, just after we'd started harvest, we lit a fire in the sitting room to relieve some of the cold and gloom.

July 25th

In a previous existence, this would have been the perfect mid-harvest day: crops too wet to touch with a combine, but fine and dry overhead, and a big cricket match to be enjoyed with the White Hunters. But my plans to pop up and umpire were scotched when the word came through that the Brockwood pitch had had just a bit too much rain yesterday, and the match was off.

The Editor called in while on pigeon patrol – despite all my texts yesterday, there were no pigeons to be seen, apparently. He'd been cheerfully challenged by Sean in New Pond Cottages, who wanted to know what the hell he has up to, scouting the field with binoculars. Once introductions were made, they had a very jolly chat. Good on Sean for keeping his eyes open.

One of the White Hunter presidents, who had been hurtling back from the West Country for the cricket match, rang to suggest a pub lunch. Hazel and I met him and his family in the Flowerpots for a ploughman's and a pint or two. As a direct result, the rest of the afternoon was fairly heavy on headache and grumbling tummy. I was quite relieved when I stumbled out to Rick and Clump to check the barley, and found it was still too soft to combine.

July 26th

A foul day. Cold, wet and windy. Diana had a couple of friends round, and they and Jonathan played Scrabble and ate spicy dips in front of a roaring fire – on July 26th! I watched some of the Grand Prix on the television, and then switched to the computer when the girls arrived. It was worth the effort, as it was the best race anyone has seen in years. Who'd have thought it?

July 27th

Gaskin's rang to sat that they wanted to deliver the new sprayer on Tuesday, and take the old one away. So I had a long day sorting the old one out. I took off all the fertiliser nozzles, and removed the nozzle filters (both of which I'm transferring to the new sprayer) and set about it with the pressure washer. It's odd to be saying farewell to a machine after only eighteen months, but its inability to apply liquid fertiliser evenly is too much of a liability on this farm. I'm not 100% convinced that the new one will do better, even if the booms will be the more traditional gullwing style instead of the multi-hinged version on the machine that's going.

While I had the cheap and cheerful pressure washer out, I gave the back end of the Deere a good clean. As usual with a modern tractor, it's all but impossible to get all the nooks and crannies done. All you do is push the dirt from one pipe-covered end of the back axle to the other, while getting a facefull of grit and oil.

I thought I'd try out the JCB loader that we've hired for loading lorries, and which Oakes Bros delivered last week. It had a flat battery. Good thing it wasn't parked up in the corn store, with a lorry waiting outside.

July 28th

Time to get the pre-harvest diesel ordered. I rang round a few suppliers as usual, and picked the cheapest. Red diesel is now 30% cheaper than it was last August. Amazing. I filled up all the vehicles I could from the main tank (Oakes Bros were out very early with a fresh battery to get the JCB going) and emptied what was left into the bowser. Another 2,500 litres in the main tank and we'll be all set to go.

We should have gone with the combine today, but the barley was still just a bit soft, and it turned out to be a chaotic day ferrying children here, there and everywhere. It wasn't helped by the Skoda going in for one of its very rare main services. We were lent a lovely courtesy car – a Fabia – but Anthony wasn't insured to drive it.

I was relieved to get really good and friendly service from the Skoda dealer. They've gone a bit sneery and all 'VW' in recent years, especially in the showroom department. I suppose they're not working as hard as they used to to sell cars (everyone seems to want a Skoda these days), but it always seems wisest to use the main dealer for servicing – and just put up with the haughty attitude. This time, however, the service was prompt, polite and efficient. Enough to restore one's faith in main dealers.

Mid-afternoon, the new sprayer arrived. It's the smallest of the big range from Amazone, and dwarfed the one that was going away. I'll probably need a bigger tractor to pull it, especially when it's loaded with 3,500 litres of liquid fertiliser. There wasn't too much to do to change, but I dare say some of the extra bits and pieces will need to be explained to me. A quick glance at the instruction book told me what we all know about modern instruction books – we'll learn nothing from that.

Meanwhile, we were ferrying children around Hampshire – Diana to Winchester to get a train to Eastleigh, Jonathan to play tennis in Petersfield, and Anthony to see a friend up in Bentley, and then the whole process reversed to pick them all up again. What was it we were really supposed to be doing today, as a cold drying wind blew through the barley? Oh yes: harvest. Oh well, we'll have a go tomorrow.

July 29th

The early alarm on my phone sounded a bit odd, and then I realised it was actually a phone call. I know proper farmers are wide awake at 6.55am, having had a side of ox and a flagon of ale for breakfast, *and* been out and done six hours' work, but I was still sound asleep. I let it go to answerphone, and treated it as an alarm call anyway. Once I was up and about more awake, I rang it back, and it was who I thought it was – the diesel delivery driver doing his 60-minute warning. Very efficient. I went and unlocked all the gates and doors ready for him. He was done and dusted by 7.30.

We made a proper early start on the barley in Rick and Clump, convinced that we'd get it finished and maybe get a couple of turns of Big Field done tonight. We got a bit held up when the first Hampshire Grain lorry of the season got lost, and headed up through Kilmeston instead of turning left at the bottom of the farm hill, so Noel was a bit late taking over from me for lunch.

While enjoying my healthy salad (and crunchy sugar-filled chewy bar), I checked the radar, only to find a band of heavy showers marching down from the north. This came as a bit of a surprise, and when they duly arrived, we had not more than an hour's work left in Rick and Clump. But when the rain comes down wet enough to keep the reel's central bar wet, it's time to stop. So we had an early finish. The big consolation is that we didn't start in Big Field, and leave a lot of straw wet, waiting to be baled.

July 30th

We made the most of the damp morning, and had a busy session weighing sheep. I helped out, trying to look like I knew what I was doing, but convinced no one.

We got another lorry of Retriever away, and made a prompt start after lunch. We could have gone a bit earlier – it had dried very quickly this morning. We finally got Rick and Clump finished, and then disconnected the chopper, and headed into Big Field. It was no surprise that the Volume was a step up in yield, but it was depressing to see how much had been hammered to the floor by the wind and rain. By dusk, we had cut about 19 acres of Big's 52.

July 31st

Another early lorry, and another reasonably prompt start, after a major refuel, grease up and window clean – just after eleven. Just as we were swapping over for lunch, the baler arrived, along with the man who had bought the bales, ready to load up and start carting them away. After months of the occasional machine in the field, it was suddenly swarming with tractors.

Mid-afternoon, I gave Robert Raimes a ring, to see what his availability was. He's in the parish combining his oilseed rape just the other side of the A272, and it might be wise for him to pop over and bash off our 87 acres – a day's work for his massive machine. It would cost a bit, but would push us back onto schedule, and save me the major job (and associated risk of physical injury) of swapping sieves and putting on the side knife.

Another lorry arrived at tea time, perfect for us all to take a breather – except Noel, who went and loaded him. We finished Big at about 6.20, and set off to open up Roe Hill. The first couple of turns were a horrible mess, and the lumps left behind by last year's drilling proved a challenge. One lump managed to break off a section – luckily, we found a couple of new bolts and nuts in the toolbox, and put another one on just as it was getting dark. Tomorrow's job is to round up a complete section repair kit and put it in the cab.

August 1st

A fine Saturday, and having managed to put Robert Raimes off until tomorrow, and with an afternoon's worth of winter barley to combine, I had a lazy morning, giving the combine a leisurely grease up and fuel up. In the meantime, Noel loaded two more lorries of Volume.

After lunch, we got stuck into the rest of the Volume in Roe Hill, and were pleasantly surprised by it. It's one of the new world-conquering hybrid barleys, which the breeders guarantee (subject to a very long list of terms and conditions) will fill your barn with a certain yield. Roe Hill was never going to reach that yield, but bearing in mind how badly it had gone in last autumn, I was pleased with what we got. I'm not sure that we'll grow it again, though – the price of the seed alone means a massive yield is needed to recover your costs. If we stick with winter barley this autumn, I'll probably go back to a conventional barley.

August 2nd

Another great flat-out Sunday. I was up very early, sweeping the barn floor at 7.30am, in anticipation of Robert Raimes' big combine turning up and having a long day in the oilseed rape. Noel popped down the hill, across the A272, and picked up Robert's header trailer, and then escorted him along the main road (very little traffic to get upset at that time on a Sunday morning), up across Godwin's, along the ridge to Clump, through the standing wheat for a few yards and into the top of Roe Hill, out of Roe Hill on to the road at the cattle barn, along the road south for a few yards, into the standing wheat in the Folly, down a tramline, and finally into White Hill. Luckily, the way Robert drives his combine it only took half an hour or so.

I toyed with the idea of converting my combine to OSR, and then joining him, but it makes sorting out the bill very confusing, so, based on his assurance that all 87 aces would be done in one day, I took up position in Godwin's barn as trailer monkey. Anthony and Noel set off to do corn cart.

All went swimmingly, until about two thirty, when I had to replace Anthony (revision for retakes beckoned). Then Noel's trailer had a puncture – a nail had embedded itself perfectly in the tread. So he replaced me, I went back to the barn, and Noel went like hell in the night to keep up with Robert's combine. By five, White Hill was finished, and after a quick disassemble, a short drive to Cheyney and a reassemble, all the oilseed rape was indeed done in one day.

There was a reasonable heap in the barn – probably about 120 tons, which is, once again, disappointing. OSR yields are still stuck at the Eighties level, and never seem to move on. I gave Robert a lift back to his truck in the Jolly Meadows in a bit of a sulk. I'd paid a fortune growing that crop, and now had paid a lot to have it combined, and it was still mediocre. And that's before we get onto the selling price at the moment.

It would have helped if the forecast still maintained that there was rain on the way, but it had changed to 'fine for a fortnight' – so I needn't have called Robert in after all. Mind you, the forecast could just as easily change again – and his view from the cab was that it needed getting in sooner rather than later. It was very ripe indeed.

Meanwhile, Colin and Matt Shaw had been into Roe Hill and baled the straw for the buyer. They were still a bit short of their target number, so some of the spring barley can go to them.

Open Mic Night in West Meon beckoned, but I would have been very late to get there, and fallen asleep at my keyboard. A quick shower and bed was a far better idea.

August 3rd

Everything that was obviously ripe had been combined. Where to go next? I kept meaning to pop out and check the spring barley and the wheat, but something always came up.

First, I realised that the deadline for October's motoring column was upon us, so I sat down and wracked my brain to remember what we thought of the SEAT a few weeks ago. That left Noel, Hazel and Jonathan to load the two lorries that were due at nine and ten. The trouble started when the nine o'clock lorry arrived at ten fifteen, and then headed down to the Drier instead of stopping at the Godwin's yard – where we were all set up to load him with oilseed rape from yesterday. The instructions couldn't have been simpler: "Upper shithole, a load of rape." Oh well; everyone shot off down the Drier Yard instead ("Lower shithole").

It was actually for the best – it gave us a chance to clear the left-hand lean-to, and so keep combining if and when I found something ripe. I dropped Diana off at work in Alresford, and met the first lorry on its way out. Anthony, hard at work revising, said he'd thought he'd heard the second lorry come in, so I assumed all was well with the world. There then came a call from the Drier, asking where the hell the second lorry was. I rang Hampshire Grain, who said the second lorry was 'about to leave', i.e. having another cup of tea and leaving in twenty minutes. I told them to scrap the second lorry, as Noel had to get away for an eye examination, and it was only fair to let him shower and shave first.

In the meantime, while comprehensively failing to write up the SEAT, I'd been on the phone to Micheldever Tyres to ask about a replacement wheel assembly to fit the grain trailers. They said they'd put one together at a reasonable price, as well as mend the old one if I brought it up there. I then remembered that I had a brand new tyre of the right size at the back of the tractor barn. Goodness knows how it got there, or when, but I took it up to Micheldever – having persuaded Jonathan to come with me and act as muscle.

We were ushered in via the exit to get to the front of the queue – they weren't busy, but they seemed to appreciate the harvest urgency. Within ten minutes, we were on our way home, with one complete brand new tyre, and one old rim with the tyre from the back of the barn mounted on it. And both of them tubeless – after years of insisting on tubes so we can repair them ourselves, I'm moving to tubeless because I haven't got the strength any more to take tyres off rims. Tubeless repair kits now dominate. Funny how life changes.

Despite having persuaded the nice people at Micheldever Tyres that there was a harvest emergency, we decided to stop at the Claas dealer just down the old Roman road and inspect the new Arion that they'd got parked outside. We dug out a surprised salesman (who was probably amazed we weren't combining) and he gave us a comprehensive guided tour. It had many good points (nice cab, great controls) but a couple of minus points (steep steps and no cab suspension). He offered to bring one out to the farm for a play, which is a rarity these days.

With everyone back at base, another lorry arrived perfectly. Hazel and Noel put the last of the Retriever in (about 18 tons) and topped him up with Volume – it's all going as feed barley, so mixing was fine. This gave me a chance, finally, to check some crops for ripeness. The spring barley seemed ready to go, as did the Stanmore wheat, although the latter could have done with a couple more days. If it was an out-and-out milling wheat, I'd be rushing up there to save the Hagberg.

While all this was going on, the Editor had set up a hide on the OSR stubble at the far end of White Hill, and was having a fairly busy time in the howling SW wind that had got up. He rang me when he saw me checking the wheat in Broom Field, and suggested that Hazel should get up there with the flatcoats and help tidy up. I drove down the Drier and relieved Hazel from her sweeping, and put it to her. She needed no second invitation, and went off like the wind in Tigger to fetch dogs and get up to White Hill.

Noel and I got the lorry finished, and finally got the driver to stop talking so we could send him on his way. Noel cleaned out the dregs from the left-hand lean-to, so that was ready to take whatever we next move into. I got home just as Team Flatcoat got back – two exhausted dogs, one delighted handler and one thrilled Editor – and all for about a dozen birds.

I never did get any combining done, although late in the evening, I thought I should do something with the combine. I popped down to behind the cattle barn, where it was parked, and did a fuel up and a grease up. It cleared my conscience a bit.

August 4th

It was oddly quiet when I got up. Hazel, Diana and Jonathan had been up for ages, and were out in the Bottom of Englands doing sheep gathering for market. They staggered in just before nine, flushed with success, and, in Diana's case, covered in mud and bruises; one lamb had tried to make a break for it, and Diana wasn't having that. A wrestling match had ensued, which Diana won. They'd got a fine bunch of lambs onto Tony's trailer, and he'd headed off to Salisbury.

There was an odd feeling about the whole idea of selling lambs at the moment, because there's a boycott being organised by the proper sheep farmers, who, like the milk producers, are being ripped off mercilessly. The idea is to withdraw all lambs from sale, and try to force some upward movement in prices. Rightly or wrongly, we sent ours anyway.

I finally finished the SEAT Leon piece, and sent it away. It wasn't my finest – it was very hard to find a theme to weave the whole thing around, but it wasn't sent straight back to me as rubbish, so I think it was OK.

By 11am, the drizzle had stopped, so I walked down to the cattle barn to pick up the combine, drove it over Roe Hill, and started the spring barley in Blackhouse Road.

It seemed wrong to be chopping the vast quantity of straw, but there's no demand at the moment, and the forecast is iffy, and we don't want vast areas of straw lying about. Diesel used to be a factor in deciding to chop or not to chop, but it's as cheap at the moment as it has been in five years. The thick bed of fluffy straw might take some incorporating, but we'll cross that bridge when we get there.

By evening, we'd done over thirty acres, and managed to load out most of the winter barley in the afternoon. One load up to Hampshire Grain on a wet morning in our own trailer and the main barn will be free for any big rush that might happen.

August 5th

Showers were imminent – or so the Met Office said. And, to be fair, the radar suggested they were right. So we had a lorry frenzy instead of combining. We cleared out Godwin's barn of a pathetic amount of oilseed rape, and then did two loads of spring barley from the left-hand lean-to. I say we, but actually it was Noel, Hazel and Jonathan. I sat round for most of the morning feeling less than well, and then decided to give the combine its 50-hour service and a fuel up – the showers still hadn't materialised beyond a few spots of rain. We finally decided to have a go at about two, and the heavens opened at four. Still, we got a couple more loads off Blackhouse Road.

Noel spent a couple of hours getting a trailer up together to take the dregs of the Volume up to Hampshire Grain. We could get a lorry in, but we pay a 'cap' fee for a mostly empty load, and the drivers complain furiously at the idea. So if it's still wet tomorrow, I'll get Noel to have a jolly trip up to Micheldever. He needs to find a trailer with working tail lights, and get the Deere's front linkage arms folded up – they've seized 'down' after all that liquid fertiliser application.

I checked out the figures from today's lorries. The oilseed rape reached a dismal 100 tons off 87 acres, but the spring barley loads continue to be top quality, which made me feel a bit better. Rufus and I adjourned to the Thomas Lord to agree loudly on politics and current affairs, and drink a toast to BBC Radio 4 and its first ever proper Climate Change Sceptic broadcast, in which they mercilessly mocked the Met Office. As if on cue, a thunderstorm blacked out all the lights in the pub. I bet they didn't forecast that.

August 6th

Everything was pretty soggy, so it was a good chance to draw breath and get a couple of wet day jobs done. Noel took the most roadworthy trailer down the Drier and filled it with the dregs of the Volume, and then set off for the long trip to Micheldever. I drove to Chilbolton to get service bits for the Deere – oil, oil filters and the like. I love the drive to Hunt's, because it takes you off 'our' Hampshire – hills and clay - and into flat chalkland Hampshire; the land of observatories, Roman roads, World War Two airfields and big open fields. There was a combine doing barley near Stockbridge, so I assume they didn't get the rain last night.

The demo Horsch Joker arrived, and looked a fancy version of a simple machine – two rows of serrated discs and a press on the back. I took it for a play on the corners and edges where I'm planning more shooting cover, and it did a good job. The main thing was that the little red tractor handled it. It'll be interesting to see what the dealer wants for it.

Noel did the service on the Deere, and then with nothing left to do, and the sun having shone for a few hours, we went back into Blackhouse Road and did another few acres. Just as we were about to knock off, the unloading auger started making unhappy noises, and then, on the last load of the day, there was a 'ping', and it gave up altogether. A quick inspection revealed that the drive chain on the right-hand side had come apart – the joiner link had lost its lock clip. Luckily, it's a tiny repair, but I had a moderately worried evening, wondering if something further down the drive line had cause the chain to fail. A bearing? A brick in the auger? We'll find out tomorrow.

August 7th

Noel loaded an early lorry, and I set off to find a new chain joining link. Rod didn't have one, so I popped into another dealer, just another couple of miles away. Luckily, after a few sharp intakes of breath and a lot of tooth sucking, they found one. There was just time to discuss with the salesman our tentative plans to replace the Massey, which should get some instant response in today's financial climate, and then it was back home. I picked up Noel from the yard, and we had the whole chain on and repaired in minutes. Thanks to Noel's height and reach, there was no need to fetch the stepladder. I put the unloading arm in gear and it went as smoothly as ever. A huge relief.

Then it was a long day in the spring barley, finishing Blackhouse Road, and doing a few turns of Behind My Love's. We started swathing the straw in BML's, and only then do you realise why the chopper was struggling to do a decent job in Blackhouse Road – the quantity of straw produced by Propino is vast.

Just as we were finishing, a hot balloon floated over Blackhouse Road and dipped down almost to the point of landing. I've been at war with hot air balloons for years, finding it outrageous that they have built a very lucrative industry based on the premise that they are entitled to fly low over our houses and farms, scaring pets and livestock, and then landing, unannounced and uninvited in our fields – and we're obliged to help them out again. The support vehicle drove past me and Sean as we leant on his gate and we all smiled at each other somewhat unconvincingly. Bastards.

August 8th

No combining this morning – I was determined to hear England win the Ashes in comfort. I dieseled up and greased up as normal, and then headed home to enjoy the radio coverage. No Sky in our house. Noel loaded another couple of lorries, and then headed off to the physio to get his bad shoulder looked at. It turned out to be typical tractor drivers' neck. Welcome to the club, Noel.

The Met Office have completely changed the forecast, and big wet weather is coming. This took us all by surprise – when really we should be used to it. We finished BML's, and then I headed back to New Pond Cottages for the foul job of removing the de-awning plates. Dust mask on, overalls on, and then you reach in and grope and wobble and shake until they come free. Once that was done, I headed up to Stanmore Pipeline via the Drier and Folly headlands (rolling down a bit of crop), round the outside of White Hill on the OSR stubble (pausing only to text the Editor about the vast flock of pigeons that was out there), and then into Broom Field. I cut a bit to get to Long Field, and then cut a headland to get to Pipeline. What a palaver.

I think it was the right thing to do. The tests from the spring barley we had cut suggested that it wasn't absolutely ripe, and so Kilmeston Road and the Hangar could wait for a bit. Meanwhile, the wheat in Pipeline was just falling out of the ear, so really didn't want to be waiting much longer. There seemed to be lots of it, too. Let's hope they all continue like this.

August 9th

A fantastic misty start led to a hot fine day. I was up in Pipeline Field fuelling up quite early – the tank was only one third empty, but the last thing I needed was to stop early tonight because of lack of fuel. I also gave the air cleaner a blow out in the yard, which should improve diesel usage.

Noel loaded the one lorry of the day with wheat. The results of this lorry (if it's crap feed wheat) might persuade me to give up on the Claire and head off to finish the quality spring barley. By 10.45 we were going, but I was in a bit of a mood. The forecast had changed completely, and there don't seem many dry days in the next week. And the baler man had texted to say he wouldn't be able to get to Behind My Love's today. I know it's only fifteen acres, and there's no hurry to clear the field, but it's a lot of straw that doesn't need to get very wet.

We had a really good run, stopping only for harvest tea with Sean and Dawn and their floppy Alsatian, who had walked up through the woods. It all came to a frustrating halt at just after six, just after we'd finished Pipeline and moved into Long Field. Something didn't feel right, and a walk round revealed a flat tyre on the rear axle.

Hugely frustrating: I had really hoped to get a good headland opened up in Long , and six-thirty on a Sunday night is no time to call out Micheldever Tyres' mobile mob. I reluctantly called it a day. I needn't have fuelled up after all. And the first load had gone in as plain feed wheat. Oh well.

More cheerful was the Editor, who'd set up a hide on the oilseed rape stubble and bagged 29 pigeons. His 'thank-you' text was a joy.

August 10ᵗʰ

Big rain a'coming, or so they said. I managed to get two short-notice lorries out – there's nothing messier than trying to load corn in pouring rain. Mud gets everywhere. Once they were done, Noel went off to shop for kitchens for the new house he's building.

I got hold of Micheldever Tyres at eight o'clock, and their man was out by nine thirty – despite us being third on his list. The new test car – a Mazda CX-3 – arrived at lunchtime, and the driver didn't need a lift to a station, which is always easier. With an afternoon free, and with Rosie's wedding next week, I popped into Petersfield for a proper haircut. And then hit Mr Sofa for the rest of the afternoon. The forecast made very depressing reading – luckily, a very jolly band rehearsal cheered me up.

August 11ᵗʰ

Hazel and Jonathan set of early in the test Mazda to buy a ram. I sat around and waited for lorries to clear room for what is expected to be the last bit of combining before we all get washed away on Thursday. Unfortunately, no lorries arrived. I rang Hampshire Grain, who apologised, and said there had been lots of breakdowns – they could get one to us later in the day – possibly. I said not to bother, and stood Noel down for the day. Thank goodness he's flexible.

The Claas dealer arrived at lunchtime with a demo tractor. You can tell things are bit doom-laden at the moment – the slightest hint of interest in new kit and there's a demo on your doorstep. I hitched on the (demo) Horsch Joker, and had another long-ish session in Rick and Clump. Heavy cloud turned to drizzle, which turned to heavy drizzle.

Hazel and Jonathan got back from Wiltshire, fairly well-travelled and very tired, having bought a ram, and Anthony was despatched to Alresford for fish and chips. The forecast is getting more terrifying by the day.

August 12ᵗʰ

Everything was still pretty sodden from yesterday's rain, but we had a very productive morning. I finished an opinion column for *Farmers Weekly*, which went through without any queries, and Hazel and Noel shifted three more loads of Claire and a load of Propino out of the drier sheds. Graham Tosdevine's man arrived to put Roundup on the peas – I nearly put him off, but it seemed to be staying dry, and there didn't look like another opportunity for a few days. Just after he finished, the sun came out and a strong SE wind got up too, so by three o'clock we were back in Long Field.

By eight thirty, we'd knocked off another twenty acres. It seemed even thicker than Pipeline, which seemed to have done about 3.7 tons/acre. I was sending a full trailer away every two acres. It was pretty soggy in mid-afternoon, but by evening it had dried enough to flow well in the tank and trailer.

I had a curious gathering of memories from Long Field: getting stuck with tractor and trailer in our very first harvest down here in 1984, the plane crash landing in 1988, and the years of Haven being grown as a continuous wheat, yielding 30 cwt/acre. It would be lovely if this harvest is good enough – even only here in the Stanmore block – to banish some of those memories.

It turned out that the straw in BML's had been baled after all – someone had nipped out and baled 53 big bales (off 14 acres!) just before the drizzle got heavy yesterday. That was a relief.

The day's curious moment came when Southern Harvesters' rep rang and asked if we were using the demo Claas. I said that we were actually combining. He asked if he could pop out and do some work with the tractor, and take some pictures for the Facebook page. Who was I to turn down such a request – especially if it meant getting a few more acres cultivated? I look forward to seeing Rick and Clump immortalised on Facebook.

With trailers safely under cover, and the Massey in the barn ready for Gaskin's to do a back axle oil change tomorrow, we went to bed awaiting the deluge.

August 13th

After all that, there was no overnight deluge – just the odd remote rumble of thunder. The air seemed white, and it was close and sticky – but no rain yet. I hadn't booked any lorries, but on the stroke of 8am the phone rang; it was Hampshire Grain, asking to send one anyway. That suited me – getting grain out of the store when the ground is still dry is a bonus.

We got one done, so I trudged out into the wheat in Drier Field (to get some phone reception) and managed to get another one within the half hour. Perfect.

I had passed a dark red car on the way down the drier, parked on the side of the road half way up Roe Hill. I raised half a hackle, but I thought little more than to note that it was a Suzuki Swift. By the time I drove back from loading the first lorry it had gone, replaced by a huge pile of rubbish. There were Red Bull cans, dozens of cigarette packets, lots of wet wipes and sandwich packets. Ah yes – it's Boomtown time!

Just to the East of Winchester is a vast natural amphitheatre. Even after a lifetime of driving round its rim on the A272 as it snakes up to Cheesefoot Head, I never fail to be impressed by the enormous three-sided bowl. The family who farm this bowl did so conventionally for many a decade, until (the story goes) the era of crop circles arrived. In the early summer, pesky aliens would sneak down into the bowl and make ever more elaborate circles and patterns in the nearly-ripe crops. Then, hundreds of members of the public would treat these crop circles as some sort of open invite to walk down and visit them.

We escaped the curse of the crop circles almost completely – something to do with the aliens being unable to get their spaceships up our tiny lanes. There was one half-hearted attempt at a circle in Kilmeston Road, but a set of car keys found near the centre suggested human input – or that aliens drive Vauxhalls.

It is said that the last straw at Cheesefoot Head was when a huge stick man was rolled into the crop, with the words 'Matt le Tiss for England' underneath. Matt le

Tissier was a Southampton footballer, whose considerable footballing talents were inexplicably overlooked by the England selectors. And our visiting aliens, having travelled countless light-years across the universe, decided that they should join in with the outrage that was seizing the south of England. For the farmer, enough was enough, and the bottom of the bowl was grassed down, and alternative uses were sought.

The most prominent diversification has been a multiday music festival every August, and this year's event covered four days and very late nights, and hosted 50,000 keen fans of the alternative music scene. They come from far and wide, and a handful of these had decided to camp in their Suzuki on the roadside last night. I think it was the Red Bull and cigarettes that gave it away.

I found a carrier bag and cleared up the mess, and couldn't help but notice several credit card receipts. One of our local police might be persuaded to do some further enquiries. They won't be available for a few days – the whole county's force is sent to Boomtown.

Just as we sheeted down the second lorry, the heavens opened, with some lively thunder. The rest of the day was spent hoping the crops don't get too hammered, and, with not much else to do, deciding to service the AGA.

At least I finally managed to get down the Flowerpots with neighbour Robert to enjoy a good moan about these inexplicable wheat yields. One of his fields, clean and dry, has yielded 11.47 tonnes/hectare. No wonder prices are in freefall.

Thanks to a few pints, I slept through any noise from Boomtown, although the easterly wind and rain probably helped to deaden any noise.

August 14th

It rained and rained and rained. And then it rained a bit more. I texted Noel: 'Sofa Day?' He replied, brilliantly 'I'm on it already'. Having dozed for much of the day, it was hard to sleep through Boomtown – which seemed particularly loud this year. I even rang up to have a word with their amusingly named 'helpline'. The men manning the 'could not give a toss' line quoted platitudes, and then hung up. It could be a long weekend.

August 15th

Everything was still sodden, but I greased up and fuelled up the combine anyway. It seemed a good chance to finish off the new game strips, though, so I hitched the tractor onto the drill, emptied out the dregs of 'Pheasant and Finch' game cover, filled it with 'Autumn Promise' and calibrated. And then, in true procrastinatory form, I gave the Deere a good wash; mind you, I couldn't see out, so it wasn't time wasted.

August 16th

Boomtown was a shocker last night, so I was up late, having hardly slept. Once I felt up to it, I nipped out with the drill, and did the new game strips either side of the new hedge between Big and Rick/Clump. These strips, long and wide ones, in the open chalkland, are my great idea to attract all of Hampshire's partridges to our shoot. I had some seed left over, so I did the west side of Cheyney and redrilled a bit of Barracuda. That's where the partridges will probably end up.

August 17th

Having held back from combining over the weekend, it was rewarding to be greeted with a great forecast for the week ahead. There might be showers on Thursday, but otherwise dry. Perfect to do some catching up.

We loaded two more lorries – one from the left-hand lean-to of spring barley, which we all thought would clear the barn, but didn't, and then took a load from the main barn of last week's soggy Claire. Both barns had about a green trailer's worth at the back, which is good for the yield numbers. I asked Noel to spread the Claire about on the floor and we'll put today's dry Claire on top, and then asked him to shovel the dregs of the spring barley into a green trailer and bring it up to Godwin's, where we'll be stacking the spring barley off Kilmeston Road and the Hangar.

The Mazda CX-3 went away at lunchtime, so we were clear to combine in the warm sunshine. We finished Long Field and hopped into Broom. The south side of Broom seemed as thick as all the other Claire, but got pretty weak where there had been a high grassweed population. Murph's huge army of massive combines and tractors moved into David's farm just across the hedge, and were a sight to behold. We all felt very old-fashioned with our little combine and two moderate tractors and trailers. We felt even more old-fashioned when we stopped at eight (even though we had finished the field) – Murph's gang went on until well past midnight.

It was easy to see why once I checked the evening forecast: dry tomorrow, then wet for the rest of the week. Hurrah for the Met Office. Clueless.

I managed to get to the last hour of the band's rehearsal – with a gig fast approaching, we decided to concentrate and play rather well. Roll on Saturday.

August 18th

It was the very worst type of harvest morning: still, overcast, with an incredible heavy dew. OK, it wasn't pouring with rain, but the effect was the same. We loaded a couple of lorries, and sat indoors feeling the worse for wear. Phil from Farol rang to ask how we'd got on with the demo Joker cultivator – I told him the truth: it had gone very well, but he wants far too much money for it, and this harvest is hardly inspiring confidence to splash out. He seemed OK with that. I asked Noel to spend an hour washing the Joker off before Farol's come and get it.

Jonathan and I went up to Stanmore and brought the combine back to the corner of White Hill, where I took the front off, ready to drive through the gateway into Springshott, and over to the far side, ready to start on the spring barley in Kilmeston Road. Jonathan drove Tigger across the pasture – the first time he'd driven it since the unfortunate episode in the tractor barn where he managed to ram it into the back of a green trailer in the barn. Two grand's worth of new bonnet and grill straightening ensued.

By two o'clock, I couldn't wait any longer, and so we made a start. The outsides were not pretty, but, once again, get into the meat of the field, and there was some nice barley, as well as a mountain of straw.

Kilmeston Road field is another one with cracking views, and from the top I was treated to the sight of a massive straw fire, somewhere to the north of Winchester. A huge plume of smoke suggested that someone somewhere was having the nightmare of fields going up in flames. Back in the days of stubble burning, the countryside had its own firebreaks, but a fire these days can travel for miles before it gets under control. When Dad was alive, I made it my business to ring him to tell him about straw fires. He would be off in search of it like a shot. Mind you, he was the man who lost all interest in farming when they banned stubble bringing.

He would also have loved the other great sight of the day: two World War Two fighters doing a mock dog fight, complete with smoke trails. It looked to be over West Meon way, and was pretty spectacular. Today is the 75th anniversary of the darkest day of the Battle of Britain, so all sort of events are going on. No doubt this was one of them.

The dew came in pretty heavily at about seven thirty, but we persevered until eight on the dot, with the combine drum thumping and complaining noisily.

Hazel reported that her throttle is playing up again – we had the same thing last winter. Both hand and foot throttles refuse to have any effect, and you get stuck with the engine at idle. Not much good for hauling heavy trailers up the farm hill to Godwin's. I'll see if I can get someone out first thing tomorrow.

August 19th
A phone call to the Massey dealer at 8am was received less than enthusiastically – they had a lot on their plate and would get out here when they could. We decided we'd have to come up with a plan that didn't involve the Massey hauling heavy trailers up the hill with the engine at idle.

I should have been bolder – the combine needed a major grease up and a fuel up, and it was past ten when I'd finished all that. Then a scud of rain came through, just enough to put doubt about an early start in my mind. It came to nothing, although Micheldever got it quite hard, according to Bill, who was still sending lorries.

So after an early lunch, we made a start. Hazel and Noel were swapping trailers, resting the heavy drawbar skids on big bits of sleeper in the Springshott pasture, which worked perfectly – Noel was doing the long and hard work, Hazel was chasing the combine. The rain arrived big time at two; I was just going through a really heavy bit of barley and the front auger jammed solid. It took ten minutes of yanking out straw and teasing with the 'vomit' button on the combine to free it up. I was wet, the straw was wet, the combine was wet – time to go home. Hello to Mr Sofa.

August 20th

It was wet – really wet. Most of the day it rained or drizzled. We managed to get two more lorries out, clearing the Claire from the big barn. Final clean and dry weight off Stanmore was 357 tons – very respectable off 98 acres, especially if you consider that about ten acres of Broom Field was dismal. It's also worth remembering the state of those fields for my first trip up there with fertiliser, when vast areas were under water. All in all, quite acceptable. And we got in and out of Stanmore without getting stuck or making a rut, which is a bonus.

Noel finally hitched on the hedge trimmer, gave it a grease up and set off to do the roadsides. We can't do field sides under new EU legislation until September, but there's plenty of roadwork to do for now.

I had a visit from a finance man, wanting to sign me up for the new sprayer. It was all a bit awkward – I had agreed a 'price to change' with Rod, but the nice man wanted a fairly steep APR. I was under the impression that it would be minimal or even 0%. I suggested he went away and had a think. He agreed to do so.

Mid-afternoon I took Diana for her first trip to Jane the Physio. She's been having neck and shoulder twinges at the café, and thought it worth looking at. Jane agreed, and gave her a good working over. It brought back memories of Dad taking me down to Bursledon to see Mr Madsen, the enigmatic osteopath who kept him going. How the world goes round.

Mr Sofa continued to beckon, and what could be better than the original *39 Steps* on BBC2? It was certainly more entertaining than the cricket highlights – the last Test of the series is a bit of a damp squib.

August 21st

It started misty and damp, but a hot sun came out and a good wind got up. It was still incredible humid, so things didn't dry up as quickly as I'd hoped. A stream of visitors stopped us from doing any harvesting – Diana had friends round for Scrabble and baking, the Editor called in with the latest thoughts on being fifty-something, and Tod and John called in to Shed 3b to pick up all the kit for the gig tomorrow night.

No grain lorries this morning, but Oakes Bros came with a replacement JCB loader. They had sold the lovely little old one we'd been using, and so had to do a swap. Noel looked a lot happier in the more modern cab, though.

The finance deal for the new sprayer was finally agreed with Rod. I bypassed the expensive finance man, and managed to persuade Rod to do a 1+2 annuals, starting at the end of September – by which time, I should have got some money in the bank. That will be at 0%, saving several hundred pounds.

Graham Tosdevine's man arrived with the huge Deere sprayer to do the spring beans in Godwin's with Roundup. They'll need a couple of weeks to go off properly.

Richard Lee rang and left a message – he's a dairy farmer from Bishop's Waltham who often turns up behind the combine with a baler. As well as his usual winter wheat straw, he now needs some spring barley straw. That would suit us fine – we can leave the hangar for him. I'll see if he's available tomorrow.

I checked the peas to see if this was our chance to get them off, but they were the consistency of Blu Tack – I couldn't see them going up the unloading auger. So the barley beckoned. We got going at half past four, and finished Kilmeston Road just after sunset. The crop got heavier and heavier as we got to the road side of the field, and the straw got thicker and thicker. I had to concentrate pretty hard: the wet weather had made the ground very soft, and the right-hand divider was pulling up the crop by the roots instead of 'dividing'. There was a lot of shuffling backwards and forwards to allow clumps of barley to slide off. At times like that, I'm grateful for hydrostatic transmission.

I rang Tod to check on progress setting up for tomorrow's wedding, and he said all was fine, but the message about needing a big stage had obviously not got through. All we had was a twelve foot by eight foot platform. I threw a bit of a tizzy about it, but Tod reassured me that it would be fine, and anyway, there's nothing to be done at this late hour.

The next panic phone call was from the bride's father, who announced that one of their cars had been broken into during the set-up for the wedding, and there was now a huge panic about security overnight. His call was at seven o'clock, and so, once again, there was little that I could do. I rang Tod to tell him, but could only leave a message. I doubt he or John would want to head all the way back to Houghton to pack everything away again, and then set up again tomorrow. We'll just have to hope for the best.

The final proof of how soft the ground was came just before we finished: coming down the hill with a full tank, I drove over a ridge, and the combine nose-dived into the dirt. A wodge of mud and straw got as far as the drum, which ground noisily to a halt. There was lots of squealing belts and a ghastly burning rubber smell. Luckily, it was a relatively simple re-start: open the concave as wide as possible, disengage the chopper (we didn't want stones sparking their way through the blades, although a good fire would have disposed of a lot of unwanted straw), reverse the drum by hand a bit with the massive spanner, and then re-engage. It thought about staying blocked a couple of times, and then cleared itself. Twenty minutes later we were out of the field and heading home.

August 22nd

It was going to be a busy Saturday. We got an early lorry of barley away from the Godwin's barn, and then we made an early start in the Hangar. Hazel came out and did a couple of turns of the headland, and then walked home, and headed off to Rosie's wedding in Houghton after lunch.

Noel and I stayed out through lunch, and finished what was probably the weakest of all the spring barley fields just after four. The sky got blacker and blacker to the south, so it was a great relief to see Richard Lee's baler arrive at three. It was tempting to have an extra early finish, but it seemed criminal to waste even a couple of hours of dry weather, so we did some high-speed table unhitching, and headed into the Panorama in the Folly. When more spots of rain came at six thirty, I'd done about seven acres of headland. I thought that was a good moment to head home and get cleaned up for the gig at the wedding.

I rang John and offered him a lift, and we drove over to Houghton, eyes peeled for harvest progress as we headed west. Every other field had a combine racing against the imminent rain.

The venue was a stunning tent next to the River Test, made even more dramatic by the flashes of lightning from approaching storms. We got going late, although the speeches were excellent, which makes hanging around that much easier. We played well – but enjoyed one of the funniest moments in our eight-year history of gigs.

The bride and I agreed that we'd do a slow number for her 'first dance'. I was sure she had said 'Need Your Love So Bad' by the sixties version of Fleetwood Mac. She was convinced she had said 'Oooh, you make loving fun', the terrible, cheesy number by the pop-lite 1980's version of Fleetwood Mac. Tod announced the first dance, the throng gathered in eager anticipation, but when we hit the very first bar, the bride and groom's faces were a picture of shock and confusion. A slow blues number was not what they had expected – worse still, they had prepared a special routine for what they thought was coming.

It could have all gone horribly wrong, but the nature of the occasion prevailed; there was a mass outbreak of 'Oh well' (as in shrugging of shoulders, not yet another Fleetwood Mac number) and the dancing started. It kept on almost relentlessly and enthusiastically until we were brought to a sudden and quite dramatic halt by the venue's owner, wary of his licencing rules. 11.30pm, and that was it. Fair enough – his house, his rules.

It was a great gig – one of our best as a five piece. We cleared up the kit, scoffed wedding cake and fancy cheeses, and got home at about 1.30am. Our patch of Hampshire, unlike Stockbridge, had stayed completely dry, and I stumbled into bed to the sound of at least two combines going in the distance. Judging by the forecast, that effort may well pay off. Would we live to regret not putting in another five or six late hours?

August 23rd

For some reason, I leapt out of bed quite early, convinced that the day would remain dry. I was sure that given seven hours without further rain, we could nip from the Folly into Chalks and get all the peas combined. Luckily, the rain arrived at about 10am and put a stop to that idea. I say 'luckily' because I was completely knackered after the gig, and if there's one combining job that needs full-on concentration, it's peas. I retired to the sofa with a duvet, and enjoyed a mixed bag of sport. The cricket was a huge let down, the Grand Prix was dull, but, as ever, the Touring Cars were fantastic. Mind you, I slept through most of everything.

August 24th

A damp start, and then a vicious black front of cloud swept in from the south. Another non-farming day.

After dropping Diana off to work in Alresford, I drove up to the doctor's to pick up yet another inhaler, only to find that they now don't take credit cards, whereas they did a few months ago. I threw a little paddy in the dispensary, and went home without it. I rang them to point out that I had found a receipt from a credit card transaction, and was assured that it had been a mistake, and they should not have allowed it. It was left to Hazel to pick it up when she fetched Diana, later in the afternoon.

The rain eased a tiny bit in the late afternoon, so I took Sasha out to Clump to check the Autumn Promise bird strips, and they were thriving in this hot wet weather. Even better news was that the peas are still standing. Let's hope that they can survive the next couple of days of monsoon – which is what is being promised.

August 25th

A damp morning turned into another deluge. I suppose we're relatively well off. There's no straw lying waiting to be baled. We're off the heavy land that does not like being driven over after four inches of rain. And the wheat that is still out there was all sown in the very late autumn and winter, so might still have some quality if it ever dries up. Only the peas have got me worried at the moment.

Noel had a long day hedge trimming again, and I sat in the office for the morning. I did a run up to Hampshire Grain with a bag of the Panorama wheat that we combined on Saturday – this may have been a bad move, because if it turns out to have been top quality, and then we find that post-rain it is rubbish, I will be even more fed up. I timed the trip to coincide picking up Diana from Caracole, and by the time I got home, the results were through: crappy feed wheat. Oh well.

It being a wet Tuesday, I rang Robert Young to suggest a beer, and we had a good moan in the Flowerpots. His Boomtown-related story was far more serious than our troubles with loss of sleep and cars disgorging rubbish by the roadside: one of the 50,000 visitors had carefully hidden a rucksack in a field near the venue. It had gone up the front of the combine and damaged the concave, stopping harvest for some time. That puts our bag of Red Bull cans in perspective.

August 26th

A clue to the day's weather arrived at 4.44am, when the whole house started to shake in a scary wind. In my semi-woken state, I couldn't tell if it was wind alone or heavy rain – it was just wind, but at about 10am the most terrifying storm arrived. The world went white with horizontal rain, a huge brown river swept the yard, and every drain and gutter overflowed. By lunchtime, the rain had narrowed to a slither of a squall line from the New Forest up to north-west London, but it just happened to be stuck over us.

There's not a lot to be done under these circumstances. Noel went hedge trimming, I sulked a lot – although we both took a break from these farming activities to rescue the postman, who had blown up his van in the New Pond puddle. Noel towed him out to the keeper's yard, and I gave him a lift back to Alresford so he could report in and pick up another van.

The deluge stopped quite suddenly at about four, and I went out to inspect the damage. Quite astonishingly, the peas weren't completely flat. They'd gone from an easily-combinable eighteen inches to about ten – not so easy, but not impossible. The ground underneath will have to dry out a bit first. The wheats were all still standing, and the forecast is now quite good. I hatched a plan to spend half a day in the Folly getting the combine shiny again while Chalks dries out, and then... Well, let's see what tomorrow brings.

August 27th

Any plans to sneak a bit of combining in – maybe this afternoon after it has dried out a bit – were scotched by a lively shower just after dawn. So we had a long morning clearing out the spring barley from the Godwin's barn. We managed three-and-a-half lorries, which took our total to ten tons over what I'd booked in, and meant a final clean and dry yield of just over 55 cwt/acre. Best of all, all of it went for grade 1 malt, except one load, which slipped to grade 2. In a grim harvest, that's good news. While the barley was going out (my back excuses me from shovelling at the moment), I took Diana into the Science Centre on this side of Winchester, for her last day of volunteering before she goes off to university. I took Sasha for her first non-farm trip out in the truck. She stuck her nose out of the part-opened window and sniffed every inch of the way. She certainly didn't make much of the mess down in the Mattingley bowl. I reckon she was picking up the scent of drugs post-Boomtown even now.

I was keen to take the pup out because she was upset at Monty not being home. He'd gone off to the vet first thing to have his nadgers off. Much as we'd love to breed with him, he'd be no good for pedigree work with his overshot jaw, and if he and Sasha bred (which would be inevitable as soon as she came on heat) we'd be trying to get rid of probably a dozen curious crossbreeds. The other reason to get him neutered is to reduce his attractiveness to the dog thieves, who care little for little things like overshot jaws.

Hazel, Noel and I then set about the tree that fell down in yesterday's deluge, lying across the fence in the back meadow. Ten minutes with a chainsaw and two sets of hands clearing up as I went, and it was done. The scary moment is when you pause before starting a job like that to consider what part of the operation is legal, and what is illegal. Have I got the right qualifications to use a chainsaw? No. Have I signed up with the Environment Agency derogation to burn the branches? Er…

Noel went back to hedge trimming, Hazel fetched a sorry Monty (complete with cone of shame), and I went and greased up the combine with Sasha – now my constant companion – who had a great time eating snails off the bottom of the combine header. They're hard on the outside, chewy on the inside.

A late session ordering red diesel produced the first sub-40p/litre quote since goodness knows when. I placed the order for next week, when we'll be rushing round like mad things in a cloud of dust. No, really, we will.

August 28th
Another heavy dew, and everything still moist from the recent rain. I suggested Noel started his bank holiday early, which he was happy with. I grabbed the stepladder and the fuel bowser, and greased up the unloading arm universal joints on the combine while refuelling. I gave it a full run up and run down (to grease the variable pulleys, like a good boy) and noticed that the self-levelling sieves had jammed at one end of their travel.

These sieves are the best things about my little combine. They are the height of simplicity: the one big upper sieve has been split into five long narrow ones that pivot to keep level. A little pendulum in the cab somewhere detects slope, and sends a signal to an electric ram that does the pivoting. It's a great feature on a small combine. I think only Claas offer anything like it, and you need deep pockets for Claas.

I rang Garwood's, and booked Luke the Combine Wizard to come out tomorrow and have a look – by now the sun had come out, and a fantastic wind was blowing, and harvest was back on the menu. I didn't want to lose any time this afternoon. They seemed happy with the idea of cancelling the appointment if the sieves sorted themselves out.

Which they promptly did. Well, not 'promptly'; I noticed, after an hour's combining in Folly, that the alarm had stopped. A quick check revealed that they were back to normal. It will be interesting to see how the sieves got on – i.e. how much corn came over the back – while in the 'full slope' position. I gratefully rang Garwood's and cancelled tomorrow's repair appointment. The rain must have got into the electric system somewhere, and dried out mid-afternoon.

Hazel and I had a good run in the Folly, finishing the Drier side, and cutting a chunk to the north of the trees in the middle. It was quite eventful. The field is now riddled with badger damage: small starter holes, huge setts, and rolled crop. What this means for the future of the Folly, I don't know. And Hazel had a fantastic shouting match from her tractor cab with a precocious teenager on a horse who refused to ride back down the road to a safe passing place.

We finished at eight, with another twenty acres done in four-and-a-half hours.

August 29th

We sent a lorry of Panorama away, which, amazingly, went as 'hard milling'. It's too much to hope that the whole lot manages that.

I spent a quick hour converting the combine for peas (perforated elevator covers, slow down the rotary separator and drum, open up sieves), took a deep breath, and set off into Chalks. It was a bit of a struggle, especially at first, when the air was still damp, but by early afternoon, they were flowing nicely. I was losing plenty over the knife – they were very ripe – but I was getting most into the tank. Noel was happy to pop out every couple of hours and empty the two trailers that he'd parked on the headland, and the day was set. By dusk, I'd have them all in the barn, Oh yes.

The 'late afternoon drizzle' arrived at three, as quite heavy rain. Peas tell you within moments that rain has arrived, and I had to abandon after having done possibly half the field. My sulk pushed new boundaries of grumpiness.

August 30th

The reason for my grumpy sulk became apparent. Another attack of bunged- up nose and sinus pain. Yet more time spent on the sofa feeling sorry for myself, while the rain continued to pour outside.

August 31st

August bank holiday was spent in much the same way – rumour has it that it was dry for some of the day, but I missed it.

September 1st

There were hints of dryness in the air, but we all knew they weren't real. So Hazel set off with Tony to the remotest parts of Wiltshire to buy more sheep, Anthony and a gang of school mates set off to Alresford showground to help with the enormous task of getting everything set up, Diana and I took Monty to the vet to check on his sore nadgers, and Noel went hedge trimming. I dropped Diana at Caracole, where she found a table and did some really constructive maths revision, or so she claimed.

Tod dropped in for a rather optimistic chat about next year's cropping – what crop would go where when the sowing season starts again. If there's one thing the last year has taught us, it's that drawing lots of beautifully coloured-in maps is often nothing more than an exercise in using crayons – fun though that is. Still, we persevered with a plan, and had the usual debates about varieties – do we stick with what we know, or choose the latest wonder crops? Do we have just one variety, or spread the risk? The Moulin catastrophe of some years ago springs to mind at this stage: a fantastic world-beating new variety of wheat that simply failed one year, and many farmers were hit very hard. We did the colouring in on a farm map, and filed it under 'probably end up in the shredder'.

In a fit of enthusiasm, I put the sprayer onto the tractor, and it promptly rained a lot.

September 2nd

It was a curious day of comings and goings.

The demo Horsch Joker got picked up (I thought it was a lot of money for a basic cultivator), and yet another load of cheap diesel arrived. Let's hope this sees us through to the end of harvest.

It was still too damp and misty to combine, so Noel kept on with the hedgetrimmer in Rick, Clump and Big Field, and I joined him out there with the sprayer, tidying up the winter barley stubbles. Dad's daily routine involved pottering round the farm checking up on the old boys whose daily routine was to set off round the farm and not get caught being idle. Dad's job would have been far easier if he'd been able to watch them from a sprayer. Not that Noel ever stops working, of course.

Shortly after lunch, everything dried out, so we reverted to combining. Off came the sprayer, on went a green trailer, and we finished off the Folly (dodging the numerous badger holes that now pothole the field), and, as it got dark, cut round the outside of Drier Field to finish a good day off at the yard. The forecast was quite good, too.

September 3rd

Good grief – a conventional harvest day. Noel was away first thing, attending a site meeting at his new house being built in Alresford, but got back in time to load another lorry of Panorama. I gave the combine a good going over, doing a full grease up and fuel up. After an early lunch we got stuck into Drier Field.

The headland was quite good – it was drilled later than the rest, but in much better conditions and at a much higher seed rate. There's a lesson there. The landwork was good in places, but thin in others, and non-existent where slugs had got to work in the wet weather. I was able to hustle the combine through those bits, and we managed thirty-eight acres. We dodged one shower early on, and some vicious black clouds skirted us to the north, but by the end of the day the corn was flowing quite well, having dried nicely.

Three ways you know you're harvesting in cold September weather: first, the grease gun feels like it's blocked; second, you find yourself looking for the heater dial in the combine's ventilation system (there isn't one), and third, the engine takes no time at all to cool to 79 degrees at the crucial end-of-day idle session.

September 4th

Our two Hampshire Grain lorries arrived later than planned, which was no great problem: the dew meant nothing was fit to combine early. So we got them loaded, had an early lunch, and cracked on into Drier Field in the afternoon. It's a nice big field with long turns, and the wheat was flowing nicely.

By early evening, we were out of Drier. I parked the combine next to New Pond Cottages, and all started getting fired up for the Show tomorrow. We won't have harvest finished in time for it (which is what we all hope for), but after a topsy-turvy year like this one, many rules and traditions have had to be abandoned.

September 5th

We did an early couple of lorries, and then shut the barn doors, locked up the tractors, tossed the combine keys into the drawer, and set about the Alresford and District Agricultural Show.

First Saturday in September: the day to gather at Tichborne Park, just south of New Alresford, and spend the whole day walking in a slow circle round all the stands. It's a show that has kept to its farming roots quite magnificently, so there's machinery and livestock, rural crafts and foods, play areas, bands, pubs, food; basically, if you don't come back home with a sore head, you shouldn't have bothered going.

The great mystery is the huge display of farm machinery. It can't pay the dealers to bring all their kit to the show – it's not like the Smithfield Show days of the glorious 1980s, when there were 'show deals' to be had, and cheques could be written at the drop of a hat. Still, it's great PR for the industry as the dealers let the public climb all over the shiny tractors and combines. I think the Trade Stand Secretary should get more credit for persuading them all in. Oh, that'll be Hazel.

We farmers drop in at as many stands as we can, grab a glass of something, maybe a nibble, exchange an insult or two and then move on to the next one. I always foolishly hit the ice cream vans on the way out for a completely unnecessary 99 flake. The mix with beer, wine, sausage rolls and warm sandwiches doesn't bear thinking about.

September 6th

To no one's surprise, it was a slightly late start. I did a huge fuel-up and grease up before another early lunch, and got all the insides set up for a return to the neglected peas in Chalks. After lunch, Jonathan gave me a lift to the combine in Pig, and I nipped into Chalks to fly through the rest of the peas. Could have been a cracking crop before the Good Lord decided to flatten them; it was now a question of getting something off and clearing the ground for the next crop to go in.

Late afternoon, I finished them. As I was rubbing the back of my neck and wincing (anyone who has combined a flat crop of peas will know why), I pondered the next move. Hop over the boundary into the beans? Nah – there's only one tradition as important as the first Saturday in September being the Alresford Show: it's that the first Sunday of the month is Open Mic Night in West Meon. So I brought the combine back to the corner of the garden, got fed and cleaned up, loaded up the Roland and had another great evening banging out some tunes.

In other news, it has been officially decided that we will spend a small fortune getting the Lupo back on the road, so Anthony can take it up to Leeds. I can hear the ghost of Granny Flindt chuckling.

September 7th

We had an early phone call from the Chairman of Kilmeston Parish Council. There have been complaints about the cultivator/telegraph pole combo that neighbour David put across Stanmore Lane after the huge burglary. I pointed out to the Chairman that it was David's doing, that he had left room for the footpath users to get round it, and (possibly rather too forcefully) that I find it ironic that the good people of Kilmeston are suddenly in favour of the legalities of footpaths, when they spend all their time wandering willy-nilly all over my farm, ignoring rights of way completely. The shell-shocked Chairman said he'd talk it through with the complainants.

Two more lorries came to clear the last of the Panorama, so I dropped Hazel off for her grain-shovel-based work out and went up the valley to check the remaining wheat. There's a bit of a panic on, after the famous high pressure that was going to be here for the whole of September (it's in an 'omega block', claimed the weather man – it'll take ages to shift) is now only going to be here for a few days. We've got five days to do a couple of hundred acres – although I doubt Bungalow will be anywhere near ripe.

The late sown wheat in Top and Bottom of Hurst Down looked frankly horrible. The straw was still green, and the heads were tiny and shrivelled. I rang Richard, who wants the straw, and suggested he come and look at it. We've got plenty in the barn left over from two years ago, and there's always the spring wheat in JA/DC, which looks slightly better.

The executive decision was to leave the wheat for a few more days to ripen, and get stuck into the beans, so we had a long afternoon in Godwin's, polishing off Big Broom and making a good hole in Middle Broom. The beans seem reasonable in quality, and look lovely. Shame the Alresford Show has gone – they would have made a good entry into the pulse competition.

Noel dug the Carrier out of the bushes, put a new bearing on it, and headed off into Chalks, which cultivated like a dream. Just the right combination of moisture and soft worked ground. Just the sort of thing to make you start thinking of autumn sowing.

September 8th

No lorries this morning, so we were able to make an earlier start in the beans. I finished Middle Broom, and popped into Child's Broom. Noel did an hour at lunch time, having finished discing Chalks, and then we flew through School and Godwin's Park. All the Godwin's block was done by five.

After a great deal of complicated logistics and resetting of combine levers, we made a start on the spring wheat in JA/DC. There seemed a lot of stuff out there, but not all in the form of grains of wheat. After four turns, it was dark, so we stopped.

A brilliant long day – probably the most we've done in one day with our little combine. Let's hope for just a few more days like it.

September 9th

Despite some nice breeze overnight, the world was still dew-soaked, which meant no chance of an early start. It was another busy morning, though. Graham Tosdevine's man came in and put 2l/ha Roundup on the oilseed rape stubble in White Hill and Cheyney. One of our straw customers arrived unannounced in the yard with a wad of cash, which was not what I wanted while trying to fill up the bowser. And, to top it all, I got a thorn in my right foot. This may sound trivial, but I had to take my right sock off, and the only time I can get a right sock back on is in the ten minutes after a shower. So I stretched and strained as much as I dared (a back injury is not what's wanted now), and collapsed in failure on the sofa, where a little doze crept up on me.

I was woken by hammering on the door. Two National Trust employees were on the doorstep wanting to do some tree lopping in Godwin's. I'm not sure what sort of sight I made, half asleep and waving a sock.

The peas went away – a lorry and a tiny bit, so about a ton to the acre. I shouldn't complain; I had written the crop off during last week's deluge. I greased up and fuelled up, and tiptoed up the Joan's Acre valley after a very early lunch.

We finished the spring wheat just after tea, and it seemed to have done moderately well. Richard came in mid-afternoon and had the whole lot baled by evening. We did ten acres of the Scout in TBHD, and even that came off better than expected. The flat land up on top seemed a particularly decent crop. We'll not know about any quality until it gets to Hampshire Grain, of course, but dry crops, mud-free combine wheels, dust flying, baler man happy – I love September combining.

September 10th

Would we get the rest of harvest done in two days? It was mighty soggy in the morning – no rain, just a heavy dew. So while Hazel and Noel loaded up a couple of lorries of Mulika, I took Anthony up to North's garage to pick up the Lupo after its major service: new cambelt and water pump, all filters, oil and plugs changed. It cost more than the car's worth, but should keep it going up north. The good news when we got back was that the Mulika had indeed survived the deluge, and gone in as low-grade milling. That should earn enough to pay for the Lupo service.

A long day in Top and Bottom of Hurst Down ensued. The slow work over in the point of the field next to Brockwood Bottom slowed us down, but at least Noel volunteered to do it over lunchtime. Niece Caroline came out for a harvest tea, with a chum and a squad of babies and toddlers. They had a lovely time crawling all over the tractor, although the combine was a bit too noisy.

We pushed on late into the evening, and got thirty-five acres done.

September 11th

Today's mission: finish harvest. We all avoided mentioning it for fear of bringing bad luck. We all just got on with a frantic busy day. Noel unloaded a lorry of seed, and then he and Hazel loaded up the last of the Mulika and a load of Scout. The Mulika, like the other two loads, made low-grade milling. The Scout didn't. I spent the early morning up in THD greasing and refuelling. So far so good; all according to schedule.

By ten fifteen, and with the straw still quite damp, we were combining. Conditions were lovely – a crystal clear blue sky, the ground was flat and dry, the turns were long. The yield was never going to burst a barn, but it was enough to make the job worthwhile. I had to remind myself that this was winter wheat sown in February. I had underestimated how much was left up there, and didn't finish until three o'clock on the dot. Mind you, it did mean we sent another trailer or two down to the barn.

There was then the longest drive possible on this farm, from the southern tip of Top of Hurst Down to Bungalow, via JA/DC, Blackhouse Road, Drier Field, Folly (where we took the header off), across Springshott, up across the Kilmeston Road (where fresh poachers' tracks suggested our expensive trenches had been less than fully effective barriers), and, finally, into Bungalow.

The stalks were green, but there were plenty of pods, so, once I'd got the table back on, I set off optimistically, but with a whomp and much screaming of belts, the whole combine bunged up solid. My fault, of course – I'd set the drum speed too low, and the drive belt was slack. Not a good start. Luckily, ten minutes with the monster spanner turning the drum backwards and some judicious use of the vomit button, and everything was clear.

The rest of the day went exactly to plan. I had to leave some of the beans that had been in the shade all year on the southern side of the field, but I flew through the rest. The ground was dry and firm, and the beans plentiful. We filled two trailers and had a bit more left over. Not bad off about twelve acres. At 6.15pm, harvest 2015 was finished. As is traditional, there was no one to celebrate with, so I raised a little cheer on my own, drained my Thermos (except for the dregs – they go on the ground for good luck), and patted the little combine on its wheel.

Noel arrived back in the field and we did the big transfer home. We got the combine

197

table hitched off and under cover, all the trailers empty and in the dry, and left the combine out next to the stand pipe ready for the big wash off. Just as it got dark, there were spots of rain.

So, what of harvest 2015? Good in parts, as they say. The winter barley was terrible, which was particularly galling because we'd put so much effort into it at the expense of the winter wheat. The oilseed rape was terrible – again, infuriating, because of all the time and effort that goes into it. The Claire winter wheat was good, but let down by a grassy Broom Field. The spring barley goes down as the success of the year – good yields and all quality. The late sown Panorama had some quality but poor yield, the Mulika was a bonus and the Scout seems to have done some quantity but no quality. The spring beans may yet be the late bonus, but the weights haven't come in yet.

I can't see us getting to our projected 2,000 tons at Hampshire Grain. We're going to be well short. Not great news when prices are tumbling, and most farmers are boasting of record yields which counteract (and caused in the first place) such low prices. It's easy to forget, though, that at the end of February, everything looked very bleak indeed, with vast swathes of the farm unsown, and most of the land under water. To get to where we are today is quite positive, with reasonable quantities and reasonable qualities. At least, that's what I have to keep telling myself.

September 12th

It takes a mighty long time to wind down from harvest. So it was another 5.30am wake up, and then an hour's not very fruitful dozing – not the most relaxing start to the first post-harvest Saturday of the year.

Jonathan had been picked to play for Churcher's College U16b rugby team, so it was the perfect opportunity to get away from the farm for the first time in ages, see some new territory, and check to see if we were the last farmers in the south of England to finish harvest. A nice long drive up the A34, then along the A303 through the terrible traffic jam at Stonehenge (odd how our ancestors' cutting-edge technology now brings our cutting-edge technology to a crawl), and up the A360 to Shrewton revealed that we might indeed be the latest finishers. The road was closed at Shrewton, so I was obliged to drive back down the A360, back past Stonehenge, then take the windy road up to Upavon, and along the southern edge of the fantastic vale of Pewsey on the Devizes road. A field of uncut beans was spotted along with a field of wheat – although the wheat was being stoked for thatching, so doesn't count.

I got to Dauntsey's just in the nick of time, and watched with great pride as Churcher's U16b got comprehensively thrashed, but they played on and on with their heads up. Jonathan took a couple of blows that would have sent him off the pitch a couple of years ago, but he soldiered on. They lost 49–0. Jonathan brought a mate home with him, and they chatted and laughed all the way home, so they must have enjoyed the game.

We headed to the Flowerpots with the Mr and Mrs Editor to mark the end of harvest, and probably talked too loudly and politically incorrectly for the whole evening. I had hoped that having a few beers would help me sleep through the noise of a big party at Hinton Ampner Place, but it was too loud for that. After a couple of hours trying to sleep, I got up at 1.30am and shut all the windows and double glazing. Two minutes later, the music stopped.

September 13th
A proper quiet Sunday. Much of the day was spent on the sofa listening to a hugely disappointing end to the cricket season.

September 14th
Lots of heavy showers meant that the end-of-harvest relief finally kicked in. We loaded lots of lorries in the rain, and Noel went out into Godwin's with the Carrier to work the ground down a bit.

A tiny domestic crisis erupted as it turned out that Anthony had failed his retakes at Leeds Uni. He looked genuinely shocked – he had been utterly convinced that he'd got through this time. A whole lot of plans were immediately in question: getting into the third year, doing the placement at a local company up there – it was a fairly fraught day.

Just before midnight, not long after a very fruitful Old Gits' rehearsal, a very noisy vehicle sped up the hill past the farm, waking me up. At almost the same moment, the phone rang. It was Sean from New Pond, pointing out that the poachers had just been all over Blackhouse Road. There was little for me to do at this stage, so I thanked him and tried to get back to sleep. The annual battle begins again, and slightly earlier than normal.

September 15th
The last of the spring beans went – there were enough to fulfil my commitment and have a couple of trailers left over for home-saved seed. All in, they must have yielded 30 cwt/acre. Only a couple of soggy loads of Scout remain.

Following last night's poacher invasion, Hazel went round the farm with a motley collection of old bales and telegraph poles, blocking as many entrances to fields as possible. Noel went out with the Carrier until it got too wet, and I started the annual chore of washing off the combine.

Once upon a time, this was done by the old combine driver, very slowly, over a couple of weeks, with a hosepipe and a hand brush. But at the end of it, the combine would be spotless. I use a pressure washer, which immediately upsets the purists ("You'll get rust in all the seams!"), but it is a lot quicker.

The challenge is to not get downhearted. You wash one bit clean, then move along a section, and promptly blast a ghastly mix of dust and grease onto the bit you've just done. Then you climb up and do the engine bay, and flush more dirt down all the bits you thought you'd finished. The secret seems to be to just persevere. Eventually, you find the grime starts to dissipate, and you're simply rinsing off tiny dregs of muck.

I didn't finish the job – a filthy storm came in from the west, and I didn't fancy being the only prominent object, standing five yards up on top of a combine in a field, while lightning started. So I packed up all the kit and headed home.

Anthony had got Leeds sorted – he'd simply drop out for a year, retake the exam, and the company taking him on as an intern have agreed to do so despite the failure. He'll simply be an intern rather than a student intern. He still seemed pretty cross about the whole affair.

September 16th

It rained a lot, although not as early and as much as they had said. Hazel and Noel had another major anti-poacher day, running round the farm with trailer loads of telegraph poles and manky big bales, blocking gateways here, there and everywhere. They're ugly, inconvenient for me when I want to pop out and do a bit of spraying, but it's the modern countryside.

Having driven over my glasses in Chalks (they fell out of my top pocket as I rolled around under the header, scraping mud off), I thought the time had come for an eye test before ordering new ones. So I got cleaned up as much as I could, and went thought the ordeal of the optometrist's examination. It's all very soporific and calm, and very easy in the semi-dark to let the eyelids droop, which would somewhat defeat the purpose of the exercise.

I always remember, in the gloom of the examination room, with a not unglamorous female optometrist just inches away, the great story of my mate Rupert undergoing the same exam, but with someone defined as officially very glamorous. "So," she asked, trying to work out the significance of his profession on her recommendations, "What do you do, sir?"

"I'm a journalist," he replied. And then, obviously somewhat befuddled by her presence, asked, instinctively "And what do you do?"

There was a slight pause. "Er, I'm an optometrist."

Luckily, I avoided anything quite as embarrassing. I was given a bit of a telling off for the state of my eyes, which, she said, looked like they had just been sandblasted. I explained that I had been pressure washing the combine only yesterday, and most of the grit and grime comes straight back in your face. She seemed thoroughly disapproving, but took the opportunity to try and sell me lots of eye care products. I politely declined. The two pairs of glasses I had ordered were expensive enough. The 'in' thing these days is to get the prescription and then do a runner to the internet and order your glasses online, thus saving a fortune. I confess I'm not brave enough, although I might ask for a copy next week when the glasses arrive, and get some tractor glasses made up nice and cheap.

Anthony had spent the day getting into a bit of a stew about leaving tomorrow, so I poked my head round his door and suggested we go for a pint half an hour before picking up Jonathan from his work stint at the pub. He surprised me by agreeing, and then being keen to go within ten minutes. So we headed for the Hinton Arms and enjoyed one of the best pints I've had in ages. I said how sad I felt for him, having had a miserable summer, with no big festival to go to, no money to earn doing corn cart, and most of the break working so hard for an inexplicable exam fail. I reiterated my suspicion that something wasn't right about the whole thing.

There's not much advice a farmer can give his son who is about to start work in an office. My gap year was spent on the farm, with a winter doing dustcart in Winchester, drayman in Eastleigh, and general dogsbody here, there and everywhere. All I suggested was that he turn up earlier than he has to, leaves later than he has to, is never afraid to ask questions, and makes small talk when necessary. It was nice to have a quiet beer with him, though.

September 17th

It's easy to think that harvest is finished when the last field is cut, but wet corn sitting in the barn counts as unfinished business. I finally persuaded Hampshire Grain to take the last loads of Scout. And had the great satisfaction of it being exactly two loads, down to the last 10 kg. It even made the Scout's yield a respectable 51 cwt/acre. No quality, of course, but easy to combine and worth all that late February sowing.

With great ceremony, firm handshakes and a hug to two, Anthony set off to Leeds – no longer a student, of course, having failed the re-take exams, but on his way to a real proper job, 8.30 till 5 and all that. There was a tear in the eye and we waved him off, not planning to see him again until Christmas.

That was the theory, anyway. Ten minutes later, the phone rang; he was stopped at Winall roundabout with an engine management warning light on. What should he do? I told him to drive home, and we'd see if North's would have a look at it. North's, of course, were delighted to let the little Lupo jump the queue, and while Anthony sat somewhat disconsolately on the PlayStation at home, they quickly found and replaced an aged and faulty sensor. By three thirty, Anthony was back on the way up north.

I missed the latter stages of this drama, as I was back at the Candover Clinic to see the consultant. It was supposed to be a follow-up to see how I had got on with the new medicines he'd suggested, and that I was supposed to have picked up via the doctor at Medstead. Unfortunately, thanks to the uber-prioritisation of harvest, I hadn't seen anyone about anything, so the trip wasn't terribly useful. I did do a carefully rehearsed speech about how significant the bronchiectasis leaflet had been, as it seemed to explain in a moment why I'd been battling joint pain and sinus infection for two decades. He looked entirely unconvinced, as consultants always do when their patients try to self-diagnose, but suggested that I go and see the local doctor to start his now rather old recommendations, and he would also refer me to the ENT specialist to discuss the endless sinus infection. This just happened to be the same ENT specialist who performed Functional Endoscopic Sinus Surgery on me in the late Nineties – in an attempt to stop the sinus pain. Full circle.

Tea was interrupted by Policeman Jon, who had called in to look at the wheel marks that poachers had left the other night, and then by Mac, who was dropping off kit ready for the big muck spread tomorrow. As a result, too much talking and not a lot else was done.

September 18th

The Great Muck Spread. Muck spreading on a little farm like ours is a flipping nuisance. There's never enough to warrant getting spreaders and contractors organised. We have been known to pile it up in a quiet corner and let Mother Nature rot it down and away over a few years. These days, such agricultural flippancy is strictly forbidden.

It was quite different thirty years ago, when from January to May the calf pens and the yard were full with eighty young cattle, who were constantly bedded up with fresh straw. By the end of March, headroom would be getting limited in the pens themselves, and so the whole lot would be mucked out. The old Super Major would be fired up (the only tractor that could fit into the pens), with a 1940's buck rake on the back, and slowly, very slowly, a vast heap would appear at the bottom of the hill. And the whole process would be repeated shortly after turnout in May.

When the Super Major blew up one year, Dad was horrified at my suggestion of hiring a man with a Bobcat. The fact that Bobcat man then managed the whole job in one day didn't improve Dad's attitude at all. I think it was the first time I realised that farming in the Eighties was nothing to do with efficiency – it was a long drawn out twelve-month exercise in finding jobs for men.

We would hire three or four old barrel spreaders later in the year, and while Ken manfully struggled to load up one using a two-wheel-drive Ford 6610, the others would be driving to some remote corner of the farm, to spread our loads. This involved trundling slowly across the field until the flails suddenly kicked in properly, and a high-speed burst would be needed to approach something remotely like an even application. Any good that the muck did for the field was probably undone by the damage done by the ruts and wheelings. The big finish involved washing out the barrel spreaders and cutting off all the string and netwrap. And this was in the days before pressure washers.

This year, we went all efficient and correct. We checked the rules on direct spreading – we've got until the end of the month – and so Noel loaded Mac's enormous rear discharge spreader, and Mac hurried off to Behind My Love's, where he disgorged and was back within ten minutes. The whole job – the back barn and the Godwin's silo – was done in under a day. Progress.

I missed out on all the fun. I was back down at the Drier, giving the combine the gentle final wash off with a hosepipe and a brush, far slower, but better at washing dirt off rather than blasting it onto another section of bodywork.

As we all got back in for tea, the phone rang. It was Anthony. My initial reaction was that the Lupo had died another death, and it had all been a terrible mistake to expect a 15-year-old car to serve as his transport, based on nothing more than sentimentalism. In fact, the news was far from doom-laden. He had taken our advice and queried his result. Someone in the department had looked into it, and a mistake had been made – he had in fact passed the exam. He was therefore still a student, his course was back to being 'Four years including a year in industry' or some such complicated description, he would still be getting money from Student Finance, and he would not have to do more retakes next summer. And the Lupo was fine. Great news all round.

An evening at Rufus' watching the opening match of the Rugby World Cup rounded the day off nicely.

September 19th

After a thoroughly low tech start to the morning, when Hazel, Jonathan and Diana went out into Englands and wormed the sheep, it all went very high tech. Jonathan and his mate assembled a computer from all the expensive components he had sourced in the internet. They seemed to know what they were doing, because it worked in the end. They claimed to have saved several hundred pounds doing it that way. Meanwhile, Diana and Hazel set off to the computer store and bought a super-duper laptop, meant to see her through uni.

The rugby fest continued. I had to abandon one game because ITV seemed to be employing Alan Partridge as a commentator, so I finished washing off the combine and left it with its skirts up to dry out ready to put away sometime tomorrow. I then watched Japan vs South Africa with sheer disbelief and amazement. If the rest of the autumn goes on like this, we're in for a joyful few weeks.

September 20th

Once again, the threat of a full day watching rugby was removed by the unbearable commentary on one match. I took the opportunity to head down the Drier and put the world's cleanest combine in the big barn. Only then did I notice that I had missed the whole of the upper section of the back. But I was all done with washing combines for this year.

Some Alan Partridge-free rugby beckoned, and Noel spent the whole day with the Carrier giving White Hill a going over. I could, and maybe should, have gone spraying, putting some Roundup on some stubbles. But didn't. I did dig out the old car ramps, put Tigger on them and climb underneath to see what sort of job putting on a replacement rear propshaft will be. The one I bought on eBay looks right, but I think I might give the job to North's.

The Editor arrived in his new(ish) Nissan Qashqai, beaming from ear to ear, having successfully dropped off child number two (of two) at Bristol University. He was full of satisfaction and relief, looking like a man who has ended a long chapter in his life. He was even happier when he headed off with a bulging bag of apples from our orchard.

September 21st

The rain came in pretty early, but Noel had enough time to head out to Joan's Acre and Dell Close and tidy up the broken bale that had been left out there, and push the fallen ash tree back into the hedge. I can now get out there and spray it, once the rain stops.

The nice man from the sprayer finance company came out for another attempt at making me pay for the new sprayer – I had thrown a hissy fit at the interest rate on the previous deal, and driven Rod to do three annuals at 0%. I could no longer get away without paying anything at all, although I did ask him not to cash the cheque until the end of the month, by when Hampshire Grain should have come up with the harvest pool money.

I nipped up to Gaskin's with the leaking ram off the hedge trimmer, and left it with them. I came home with a lightweight PTO shaft for the new sprayer. The present one is an absurd monstrosity, more suitable for driving an eight-metre power harrow, not a diaphragm pump. It has a double set of UJs at the tractor end, guaranteed to do one's back in every time the sprayer gets hitched on.

The rain came on fairly heavy by lunchtime, so Noel gave the Terradisc an overhaul, and I organised a couple of cars for the pre-Christmas rush of deadlines.

Evening was spent waiting for news from Leeds, where Anthony had spent his first day in a proper job. He rang at about eight, having had a nap after a very busy day. They had made him very welcome, and set him to work researching the internet for potential stockists of their range of country clothing. Sounds perfect for him.

September 22nd

Lots more rain, so I texted Noel to suggest a sofa day. He was quite happy with that. Hazel's routine sheep check turned into a mini crisis as one of the new sheep in the back meadow was at death's door, and another was less than well. This wave of wet weather isn't doing them any good, by the sound of it. And sheep have a horrible habit of telling you they're ill only when there's not a lot that can be done. I left Hazel and Tony to sort it out.

Policewoman Lyn came round with her new PSCO to collect the bag of litter that has been in the back of Tigger since the Boomtown sleepover incident. As usual, a 'pop in' turned into a lengthy natter and tea-drinking session.

The big debate of the day was with Chris, our land agent. Do we go for a rent review, with a view to getting a reduction? As tenant farmers on an Agricultural Holdings Act tenancy, our rent can be reviewed at intervals of not less than three years. Ours was last changed in September 2012, so could have been changed again this month, However, the party that wants the change (and over the years that has most often been the landlord) has to serve an official notice not less than twelve months before the change – and the National Trust didn't do so last year. Our rent stays the same, therefore, for the next farming year.

The stunning collapse in produce prices got us thinking – could this be a year to serve a notice to the Trust, and try to get a reduction, starting Michaelmas 2016? Chris, when I finally got hold of him after numerous phone calls and emails, wasn't convinced. The jury is still out. We mostly-arable farmers are still doing OK, and the savings that could be made might not justify the stress and costs of a review. Having had a couple of reviews over my career, I know what he means. It hangs over your head horribly, sometimes for months. It's true that some were done amicably over a cup of coffee over the kitchen table, but some take months of pointless and belligerent analysis by Cirencester's finest.

His advice was to not serve a notice this year. If the slump continues, we'll do one next year – his parting shot was that the wise heads in the know are suggesting that slump ain't going to be going much longer anyway. We'll see.

Fired up with enthusiasm for a farming boom, I hit the Flowerpots with Robert, who had fallen victim to yet another chest infection, He took the best part of a year to shake off the last one, and a session stacking corn in the Merlo with the side window open (broken air conditioning, apparently) has been enough to kick it all off again. We had to avoid too much silliness, which is easier said than done. Robert gave a coin he'd found to the metal detector man who props up the other end of the bar on a Tuesday. "Ah," said metal detector man, "I can see a squirrel on this side of the coin." There then followed a slightly drunk historical appreciation of King Tufty the First, who escaped the invading French by scurrying up the far side of tree trunks. A massive coughing fit ensued.

Back home, Hazel had had reports from picker-up Julie of someone chainsawing in the semi-darkness, at the end of Stanmore Lane. This was baffling on all counts; why would someone be sawing wood up there when the roadsides are littered with free wood from last autumn's storms? The trouble is, by 1am, as a couple of pints (mixed with three packets of peanuts) churn their way around my system, a complete theory had developed: the poachers who cleaned out poor Matt's garage the other day are sawing up the telegraph poles to make way for another raid. Perhaps they'll do it tonight. What was that noise? Is that a vehicle driving over Stanmore Long Field...?

September 23rd

A quick trip up to Stanmore in the early frosty sunshine revealed absolutely nothing. No wheel marks, no sawn logs – nothing at all. I had a quick chat with Hazel's Wednesday dog-walking gang, and then hit the office again, finally finishing the next Farmers' Weekly opinion piece.

Noel took off the Carrier, and hitched onto the drill, ready for me to overhaul the main pivot pin. He then, with much effort and cursing, put the main ram back on the hedge trimmer, only to find it still leaked. So he took it back off again, with much effort and cursing, called it a day here, and went off to do stuff with his own sheep.

I started work on the pivot, and found that the main pin needed replacing as well as the two cast-iron bushes. It'll do for now, but I got one ordered from Oakes Bros on the phone. To finish the day, I took the hedge trimmer ram back to Rod's for them to have another go at welding up the leak, and went on to Petersfield to pick up Jonathan.

More excellent rugby beckoned in the evening.

September 24th

After another deluge last night, Noel agreed to have another day off, and keep shopping for kitchens for his new house. I had another office session, trying to get my head round the maps we've got to do for the ministry by the end of the month, registering the 'permanently ineligible features' in the corners of fields. It beggars belief that after all the years of mapping and satellites, we are still under obligation to tell the Rural Payment Agency what's going on in the corners of our fields. Hazel spent the morning getting some pens ready for partridges, which are due soon.

The great news was that Diana passed her driving test, at the third attempt. The daft thing is that she isn't really going to have the chance to make the most of it – she should be off to Durham in a few days' time. Still, it's another confidence booster.

We hit the Hinton Arms for a celebratory evening meal, and all came back ridiculously overfed. I could hardly sleep for being so full.

September 25th

Noel had another go at putting the big ram back on the hedge trimmer, and to no one's surprise, it still leaked. I asked him if he had anything else he could be doing, and, thankfully, he did. I was left pondering whether we should have bought a new ram in the first place, rather than these endless attempts to mend one that is obviously knackered.

Tod arrived for another Autumn Strategy Meeting. Having abandoned the idea of oilseed rape in Rick/Clump and Big, we're already onto Version 2 of our autumn plan. I suggested that if we get a lovely open autumn (which some pundits are predicting), we ought to shift the winter beans from the Stanmore block to Rick/Clump and Big, and put a second wheat in Stanmore. We did that with Panorama a couple of years ago, and it was a great success. It cured me of the terror of second wheat which was the result of growing continuous Haven up there in the 1980s. We never did get over the 'take all barrier', with yields running at a ton to the acre in some years. Tod pointed out that dropping oilseed rape this year may be a good decision – many farmers are struggling to get it growing, after a cold wet August and the neonicotinoid ban. Even better news was that the band have got another gig at the end of October.

A hundred partridges arrived late morning, and we loaded them onto Pig and set off round the farm to put them into the carefully prepared pens. We put one box behind the cattle barn, one in the Folly, and the last up in Kilmeston Road. The plan is to leave them in for a couple of nights – hoping Mr Fox doesn't find them – and turn them out in dribs and drabs. I suspect we will abandon the 'dribs and drabs' bit, and let them all go in one whoosh. Partridge man asked how the pheasants were getting on, and was quite reassuring when Hazel pointed out we couldn't find many of them. "Don't panic," he said. "They're out there somewhere."

The forecast continued to improve, so I hitched off the not-quite reassembled drill, and put on the sprayer, ready to put Roundup on the fields where the winter barley is going – TBHD, Joan's Acre and Dell Close. Well, that's the plan – at the moment.

September 26th

There comes a stage when you just have to put the Rugby World Cup to one side, and go and do some work in the fabulous September sunshine. So I did two tanks of Roundup. I used the opportunity to do some on-the-go setting up of the new sprayer's calibration, which thinks the fields are only about 80% of what they should be. After three fields, the figure was more consistent – the fields were 22.3% larger than the sprayer reckoned they were. I changed the 'impulses/100m' setting by that factor (the wrong way, and then the right way) and noticed that the 'sprayer speed' reading was nearly what the tractor said it was. Somewhere on the floor of the tractor is a little satellite box – I bought it last year for parallel guidance when tramlines are invisible. It dawned on me, just as I'd finished a good dose on Roe Hill, that it gives a really accurate speed reading. Next time I'm out I'll use that as a base figure. It's a shame all this work wasn't done by Amazone, but there we go.

The lure of the rugby was too much by now, so I hit the sofa for an entertaining Samoa vs South Africa, and then went down to Rufus' for the big England game. Poor old Rufus was just back from his father-in-law's funeral, and still recovering from having had a car crash on Monday. Someone had driven straight across his bows up at the notorious Preshaw crossroads, and he'd t-boned it. No airbags in his old Range Rover, so both he and his boy were pretty sore. The other party had held up their hands at once and admitted responsibility, so Rufus is spared any more insurance ordeals. The old Rangie is a goner, and he's in a nice Hyundai i35.

Things weren't made much better when England lost a thrilling match, despite most of the Welsh team being in casualty.

September 27th
Yet another fine day, so it wasn't really possible to put off drilling any longer. I had a very long morning attacking the Horsch from all angles. The front hinge pin needed reinserting (I'm still waiting for the new one from Oakes Bros), the air pipe needed to be reconnected, and then all the work I'd done for sowing game strips in the summer needed sorting out. I removed the duct tape blocks I'd put on six of the outlets in the hopper, and reconnected the pipes. Several pipes had also come out of their coulters, so they needed sorting out. The low speed feed reel was placed with the wheat version, and a new rubber flap went in, next to the rotor.

Finally, I was ready to calibrate for Claire.

By three o'clock, I was out in White Hill in stunning sunshine and fabulous ground conditions, doing a huge headland and a nice bunch of landwork before the tonne of seed I'd put in ran out. The seed rate was a bit too low so I'll have to step it up a bit when I next get out there.

Another one of Hazel's precious sheep died – but the word is that there is a plague of fly strike going through sheep everywhere. Only a slight consolation.

September 28th
I finally got the 'permanently ineligible features' map away by registered post, and then got on with real farming. Out in White Hill, I had a really good long run, getting forty acres done in fabulous conditions. Let's hope it goes on like this for the whole autumn.

At band rehearsal, two gigs we thought were dead certain have been shelved. One because there's World Cup rugby on that night, and many people come to that pub to watch it, and one because the hosts would rather have a disco. Shame on them. What's the old saying: every time you book a disco over live music, a fairy dies. Something like that.

Noel had a good run with the Terradisc, getting Godwin's finished.

September 29th
Today is Michaelmas Day, the official start of the new farming year, and, it has to be said, it wasn't the greatest first day of my 25th farming year. The next Mercedes press car turned up unannounced, and without a wingman, so I had to give him a lift to Petersfield. I had

hoped to be out drilling nice and early, but he put a stop to that. I finally got out to White Hill. Late morning, I finally got into Rough Field, but got hit by The Curse. A hydraulic pipe burst – the one that keeps the drill 'up', so I was lucky it didn't burst on the road. It would have made a mess of the lane as a fully loaded machine dragged its tungsten tips along the tarmac.

I dragged the drill round the headland, with the seed feed 'off', disconnected the pipe, and rushed off to Rod's for a repair, pausing on the way to pick up the bloody hedge trimmer ram, so they could have another go at welding up the leak. Dave managed to get a new pipe made up, and I got home and finished Rough Field just as Noel arrived in the field to roll it. Perfect. I nipped up the road into Cheyney, and bashed that one off, too. It was not quite so easy – the Terradiscing hadn't gone so well, and the field was fairly corrugated. I had to go a bit slower than normal, but finished with a bit of seed left over, perfect to double sow the south headland.

Back home, Hazel had finished giving Tigger a really good clean, ready for the big service tomorrow, and we drove up to North's to drop it off just as it was getting dark. We only just made it; Tigger's propshaft was completely seized, and the whole car was shaking dangerously as we headed up the A272. Not a day too soon.

September 30th

Having finished the Claire, it was time to switch over to Scout. I would have started the winter barley but the small technical error that the seed hadn't actually arrived prevented that. I was shuffling bags and tractors around the yard when a Citroen Picasso stopped me on the road. "This is Monkwood, isn't it?" The driver – he looked like an odd-job/maintenance man – had an address and a phone-based satnav, which was inexplicably directing him to the middle of Hinton Ampner. I tried explaining to him that he was a good five miles away, and he got quite tetchy. In the end, I sent him to Alresford, and suggested that the satnav might work properly from there.

Once I had dealt with lost strangers, I calibrated the drill for Scout, and hit Chalks, which went like a dream. It reminded me why I like to grow peas – the seedbed they leave, not to mention the nice flush of residual nitrogen. The top and bottom shooting strips were heaving with birds – loads of cock pheasants in the bottom one, which was odd, because we certainly hadn't put them there. It was all drilled by four o'clock.

It would have been sooner, but the phone kept ringing. There was a very embarrassed transport company, pointing out that the barley would be here tomorrow afternoon (I'd rung up and done some shouting first thing). Then the Devizes-based dealer who had sold me the big rotavator over the internet rang to say delivery would be next week. And I rang North's for a progress report on Tigger – I'd been expecting a call all afternoon to say that the eBay-sourced propshaft was no good. I'm such a pessimist. They'd been held up on a previous car, and wanted to keep mine in for another day. I was happy with that – I'll be stuck in the tractor for a couple of days yet.

After finishing Chalks, I popped into Big Broom, and did about fifteen acres, to take the day's tally to over fifty. I thought I'd reward myself after such a good day with an evening's rugby, but there was another technical error: there was none on tonight.

October 1st

The frantic scramble to get as much drilling done before the long trip to Durham Uni continued. The weather helped, with today being another stunning bright day, although the howling easterly wind stopped Graham from coming in to do a bit of pre-emergence spraying. It's amazing how essential pre-emergence spraying has become. When I started, it was almost unheard of. Over the years, the grassweed problem has exploded, just as our armoury has dwindled. Getting a good dose of Liberator/Defy on asap after drilling is now the only remotely reliable way of dealing with the problem. So it's worth booking a contractor to get onto the field as soon as the roller has left it. I'm glad Graham's team are so easily available.

I kept going in Godwin's, making a reasonably early start, and finishing Big Broom just before lunch. I was doing my hourly walk-around/check when I spotted that my repair work back in the spring – a new bracket to hold on the following harrows – had fallen off again, and the only thing holding the harrows together was the selection of zip ties I'd put on back in February. Just as I was counting my blessings at having left them on as an insurance policy, I happened to spot the bracket, lying on the headland where it had fallen off. Very fortunate indeed, even if one of the bolts had gone missing somewhere else. I put another zip tie on, and an extra bit of baler twine, and carried on.

The ground in Godwin's was getting pretty hard, and I did briefly contemplate leaving the last fields until after the rain comes, but last year's four-month washout is still fresh in the memory. I pushed on into Middle Broom, finishing it just before tea, and made a start on Child's Broom.

Noel, meanwhile, was doing a bit of fencing patching in the morning, then rolling behind the drill. He then switched to rolling in front of the drill, in Godwin's Park, where his Terradiscing had baked dry. He also unloaded the winter barley seed, which finally arrived just after tea.

The saga of getting Tigger repaired continued. I rang North's who said things were progressing – they were still waiting for a new brake pipe, and the eBay propshaft was wrong. Luckily, they had matched the good end of the old one with the 'right' end of the new one, and made one that fitted. Quite a relief.

After a quick tea and a shower, France vs Canada was a thriller.

October 2nd

I set myself a pre-Durham mission for today: to get Godwin's finished. And, remarkably, I achieved it – but not as smoothly as I'd hoped. I got safely out of Child's Broom, and headed east to Godwin's Park. It's not a huge field, and it's one of the only flat ones on the farm, but it's an awkward shape, and it always takes longer than you think.

The dear little Horsch drill started to shed bits as we progressed across the field: shear bolts kept snapping, and I had the horrible 'marker arm foldback' syndrome again, only this time it managed to burst one of the front depth wheels. Luckily, this is more of a depth 'assisting' wheel, so it made little difference.

After a long satisfying day, the whole Godwin's block was finished, and the Park itself looked an absolute treat. I hauled the bruised and battered drill back along the track back home.

All we had to do then was pop up to North's and fetch Tigger, complete with half-new prop shaft, now running as smooth as silk. And that was our cue to put farming on the back burner for a bit, and start finalising plans for the long trip north. And for someone like me, who doesn't get out much, that can be a bit scary.

October 3rd

Even though I stayed out of the tractor, it was still a busy Saturday. My plan to settle down and enjoy some more rugby on the television kept on being foiled by visitors. Some of them were planned or not unexpected; Graham's sprayer came in and did some vital pre-emergence on White Hill, and then, because he was here, gave the Stanmore stubbles a good dose of Roundup. And the Editor was on patrol for some pigeons on the freshly sown fields.

The big surprise came when a strange car parked in the yard, and a huge figure of a man climbed out. He seemed hesitant as he walked across the gravel, until a huge grin broke out when we recognised each other through the open window. It was, the land agent in charge of Hinton Ampner when we took over the farm in 1991.

A frenzy of coffee and nostalgia endued. He'd left the Trust some years after the takeover, and now looked after a private estate somewhere in the south-east, but fancied a visit to Hinton, and thought he'd drop in. We had a fantastic morning comparing notes about those dark days of Flindt vs Flindt (the battle to take over from Dad was not easy or fun), and the notorious tenant at Hinton Ampner House who had caused us so much stress. A quarter of a century on, we can laugh about it, which we did, and we parted on the best of terms – unlike (it should be said) some of our meetings 25 years ago.

A lot of rugby was missed as a result, though, and I managed to keep clear of the final preparations for the trip up to Durham. Probably no bad thing.

October 4th

As usual, whenever I know I've got to get up early, it means I can't sleep. I was wide awake at about 4am, and then managed an hour or so unsuccessfully dozing, before deciding it was a waste of time, and got up. It did mean that we actually managed to set off early; to be on the A272 at eight is some sort of record for me.

It was the most stunning autumn morning, and a fantastic drive up to Durham. The roads were clear and reasonably empty, we did a couple of comfort breaks, and everyone stayed calm and unruffled. We unloaded Diana and her stuff into a 70's accommodation block in Gilesgate, enjoyed a lovely meet-and-greet session with her 'mentors', and very quickly realised that Diana was already feeling at home. We said our goodbyes and headed out to the hotel.

October 5th

I'm not a good sleeper in a strange bed, but there was something excellent about this one. I slept fantastically, and was up ripping off the sheets to find the make of the mattress almost as soon as I woke. After a late breakfast, we set off south. There was more nostalgia on the sections on A1 that have remained untouched in over thirty years, then it was time to settle down for a slightly more crowded drive back. There were one or two hold-ups too, and some fairly heavy rain, so we were home at three.

October 6th

Another dreadful wet day. I cheered myself up with lots of writing, and a drive round eastern Hampshire. First the surgery for yet more prescriptions, then on to Rod's for the hedge trimmer hydraulic ram that is defying all attempts to mend it, and pick up some oil and filters to give our little Massey Ferguson 5455 loader tractor a bit of a service. He isn't a Massey dealer any more, but still carries many of the everyday parts. Then it was on further down the Froxfield road to the official Massey dealers to get new hydraulic connectors for the same tractor. The old ones have been dribbling away for some time, and it's spooky how much oil can vanish from the rear axle while you're not looking.

Back home, Noel and Hazel were in the middle of sorting cattle for the TB test, so I made my excuses (livestock not my department, etc., etc.) and set about servicing the Massey. All went well until the restart: it would fire up, then die. Over and over again. I tried bleeding, assuming it was an air lock – but nothing. I gave up and rang Rod's – their skills as ex-Massey dealers would nail it, surely? Little did I know that the most extraordinary couple of weeks in my 34-year farming career were imminent...

Not long after I got back from an uneventful Tuesday night pub trip with Robert, the phone rang, and it was Mike the Keeper. Did we know that there was a vehicle driving round the Joan's Acre woods? I didn't, of course, but jumped back in Tigger to go and investigate. He was outside Joan's Acre House, waiting and watching the woods. We discussed what on earth was going on; it's not poacher territory – just some lovely woodland with wide rides running through it. All was silent by now, though, and Mike decided to head home. I parked up quietly and waited for a bit longer.

My patience was rewarded after another ten minutes when, quite bizarrely, a classic Mini came hurtling down the track out of the woods with a speed and nimbleness straight out of *The Italian Job* (the original, not the shite one). It took off down the road to West Meon, and I pulled out from my hiding place – lights off – and chased it. After a few hundred yards, I switched my lights on, and scared the living bejeezus out of them – they had no idea I was there.

I know this because they stopped sometime later; I wouldn't let them get away (a Mini driven by strangers to the parish will never shake off a Terracan driven by a road-knowing local), and they pulled over. I asked what the hell they were doing driving a Mini round National Trust woodland in the dead of night, even if their rallying skills did seem mighty impressive. They shouldn't complain if they get mistaken for poachers, I told them in my best grumpy voice. There were lots of apologies, and pleas of "we didn't know!". As if you have to 'know'.

October 7th

Everything was sodden, so we all had a sofa day. Well, I did for a bit, and then the diesel lorry arrived, ringing from the gate to say he was here, rather than from half an hour away to give us notice. Then a spray delivery arrived, with the driver parking outside the spraystore and ringing to say he couldn't find the spraystore. Then Rod's engineer turned up to try and restart the Massey 5455, still stuck in the doorway of the barn.

He found a leak in the bowl of the second fuel filter, and then the tractor started fine. And then stopped dead, and refused to start for the whole of the rest of that day. Come dusk, and the poor fellow was still struggling to find out what had happened. It could be an expensive job.

I sat indoors and tried a hundred times to write up the Fiat that we had out ages ago, and failed completely. Hazel had a soggy dog walk with Caroline, then a good session with Monty at training.

A walk across White Hill gave me a fright – the slugs were out in force. We've got plenty of pellets in stock, so I tried and failed to ring neighbour Robert to see if his machine was up and running. Having failed to make contact, I tried Graham, who said he'd be in tomorrow.

Priorities were re-established by the news of a very old friend having advanced breast cancer. We truly are entering the old ages.

October 8th

I've had better birthdays. They have usually been spent sowing barley, but there was no chance of that this year. The loader tractor was still stuck in the doorway of the tractor barn, broken down.

Rod's man came out and spent another couple of hours on it, before admitting defeat and saying it would be a main dealer job, i.e. that a laptop diagnosis would be needed.

I rang the local main dealer, who arrived just before lunch. Unfortunately, they sent someone who didn't seem to have a clue what he was doing, and covered it up with belligerence and rudeness. I popped out every half an hour to see how he was getting on, and came away crosser and crosser each time. On my last trip, we had a major shouting match about whether I should be paying for the time he was taking to wait for his laptop to be recharged. I suggested he go away and someone who knew how to diagnose the fault in a broken-down tractor should get out here asap.

In between half-hourly shouting matches, I was desperately trying to get the December motoring column written. I had a hundred goes at the Fiat 500x, and just couldn't get it started properly, so switched to the Mercedes that we'd used to get to Durham. It flowed beautifully, and within an hour I had a finely crafted, witty and amusing mini-history of our trip north. Five minutes later, it arrived back from *The Field* with a curt "Er, no. Have another go, and concentrate more on the car." Luckily, thanks to the astonishing lack of farm work that was possible, I had a rewrite done in another couple of hours, and, even better, *The Field* thought it acceptable.

Meanwhile, there was an outbreak of efficiency as Graham's slug spreader man arrived, and put 5 kg/ha of pellets on the Claire wheat. It was nice to see our old ATV being used – he had bought it off Rod after we traded it in for Pig.

After lunch, the Massey main dealers were back, in a team of two, with a fully charged laptop. As we all set off in the early evening to the Horse and Groom in Alresford for a quiet birthday meal, they were still in the barn desperately trying to find out what was wrong with the tractor. This is going to be one very expensive repair job.

I cheered up once we got to the pub. The Horse and Groom was 'home' for Alresford Rugby Club back in the mid-1990s, when I was still propping for them. It has had the most fantastic makeover, and there's no sign of the holes in the ceiling that somehow resulted from lively evenings there. I told Jonathan that he was sitting only feet away from where I once stood on a chair, bollock naked, singing 'Sunshine Mountain'. Or was it 'Father Abraham'? Luckily, Jonathan had finished his meal.

October 9th

The Massey main dealers spent another long and expensive couple of hours playing with the tractor, before deciding that the ECU was faulty. It would have to come off, and be sent away to Perkins. It might come back on Monday, but then again, it might not. This left me contemplating the drilling campaign. I can't do much without a loader tractor, and if I can find a tractor (Noel kindly suggested we could use his), it will have to work its way round the 5455, parked helplessly in the entrance to the tractor barn.

Right on the promised dot of ten o'clock the internet-bought three-metre rotavator arrived. While it was being unloaded by crane, I gave it a good looking over, and was pleased that it appeared better in the metal than it did on the internet. Without the prospect of any drilling, Noel hitched it onto the Deere, did some work on the PTO to make it fit, and set off to Bungalow to give the bean stubble, and the area of green uncut beans, a good mulching in.

I was still sulking with all the tractor breakdown stuff, so headed off to White Hill to enjoy the slug carnage – which is always satisfying. Bad news for veggies, though.

The TB test reading session went well, though – which is always a relief.

October 10th

Another fine Saturday brought a dilemma. We have no loader tractor, so I can't go drilling unless we organise a replacement. With the fantastic forecast, I decided it wasn't worth the trouble of doing so, so asked Noel, once he'd finished with the new rotavator in Bungalow, to take the Carrier up to JA, DC and TBHD, and run over the ground before the winter barley. It would dry it out a bit and make the drill go better, when I finally get there. It would also allow me to sit indoors, watch lots of rugby, and get psyched up for tonight's gig.

Two large cheques arrived from the taxman, which baffled us a bit – something to do with overpayment last time we sent them anything. We dug out the letter from the accountant which was supposed to explain everything, but it just made things more confusing. A great thick fog descends upon me when tax matters come up, so I leave the whole thing trustingly to the accountant, and hope he's doing everything right.

Keeper Mike rang from next door to say they'd had the poachers all over the farm last night – had I had any visits? I said I hadn't been out today, but sneaked out between rugby matches to have a look, and indeed they had given Big Field and Rick/Clump a good going over. Interestingly, they entered and left by the only open gateway, the one next to Sean and Dawn's. They happened to be out in their garden, so we had a good moan about it, and made yet more provisional plans for gates here, there and everywhere.

All in all, though, a more cheerful day, made better by cheerful news and texts from Diana in Durham, and a truly great gig in the Greatham Inn. We'd expected a bar full of rugby buffs, cross because we wanted to play, but it was anything but. The rugby was on the telly in the corner, and many watched it and listened to us at the same time, but once that had finished, we had a full pub dancing. And we played very well – all those Monday nights in Shed 3b do really serve a purpose.

October 11th
Choice A: Despite the sore head from last night, somehow organise a way of putting seed in the drill, and go and spend Sunday sowing.
Choice B: Lie in, take some paracetamol, then enjoy a feast of rugby.
Choice B won.

October 12th
Fired up with enthusiasm to get some farming done, we spent the whole morning on the phones. The Massey dealers had still made no progress with the 5455, so I chased up a neighbour to pop round with his Merlo and do me a 'load up' at lunchtime. Meanwhile we rang the chimney sweep to give the fires an autumn clean up – the evenings have suddenly got very cold in a dry north wind. I rang the lettings agents to check that they would do the formal checking out of our tenant from the cottage, which they already had in hand.

Next up was the landlord, to arrange a meeting to discuss them having the cottage back, and finally a query to the medical team looking into the bronchiectasis: would BUPA pay for another visit to the sinus surgeon, when anything connected with sinuses was excluded on my policy?

Having sorted all that lot out (or left an assortment of messages), I took the Carrier and the front weights off the Deere, got the drill on, and persuaded Robert

Raimes to send up his man in a Merlo to load up the rest of the Scout. Thanks to the Merlo's nimbleness, he was able to shift a whole lot of assorted clutter and wheedle his way round the stricken Massey. It was all done in five minutes.

I headed off to Bungalow with about 1,250 kg of seed, and did my sums. It was 5.7ha last time I drilled the whole lot, and I've done a wild bird shooting strip since then, so down to 5.3 ha. The slightly dodgy calculator said 236 kg/ha. There then followed a moment which old farmers recognise: something told me to put a different figure in the drill's control box. I don't know why, but I entered 230 kg/ha. It could be experience, it could be a fear of running out early and having to go all the way back for a bag of a different variety – whatever. 230 kg/ha it was.

Bungalow drilled beautifully. The new rotavator had done a fantastic job, and the soil was a dream-like consistency. It was almost enough to banish the terrible memories of struggling through quagmires in the mid-1980s, two ploughs, power harrow and separate Bamlett drill, normally in mid-November. The field looked a picture when I finished. A good roll, and it will be as good as I've ever seen it.

Best of all, the calibration was perfect. I finished next to the houses with only a couple of handfuls of seed still in the drill. A good day.

October 13th

It was an official bugger-all day. The loader still wasn't working, so we treated ourselves to a day off. Noel went shopping in Swindon for kitchens – again – and I sat indoors and did some writing.

Phil from Farol dropped in for a cuppa and a long session of philosophy about the state of the industry. Like everyone else, they are suffering in the sales department, but repairs and servicing are picking up as people hang onto kit for longer. Not the best thing to say to me with our apparently unrepairable tractor still blocking the main barn entrance.

A long pub trip with Robert – and a letter to confirm that the cattle had passed the TB tests – made the day end slightly more cheerfully.

October 14th

There was no sign of any repair happening to the loader, so I took Noel up on his offer of using his little Case IH tractor loader. He brought it over from its base in Alresford, put some weights on the back and had a long session manoeuvring it in the little space in the barn to get to the winter barley seed. He only had a muck grab, and our front implements wouldn't fit, being Mailleux kit from the mid-1990s. But the grab was good enough to lift a bag, and get it over the side of the drill, so we put two bags in, and he then took a trailer-load down the Drier Yard. I had a quick calibrate and got ready to head out after lunch.

Noel's a bit of a fencing pro, so I asked him to start work repairing the rotten gatepost at the top of the back-door path. It had finally given way some days ago under the onslaught of a trio of excited dogs trying to bash the gate open.

I headed out for the long drive to JA/DC, via gateways that weren't blocked by telegraph poles, and did the headland and a chunk of landwork. I was interrupted by a mysterious phone call: we had been selected for a full sheep inspection, and the nice lady doing it wanted to have a bit of a chat about the whens and wherefores. The reception on the phone is terrible in the Joan's Acre valley, so we lost connection several times. I suspect she thought I was trying to lose her, so that no appointment could be arranged – it had to be done in 48 hours from the time of the call. She persevered, and we finally connected enough to get a date sorted. I rang Hazel with the terrifying news, but she seemed confident that all would be in order.

I stopped reasonably early, because the Growmore Club Quiz started tonight. By 8pm, two teams of farmers were sitting facing each other along a long narrow table in the Pub with No Name in Colemore, answering a quiz round about farming, general knowledge and current affairs. Then we had a debating round (a hurriedly prepared 90-second speech on a random topic), and then a snap quiz round, one team member against his opposite number. All done in the lightest of spirits, and after sandwiches and a beer or two, all home by ten. There's a great feature to be done in *Farmers Weekly* one day about the Growmore Club Quiz.

Hazel was poring over paperwork on the kitchen table when I got home, and I was asleep before she finished. I suspect sheep things might be not quite as in order as was first thought.

October 15th

We were getting towards the end of an incredibly frustrating week, waiting to find if our loader tractor would be mended. But today (we were assured) would be the end of it all. Today, well before noon, the ECU would be arriving at the local Massey dealers, ready to be whisked down to our barn and refitted to the stricken tractor. And away we'd go, with proper seed loading and high-speed drilling. I leapt out of bed (as well as I could after last night's excesses) and opened the tractor barn to speed proceedings even further.

The phone rang at 9.20am and it was the main dealer's rep. Unfortunately, the highly respectable overnight parcel company seemed to have forgotten to pick up the ECU yesterday, and it was still with the re-mappers. Nothing could be done. I had a bit of a moment, suggesting that someone somewhere was trying to pull a fast one and actually there was nothing but incompetence at play. Things got very heated, and I nearly hung up, but suggested that they get on and do the best they can.

We would have to carry on with what we had, so I asked Noel to drop another couple of bags in the drill down at the Drier Yard, and I popped out mid-morning to finish JA and DC. Once again, I was surprised with how well they drilled, although (whisper it) they'll be needing a rain later.

Graeme the vet popped over at lunchtime, and gave the dogs their jabs – not sure why we were treated to a visit, but I suspect a good gossip was needed, and he probably fancied a trip away from the surgery. It meant I wasn't back out in the tractor until three, though. I ran out of seed just before five, and ambled back to the drier yard, having started in the very short work in BHD. I'd decided to 'go straight in' with no cultivation at all and it was – once again – going in far better than I had hoped. A good roll afterwards would make

216

a nice job of it.

Noel finished the gatepost to the back-door path, and took his little tractor off to Bungalow and rolled that – without getting stuck, which is always a bonus. That little field of wheat has had the best start possible: good bean crop, slow rotavate, drill in perfect conditions, roll. It's all downhill from here. He then popped out after tea and put two more bags in the drill, ready for me to make an early start tomorrow. The incentive to get out early will be to avoid the mood when the expensive new ECU is put back on the Massey, and it still doesn't start. Pessimists – we're never disappointed.

The Sheep Inspector duly arrived, waved her magic stick over the sheep to check electronic ear tags, looked at the movement books and other assorted records, and announced that everything was hunky-dory. She then announced that my *Farmers Weekly* articles were the best thing in the magazine. She can come and inspect our livestock any time.

October 16th

Dawn from New Pond was on the phone well before 8am; she'd seen a Mitsubishi go up into the woods, and was a bit worried. I reassured her that it was Jim the Deerman doing his rounds, and not poachers out unusually early. Jim himself then rang, offering a freshly shot deer – I had to work quite hard to turn it down. He was convinced that we would like nothing more than several stone of freshly gutted, still bleeding carcass hanging in the house. All I remember from the last one we had was that it didn't actually taste very nice.

I asked how he had got on, pointing out that we were becoming overrun with deer. He apologised, and said his mission as a deer control man is now entirely compromised by walkers, even from the crack of dawn. "You ought to see the people out walking over your fields!" he said, which didn't put me in the best of moods.

My mood didn't improve much when the absolutely dead certain, non-failing, guaranteed pre-9am delivery of the part for the Massey failed to materialise. No one got in touch to tell me as much; the first I knew was when I'd made another early-ish start on the winter barley in TBHD, and Noel bought another load of seed out. "No, nothing's happened," he said. "Tractor's still in pieces in the barn." Thank goodness he's happy for us to keep using his little beast. I finally got hold of someone at the dealer who said that the part hadn't arrived, but it was due in, ooh, literally, the next five minutes. In fact, there was a mechanic sitting waiting for it. His time, no doubt, to be added to my already humungous bill. At tea time, I rang the rep, and asked for his version of what the bloody hell was going on. I was treated to a gobsmacking range of excuses and drivel. I made a note to try and find the Claas quote we had some months ago.

He rang again, quite late, and left a message to say that, wonder of wonders, the part had arrived. Unfortunately, they wouldn't be out to fit it tomorrow, because it's Saturday tomorrow, and the re-mappers have to be available on the phone to help set up the new part, and they don't work on Saturdays. But they'll all be piling out here first thing on Monday – assuming aliens from the planet Zog don't break into the workshop and nick the ECU. If they did, it wouldn't surprise me in the least.

Tod and I had a long discussion about ordering more wheat seed. In theory, if we have a good run tomorrow, we'll finish all the scheduled wheat and barley, but that will be only 220 acres of wheat (early sown first wheat, admittedly), and the Good Lord seems to be presenting us with an opportunity to put a second wheat up in Stanmore. We might have a slot to get up there and direct drill some Panorama, which we tried as a second wheat a couple of years ago and was a great success. We'll get it Latitude treated, which is supposed to help, and hope it stays dry long enough. Last year's nightmare of a six-month winter wheat drilling campaign is still fresh in the mind. The decision was made: we'll go for it.

October 17th

Rugby World Cup quarter-final day, so the mission was to finish the winter barley sowing in TBHD. Luckily, Noel had topped up the drill with seed last night, so when he arrived in the yard mid-morning and found that his little tractor had a front puncture, it didn't affect me out in Hurst Down. He took the tyre and wheel off, flung it into his pickup, and whizzed off to Micheldever Tyres. Bizarrely, there was no queue, and he was back out in the field just in time to refill me by late morning.

Once again, the seed ran out almost to perfection. I had enough to do a ninth turn of headland (which I decided to do last in this field) and there was just a handful of seed in the Horsch when that was all done. Noel finished rolling, and we had the field emptied of assorted vehicles and trailers in time for most of the evening's rugby. Very satisfying.

October 18th

A nice lazy Sunday. Hazel took Sasha to dog training, and I walked the other two dogs for a nice long loop down to the Drier and back. I couldn't help thinking that the Claire in White Hill needed a good rain, but put the thought from my mind as quickly as possible. Then it was a feast of rugby for the whole afternoon.

Late in the evening, I sat down and collected all the facts and figures to do with the ECU on the tractor, and sent it off to the local main dealer who had been trying – and failing – to mend it. I'd had so many conflicting messages about when it would be ready, where it had got to and what was wrong with it, and I needed to get on record all the claims and promises. I pressed send, and thought little more of it.

October 19th

Probably not the best idea to send that email yesterday. Shortly after 8am, the Massey dealer's rep was on the phone, and we had the most unpleasant phone conversation I can remember having with anyone ever.

It had come to their attention (he said) that I had let Gaskin's look at the tractor before asking them to try to sort it out.

"True," I confessed.

"This is totally unacceptable to us," he raged. "Our mechanic will come out this morning, refit the ECU, and leave the tractor as we found it, and walk away from the job. We want nothing more to do with it. We will, however, not charge for the work."

I was somewhat taken aback by this, and had visions of the tractor being stuck in the doorway to the barn for weeks to come. I tried to push him for the reason for the toys being thrown out of the pram: was it really because I had tried someone else? He wouldn't say – he had been told by his boss to cut us off, and would say no more.

"Well, at least suggest someone who might be able to mend it," I insisted.

"Try Romsey Agricultural Machinery," he barked.

And that was that. My first phone call was to Gaskin's, to tap Rod's view. He said it didn't surprise him, but it's not a position he would have adopted. Anyway, he'd be in the area later, and he'd drop off some brochures for the Kubota…

My second phone call was to Massey Ferguson customer services. All was going well as I explained the situation, and sympathetic noises were being made, until I mentioned the name of the main dealer, at which point there was a sharp intake of breath, and a hurried "I need to speak to my manager!" Needless to say, I heard nothing more all day.

The third call was to Romsey Agricultural Machinery. I fell out with them some years ago, funnily enough over servicing the same tractor (which they had actually sold us in 2009). So I put on my best grovelling voice. It worked. They said they would be delighted to come out and have a look – their mechanic would be out within the hour.

In the meantime, the main dealer's man came out, and seemed slightly nervous, so I did more apologising to him for getting him in the middle of the whole silly spat. He then dropped a bit of a bombshell: the ECU had come back from the service centre with 'nothing wrong' written on it. After all that talk of re-mapping… well I never did. He very kindly stayed on for some time after he'd fitted the ECU back on, trying to find the real fault, but admitted defeat, packed up his kit and left us.

He must have passed the mechanic from Romsey Agricultural Machinery on his way down the hill, for it was only a matter of minutes before the doors to the barn were reopened, and a man in smart overalls was preparing to dive under the 5455's bonnet. We had a laugh about the whole situation, and then he listened carefully and patiently to the symptoms.

"Right," he said purposefully. "Only one thing to do. If the ECU is fine, it's something simpler, and we'll start this end and work our way along until we find it." The first time I popped in to see how he was getting on he had all the filters off, including the high-tech extra heavy duty one tucked at the rear right of the engine. Had he found anything? "There seemed to be an airlock in that last one, but I'm not sure that's what it is," he said. Twenty minutes later, there was an engine running. And stopping, and running, and stopping. I popped in again. He had his hand on the wiring that came off the water sensor attached to the bottom of the second diesel filter. As he wiggled it, he could stop the engine. He had a very large smile on his face. Ten minutes later, with the frayed wires taped up, and no longer shorting out and thereby telling the ECU to stop the engine, the whole job was finished, and he was on his way back to Romsey. Huge relief and back-slapping all round. The moral of the story? Be more careful with wires when changing filters.

Finally – finally – we could get on and do some other jobs. It was hard work trying to concentrate, what with the steam coming out of my ears. But we managed to vaccinate some sheep, and get some cattle moved using Robert's fantastic low-loading cattle trailer. Meanwhile, Graham Tosdevine's man was in doing some vital pre-emergence herbicide application. An unusual but busy day.

As I dozed off, my mind still spinning from the hideous saga of getting the tractor mended, I couldn't help replaying in my head the final scene from *Burn After Reading*. Damned if I know what we did wrong, but we sure as heck better not do it again. Or something like that.

October 20th

An early email came through from Mark the Landlord. One of our neighbours in Kilmeston had been badgering the Trust to buy a bit of Bungalow Field for their garden. As is the way with the white settlers of Hampshire, they are insistent. Mark had done his best to tell them that it would be too difficult in the era of BPS/ELS/AHA et al, and he doubted that I would be keen, but they just would not take a 'no' from him. So he was asking us for our view and the inevitable 'no'. I was delighted to furnish him with several paragraphs of 'no'.

Rod the Kubota dealer was dead keen to strike while the iron was hot – he was on the phone at 9.10am, having already got a quote together to replace the Massey with the most ugly machine you ever saw in your life, the M135GX. A very fair quote it was too, but I wasn't going to rush into signing anything until I've at least had a go in one.

Hazel set off very early for her first day's picking-up of the new season, at Barrow Hill with Monty. She asked me to check the cattle were OK down in the bottom of Englands, so I took Fred and Sasha to see how they were. They seemed a bit baffled by the little plastic sheep water trough, so I showed them where the big one was, and they seemed grateful. I looped back round Godwin's to enjoy the fine-looking Scout and make the most of the last of the stunning October days.

Richard from Tosdevine's arrived to finish the pre-emergence herbicide on the Scout, so I was pleased to be off the field before he started with the unbearably smelly Liberator/Defy mixture. I warned him to be aware of the many footpaths in Godwin's, and to be prepared to stop for a minute or two to let people through – and to be ready for an angry gesture or two that the walkers now feel happy to make at us as we go about our job.

Then it was back to medical matters – off to the Basingstoke Clinic to see the ENT man, to get his thoughts on the bronchiectasis and how it seems to mean constant colds and sinus pain. I rang BUPA to get the authorisation number, half expecting them to say 'no'. I'd been in the middle of one of the most severe sinus infections when I joined BUPA, so it was the one and only excluded condition. But BUPA seemed happy to give the all-important eight-digit number, so I had a lovely drive to Basingstoke in the Mazda.

Those sinus-infected pre-BUPA days were dark indeed. I was battling with the pain and toothache, and the start of terrifying digestive problems caused by scattergun antibiotic use. The doctors had suggested replacing all the white fillings I had with traditional amalgam, to see if that was the problem. It wasn't. When they suggested 'functional endoscopic sinus surgery' to drill away some 'bodywork' and clear the airwaves, I was so desperate for something to work, I paid for it privately out of my own pocket. It was a bit of a messy failure. Not only was the Test Match at Sabina Park abandoned after only a few overs – I'd carefully chosen a date so that I could enjoy some live cricket while recuperating – but the operation failed to stop the sinus problems. The surgery was done by the same ENT man at the Hampshire Clinic.

Eighteen years later, I was back in his office, discussing the whole bronchiectasis saga. It was much more a social visit this time – he was a regular on the old shoot as a fully paid-up member of the Candover Mafia. After a good gossip, we got back to medical matters, and he suggested that it might be a case of chicken and egg. Sinus problems might not just be caused by the bronchiectasis, they might also be making it worse when they arise first. There was then a session with a camera up my nose, projecting crystal clear pictures onto a monitor. I had a guided tour of the cheekbone sinuses, the ones at the top of the nose, the bottom of the Eustachian tube, and a view of the back of the throat. All looked well – I just happened to be in good nasal health this week, with a sense of smell and clear airways. He could even show me the work he'd done almost twenty years ago. However, he did find several polyps, and quickly decided that these could be adding to the whole issue, restricting flow and blocking sinuses. Solution: yet more steroids. We said our goodbyes and I put the roof down on the Mazda and headed back down the Candover valley dreading yet more sprays and drops, and couldn't help notice how good an MX-5 was at clearing the head.

Back home, I rang Gordon the landlord to ask if he was still on for a late afternoon chat. He was over in a matter of minutes, and looked as if he needed a light-hearted argument, which we duly had. I said we'd have a cottage empty in a couple of weeks (all being well), and asked what sort of deal could we do on giving it back. We went through all the usual stuff about public access, and he once again promised to look into signs and fences. He went away much more cheerful that when he arrived.

Hazel and Monty arrived back from Barrow Hill suitably knackered, having had a great day in the sunshine. Hazel is now officially 'a keeper' (as in someone who looks after game birds, not just as a good girl to be held on to). As such, she was entitled to two things at Barrow Hill. First, an extra layer of top-quality abuse, and, second, a walkie-talkie for the day. An honour, indeed.

October 21st

It was bloomin' wet again. I unloaded the late-ordered seed, ready for a rather optimistic extra few acres to go up in Stanmore. Tod came round to check on everything, and seemed happy. Apart from that, we sat indoors and watched the rain.

October 22nd

A long walk across White Hill revealed the slugs were back hard at it, wrecking the growing crop. A walk across Broom Field made me question the wisdom of the extra seed we'd bought. It's going to take some draining to get any sowing done up there.

I did a bit of work on the drill, nonetheless. I put the tyres back on the press, and checked out the state of the right-hand marker arm holder. It had a huge crack in it, and didn't look as though it was going to manage to hold out much longer. I took it off and whipped it up to Rod's for a bit of repair, and also to get a bar welded on to stop the arm falling forward after the shear bolt breaks. The bolt snaps while in work, but stays in its hole long enough for the arm to go vertical. Once the arm is vertical, the bolt falls out, and the arm falls forward, then gets folded back underneath the drill. I've been through five or six marker arms, and they're not cheap. The little bit of adaptation should put a stop to that. If we ever get back out into the field.

October 23rd

Gaskin's had done a super job welding up the marker arm holder on the Horsch, and I spent a bit of time in the morning putting it back on, and then contemplated making a start in Stanmore sowing the late Panorama. Working on the principal that going in well and late is better than early and messily, I put it off again.

Instead, with Jonathan home on half term, we decided to say a big goodbye to the grand piano. It has been sitting in the corner of the dining room for years – longer than we've been in the farmhouse. I bought it in the mid-1980s, soon after we came back from university. It came from one of the fabulous grand houses in Wickham Square, and cost me a few hundred pounds. Moving it to the little farm bungalow where we lived then was almost as expensive. I played it endlessly, teaching myself to tune it (which it needed frequently, with all those loose pins), and then supplemented it in 1995 with an electric Roland. The first pregnancy had meant the end of skiing plans, and the money 'saved' went on the Roland.

Along came a second baby, and the main sitting room in the bungalow had to be subdivided to make another office, and then there was no room for the piano any more. At the same time, I sent it away to be comprehensively restored: new strings, dampers, hammers, and the insides given a fantastic spruce up. When the time came to return it, I sent it to the farmhouse, where there was plenty of room, and where, we had hoped, we'd be moving in soon – even if my parents had failed to get the hint.

The Brinsmead piano did the trick. Just before setting off on the twice-yearly holiday to Jersey, my mother announced that, when they came back, they'd be moving into the bungalow. And while she had been babysitting for us one evening, she had colour-coded the doorways with different stickers. While she and Dad were away, we were to move all the furniture with red stickers into the red room, the blue into the blue room, and so on. We called in a couple of helpers, and did the move in a couple of days with tractor and low trailers.

The poor old grand piano hasn't been used much since then. Electric pianos kept arriving, and the last time the Brinsmead was played in anger was at Anthony's 18th birthday, when a long drunken version of 'Skyfall' could be heard.

So, how do you get a grand piano out of the house? We took the lid off, took the action out, lifted one end up using the farm hi-lift trolley jack, and lowered it onto its side on two fencing posts. Off came the legs, and then we jacked it up again, and slid a 'piano dolly', hired for twenty quid that morning, under the massive body, and we were ready to roll. Which it did, surprisingly easily, out of the back door and up into the yard. Thence it was a short and undignified trip on the front of the loader to the bonfire, where it was dropped, unceremoniously for the camera, several times, but simply refused to do anything but go 'bong' dramatically. A sad end – and, yes, I had tried selling it. But the dramatic increase in space in the dining room made the exercise worthwhile. We'd better get good turnouts for the shoot lunches after all that.

Just after 11pm, the poachers were back. The sound of engines being revved up and down in a distinctly off-road way stirred me just as I was finally dropping off. A cursory glance out of the window revealed the inevitable lights in White Hill, so I headed downstairs, out into the yard and into the Top of Englands, from where I could watch them hurtling backwards and forwards across my poor fragile wheat. A 999 call was taken sympathetically, and I gave the poaching codeword, but expected little more – not at this time on a Friday night.

Two minutes later, I was rung back, and a very urgent voice wanted to confirm details. Odd, I thought. A couple of minutes later, a police car sped into the village, crewed by two. They stopped next to me outside the farmhouse, and I sent them towards White Hill, pointing out the lamp that could still be seen working the fields, although by now it had moved on to David's farm, south of mine. A couple of minutes later, another car arrived, with a policewoman on board. She stopped for a chat, and then acted as a sort of liaison officer between me – directing operations from the Top of Englands – and yet more cars which arrived from everywhere.

The really curious moment was at about midnight, when up Farm Hill came a Discovery, souped up to the roofline, with extra lights and massive tyres, covered in mud, and doing about sixty miles an hour. It came screeching to a halt at the sight of the policewoman and her car, not to mention me in my jimjams. There then followed a curious standoff – I was convinced that it was the poachers, and told the WPC as much. So she (and I) approached it with a certain amount of nervousness. It turned out to be a pair of classic *Fast Show* 'Let's Off Road!' types who were indulging in their hobby of midnight green laning. They got a thorough going over by the WPC, and I then gave them a bit of an earful about driving around the countryside doing a great poacher impersonation at this time of year. They looked a bit shell-shocked at what seemed to be a major police operation.

Within half an hour of my 999 call, the two panda cars were joined by Jon in his marked Land Rover, a plain estate car full of dogs, and two very burly lads in a plain Discovery. Team Disco were thrilled when I suggested that we go down and open the gate to White Hill, and they could tiptoe round the outside – the lamping lights had by now gone, and I was convinced that they had spotted the array of police car lights, and had tucked up in a corner. I got a lift down to the gate with the single policewoman, who seemed not to care that I was still in jimjams and dressing gown, and Team Disco set off round the wheat, sticking resolutely to the headland tramline which I had pointed out to them.

It soon became obvious that Team Poacher were nowhere to be seen – I reckon, looking back, that they had sneaked out down Stanmore Lane. They had moved the telegraph pole/cultivator combi to get in, so they might have sneaked back out at some time. Very frustrating. A call then flooded everyone's radios about a fight and a robbery in Winchester, and, not surprisingly, that took precedence. It was left to Jon to give me a lift home in his Land Rover. I just had to ask him about the phenomenal turnout; what was going on? "Those up high are very unhappy about what's going on," he explained. "We're determined to get them. I'm only sorry we didn't manage to book the helicopter this time!"

Half the Hampshire Constabulary then left, leaving me on my own outside the farmhouse. I spent half an hour back out in the Top of England's, half expecting to see the poachers light up and drive off, but nothing happened. So I headed to bed. It was getting on towards 2am.

October 24th

A drive round revealed wheel marks all over White Hill. The straight line stuff hadn't done much damage, but the sweeping turns as their dogs closed in on a hare had ripped up great long ruts in the wheat. A walk up Stanmore Lane revealed that they had indeed used it for access, and getting onto David's farm, but also revealed that someone had neatly trimmed the grass. Really? Conscientious poachers worried about their damage, so they trimmed the footpath grass? Hmm – not sure about that. The poachers had also been all over Big Field and Rick/Clump again, using the entrance right next to Sean's house. He rang my mobile as I was checking the winter barley – untouched, thankfully – so I turned round for a chat.

We decided to start planning new gates across the track next to his house. On a lighter note, as they say, he said he had a chum who would be interested in buying our Massey, if we were in the mood to sell it. I said I'd check with Rod first, as I don't want to fall out with yet another dealer.

I rang David when I got back in, and told him to check his fields. Within an hour, he was in our yard (in his incredibly old and beaten up Land Rover which would provoke another 999 call if you didn't know it was him), saying that they had been over every one of his fields in Kilmeston. He also pointed out that the council had sent round a mowing team just yesterday to trim the grass on the footpaths. They were contractors from Guildford way, which would explain why they mowed the track right up to Long Field, instead of stopping at the end of the footpath. Not much use in my ongoing attempts to block the path. David and I mulled over all sorts of ways of blocking the track – it is too narrow for modern machinery, so a lump of something up there isn't going to inconvenience farming activities.

Tod was in, unloading the band kit into Shed 3b, and he asked if he could go down the Drier and start dismantling the last of the old wooden grain sides that he'd got his eye on. I said that would be fine, but to watch out for swarms of police cars descending on him if Sean spots a strange vehicle down at the barn. We're all a bit jumpy at the moment.

The first rugby World Cup semi was tight, but entertaining – when I got to it. I had Anthony on the phone chatting away excitedly about his work up in Leeds, and then the local poppy-seller on the doorstep. I told her about the new shoot, and suggested she might want to come beating again. She was one of the nicest of the old beaters, always taking care of our children when they were sent to join the beating line. It would be lovely for her to come along again.

Hazel had spent the whole day picking-up at Tim Sykes' shoot at Hambledon, and she and Fred had a great day. Fred, despite being a 'double digit flatcoat' went like a train all day, and did one or two master retrieves – one of which earned applause from the onlookers.

October 25th

There was quite hard frost – I hoped the new sprayer was OK. It would be just typical to end up with burst pipes after only a hundred or so acres done with it.

Hazel was away with a dog again – this time to Newbury Lodge for another session with Sasha. She had emailed to cry off now that Sasha was on heat, but they told her to come along anyway. Good training for her and all the other dogs, apparently.

I took the flatcoats out for a loop round Chalks and the Godwin's block, pleased to see a multitude of pheasants lining the edge of the top strips, and melting into it as we approached the tennis court. I met a couple of archetypal trophy wives walking the path at the top of Chalks – blonde, sunglasses, one with a baby in a front sling, one with a sevenish-year-old boy. The dogs trotted over to say hello, but the trophy wives stared resolutely ahead, afraid to move their heads, and just kept going. I got a wave from the little boy though. All that block of Scout looked fantastic – far better than the earlier drilled Claire, even without all the poacher wheel marks in it.

Another vintage public access moment when I heard pheasants shouting and flying out of the aforementioned shooting strip. I spotted two figures on the edge of the tennis court. They had got lost – you do surprise me, Madam – and were trying to find Hinton Ampner House. I sent them down the hill and onto the road. Let's hope this doesn't happen on Thursday.

A quick drive down to the Drier revealed Tod and Dan having the time of their lives, working lights all set up and angle grinders screaming their way through half-century-old bolts. It soon turned into a tour of the whole drying and cleaning set-up, still in the state it was left the last time I used it – goodness knows when that was. I talked them through the numerous intake conveyors and elevators, the old Alvan Blanch double flow drier (which the manufacturer still reminds me every year is due a service; it would take more than a service to get it going now). Just as I was finishing the story of how I drove a Class Protector 6 through the end of the building, I heard voices, and found the Editor and his wife snooping round to see what was going on – and asking if a lift home would be possible. Of course it would.

So it was home for tea and biscuits, a raid on the unbelievable apple crop, and a half-hour session trying to persuade her to splash out on a new steering rack for their aged Toyota. Yes, it may be expensive, but if you can't turn the corner…

The second World Cup semi was exciting but ultimately one-sided. Then the evening got dark an hour early. Horrid.

October 26th

Not the greatest of Mondays. In a fit of enthusiasm, I hitched onto the drill, filled up with a ton of Panorama, calibrated and headed off for the long drive to Pipeline. Within ten yards, there was a problem: the 'motor overload' buzzer went off. I assumed it was just sticky with a ton of wheat on top of it, and went to free it by hand. It was very stiff, almost as if there was something more serious going on. I turned it by hand again, and tried the motor override button, but it still jammed.

Time to investigate it properly. I took off the motor and ran it on its own – it was fine. I took off the support on the right-hand side – it was running smoothly. The roller was now sitting on its own in the base of the hopper, and felt very jerky and unhappy as I turned it. Something must have fallen into the hopper, and was making it jam. I twisted it and wobbled it, acutely aware that quite a pile of bright red treated seed was building up under the drill. I slid it nearly all the way out and back in again, hoping that the obstruction would fall out, and reassembled the support bearing and the motor. It still didn't feel very smooth, so I decided to head home and call an expert. It seemed wise to drive through the pile of seed with the drill down to spread it about, so I did a big loop and swept over the top of the heap. The feed roller promptly started working properly, with no alarms or buzzers. So I kept going, doing the short headland next to Long Field, thrilled at suddenly and unexpectedly making progress.

It didn't last. As soon as I got into where there had been a heavy crop, the straw bunged up under the drill, proving too much for even the high-clearance Horsch. Four or five huge lumps of trash were enough to revert to my original decision, and head home in a huff.

In an attempt to cheer myself up, I took Jonathan up to Trailertek in Micheldever, with a view to buying a little tow-behind trailer for Pig. This would be very handy come lambing time, and even handier on the shoot, if we need to move a few people by vehicle. They had one or two that looked perfect, and I very nearly bought one – but decided against it at the last moment. I think it might have to wait until the spring.

Band rehearsal was cancelled, which was a shame.

October 27th

Thirty-one years ago today was a frosty Saturday. Hazel and I, and a couple of friends, went off to Winchester Registry Office and she and I got married. We went to the Bush in Ovington for a pub lunch, and then came back and tried to mend Gordon's inboard brakes on his Alfasud. Not very romantic, but the 'correct' wedding would have meant getting team Flindt over to County Down. I never could see that happening in the mid-1980s.

Ernie and I were working together down at the Drier the week before the wedding, bagging the beans in hundredweight paper sacks, ready for the pigeon fanciers to buy. I told him about the wedding, and he was thrilled – but what did we want for a wedding present? I laughed and said a can of beer. At about 6.30 on the Saturday morning, there were footsteps outside the front door of the bungalow where we lived, and a four-pack of lager appeared on the step, with a card.

Ernie and his brother Ken were sowing wheat in Kilmeston Road on that day. Ken always mentioned that he badly skinned his knuckles trying to clear mud from the cage roller on the Maschio power harrow. The cold day made the pain much worse.

At least they were drilling, which is more than I did today. I sat around trying to work on two articles, and failed to do both. I did lots of dog walking instead, and discussed revised drilling plans for Stanmore with Tod. I'm dreading another long autumn of unfinished business.

October 28th

Wet start, then fine and dry – should have gone spraying. Instead, we spent the whole day getting ready for the first shoot of the season. It was nerve-wracking last year, when we were just shooting the odds and sods that had accumulated over three 'unshot' seasons. This year was even worse – we've actually done some preparation. There are shooting strips and pheasants. Goodness knows what will happen.

At tea time, Tania and Guy arrived, old chums from the 80s, and their son Wilfred, who is my godson. Just the sort of team to help launch the all-new Hinton Shoot. Guy very kindly brought a 250-box of unopened Hinton Ampner Special cartridges, which he'd bought when I was ordering them by the thousand back in the early days of the big syndicate shoot. We used to get them from Hull Cartridge – the boxes had a different colour each year, but always with a line drawing of Growler, the shoot captain's favourite Labradoodle, on the front. The cartridges themselves were marked 'Hinton Ampner High Partridge' in a post-ironic way, and 'Piaculum', which any fule kno is Latin for 'scapegoat'. Well, it used to make us laugh, anyway.

When I was organising the bespoke printing, Hull Cartridge demanded to know what 'Piaculum' meant, and refused to go ahead with the order until I had told them. It turned out that they had once sent out 10,000 cartridges with the Latin for 'If it moves shoot it or fuck it' on the side. They weren't going to do that again.

We abandoned the idea of going to the pub, not least because it's curry night in the Pots – and three or four beers wouldn't be wise if we're out all day tomorrow. So we stayed in and were very civilised.

October 29th

The first shoot of the new season, and our first season with our own bought-in birds roaming the farm. High tension as Roger turned up to complete the gun line-up, and John and Julie arrived to complete the dog line. Actually, there was no tension at all. The mood was still very light-hearted.

The rain arrived, complete with howling wind, at about 9.30am, but we set off anyway, striding purposefully along the back bridleway to the Chalks dell, ready to start to sweep the new mile-long 'S' of cover.

Not much happened for some time. A few birds got up in a flush from the north strip of Chalks, but none to shoot at, and nothing happened in 'Keepers Secret Drive'. Chalks south was a different matter: we did it in two blocks, and the first block we walked from one end to the other. There was a flood of birds hopping and running into the second block, although a couple flew out and we were off the mark. For the second block of Chalks south, we sent two guns and two beaters in Pig to the far end, and we walked toward each other. Suddenly, we were in business, with 22 shots and a nice handful of birds – some of them seriously difficult.

Next was the copse in Clump. I sent two guns up to the top, Roger walked up in Roe Hill, and I walked in Clump Field, ready to intercept any Trust walkers. There were none to be seen – no surprise, bearing in mind the wind and rain were really up by now – but I had the oddest confused pheasant fly straight over me from the south end of the field, almost going for me – he lost. The beating team worked their way up the copse, into the gale, and the rain got stronger and stronger. Suddenly, there was a fountain of birds, rising up at the far end, and doubling back – mostly over me, I'm ashamed to admit. But everyone got a few shots in.

It didn't take long, as we stood dripping wet in the top of BOMS, to decide to head for the Drier Yard, where at first light I had parked Tigger complete with food and drink. Hazel and Julie both headed off to change dogs, and we stood in the right-hand lean-to and tried to dry off a bit.

Just as I was mooting the option of knocking off for the day, the rain eased a bit, so, with everyone fed and watered, and with fresh dogs raring to go, we yomped across Drier Field to do George's. There seemed to be lots of birds when we arrived (mostly cock birds squabbling in the dead beech), but not a single thing flew out over us. George's obviously only works with a healthy line of beaters.

Undeterred, and feeling a lot more upbeat now that the rain had ceased, we crossed through the woods and took our position for Barracuda. Three birds came soaring out in the gale, and we got two.

Folly proved more fruitful. We were nattering away like old women at the bottom of the strip of trees when Team Dog got on the radio to tell us to get into proper positions – Hazel could see a mass of pheasant heads among the trees. She was right, although many of them curled back with the gale. All those worries about the badgers colonising the Folly trees proved unfounded.

To finish we did Bob's Wood. The strangest thing happened. While I was half-beating alongside the bridleway, a nettle plant wrapped itself around my shoulders, stinging both sides of my neck. Try as I might, I couldn't work out how it had got there, but assumed it had been flicked up by my beating stick. And, try as I might, I couldn't get it off. Just as I was about to down tools to unwrap it properly, someone yanked it off forcefully. I turned round to see who the practical joker was. There was no one. Very spooky indeed.

Enough flew out of Bob's Wood to make sure that everyone had a good day. We ended up with 19 with 79 shots – exactly the sort of numbers I'd been hoping for. Loads of birds were out there, and we weren't soaked through. Perfect. After a wholesome tea, a few glasses of this and that, everyone went their ways, and we all had a ridiculously early bed.

October 30th

That shoot was the most exercise I'd had in weeks, so I was a wreck this morning. I really, really must start some sort of fitness campaign. Hazel and I had both ended up with wet feet yesterday, so, once recovered, we took a trip into the Countrystore and treated ourselves to new wellies. And some new socks. And a new cartridge belt. By the time we reached the till, several hundred pounds had been spent.

Just as I was finishing off the long haul in the bathroom before bed, I thought I heard the distinctive sound of a Subaru. It seemed close, but the wind was coming strongly from the east, so I decided not to investigate it further. It must just have been traffic on the A32.

October 31st

Nope, it wasn't A32 traffic: it was the poachers, and how. The blighters had made a hell of a mess in Chalks, especially up on top, and then done a fairly comprehensive tour of Godwin's. The bales we'd put down on the exit onto the main road had almost worked. They had had to get out of their Subaru and roll one out of the way to make it off the farm.

Not surprisingly, I could hardly sleep that night, convinced I could hear engines roaring again. I even jumped out of bed and spent ten minutes listening out by the back barn. The car noise was definitely coming from the A32 this time, so I needn't have got up. I was treated to a fabulous misty moon and a stunning fireball – an Orionid? – for my troubles.

One better bit of news was that our cottage tenant had moved out successfully. We have got to start looking for a new one, of course, and in the meantime, we're down nearly a grand a month.

November 1st

A really misty and quiet Sunday. Everyone was up late. Hazel went off to dog training with Sasha, and Jonathan and I tried the Chalky Hill clay shoot – it was heaving, so we decided, rather pathetically, to go home.

I did a big walk round the winter barley in Hurst Down, quite pleased with the way it is getting away. I took a little detour down into the Hurst Down chalk dell, which is always fun. It's a vast hole in the ground, dug out over God-knows how many years, and then abandoned at some date, probably in the late 19th century.

The gently sloping ramp is still obvious, and I often wonder if a session with a metal detector would reveal anything. It would be lovely to know exactly how these holes were dug; shovels and carts, I assume. A heck of a lot of manual work. I once heard that livestock were over-wintered in the dell, and then a mix of muck, straw and chalk would be dug out and spread in the spring. Not sure if that's true, though. I'd also love to date it properly, maybe by checking the rings of a tree that has obviously been growing since the pit was abandoned. Another clue would be to trawl all the old OS maps that are available online, and see when it switched from 'chalk pit' to 'old chalk pit'. And finally, I'd love to measure the diameter of the hole, and its depth, and work out just how many tons of chalk were removed. And all by hand.

There was once a huge dell in Roe Hill, just inside the top gateway. Ian and I used to go and play in it when we were small. There was all sorts in it then, as it was a convenient rubbish tip for the whole village. Somewhere in the attic is a speedometer marked in Russian than I took off an old motorbike I found down there. In the mid-1980s, Dad decided that it got in the way of arable farming – mind you, he had to wait until Lord Sherborne had died; the original tenancy agreement specified that Roe Hill should remain pasture, as it could be seen from Hinton Ampner House.

Ken was despatched with the trusty chainsaw to fell all the trees on the edge of the dell. Terry the crawlerman was booked to come in with his Caterpillar and bulldoze the stumps into the bottom of the dell. Ah, the good old 1980s.

The next part of the story still fills me with incredulity, as the chance of it happening seems miniscule. Ken happened to be down at the Cheriton Crossroads filling station when a lorry driver, loaded with chalk from a Winchester building development, called in to ask for directions to a landfill site. Ken, in an outbreak of initiative, told him we were looking to fill a hole just next to a road – why didn't he bring it up to us? Over the next week or two, an endless stream of lorries brought hundreds of loads of chalk up to Roe Hill, and proceeded to fill a hole that must have taken decades, perhaps over a hundred years, to dig. I was put in charge of telling them when to stop, and once I thought we'd reached four or five feet above field level, I called a halt. Thirty years later, the chalk has slumped, and the dell is still marked as a dip in the ground.

It seems so bizarre (big hole in ground awaiting filling, lorry with suitable filling material gets lost in Cheriton, meets Ken) that I occasionally think that Dad had actually booked the chalk, and decided not to tell me. But we'll never know. I still regret not asking them to stockpile chalk anywhere possible on the farm. You can never have enough of it.

Looking back, it also seems bizarre that we could do such things. We could cut down trees at random, bulldoze stumps, accept countless thousands of tons of what would now be waste, and redraw the shape of a field. And there wasn't a scrap of paperwork. Those days were truly the last of a golden era.

November 2nd

Rod came over with a demo Kubota tractor, which I confess was less than impressive. One day, Kubota will rule the world, but they'll have to sort out some fairly fundamental ergonomics first. Starter key down in front of your legs at calf level? No. Radio rear right of the cab, at waist level, pointing upwards for all the dust and dirt to fall into? No.

I went to the doctor's in Medstead – again – but this time it was to look at the right shoulder. As usual, it was a cursory inspection, and then a recommendation of a private specialist in Winchester, who should have an appointment available within days. It's a curious thing, this private medicine.

Back home, it was all go. Neighbour David called in for a discussion on poachers, and what we could do about them. More bales and blockades seem to be the only answer. Tenant John was round to announce that his boiler had blown up – that's our job to replace. And the 'Move out inspectors', checking the now-empty cottage had found a rather long list of what we'll call 'issues'. It's a good thing we're using professional letting agents to handle what might be a bit of a barney over returning the deposit.

November 3rd

Hazel set off for Barrow Hill shoot with Monty, so I sat down and had another go at the Fiat 500X review. It was here months ago, so I was glad that I'd made copious notes at the time – always a good idea. Policeman Jon called in for a cuppa and a chat, having been to see neighbour David, who is also spitting teeth about the poachers driving over his fields. As a result, it took longer than I'd planned to finish the Fiat article. And still it rains.

November 4th

Still it rains, and still there's a barn full of unsown wheat and beans. Oh well.

A couple of minute's browsing of the accounts book revealed that I was way behind with my invoicing for writing work. Sixteen articles had been sent to *The Field* and *Farmers' Weekly* without invoices. I hope there's no get-out clause that says articles won't be paid for after a certain length of time.

The problem isn't just one of poor office management – it's that I still can't believe that I'm owed money for these articles. Writing them isn't hard work; sometimes it takes a few hours, sometimes they fly off the keyboard in a matter of minutes. I suppose I'm blessed in that way. But I still pinch myself every time a cheque arrives. It's still as much of a thrill now as it was when I got my first opinion piece in *Farmers' Weekly* back in July 1998.

After lunch, I jumped into the test MG and headed up to Lord Wandsworth College to watch Jonathan play in an U16b match. Churcher's were brilliant, winning 24– 0, and Jonathan has grown into his rugby (literally and metaphorically) with every game. He was given plenty of crash ball duties, but each time seemed just a bit hesitant. On the way home, I tried to persuade him to revel in his bulk in future, and boss the game a bit. The great sadness is that he's in his last rugby term at Churcher's, and Pete Symmonds College (where he'll be going for his A levels) only runs serious top-flight rugby sides. I'll have to cherish every one of the last few games he's got now.

November 5th

Hazel and I did an inspection of Stanmore Lane, and found that the Friday night poachers had indeed tried to get onto it, and were thwarted by the bale she had put across it. A small satisfaction, keeping them out of White Hill. Hazel and the dogs went on for a rain-soaked yomp, and I drove round to the winter barley in TBHD. It was all there, with only a few traces of slugs. Joan's Acres and Dell Close looked brilliant, but Hurst Down will look better once it gets above the standing wheat stubble. Mind you, that could take months.

I had a quick chat with one of Murph's men, swapping stories of drilling progress and poacher damage. They, of course, are all up together, having done their winter beans before the weather broke. The purists would say that's a bit early, but let's wait and see if the weather allows us to get ours in before the new year.

After an early lunch, I popped into a rain-soaked Petersfield in the MG6 for a haircut. To complete the old git sort of day, it was off to the Thomas Lord with Rufus for a pint or two and a routine whine and a whinge.

November 6th

More rain. Rod Gaskin came out to the farm to pick the Kubota that had been sitting all but unused in the yard. Over a cuppa, I tried to explain that much as I wanted a non-Adblue tractor with a five-year warranty, and I would have loved to have bought one off him, I couldn't possibly live with the Kubota's car-crash ergonomics. I think he guessed that anyway.

The rest of the day was just wet and horrible. I confess that the sofa and a warm fire beckoned.

November 7th

After much debate about which flatcoat to take to Hambledon, Hazel set off with Fred, working in the principle that he hasn't got many seasons left. I wished them luck as they set of into the deluge and gales.

It was hairy enough driving over Cheesefoot Head to visit Sarum Road for yet more medical investigation, this time on the right shoulder. It hasn't been fully right since I did something to it last spring, and the shoot the other day had stirred it up a bit. The consultant – rare as one who is polite and listens – seemed more shocked by my general skeletal health than just the shoulder, but recommended an MRI scan as soon as possible for the latter. I couldn't help chuckling at the possibility of having just one day's shooting on our own proper shoot before succumbing to injury.

I wasn't long through the back door when the phone rang – it was Ali from Blackhouse, begging for help with a fallen tree across the drive. It's moments like this that make farmers popular; we've got tractors and saws, and an unswerving dedication to our white settler neighbours. Rufus was already there waving his Stihl when I arrived in the loader, and it took the two of us not many minutes to clear the way. I wasn't sure that restarting his saw for him was wise. Possible the worst thing you can do with a bad shoulder.

The rain wrecked my chances of watching Jonathan play rugby – the pitches were waterlogged. I did have the delight of taking him up to a party in the posh houses of Hindhead, and then picking him up, thoroughly sozzled, just after midnight.

It is one of the greatest worries any father can have: what will my son be like when drunk? Will he be aggressive, sleepy, or morose (like his father)? Jonathan turned out to be a cheerful 'looper', earnestly admitting "I'm going to be honest with you, Dad – I can't tell a lie. I think I may have drunk a bit too much." The fun bit was that he repeated himself every five minutes all the way back down the A3. I was very proud.

November 8th

Having got in at 1.30am, I treated myself to a lie-in. Hazel, despite having got soaked yesterday, was off training with Sasha at some unearthly hour, and poked her head round the bedroom door to say goodbye. Jonathan, despite being well sozzled last night, was up early too, which made me very jealous. How we miss the recovery powers of youth.

I also miss the ability to lie in without developing a monster headache. Mine kicked in about ten minutes after I finally got up, and hung around for the best part of the day. Good thing it was too wet and windy to do anything but lie around and feel sorry for myself.

November 9th

At about 1.30 in the morning, Cain the cat thought he needed a pee. He'd had a lovely long evening on the armchair in the downstairs loo, and had avoided being turfed out at everyone else's bedtime. But the time had come to find someone to let him out. He sneaked up the back stairs and started bashing the old door at the top.

I was woken by the thumping noises coming from somewhere, but was sure it was the wind blowing one of the old sash windows. There was then another thump at a wind-free moment, accompanied by a distinctive meow. That was my cue to get up and find the blighter. He was thrilled to see me, rolling around and biffing my outstretched hands as I picked him up. His ejection through the back door may have changed his mood.

Back in bed, wide awake, and every owl in the parish decided that a parliament should be held just outside our window. It was nearly 5am by the time they reached a decision, and I finally dozed off.

And the day itself? It was wet, of course.

November 10th

It looked almost dry. Well, a bit dry. Unfortunately, the wind that had done the drying was still howling, so no chance of any spraying. Another frustrating November day.

I did a big loop of the winter barley, which is loving the warm temperatures, and seems to be escaping the slugs. It's being hit quite hard by the pre-em chemical, showing signs of yellowing, but, as Tod always likes to point out, it shows the spray is doing its job.

A couple of heating engineers came to do quotes for John's central heating. One was a local company we've used for a year or two, and one was the Trust's own man, who had done lots of work for them here and there. I will be interested to see their quotes.

In the afternoon, I sat down with the spray records, and the fertiliser records, and the sowing book, and started the long drawn out procedure of costing the expenditure on each field, and thereby each crop. It's the first stage of producing some accounts. Proper farmers have the whole lot on electronic records, ready to be produced at the press of a button. I keep everything on bits of paper, and have to set aside several afternoons with a calculator to do it. I did well with my task this afternoon, and so rewarded myself with a trip to the Pots with Robert.

November 11th

Hazel took Monty away for a training day, and I had a long session in the office, organising a skip. Years – decades – of not throwing anything away has got to stop, and we've decided that a skip or two, or ten, will be the way to go. I found a friendly skip company who reckoned they'll be out tomorrow, but we'll see. Tod came round again, and we checked the hordes of slugs in the wheat in White Hill. They were serious enough to justify an emergency call to Graham to see if his man was available.

This week's Growmore Club Quiz was down in Upham, in a little pub that used to be Tod's local when he lived down this way. We did well in the quiz, and it was good to see both of Tod's sons at the event. I think I managed to get myself booked for a speaking engagement in October next year. One of the opposition team members is organising a huge dinner dance next autumn at Salisbury Racecourse, and they need a speaker. I said I'd have a think, but might insist that they book the band as the same time. He said he'd have a think. We went our ways, both thinking.

November 12th

The unbelievably efficient skip company rang at 7.40am, to say that the lorry was on the way, and by 9am, a slightly knocked-about green and yellow skip was dropped outside the tractor barn, ready to be filled with thirty years' worth of stuff from all round the farm. I just hope it's big enough.

The next arrival was Graham's slug pellet man, who was in by nine thirty, ready to do the heavy land in White Hill and Cheyney, where the slugs are continuing to massacre the early drilled Claire. On a damp, occasionally rainy morning like this, there is no better feeling than booking someone else to do the pelleting.

The skip was soon called into action, as Hazel set about the garage with a vengeance. All sorts of old armchairs and bits of carpet went out. It was a good thing that I wasn't helping – there would have been a mass outbreak of "you can't throw that out!". The problem with living on a farm, with its endless space and corners, is that little gets thrown away. Something tells me that a second skip will be in order quite soon.

November 13th
The great challenge of an MRI scan is lying still. It's bad enough relaxing after being wound up by medical staff (even the private ones at the Candover Clinic) insisting on calling you by your mostly unused Christian name – 'Charles' – and in a tone of voice that suggests they think you're a bit simple. But then they ask you to lie still in a narrow tube, with the bare minimum of head support (not good with a dodgy neck) and some garbled instructions (yes, they've repeated it all to two dozen patients today, but it's still the first time I've heard it), while the clever bit of kit thrums and thumps its way through a comprehensive survey of your shoulder. At least it should give a definite answer as to what's going on in there.

November 14th
It rained a great deal.

November 15th
Dry, but very windy. Jonathan and I got tooled up, pumped up Tigger's front tyre, picked up the Editor, and headed off to Froxfield, to try the Petersfield Gun Club – a clay shoot based in a small wood near the Pub With No Name. It's one I've never shot before, but he has been before and rated it very highly.

We had a fantastic morning. A lot of work had gone into making the most of the available space, and the layout was challenging and interesting. We all shot well, with Jonathan still handling his Browning 20 bore well – even though he has grown several inches since he last used it.

The afternoon was spent snoozing on the sofa, in front of a very boring Formula One race.

November 16th
There is no job more melancholy than looking for a lost pet. It has been several days since anyone saw Cain the cat, so I thought the time had come to start checking barns. I'm still haunted by the memory of finding what I thought was a Frisbee at the bottom of an elevator pit in the Drier barn, only to realise that it was the dried up remains of a cat, perfectly curled up in a circle, where it had died. The idea of it mewing at the bottom of a 30-foot shaft for God knows how long until it died of hunger and thirst

still makes me choke up. I checked as many barns and yards as I could, but found nothing. I walked a short stretch of road, and still found nothing. At least no body is better than something squashed by the side of the road.

Monty and I went and walked the winter barley, leaving Sasha and Fred to accompany Hazel on her walk with a friend. Then I went up to Rod's to see if they'd got the right bit to mend my vital farm compressor. A certain amount of confusion (my fault) about 5/8" and 5/8" BSP meant that they hadn't got the right connector. So we plucked something off the shelf in its stead, and brought that home. It was too short.

My quest took me to Alresford Builders Merchants, the old-fashioned warren of builders' bits and pieces tucked away in an alley off Broad Street. No luck there – I was now looking for a ¼" BSPT/ 3/8" BSP reducer, for the record – so I drove to Winnall. The new massive soulless Wickes had nothing remotely like it. In the shadow of Wickes is a trade park with at least three plumbing supply shops, all of them no doubt feeling the pain of the megastore's recent arrival. The first tried to help, assembling an assortment of adaptors and sleeves, but to no avail. The second had exactly what I wanted, and after enjoying a deep discussion of the sheer agony of the new Ellie Goulding single which was playing loudly on the radio (the man behind the counter and I agreed that she's set new boundaries in irritating songs – beating the atrocious 'Love Me Like You Do'), I handed over the princely sum of £1.21, and headed home.

On the way home, I stopped in Alresford and picked up my glasses. Now, if there's one thing I've learned in the ten or so years that I've farmed and worn glasses, it's that farming and glasses don't mix. The reason I had to get my new ones is that my last pair fell out of my top pocket while I was rolling under the combine header scraping mud off. I then drove over them. Mind you, they were scratched beyond reasonable use anyway. And that's the problem: farm pockets, tractor floors and toolboxes, and barn worktops are not the places to keep expensive glasses. The trouble is, I don't wear them all the time; I have to take them off when doing long-distance stuff, like driving the tractor. And within moments, there are dozens of tiny scratches on them. Within a year, they're almost useless. One day, I'll develop frames that aren't so much frames as tubes, so no matter what you do with your glasses, nothing can touch – and scratch – the glass. One day.

November 17th

Another foul, wet and windy day. I was invaded late morning by two reps from the New Holland dealer and a product manager from New Holland itself. They had noticed – somewhat belatedly – that my annual payments on the combine had finished, and so felt they should come out and talk about a replacement. I had absolutely no intention at all to fork out on a new one, so was fairly rude to start with. Are they still 'built' in Poland? Have they learnt how to put the pieces together properly yet? The poor product manager winced a bit, as if he hadn't been briefed on the first dreadful couple of years I had with my TC5070. I pointed out that I couldn't possibly part with it now, because we'd finally ironed out all the bugs.

Once I'd finished lecturing them on the dreadful quality of their product, I took them down the Drier to give the old one a check over with a view to a trade-in. My act sort of slipped a bit, as I found myself raving about how it was the perfect combine for this size of farm, with lots of clever features that no one else does at this price and size. I ended up sounding like New Holland's biggest fan, which was not my intention at the start of the day. I found myself retelling the story of what clinched the deal: in the brochure was a double-page picture of the combine driver climbing out of his cab to greet his tea-bearing family. That struck a chord with me.

A very jolly evening in the pub with neigbour Robert included him telling the story of his Land Rover breaking down up on Ganderdown. A Land Rover breaking down is hardly news, but it was the aftermath that had us chuckling. A passer-by lent him a mobile phone, but with a flat battery, so he couldn't summon a lift. He was left to walk home, which should have been no problem – it's downhill all the way from Ganderdown to Tichborne. Unfortunately, he had the new family poodle in the back of the Land Rover, and had to walk all the way with the fluffiest dog in Hampshire mincing along beside him. I'd have paid good money to see that.

Dozing off in a haze of beer and peanuts, there was still something not quite right about the day, but I couldn't quite nail it. Oh well.

November 18th

In the middle of my porridge, it hit me. I should have been shooting up near Basingstoke yesterday. It was the most terrible feeling – I had committed possibly the very worst of shooting gaffes. I was furious with myself. I rang my inviter at 7.50am, hoping to catch him before he went out doing proper farming, and luckily, he was there. I owned up at once; I had simply forgotten. No excuses – sheer idiocy on my part. He seemed OK, or too polite to say otherwise.

I spent the rest of the day in a foul mood, kicking myself. In an attempt to redeem myself, I knuckled down and finally got the crop valuations done – an annual chore that needs all Tod's spraying records, all the final chemical prices, all the fertiliser records, and the seed prices. If I were a proper farmer, I'd have it all ready to go at the end of the farming year at the press off a computer button. But because I'm not, I have to wrestle with reams of paper for hours. Anyway, I got the job done. If I were a proper farmer, I wouldn't be still waiting for the weather to dry up so I can finish the autumn's work.

Jonathan spent the day in bed, crippled by headaches. There's a lot of it going round, as we always seem to say at this time of year.

In the evening, Rufus and I hit the Fox in Bramdean – I needed to get out of the house while Hazel and the rest of her book club discussed something worthy, once they'd finished sharing notes on the latest crises involving children and universities.

November 19th

After breakfast, I sat down and wrote an early Christmas card for my not-quite-shoot-host, and filled it with the grovelliest apology I could come up with. I then taped it to the decent bottle of wine that Hazel had bought yesterday, and drove up to his farm. I found their bungalow and tried to raise someone. An open side door led to no one but a curious wolfhound, so I tiptoed back out of there. At the front door, a black lab appeared from the garden and checked me out, but no sign of a householder. I draped the bottle and card, in a plastic bag, over the gate handle, and left. On the way out through the farmyard, I accosted someone on their way out with a slug pelleter, and checked that I'd got the right house. I just hope my grovelling makes the grade.

Poor old Jonathan was still wracked with headaches, so we sent him back to bed. He's also despondent about his missing cat. Every passing day without Cain coming home suggests that one of the sweetest cats I've ever known has met his end somewhere. Let's just hope it wasn't unpleasant. But, as Jonathan said, finding a body would mean closure.

I finally got the compressor reassembled, and it still didn't work. All that faffing about with new switches and effing reducers and PTFE tape and driving round half of Hampshire for a £1 bit had been a complete waste of time.

November 20th

Finally, an outbreak of hands-on farming. Hazel decided that the Bottom of Englands was taking too much of a hammering with the cattle and sheep in it, so decided that we'd bring the cattle up to the Godwin's barn. There was a short debate on the pros and cons of bringing them on foot (or hoof) up to the Top of England, out onto the road, along the road for a bit, and down through Godwin's yard. It was a very short debate, and ended with me texting Robert Raimes to ask if his low-loading cattle trailer was available at very short notice. Luckily, it was. Noel was available to help, too, so we asked him to pop down to Tichborne and get the trailer while Hazel did some preparation with hurdles.

As is usual with Hazel's tame cattle, it took an age to get them to get onto the trailer. They just stood around and looked at us in their half-ton of cuddliness way. I couldn't help thinking, as Noel and I lifted and pushed the last one in limb by limb, that it's a good thing my shoulder is going to be diagnosed fully tomorrow.

We spent the afternoon trying to sort out the water supply to the little barn/lean-to where the cattle were now enjoying the warmth and dry. The aged black pipe had perished on a tight bend, so it meant another trip across Hampshire – this time to APM to get an assortment of fittings and converters, in the hope of reconnecting the water supply. By the time I got back, it was darkening, so the cattle had to make do with a full trough for the night.

The rain and cloud that has been pestering us for endless weeks suddenly cleared, and everyone's mood seemed to lift a bit. The wind picked up a bit and started to dry the yard. Was this the start of the long dry spell that is going to allow us to catch up? The deluge that greeted the dogs last thing as they did their pees suggested 'no'.

November 21st

A howling northerly brought rain and great slushy flakes of snow early. A mid-morning flickering of the power suggested that a tree was down somewhere. And as Hazel set off to get the papers, she found it: just outside Godwin's barn, on the bend, the tree had blown over onto the cables, stretching them down and making the neighbouring poles lean over at a scary angle. I walked out and had a look, and wondered if this was another one of those situations where the farmer is expected to put the work in for the greater good. I decided this was not my department.

After ten minutes trawling the old-fashioned phone book for the right emergency number (is it still Southern Electricity? SEB? SSE? Scottish at Southern?), I found the one I wanted on the internet (thank goodness the power hadn't gone altogether) and rang it in. The nice lady was very grateful, and said that, yes, they were indeed having a busy morning. Within an hour, a gang had arrived and started work.

By late morning, the clouds had cleared, and a sparkling low sunshine ensued. I drove into the private hospital in Sarum Road to hear the results of last week's MRI scan. The consultant had no real surprises. The bit at the end of the collar bone was a bit knackered, the front tendons weren't very happy, but he was a bit surprised to see considerable damage to the tendon that lifts the arm away from the body. It looked as if it had been badly torn, and some time ago. I had to explain that that was probably the work of Beaver Johnston, an Alnwick and England B prop, who got tired of my cockiness when I was loose-head for Newcastle Uni in October 1981, and decided I had to end up on the floor. My shoulder stayed up, wrapped round the hooker's back – or so it felt. It was nice to get a proper diagnosis, 34 years on.

He pumped the shoulder with what felt like a pint of painkiller and steroids, and sent me on my way, suggesting another visit in a fortnight to check on progress, and a referral to a surgeon if the old torn ligament really needed mending properly. I might do it after my lungs and sinuses and hips and…

The wind got stronger and stronger, and it got colder and colder. The Editor called in after trying some pigeons – he got three with three in the middle of Big Field, then they all vanished. Plausible, but I reckon the chill wind drove even him indoors.

The forecast was for the first serious frost of the winter, so I slowly and carefully (thanks to the shoulder) put the sprayer on the tractor, and backed it into the relative warmth of Godwin's barn. I damaged my brand-new Gem sprayer in 2005 by leaving it out in the frost, and that was a simple one to repair. The new high-tech Amazone might be slightly more complicated.

November 22nd

It took me four hours to shift the Sunday lie-in headache, and I felt so good when it had gone (like hitting yourself on the head with a hammer) I thought I should make the most of the stunning day and get some spraying done. I got a good dose of Roundup on the Folly and Roe Hill.

Hazel and Jonathan (and Monty) did the rounds of pheasant feeders, and came back chilled to the bone.

November 23rd

When she was down at the Cheriton shop, picking up the papers, Hazel spotted a postcard in the window: 'Black and white cat found. Ring this number....' She duly did, and a lady told the story of finding a sleek black and white cat at the bottom of Goodwin's, next to the A272, stunned and bleeding from the nose, but not obviously injured. She picked it up and took it to Cedar Vet in Alresford. And as far as she knew it was still there.

As soon as Hazel told me this story, I rang the vet. Yes, they still had it, but only just. Its hand-over to the Cat Rehoming League (or something like it) was imminent. I asked when we could come and look at it. Late morning, they said. We couldn't wait that long; Hazel grabbed the cat box and set off.

Half an hour later, she was back, with a slightly befuddled looking Cain yowling from inside the box. Huge relief all round. We're getting soppy in our old age. Cain was slightly the worse for wear, looking thin and less glossy, and obviously quite sore around the ribs. We set up a litter tray and decided to keep him in for a few days, and fatten him up again.

A good day was rounded off with me managing to get another tank of spray on – this time on the Hangar and Kilmeston Road. A good 3l/ha dose of Roundup ready for whatever eventually goes out there. If it ever stops raining.

Only Tod turned up for band rehearsal, so he and I did a couple of songs and then abandoned. Not sure quite what happened in that department. Still, if we do get the New Year gig he's trying to sort out, we've still got a couple of months to rehearse.

November 24th

Poor old Hazel started to go down with a cold – and that is a rarity. Maybe she did get chilled too much on Sunday thundering round the farm on Pig.

I headed into Winchester for my six-monthly dentist appointment. Parking was a nightmare. The Christmas rush has started, and the closure of one of the multi-storey car parks in the centre of town has caused chaos. I finally squeezed into a slot in the North Walls car park, and hurried down Parchment Street. Thankfully, there was little to report – more wear and tear, but no work needed, for now.

There was yet another visit from the landlord to discuss their huge plan to rip up Englands and install a waste treatment and drainage system. We took one look at the details, and realised that this was beyond our league. This would have to be passed to land agent Chris to handle. There will be land permanently taken away, an unspecified area ripped up for an unspecified length of time, fences moved, cattle and sheep plans disrupted… Let's let the pros sort this one out.

November 25th
Neighbour Robert very kindly invited me to shoot on a day he'd bought at Shorley, directly next door to us. This is a proper, old-fashioned shoot, with a huge bag, and four or five drives where a loader would be handy. Things got off to an iffy start, when the very first cartridge misfired. It was one of the Hinton Ampner specials that Guy had brought a couple of weeks ago, and the loud 'click' without a bang sent a bit of a panic through me. Were they all going to misfire, being of a good age? Or was it the gun? And once you start thinking negative thoughts, everything goes to pieces. Shooting, like cricket, is a mental game.

Luckily, I got better towards the end of the first drive, and started hitting almost everything. In fact we all did, and the bag limit was reached quite early, so tea was brought forward – or so it seemed. We all ate far too much. I staggered home, optimistically put the hosepipe into the water tank – in case there was a chance of doing some spraying tomorrow –and hit the sofa.

November 26th
A bit of a dilemma day: it was dull but calm, with hints of drizzle in the air. Should I go and do a couple more tanks of Roundup (my last legal day to do so), or have a quiet morning recovering from the shoot, and then hit the road to Marlborough for the Tenant Farmers Association meeting?

The decision was made when I checked the water tank in the yard. The pipe had slipped out and bucked over at some time in the night, so the tank was still virtually empty. Not really any chance of spraying today.

I drove up the A34 and headed left down the A4 to Marlborough, where the TFA were hosting a gathering in the slightly cramped conference room of a golf club. It was a fairly technical meeting, with lots of talk of rent negotiations and model clauses, and I was feeling a bit sorry for myself after yesterday. I did kick myself for not insisting we start a rent review last Michaelmas, but perhaps things are going to pick up soon.

However, when the combine dealer rang just after I got back to ask about the quote he'd sent, I had no hesitation in saying 'Thanks, but no thanks!'. The cost to change had me spluttering when it had come through some days ago, convincing me that the old policy of hanging onto them for fifteen years and going mad on good maintenance is a far cheaper way to run a combine. Luckily, finances are not so bad as to rule out yet another pub trip with Robert that night. That truly would be the end of the world.

November 27th
Rumour has it that the Single Farm Payment cheques are going to be 'lost in the post' for some time. There is, apparently, little hope that the vital five-figure cheque, on

which we've come to depend so much, will flop into our bank accounts on December 1st – as it has for the last few years. If this is indeed true, we'll be needing to do some weapons-grade grovelling to the bank to extend the overdraft, and for that, we'll need some up-to-date accounts. So I sat down with a purpose and finished off all the annoying fiddly bits of the figures – things like the bought-and-sold sums, and the valuation of a handful of bales in the barn. All that was left after that was to jump in the car, fly down the A3(M), along the A27, and into Havant to drop the books off. As usual, it was just an exchange of pleasantries with the receptionists, and then back home again.

I should have a rough idea of how the accounts will turn out, but, as is always the case, I haven't a clue. The long pool from harvest 2014 did well, but the harvest pool from this year didn't do so well. In an ideal world, we'd have accounts that were a little less spectacularly good than they were for 2013/4 (which caused some terrifying tax bills and the loss of our 'poor farmer' discount at Churcher's College), but were good enough to keep the bank happy. Time alone will tell.

November 28th

I love farm plumbing. It's always a challenge to see what we've got in the plumbing box, and try and make it do what we want it to do. The time has come to sort out the trough in the Godwin's silo, which has a major leak, and Hazel's dozen big bullocks are running short of water a bit too much. We spent a very jolly morning playing around with Stillsons and PTFE tape and ¾"/½" reducers and nipples, and took several hours to mend anything. It didn't help that the dogs kept running off with anything that they felt wasn't vital, and the cattle themselves couldn't help but investigate what was going on. Winding PTFE on a joint isn't that easy with a ton of Angus-cross in your armpit.

There's talk of colder weather on the way – at last – so we had a long session in the Godwin's barn sawing up some logs.

It's all good farm work, but it's not putting any seed in the ground, which is what we really want to do.

November 29th

It rained a lot, so I snoozed on the sofa while watching the Grand Prix.

November 30th

It pelted down in the morning, but I managed a fairly slippery walk all over Hurst Down, checking on the poor winter barley. It was just about holding up, but will need some fertiliser pretty promptly in the spring to give it a kick-start.

Hazel and I thought we'd treat ourselves to an exciting day out, so we drove off to Alton to visit a lighting warehouse, to choose some new fixtures to replace the old and wonky ones on many of the farmhouse walls. Just as we were leaving, however, there was a worried phone call from Mike the Keeper, warning us of a silver Frontera that was doing the rounds of the parish. It was the usual scenario: burly men and long dogs. I had a brief look out of the farmhouse windows, but saw nothing, so we set off up the A32.

The warehouse was rather hot, and full of a billion lights and designs, but all of them were rather over our budget – I think Homebase beckons. And then, just as we were leaving the car park, a muddy Frontera loaded with burly men and long dogs drove past – an astonishing coincidence. It was sorely tempting to swing out after them and follow, but, just for once, I couldn't be bothered. I did email our close encounter to the Police once I got in, though.

December 1ˢᵗ

Not much chance of a bright new optimistic month. It was another sodden day. Hazel and Monty bravely set off to Barrow Hill for a day's drenched picking-up. I stared at a screen for most of the day, trying to get the next opinion piece done, and ventured out a couple of times to give the other two dogs a chance to stretch their legs.

December 2ⁿᵈ

Finally got the opinion piece for *Farmers Weekly* done, and sent it off down the wires. I spent an hour taking the old compressor to pieces, but could find nothing obvious wrong with it. Is it worth the cost of lots of investigating and spare parts? As with almost every gadget, it will probably be cheaper to order a new one, and throw the old one in the scrap skip. In an attempt to do something constructive, I took the depth wheel off the plough – it had burst on the very last few yards of Chalks back in the spring – and ordered a replacement tube from Micheldever Tyres.

December 3ʳᵈ

My collection of tyres that needed mending had got to a stage where a trip up to Micheldever Tyres was justified. I loaded up Tigger with the depth wheel off the plough, the front depth wheel off the Horsch (although it's a floating wheel so does very little 'control'), and one of the packer wheels off the back off the Horsch. Once again, I was able to drive round the back, bypassing the long queue, and get the whole lot done quite quickly.

Back home, I hitched the sprayer off the Deere in the Godwin's barn, put the weights on the front, and put the plough on the back, ready to go and turn some soil over – if I can find any that's dry enough.

Hazel spent the day filling the new skip with stuff from the tractor barn. It became obvious quite quickly that this will not be a one-skip job. It looks like a stream of them will be needed. We'll have to enforce the three-year rule, too. If it hasn't been touched or needed in three years, it goes in the skip. Trouble is, as you get older, that 'three-year' can stretch out a bit. Four, then five, then six…

December 4ᵗʰ

Hellard's, the letting agents in Alresford, were desperately keen for us to meet the couple who are hoping to move into the empty cottage, claiming that they would be the perfect family to move in. They are also the only people to have responded to the advert, and this is a quiet time of year. The advice was to grab them with both hands, even if they have got to serve more notice than usual in their present property. They were indeed a lovely couple with two small children, and we chatted for twenty minutes in the empty little kitchen, and then sent them on their way. As soon as I got back in, I rang Hellard's and agreed. Let's have 'em.

Next job was to finish writing up the MG6, which was a couple of days overdue. Luckily, the mental tubes cleared, and it flowed quite well – then again, it might be sent back with 'rubbish' written all over it.

By now, I'd run out of excuses for not going and making a start on the ploughing, so I drove all the way out to BML's and got going. Conditions weren't great – the light soil was loose and wet, and the mouldboards were rusty. I really must learn to recoat them halfway through the non-ploughing season. I spent much of the afternoon trying to set the Deere's draft sensitivity as low as possible. Even just 'one click' away from full 'position' setting is enough to send the three-point linkage overreacting to changes in draft, and the plough bouncing up and down. Mind you, I was going across last year's crap ploughing, which was anything but level.

I nearly swapped from BML's to Roe Hill, mainly to see if a bit of tough ground would do some mouldboard polishing, but also because it's Friday, the ground is getting firmer, and it's blowing a gale. Just the night for some poacher action.

How right I was. As I was just about to jump into bed, I paused for a minute at the bedroom window. And there, sure enough, were lights flashing in the Folly. For a brief moment, I contemplated keeping my head down, and letting them get on with it, but my Inner Policeman won out, and I 999-ed it. After a minute or two watching the lights from the bedroom, it dawned on me that I'd be better use out on the road, ready to direct incoming police vehicles, if we were going to get any.

As soon as I got to the road in front of the house, I saw the poachers' car speed up Roe Hill, off towards New Pond. This suggested that they were on their way to Big Field, so I switched position, and headed for the corner of the old tennis court. There were no lights to be seen anywhere for five minutes, and I was just on my way back in when a vehicle headed back towards Roe Hill from New Pond. It slowed down, found a gap in the trees, and launched itself into the Roe Hill stubble. It rampaged around Roe Hill, and then crossed into Chalks, through the gap at the far end (these boys know our farm very well) and carried on chasing and killing hares in the wheat.

By now, the first of the police cars were arriving, and I tried to talk them in – officially the most difficult job in the world. They are using satnavs and postcodes and I'm trying to say, "They're in the field on the left of the junction." Almost impossible. The poachers, meanwhile, gathered that they'd been rumbled, and switched off all their lights. It became even harder to direct the police cars, who were driving dark lanes in a strange part of the countryside, with instructions coming to them secondhand from the control room.

The poachers drove very slowly up to the top of Chalks, only thirty yards from where I was standing, in my best jimjams, clutching what I hoped was an unlit phone. Then they crept along the top of Chalks, down to the gap into Roe Hill and sat quiet for few more moments. Police cars came and went again, and the poachers took their chance in a gap in constabulary traffic, shot out through the hedge again onto the road, and sped off towards New Pond – again. I rang their latest movements into 999, and watched for a few more moments.

It was probably another ten minutes, but I was rather hoping to see flashing blue lights in the distance – something, anything to suggest we'd had a result. I saw nothing, and so went to bed.

Just as I had got the adrenaline levels down and dozed off, the phone rang. It was a sergeant announcing that they had indeed got the vehicle and the dogs, but none of the occupants. Any chance of coming round for a statement? "Er, no, not now!" I said, and turned the phone off.

December 5th

The aftermath of last night's events started early. The phone rang just after breakfast. It was Policeman Jon, elated. The car, an old Jeep Cherokee had been abandoned after a long police chase, in a petting farm in Swanmore. The dogs had also been abandoned, but all the car's occupants had got away.

That was all the good news. The bad, or sad, news was that the dogs, running wild in the paddocks, had killed a pet reindeer and injured another. And a rabbit. It was astonishing to watch the reaction on the internet, as outrage spread from Facebook page to Facebook page. I couldn't help thinking that the death of a pet reindeer just before Christmas could just be some sort of tipping point in the war against poachers.

A local PCSO came round to fill in some of the details, and promised that Jon would be round for a longer statement later on. She asked if I could pop out and get some pictures of slaughtered hares and send them to her, so I nipped out in Pig, and found a trail of ripped apart animals across Chalks.

Ian the drummer called in to pick up one of John's Christmas trees, and needed a hand loading it, thanks to his injured shoulder. It seemed silly for him to drive all that way from Godalming just for that, so he stopped for a chat and a cup of tea.

December 6th

Giving a statement to police is not a five-minute job. I knew they'd be out, so I had typed a neat version of events, thinking that that might save an hour or two. My neatly typed statement was carefully put to one side by Policeman Jon, and utterly ignored.

Instead, we settled down to do five pages of scraggy handwritten statement, carefully phrased as only a police statement can be, designed to inform and sway anyone listening to it. There was lots of background and history, plenty of emotional stuff about fearing for my family's safety, and, of course, a step-by-step retelling of the actual events of Friday night. You do it, of course, with the fervent hope that you're not called upon to testify against these violent thugs.

Once that was done, and I'd had a nice little Sunday afternoon kip, I started packing up pianos and amps, and getting ready for Open Mic Night. But once again, it was not to be. Mike the Keeper was on the phone, just as I was about to set off, with a report of flashlights going all over Big Field, Rick and Clump. I couldn't believe it, until I tiptoed down onto the tennis court, and saw brilliant beams of light heading up towards Godwin's Broom from Clump. I walked out into the pasture in the Back Meadow, and watched. There were definitely two torches, and they seemed to be doing the edges of Godwin's – it was hard to tell in the thick mist.

Keeper Mike was on board with a police patrol car, and was hurtling backwards and forward from New Pond to Bramdean, desperately trying to catch them – whoever they were. I was trying to give clues in the darkness, aided by the now occasional flashing torch beams, but hindered by the calls I had to make to say sorry for missing yet another Open Mic Night. By the time I got back in, I was wet, cold and cross.

December 7th

There was no evidence of further hare-chasing anywhere to be seen. I spent much of the morning checking out the stubbles, and apart from tracks that looked reasonably fresh, there was nothing to suggest that our poacher friends had suddenly decided to take the healthy option. I ended up convinced that it was just walkers having a yomp across my fields in the dark. Not a lot can be done, really.

I spent the afternoon in BML's desperately trying to make a good job of some ploughing, and not really succeeding. At some stage, I'm going to have to cut up the enormous oak that blew down in the St Jude's Day storm last year. It is clogging up the western headland, and while I've managed to plough round it for a year, I think I ought to get on and clear it. I'll have a word with Shawn at New Pond – he'll have better kit than my 16" chainsaw. In my ideal world, I have a Woodmizer down at the Drier, which I'd use to plank all the fallen wood round the estate, but I think that's just a dream.

December 8th

Hazel overslept, so I took Jonathan down to the West Meon Hut pub car park, where the Churcher's College bus picks him and a couple of other local children up. It's only a mile or two away, but it's a different world. I always used to say that farmers should spend a day or two in London every year to remind themselves of what some of the rest of the world is like. Well, if London is a bit of a hassle, there's always the West Meon Hut crossroads at 7.45am. Four long queues of traffic waiting for the lights to change their way. Then the roar and fury as each queue sets off, everything from vast delivery lorries to executive saloon, all full of the sullen faces of commuters in autopilot. It didn't help that the rain was stair-rodding it down, making the whole grim scene a whole lot grimmer.

Get there an hour earlier, as Hazel has done for school trip drop-offs, and the vehicles are slightly different. It's the building trade on the move to work – the shop is full of burly men in shorts and vests, stocking up on Costa coffees, and hardly a word of English spoken. Truly a world away from the farm.

We'd booked the use of John's trailer to get a couple of second-hand sofas that Hazel had bought on eBay. Most of the year, getting hold of it isn't difficult – it sits outside Shed 3b, mostly unused – but this being Christmas tree season, and John being heavily into the supply of them, we had to find a day that suited him. We hitched it onto Tigger, found the spare number plate, checked the lights, and set off for Twyford.

The seller was a very young-looking granny, undergoing a bit of a life change (much talk of 'he' and 'him' in a dismissive tone – a divorce in the offing?) and moving to a smaller house. Two huge sofas, very similar to our present one, but longer and cleaner, had to go. We looked at them for some minutes, before working out how they dismantled. Three long bolts had to be undone. Luckily she found some tools, and after an hour, the four halves were in the trailer, covered with an assortment of old rugs and roped down. The tiny sum of £100 was handed over, and we set off in a very convenient inter-shower dry interlude for home. Four lumps of sofa were unloaded into the recently-cleared garage, and the trailer was ready for another batch of Christmas trees. All that remains is to decide what to do with the old chairs and sofa in the sitting room.

In the afternoon, it was back to see the surgeon in Winchester for an update on the shoulder. There was little to report – it was comfortable, with only a slight ache down the front. Sleeping – the acid test for a shoulder – was fine. His instructions were to rest it for longer, if possible. Was I up to much on the farm? Not a lot, I said. A bit of ploughing, a bit of sofa moving – and then there's chasing poachers. At the mention of poachers, the incredibly quiet and mild-mannered doctor exploded into a range of most impolite expletives. It was quite a shock. He lives near a river, which our poacher friends delight in clearing out at regular intervals. They're nothing but a curse to us all.

Before leaving, I thought I'd mention the right hip again, which is still in a right mess. Lots of assorted surgeons have grabbed a knee, wiggled a leg and exclaimed "New hip!" with glee as I winced with pain. What I really want, before I commit to such a major operation, is evidence. I want someone to show me an X-ray, point out the problem and explain to me why nothing other than a new hip will do. "We'll do an X-ray right now," he said, signed a chit, and sent me down a corridor, where new X-rays were done. We'll see what they say.

Just after dark, I enjoyed a starlit walk round Godwin's and Chalks, to stretch my legs, look out for Geminids, and possibly catch up with the night-walkers from a few nights ago. I didn't stay out for long – it was too cold. And there's something we haven't said very often this autumn.

December 9th

The latest test car, the new Volvo XC90, arrived at 8.15am, complete with plenty of pre-warning by the driver, and a wingman to take him away. Perfect. How all test cars should be delivered. I stood and looked at it for a minute or two, forming a few of those oh-so-important first opinions, but then decided that farming should take some sort of priority. I headed out to BML's for a bit more soggy ploughing.

The perfect antidote to the dark miserable December days is the mid-week Growmore Club Quiz, so I picked up John and we headed up to the No Name at Froxfield with high hopes and cheerful expectations. Unfortunately, we got thrashed. Because we were sore losers, we even grumbled a bit about the unevenness of the questions. The side that went first (or it might have been second) got all the easy questions. Someone pointed out that the nice lady who spends countless hours setting the questions happened to be there that night, so we quickly stopped moaning and became magnanimous in defeat.

December 10th

The rain finally got the better of our old-fashioned cess pit, seeping in through the Victorian brickwork, and the fine pong of poo started wafting up the garden. It was time for Botley Cleansing to come out and suck as much as they could out of it. It's a messy, unpleasant job at the best of times, but with slippery ground and a set of slightly dodgy manhole covers, it must be even more unpleasant.

In the afternoon, we hosted another batch of trainee RPA inspectors who were on a training course at Sparsholt College. Once again, they were a thoroughly pleasant bunch (save one, who kept interjecting while I was trying to talk – "He won't last," said the man in charge, as he and I held onto the dogs while the rest checked out the sheep.) and as the day went on, the event got more and more jolly, and by the time we sent them on their way in the Sparsholt College minibus, we were all the best of friends. Let's hope it stays that way if we get inspected.

December 11th

It was very wet again. I took the dogs for a long walk in the morning, and then had a session with land agent Chris to discuss the big issues that I'm planning to take up with the Trust. There's the public access, just for a change, and the new sewage plans in the bottom of Englands. His advice was to dig in our heels a bit over the latter to get what we want with the former. The terms of the tenancy agreement are pretty clear: we have to let them do the digging they want, but in theory it's a year's notice before they can take land off us. If they're in a hurry, then they might jump a bit on the public access issue. He said he'd go away and re-read the agreement just to check we weren't subject to any clauses that would change his mind.

December 12th

The West Meon Players are another of the amateur dramatics clubs that thrive in this country, and, like most of the many clubs and societies in West Meon, are particularly strong and talented. They have a Christmas meal around this time of year, and we Open Mic Night regulars provided the entertainment last year. This involved playing along to anyone on the room who wanted to get up and sing. Last year's was spectacularly well attended, and ended in a fantastic mish-mash of songs and dancing. Tonight's was a bit quiet by comparison. There's a definite feeling of 'down' in the air, and I think it's the continuous rain. It was still fun, but people left a lot earlier and were generally quieter. I suspect that last's years was an exception.

Anthony made the long drive home from Leeds. It wasn't his trip home for Christmas, because he has plans to go back up to work for a few days. He called in at Durham to pick up some stuff from Diana, and was about to head north to Newcastle to see some friends, but the first real snow of the year had arrived, so he wisely headed south instead. Even then, the Lupo had a bit of a struggle in places, but it's the perfect narrow-tyred snow car, and he was home safely in the early evening.

December 13ᵗʰ

A quiet Sunday. I was on my way up to Kilmeston to help a friend with the wiring loom on his refurbished Ford 3000, when I saw a couple of people in the bottom of Roe Hill. They were wandering around in circles, looking at the ground. I stopped to see if I could help. Had they lost something? Were they lost?

No, they weren't lost – they were confused. They had seen the brand-new finger post pointing up across the field, but it didn't match what looked like the path across the stubble. The angle seemed slightly 'out'. I assured them that the track was indeed the footpath, and accused him, light-heartedly, of being an engineer. No one else would be so precise about little things like a sign's angle. "Nearly right," he laughed. "I'm an architect!"

In Kilmeston, we had a very jolly afternoon playing with the vintage tractor, trying to match the wiring loom to the few electrical components on the Ford, helped, or hindered, by the wiring diagram in the old handbook. We managed it after a couple of hours, just as it was getting dark, and adjourned to their lovely house for tea 'n' cakes. In forty years' time, will two amateurs be able to rewire a Fendt 916 in an afternoon, armed only with a bit of auto electrical knowledge and some boyish enthusiasm? Somehow I don't think so.

December 14ᵗʰ

It isn't often that I get to leave the parish – it's the curse of the 'hands-on' farmer. But today I had a lovely day out to do some research for a motoring article. Even better, I had good company for the trip. I'd decided to do a write-up of a company up near Oxford that overhauls Mk 1 Range Rovers, and there's no bigger Range Rover nerd than Guy. I'd warned him that the trip would be today, so he'd reorganised his busy army schedule, and arrived here mid-morning. We jumped into the test XC90 and headed up the A34 like a couple of schoolchildren.

Being a gadget freak, Guy very soon tapped into the Volvo's electronics, and got his phone talking to the car, and thence to the outside world. I was then treated to several hilarious but no doubt very important army conversations, which seemed to revolve solely around where the next drinks party should be held. It's very odd to hear someone I've known as 'Guy' for 20 years being addressed as 'Colonel'. The army works in odd ways.

Having done my usual 'I have memorised the route and don't need an atlas' routine, I managed to get hopelessly lost, forgetting – or not spotting – that the A40 can only be accessed by going into Oxford and then back out again. We were halfway to Chipping Norton before I realised my mistake. Asking Guy to input the postcode (using the handwriting recognition screen) for our destination was hopeless. His Parkinson's (not usually a laughing matter) meant that we were lucky to stay this side of the Channel. I might use that line in the write-up of the Volvo – with Guy's permission.

The Range Rover restorers were quite something. A large-ish yard, crammed with wrecks of all sorts and sizes, and then, parked neatly along one wall, a row of perfectly restored Mk 1s. We had a very detailed tour of how a typical wreck became the beautiful finished product, right from bare metal strip down to fancy new engines and suspension. Both Guy and I had a lovely time. There was a long and good tempered row with our host about the correct wing/door mirror on a very early three door. I confess I decided to sit that one out.

I took lots of pictures, made lots of notes, and we set off home in time for a bite to eat, and Guy set off home for Bovington. We made a few ambitious plans for me to have a play with some of the toys down there, and see if we can get something suitable for *The Field*. A session on the ranges with a serious gun would be just the job.

December 15th
Still it's too wet to do anything. I popped into Winchester to pick up some new Chelsea boots that I ordered over the internet. Hazel had a long day picking-up at Barrow Hill. In the evening, I had a lift from Anthony to the pub, and a lift home, too. Very civilised, and meant I had a pint or two more than I should have done.

A curious feeling of resignation has started to creep over us – there's really no chance of getting any physical farm work done before Christmas, and hence the New Year. There's really no point in watching the forecast anymore; let's just shrug our shoulders and accept that when it stops raining, it'll stop. But not until then.

December 16th
There was another deluge last night, so it was perfect to take the new XC90 round Drier Field and up into the woods for a bit of an off-road test. As usual, it was on road-biased tyres which struggled a bit, with the onboard computers chatting away, trying to handle the sodden Hampshire clay. I chickened out of going too far into the woods, did a ten-point turn and headed home. My little trip showed how many pheasants there were still lurking in the woodland edges, though. Let's hope we find them tomorrow.

December 17th
Another shoot, and the best one so far. A team of crack guns – neighbour Robert, the Ministry Vet, the Ford 3000 owner, (and me), and a minimal team of four stick/dog wavers. We put Jonathan in charge of Pig, to carry neighbour Robert from peg to peg. Last year, Robert had to cry off with his bad lungs, and I wasn't going to let that happen again.

It was breezy and pretty damp to start with, but the day improved and there were some really fine birds flying. Highlight of the day was Robert shooting our first ever partridge at the top of Clump. There was much cheering and celebrating, complete with a highly posed picture. I must get it printed up and framed before my next trip to the Pots with him. Will it be the only partridge (out of a hundred put down) of the season?

Another sign of improving fitness: instead of hitting the sofa for the evening, I hit the Thomas Lord with Rufus for a beer or two.

December 18th

A bit of recovery time was needed in the morning – luckily, Friday means *Farmers Weekly*, although there was a very rude letter about me in it. It was from a global warming fanatic, very upset at my article about the madness of diesel generators providing back-up for 'green' energy schemes like solar and wind. As is usual, there was very little constructive argument, just a stream of *ad hominem* insults. Hardly Soctratean level of argument.

December 19th

Hazel and Fred spent the day picking-up at Tim's shoot, and I had yet another lazy day. I took the other dogs for a long yomp round the farm, trying to convince myself that the ground really will dry out one day. All the forlorn staring at the stubble paid off when I found the walkie-talkie that had gone missing on the shoot the other day. Despite being on the ground in the dirt and the damp, it was still working. Jonathan jumped in Pig and checked on all the pheasant feeders, topping them up and refilling the water bowls.

Diana finally made it back from Durham. I had a very enjoyable nerd session, tracking her progress south on the internet, and was thrilled to see a bouncy bright teenager emerge from the station. Uni is obviously suiting her.

December 20th

A bright morning, almost dry enough to go out and do a bit of ploughing, but a nice-ish Sunday is really not the day to head out to the Hangar and do some farm work. It's one of the fields that has entered popular local culture as 'open to anyone', and it's just not worth the hassle of chasing people round the field all day.

Instead, we enjoyed a debrief from Diana about her first term at Durham. She seems to be really enjoying it, and one of her proudest possessions a preppy 'HildBede' jacket. I was thrilled to see it – a real sign of a sense of belonging. A huge relief all round. She and Jonathan popped into Winchester to see the new Star Wars film. Funny to think that we were doing the same thing at her age. Not much changes.

December 21st

I can never work out if today is really the shortest day – sometimes it is, sometimes it isn't. It started bright enough for the kitchen to be flooded with lovely low sunshine while we had breakfast. It was dry enough outside for me to give some thought to getting in the tractor, and maybe doing a bit of ploughing in the Hangar.

It didn't last, of course. Just as Hazel and all the dogs got back from their morning walk, the heavens opened, giving another deluge that went on and off for the rest of the day. Jonathan and I set off to the Rod Box to get Hazel's Christmas present: a filleting knife complete with a safety glove. We did Dad's favourite drive: to Alresford, up New Farm Road for a bit of whatever with his lady friend, and then up the Itchen Valley. We passed the haunted farmhouse at Ladycroft (where a farmer was shot during an armed exchange with police during the war. He had refused to let the WarAg take it over, and the showdown was tragic and brutal).

The Rod Box is lovely and old-fashioned, terribly helpful, but unfortunately completely out of cartridges. I owed Guy a box for the old 'Hinton Ampner Specials' he had returned to me. So, having paid for the knife, we drove on to the Countrystore and bought a box there.

December 22nd

Wet again. Hazel bravely set off for a walk with the dogs, which left Jonathan and me in charge when Sainsbury's did a home delivery, so it was fairly chaotic. It didn't help that the boys at the warehouse (or wherever it is that our orders were put together) must have been in the middle of their Christmas party when Hazel's order came through; milk cartons were smashed and egg boxes had been dropped. The poor fellow doing the delivery spent an awful lot of time apologising and beeping refunds on his gadget. The home delivery idea is huge these days, having not existed fifteen years ago – competition is fierce, so a tray of groceries dripping in milk and egg white doesn't earn many plus points for Sainsbury's. I always chuckle at the return of home deliveries. In the early sixties, my mother would ring an order to Airey's shop down at the Hinton Marsh (as it was then) crossroads, and a young Bill would deliver it on his bike. I bet he didn't smash any eggs.

Sister Liz called in for what has become a bit of a Christmas tradition – she delivers huge bags of outrageously expensive presents for the children, has a bit of lunch, catches up with all the Hinton gossip, and then drives all the way back to Gloucester. I had a slightly shorter drive down to Havant to pick up the VAT-related books from the accountant, with a view to getting a substantial VAT reclaim in as soon as possible. A pub trip with neighbour Robert rounded off yet another drenched day.

December 23rd

A lovely sunny and warm day. I should have gone out and done some ploughing, but Tod was offering a bit of a pre-Christmas lunchtime beer at the Hinton Arms. John was up for it too, and both Robert Raimes and Robert Young weren't too difficult to entice along. Poor old Tod picked up the whole tab.

I wasn't fit for much by the time we got home, and I couldn't even hit the sofa – Diana had two mates round for a gossip and a selection of games, so the sitting room was out of bounds. I made a slightly woozy start doing the VAT instead.

December 24th

The long dry spell (i.e. 36 hours) lasted until about lunchtime, when the heavens opened again. I popped up to the Medstead surgery to get another batch of the two inhalers that have become such a crucial part of life now – so much so that I was desperate to avoid the chance of running out at some stage over the long Christmas break. Anthony safely negotiated the long drive down from Leeds again. I'm really thrilled that he seems to just enjoy driving.

I managed a slightly slippery walk with the dogs, and then we all settled down for an early pre-Christmas night. Unfortunately, the bells at Hinton Ampner church started at 11.30pm, summoning the faithful who couldn't contain their Yuletide excitement, and rushed through the lanes in their Audis to welcome in the Holy day. My thoughts, as I tried to get to sleep, were less than Christian.

December 25th

I miss the excitement of Christmas with small children so much. It's all rather dull by comparison. Jonathan got up reasonably early, in fairly high spirits, but the other two were firmly stuck in bed. Jonathan and I took the dogs for a nice early walk in the dry and the wind. We nearly came unstuck when all three greeted a lady walker all dressed up in cagoule, gaiters and backpack – I confess I thought we'd be the only ones out there at this time on this particular day, but I suppose she wanted to spend her Christmas Day her way. Everyone was up and raring to go by eleven, and the present opening frenzy started soon after that. There were sweaters, shoes, shooting waistcoats and the usual plethora of electrical goodies and gadgets. And, of course, the little jar of strawberry crème Quality Streets…

Many years ago, when I was but a nipper, I used to try and hog all the strawberry crème Quality Streets. And I used to get in a right rage if anyone else had them. One Christmas, Mum had bought the usual monster tin, and someone carefully went through the tin and removed the strawberry ones. I never saw any of them. In an impotent rage, I wrote on the lid: 'Someone has nicked all the strawberry ones, and it WASN'T ME!'. That tin hung around the house for decades, long enough for my children to ask what the slightly battered message was all about. So I sat and told them the whole sorry saga, acting up the sorrow and rage, until I suddenly realised that I was really crying – tears pouring down my cheeks. It was 1969 all over again. How we laughed, and cried.

My Christmas present that year was a glass jar full of *only* strawberry crème Quality Street. I wasn't expecting it, the year after I'd told my children that story, and I confess that once again, a tear or two arrived. And the same jar has been carefully reused and refilled every Christmas since, and this year was no exception. The only difference is that I genuinely didn't spot it coming – I had no idea that yet another jar-load was wrapped up under the tree. I had even failed to put two and two together when rummaging through the two open tins of Quality Street – I just thought it seemed odd that I couldn't find any strawberry ones. I must be getting old.

Christmas lunch was excellent, somehow made more significant with everyone home. The enormous turkey hardly stood a chance against five Flindts; if it didn't want to be eaten that fast, it shouldn't have tasted that good.

After a final frenzy on the presents, we sat down to a long game of Cards

Against Humanity, which was as disgraceful as ever. I took great pleasure in making a bit of a speech once it was over. "Now look here," I said. "You are all getting the nasty habit of calling me a racist, sexist, misogynistic pig. You have all spent three hours making racist, sexist and misogynistic jokes, and laughing at them. You can no longer call me any of those names again." All I got for my trouble was a hail of Quality Street wrappers – but no strawberry ones. I'd eaten all those.

Monopoly beckoned after a completely unnecessary tea. We have several versions, including a 'make your own', which includes fields and barns, and tonight we used the modern London one, but I still miss the classic version. Diana won hands down, which is rare. Usually Anthony cleans up.

A top-notch Christmas day. Sadly, the little baby Jesus failed to get a mention.

December 26th

One should get into some sort of outdoor activity on Boxing Day. Go and cheer the hunt, or have a shoot, or enjoy a healthy walk around the farm. Not us Flindts – we just kept eating. There was a bit of exercise – a huge game of racing demon. As usual, the cards flew everywhere, as did the many accusations of cheating. There was a curious moment when Hazel put her medley CD on in the background – Jonathan had compiled it as a Christmas present from her list of all-time favourites. There was an amazing inter-generational row as all three children complained that all the singers were flat and sharp. It dawned on me that today's yoof will not have heard a recording from the late seventies, when voices were normal, natural, and slightly fallible.

We finally tired of board games, and settled down for what I'd hoped would be the Christmas television treat: the latest from Aardman Animations. Somehow, it was a great disappointment.

December 27th

The post-Christmas lull was livened by two computers breaking down. Diana's almost-new £800 laptop conked out, and will have to go back, and Hazel's rather more aged desktop threw a bit of a wobbly. It's only when these machines aren't working that you realise our reliance on them, for work and play. I genuinely can't imagine what it was like without the morning routine of checking weather, emails, Pound vs Euro exchange rate, wheat prices, Russian Babes... And it's not as if those days are far away. It was only sixteen years ago that we got onto the internet for the first time.

December 28th

It seemed almost dry enough to go out and clear the tubes with a bit of ploughing, but not quite, so I made a start on the VAT. In the middle of one of my trips away from the desk, a nice man rang the landline and the mobile, wishing us a very happy new year. I had no idea who it was, and googled the number. Still no idea. So I rang it back, and explained that I didn't think he'd meant to ring us. He was trying to get hold of someone in Otterbourne, and was terribly sorry. We wished each other a very happy new year anyway, and parted the best of strangers.

The weather stayed dry enough to suggest a bit of ploughing the chalky land on the Hangar might be in order, and it went very well. I started up against the top headland, pushing the land uphill, and managed to get about a third of it done by dusk. The mouldboards still refused to shine up, but a bit of stiff ground should be needed for that, and there's none available. Still, at least I remembered how to drive the tractor

December 29th

The day of our Christmas-ish shoot, and it started with another four-hour deluge. Luckily, by the time the Editor's family had arrived, things had dried up a bit. By 10am, five Flindts, his family of four, and picker-up Julie were in the yard, ready for action.

We thought we'd try doing the far end of the farm, starting at Blackhouse Farm and working our way back. It wasn't a great success to start with, with bugger all flying out of the hedgerows. By the time we'd done the Blackhouse Wood, the boundaries of Pipeline and the boundaries of Long Field, the bag was a dismal three – all shot by me.

Two things cheered me up enormously as I walked round the outside of Pipeline and Long Field. The first was the discovery that the few acres I did sow in Pipeline back in the early autumn have failed completely. It was a huge relief that I didn't force in all 98 acres. The second was what I saw when I tiptoed through the hedge and walked up Murph's side of the hedgerow: his wheat, put in properly by a team of proper professional farmers was suffering too. Not to the same extent as my little patch, i.e. total wipe-out, but a good 50% seemed to be gone or almost gone. Farmers never ever take delight in the misfortune of their neighbours, but it made me feel slightly less incompetent.

Barracuda drive proved a bit more successful, with some serious high birds coming out, and four or five coming down. We yomped back across Drier to the yard, and had our elevenses break. George's should have been better, but most of the birds leaked. Bob's Wood and the Folly finally came up with some respectable shooting, and by the time we made it home, the bag was the perfect 20. Jonathan was the only one not to have hit anything, but he will, one day.

What with it being a fine day (in the end) in the middle of the long Christmas/ New Year break, I thought we'd have more issues with Trust visitors than we did. We were glared at by some cagoule-clad walkers while we did Bob's Wood, and some brightly coloured yompers were halfway across Folly Field as we started that drive. Two walkers coming along Dark Lane from the Springshott end stopped and looked worried. I halted the drive, and jogged down to ask if they wanted to get past, now that we'd stopped for them. They seemed happy to turn round and go back the way they'd come. We await a flurry of complaints being filed with National Trust headquarters.

A long, relaxed and thoroughly silly tea was followed by a pub trip with the Editor and Robert – I must be getting fitter. Only a year ago I would have been sentenced to a long evening snoozing on the sofa, not emptying the Flowerpots with two chums talking possibly a bit too loudly about the joys of shooting.

December 30th

I've been calling the bank every couple of days since the first of the month, in the hope that our subsidy money will have arrived. I forget what it's called this year – I think it's the Basic Payment Scheme. I should know after all the shenanigans in the spring. Because we refuse to do online banking I have to jump through all sorts of security questions and then finally talk to a real live person at the end of the telephone line. I always get there in the end, even if it does take ages. Just like my large cheque.

It's a touchy subject, of course. We farmers are now being pummelled into a submissive 'Yes, sir, thank you, sir' attitude when it comes to our subsidies. We must be pathetically grateful and not kick up a fuss if the Rural Payment Agency decides to make yet another unholy mess of the whole scheme. You have to be a tad careful about discussing it – keep the conversation to among other farmers only, and even then keep your voice down. I made the mistake recently of raising the topic with what I thought was a friendly contractor, and got both barrels of 'we have to work all day with no subsidies!'.

There's no sign of it arriving yet, but the bank manager did ring halfway through yesterday's shoot. I ignored the call, but secretly hoped it was him calling to say that a large five-figure sum had thudded its way into my account, halving the overdraft. This morning I 'returned' the call by email, and he rang back almost instantly. Alas, the money wasn't there but he wanted to talk about the overdraft limit for the next six months, or even the whole year. There were two problems with me trying to suggest what sort of limit we'd need: the first was that the books are all still at the accountant, so it would be impossible to come up with a meaningful cash flow. The second is that there's a real possibility of the big subsidy not arriving for a couple of months, in which case the overdraft limit will need to be a lot higher than we'd all planned. Ah, said the bank manager, all that's taken care of: the bank will be organising a separate loan at standard overdraft rate up to the value of two-thirds of the Basic Farm Payment. All the bank would need is a copy of our proof of submission. "That's all very well," I thought to myself. "Where the hell would that be?"

It was only after he'd hung up that I remembered that the books had in fact come back from Havant. Still, I was dammed if I was going to start doing cash flows just before New Year. If this weather goes on, there will be plenty of chances for more long drawn out office sessions.

December 31ˢᵗ

Today sort of summed up the whole year. We were all up a bit late, having been kept awake by the fierce wind and rains overnight. The whole house shook, and couldn't decide if it was Jonathan and his mates rampaging around downstairs or the roof about to come off. It was enough to stop me from sleeping.

That was my excuse for making such a cock up of the November's VAT in the morning, anyway. It took several attempts to get the figures to add up, with 27p being written in as 72p, and then a credit charge sneaking in where it should have been deducted. In the end I nailed it, and sent in an electronic claim for almost exactly six grand – a huge one, but the Hampshire Grain first payment involved a sizeable bill for all the drying during the wet harvest, and there was £4.5K involved there.

Tony the shepherd called in for a chat (but no tea – he doesn't drink tea or coffee) and some car-buying advice, which is a lovely compliment. His other half's Land Rover has expired, and they're looking for something to replace it. Always a fun challenge. Budget – £3,500. Off-roader – well, 4WD would be handy. Bigger than an estate car, but smaller than the Shoguns of this world. I sent him on his way with my recommendation: a Hyundai Tucson.

It had dried up nicely by now, so I headed out to the Hangar with the plough to do another afternoon out there. It was mighty soggy for the first turn up and over, but dried up thereafter. It was hugely disappointing to find that the couch out there still hadn't died despite 3l/ha of Roundup some weeks ago, and in places was thick enough to block the plough and make a mess of what was beginning to look an almost professional job. By four it was getting dark – prematurely, I thought, but then the heavens opened. I just about got the plough cleaned and got home, but once in the yard, the wildest hailstorm you ever saw swept through. I tried to get indoors, but had to take shelter from the stinging downpour in the calf pens. It eventually relented a bit back to rain, and I had to sprint through the brown torrent that was flooding across the yard, and I burst through the back door melodramatically, drenched. Unfortunately, there was no one to appreciate my entrance. Oh well – I went upstairs and changed my dripping clothing, and, with Jools Holland and a couple of alcoholic ginger beers lined up for the evening, decided to call it a day, a week, a month – indeed, a farming year.